This book is dedicated to my mother Lim Heng Keow. *The Hainanese bridge that crossed the ocean.* She was so important to me. She taught me what food is all about.

And also what life is all about.

TONY
COOK

I would like to acknowledge the traditional owners of the land on which I live, work and teach, the Dja Dja Wurrung people. Recipes, stories and knowledge have been shared on this land for tens of thousands of years.

TAN'S
ASIAN
ING
CLASS

murdoch books
Sydney | London

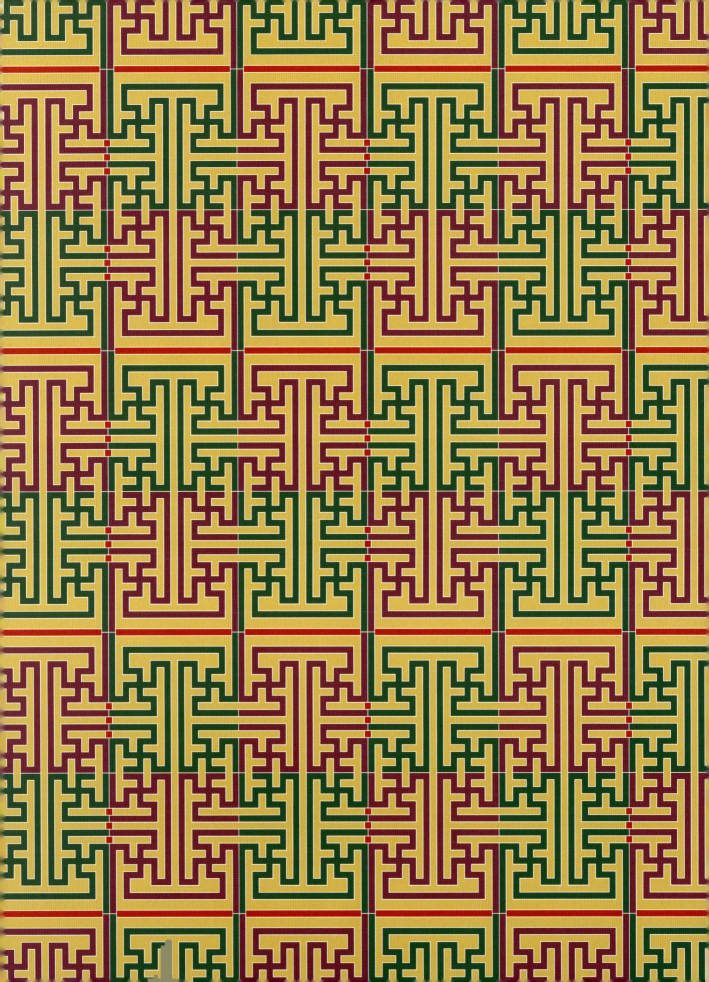

RECIPE LIST	6
INTRODUCTION	8
My Asian Kitchen	14

NOODLES AND RICE — 33
The Story of Noodles — 34

DIM SUM, DUMPLINGS, BUNS AND SNACKS — 65
The Right Oil for the Task — 82

MEAT — 117
Spice Histories, Pastes and Powders — 136

POULTRY — 161
Superior Stocks — 162
The Art of Duck — 170

SEAFOOD — 205
Hot Wok, Cold Oil — 228

VEGETABLES — 247
Mastering Stir-fry — 256

SWEETS — 287

ACKNOWLEDGMENTS	319
FURTHER READING	320
INDEX	321

RECIPE LIST

NOODLES AND RICE

Char Kway Teow	37
Asam Laksa	38
Stir-Fried Squid Ink Noodles with Prawns, Lap Cheong and Tomato	39
Prosperity Toss *Yee Sang*	41
Laksa Lemak	42
Fried Rice with Chicken, Salted Fish and Bean Shoots	43
Cantonese Fried Rice	44
Chinese Olive Fried Rice	45
Fried Rice with Pineapple *Kao Pat Sapparot*	46
Glass Noodles with Pan-Fried Fish and Saffron Broth	48
Jewelled-Rice Congee with Sweetcorn and Whitebait Fritters	49
Glass Noodles with Minced Pork, Shiitake and Garlic Chives	50
Nasi Lemak	52
Traders' Rice *Nasi Dagang*	53
Rose-Scented Chicken Biryani *Nasi Biryani*	54
Soba Noodles with Seafood	58
Hae Mee *Pork and Prawn Noodle Soup*	59
Chinese Bolognese *Zhajiang Mian*	61
Spicy Mung Bean Noodle Salad *Liang Fen*	62
Stir-Fried Vegetarian Hokkien Noodles	63

DIM SUM, DUMPLINGS, BUNS AND SNACKS

Mushroom Dumplings with Curry Oil	66
Pearl Balls	68
Lamb Dumplings, Xi'an Style	69
Chicken and Prawn Windmill Dumplings *Gai Ha Gao*	71
Deep-Fried Glutinous Rice Dumplings *Hum Sui Gok*	72
Steamed Chicken Bao *Gai Bao*	73
Rice Rolls with Pork and Wood-Ear Mushrooms *Banh Cuon*	74
Thai Duck Curry Dumplings	77
Chiu Chow Dumplings	78
Pork and Chinese Cabbage Dumplings *Shuijiao*	80
Har Gow *Prawn Dumplings*	84
Taiwan Pepper Buns *Hu Jiao Bing*	86
Crisp Beancurd Skin Dumplings *Fu Pei Guen*	87
Xiao Long Bao *Soup Dumplings*	88
Squid-Ink Potstickers	90
Steamed Pork Buns with Fermented Black Beans and Chilli	92
Char Siu *Barbecued Pork*	93
Char Siu Sou *Flaky Barbecue Pork Pastries*	94
Potsticker Dumplings *Wor Tip*	96
Steamed Pork Spare-Ribs *Jing Pai Kwat*	97
Zucchini Dumplings	99
Chawanmushi with Shellfish Oil and Crab Meat	100
Spring Onion Pancakes *Chung Yew Bing*	103
Roti John	104
Roti Canai	106
Roti Jala	108
Top Hats *Kuih Pie Tee*	109
Scrambled Eggs with Curry Leaves and Green Chillies	110
Peanut Crackers *Rempeyek Kacang*	112
Kaya *Coconut Jam*	113
Sesame Doughnut with Custard and Chocolate *Jin Deui*	114
Egg Tart *Dan Tat*	115

MEAT

Beef Rendang	119
Alice's Ultimate Meat Patties	120
My Family's Beef Brisket	123
Balinese Dry-Spiced Shredded Beef *Balinese Serunding*	124
Thai Grilled Beef Salad *Yam Neur*	125
Eggplant with Minced Pork	126
Beef Salad with Roasted Beetroot, Preserved Lemon and Herb Dressing	128
Pork Chop Bun, Macanese Style *Ju Pa Bao*	129
Xinjiang Lamb Skewers *Yang Rou Chuanr*	131
Nyonya Pork Satay	132
Macanese Beef 'Curry' with Daikon	138
Massaman Curry of Beef *Gaeng Massaman*	139
Beef Fillet with Sichuan Sauce	141
Penang Nyonya Braised Pork *Hong Bak*	142
Vietnamese Shaking Beef *Bo Luc Lac*	145
Beef with Mandarin Peel	146
Stir-Fried Lamb with Spring Onions and Steamed Buns *Cong Pao Yang Rou*	147
Beef Cooked in Sweet Soy Sauce *Semur*	148
Braised Pork Belly with Soy Sauce *Nyonya Tau Yu Bak*	151
Braised Lamb with Beancurd Sticks and Tangerine Peel *Foo Jook Yeong Yuk Bo*	152
Sichuan Twice-Cooked Pork *Hui Guo Rou*	153
Roast Lamb with Saffron and Tandoori Spices	155
Balinese Roast Pork *Babi Guling – Be Celeng*	157
Tamarind Pork *Babi Asam*	158

POULTRY

Stir-Fried Chicken with Ginger and Wood-Ear Mushrooms *Gai Phad King*	164
Isaan-Style Grilled Chicken Wings *Gai Yang*	167
Drunken Chicken with Shaved Ice *Zui Ji*	168
Duck Breast with Sweet Osmanthus Sauce and Baby Bamboo Shoots	173
Teochew Duck *Lor Ark*	174
Thai Red Duck Curry with Lychee	175
Grilled Chicken with Savoury Coconut Sauce *Ayam Percik*	176
Chicken with Black Bean Sauce	181
Balinese-Style Roast Spatchcock with Glutinous Rice	182
Slow-Cooked Duck with Cumin and Black Pepper *Itik Golek*	183
Roast Stuffed Spatchcock with Daikon	186
Braised Chicken with Lemongrass *Ga Xao Xa Ot*	187
My Mother's Roast Chicken	189
Fragrant Duck, Shanxi Style *Shanxi Ya*	190
Balinese Roast Duck *Bebek Betutu*	191
Slow-Cooked Duck with Fragrant Stuffing – the Duck that Won 1000 Hearts	192
Kung Pao Chicken *Gong Bao Ji Ding*	194
Curry Kapitan	197
Vietnamese Honey-Roasted Quail *Chim Cut Ran*	198
Chicken Buah Keluak *Ayam Buah Keluak*	199
Stir-Fried Chicken with Cashew Nuts	201
Slow-Cooked Spatchcock with Jicama, Brussels Sprouts and Vadouvan	202
Fried Chicken, Nyonya Style *Inche Kabin*	203

SEAFOOD

Oysters with My Dressing	206
Thai Green Papaya Salad *Som Tam*	209
Shellfish with Garlic, Coriander and Thai Basil	210
Singapore Chilli Crab	211
Stir-Fried Pipis with Malaysian Flavours *Kam Heong La La*	214
Calamari and Green Mango Salad	217
Spicy Pomelo and Prawn Salad *Yam Som-O*	218
Watermelon with Crisp Fish	219
Vietnamese Stuffed Squid or Calamari	220
Steamed Seafood Pudding *Otak-Otak*	221
Grilled Scallops with Sweetcorn Sauce and Curry Leaves	222
Butter Prawns *Nai Yow Ha*	225
Steamed Prawns with Pickled Leeks, Ginger and Spring Onions	226
Oyster Omelette with Chilli Sauce	227
Steamed Mussels with XO Sauce	232
Penang Nyonya Fish 'Curry' with Spicy Tamarind Sauce *Gulai Ikan*	235
Stir-Fried Prawns with Duck-Liver Sausage	236
Typhoon Shelter Crab	237
Pan-Fried Snapper with Vinegar Sambal	239
Fish Head Curry *Kari Kepala Ikan*	241
Five-Spice 'Smoked' Fish with Broad Bean Mash and Spicy Witlof Salad	242

VEGETABLES

Char Siu Cauliflower	248
Lemongrass Tofu	251
Spicy Sichuan Mung Bean Noodles	252
Grilled Eggplant Salad with Chilli Jam *Yam Makua Pow*	254
Stir-Fried Chinese Spinach or Amaranth	255
Stir-Fried Mixed Vegetables	259
Stir-Fried Bean Shoots with Salted Fish	260
Wood-Ear Mushrooms and Shredded Chicken, Nyonya Style *Kerabu Bok Nee*	261
Edible Chrysanthemum Leaf and Tofu Salad	262
Gai Lan with Lotus Root or Beef	263
Grilled Asparagus with Walnut Pesto	264
Pineapple Curry *Pajeri Nenas*	265
My Dhal	266
Rajasthani Watermelon Curry	269
Sri Lankan Spicy Cashew Curry	270
Pol Sambol	271
Seitan	272
Stir-Fried Seitan with Mushrooms and Capsicum	273
Steamed Rice Cake *Chwee Kuih*	274
Spicy Fried Tempeh *Sambal Tempe*	275
Roast Potatoes with Fermented Bean Sauce	276
Taro Gnocchi Two Ways	278
Silken Tofu with Roasted Capsicum and Fermented Chilli	280
Spicy Pickled Chinese Cabbage	281
Pickled Young Ginger	282
Pickled Green Chillies	283
Penang Nyonya Pickles *Acar Awak*	284

SWEETS

Pandan Panna Cotta with Red Rubies	288
Watermelon Granita with Coconut Jelly and Berry Compote	291
Matcha Ice-Cream with Sago and Dried Persimmon	293
Kulfi Ice-Cream	294
Fluffy Pancakes with Roasted Peanuts and Sesame Seeds *Ban Chang Kuih*	295
Pandan Crêpes with Coconut Filling *Kuih Dadar*	297
Glutinous Rice with Coconut Custard *Pulut Serikaya*	298
Rhubarb, Cardamom and Rosewater Sorbet, Boozy Watermelon and Sago	300
Black Rice Pudding with Roasted-Coconut Ice-Cream *Bubur Pulut Hitam*	302
Indian Rice Pudding *Payasam*	303
Sri Lankan Coconut Custard with Pear and Persimmon *Watalappan*	304
Chinese Almond Biscuits *Hang Yen Paeng*	305
Makrut Lime Leaf Crème Brûlée	307
Onde Onde	308
Snow Skin Moon Cake with Custard Filling	311
Pineapple Tarts	312
Rhubarb Crumble with Rhubarb Sorbet	313
Cheesecake with Red Fermented Tofu	315
Pandan Chiffon Cake	316

INTRODUCTION

I grew up in Kuantan, a town on the east coast of Peninsular Malaysia. Like many towns and cities in Malaysia, Kuantan is a melting pot of cultures. As the capital of the state of Pahang, it attracted Chinese, Indian and Malay settlers, and they brought with them their cultures and culinary traditions. From my Indian-Tamil neighbours, I learnt how to eat rotis and chapatis. My Malay neighbours taught me how to cook beef rendang and all sorts of kuihs – sweet or savoury snacks made from rice flour, nuts and fruits. From my Peranakan neighbours, I learnt how to appreciate chicken cooked with buah keluak, a nut from an indigenous tree grown throughout Southeast Asia.

The consequence of this upbringing in a country that has a confluence of influences?

> I developed not only a sophisticated and seasoned palate, but also a deep understanding of food and culture, its fluidity and its changeable nature depending on place, people and movement.

Take my family. My parents are Hainanese and their forefathers came to Malaysia as part of the Chinese diaspora. The Hainanese, the last wave of migrants to reach Malaysia, had few career options open to them, so many ended up running coffee shops and working for the British colonials as cooks and housekeepers.

My father managed a government 'rest house', a term used to refer to hotel-like residences reserved mainly for British colonials, while my mother was the cook. Mum didn't speak a word of English, but she was intuitive and learnt rapidly how to make roasts, tea cakes and curry tiffin (the elaborate or grand Sunday lunches that included chicken curry, roasts, lentils, chutneys, mulligatawny soup and trifle, which were carried over from British India) from the wives of British officials. It is from her that I developed an appreciation for Western food.

Despite these humble beginnings, my parents eventually ended up opening the first modern hotel with a Chinese restaurant in Kuantan in the late 1950s. My father employed the best Cantonese chefs and the restaurant was a resounding success. Our dining table, therefore, was a mosaic of Chinese dishes from Hainan island and Guangzhou, along with my mother's curries. Life as a Chinese person is centred around food, but in my case it was immersive. I was the unofficial apprentice, which meant that I had to dress chickens, gut fish and clean vegetables. I can also remember how I was made to peel what seemed to be mountains of prawns for wedding banquets; if I close my eyes, I can still smell the prawns on my fingers.

My father, being a hard taskmaster, would often quiz me during mealtimes, having me analyse what ingredients each dish contained and how they tasted.

> I can still tell the difference between a piece of cassia bark and a cinnamon quill by scent alone.

Those were my formative years. Trips with my mother to the local wet market to select the best chillies to grind into sauces for Buddhist-Taoist feast days. Poking at fresh seafood hauled in from the South China Sea so I could learn to identify the best. Spending time in the kitchen at my sister's café making kaya, the coconut-egg jam she was famous for, and grinding spices and other aromatics to make her legendary laksa.

ASIAN CULINARY HISTORIES

Asia is a vast region in which more than half the world's population live. Its geography is as varied as the people who live in it, and the food reflects this. As my upbringing shows, being Malaysian can mean many things, and the food I grew up eating, although in many ways typically Malaysian, has ties to other cultures, regions, people and ingredients. It's the same across Asia. Food is never static. Who would have thought that chilli, an ingredient that came from Central America as late as possibly 1499 could so fundamentally change the cuisines of India, Southeast Asia and China, for example?

Have you ever crushed the fresh leaf of a pandan plant and wondered why it is known as the 'vanilla of Asia'? Or why this fragrant herb is used in sweet and savoury dishes across the continent, including in beds of rice in Thailand and Indonesia? If you haven't, check out my pandan chiffon cake (page 316) and when you do, you'll be seduced by the intoxicating flavour of this innocuous-looking leaf. If you happen to tuck into a bowl of chicken rice in Thailand, Malaysia or Singapore, chances are you'll encounter the scent of pandan leaf; without it, the rice is just dull. Have you also wondered why lemongrass, a member of the grass family, is so fundamental to Thai, Malaysian, Vietnamese and other Southeast Asian cuisines, but hardly used in the Indian subcontinent? Have you questioned why stir-frying is such an integral part of the cuisine in so many Southeast Asian countries? Or why Indian curry powders pop up in Japanese, Macanese and Malaysian dishes?

The answers are fascinating. For example, before the age of the internet and modern travel, in the 5th century BCE even, two of the world's greatest culinary cultures, India and China, were already exchanging their wares of silks and porcelain for pepper, cloves, nutmeg and cassia in the kingdoms now known as Vietnam, Indonesia and Thailand. Later, in the 15th century, there were permanent Indian and Chinese communities in the region, bringing their own influences: from the Chinese, local communities soon added noodles and soy sauce to their repertoire; and from the Indians, especially those from South India, rotis or flatbreads and curries.

Noodle dishes in the region have long since taken on identities of their own, with a broad spectrum of variations across communities and borders. Curry laksa and asam laksa are two such wonders. Much loved by Indonesians, Malaysians and Singaporeans, these delicious, soupy dishes taste completely different to each other, even though they share a common name – apparently laksa is a Sanskrit word meaning 'a lot', because many herbs and spices are included in making laksa. Curry laksa, also called laksa lemak (the word lemak meaning 'rich with the creaminess of coconut milk'), is made with a spice paste consisting of the indispensable lemongrass and chillies, among other ingredients like galangal and turmeric, whereas asam (meaning 'sour') laksa is also made with lemongrass and chillies but includes tamarind paste, the tangy sweet pulp of a fruit from Africa, probably brought to Southeast Asia by Arab or Indian traders eons ago.

These examples and so many more illustrate the depth of culinary traditions and the wealth of ingredients that exist in Asia.

> For me, considering the food of Asia is like walking into an emporium of spices and creative ideas that have been germinating for thousands of years.

Who would have thought that 'Indianised' kingdoms like Indonesia and Cambodia would not only inherit religion and philosophy, but also spice pastes and blends to enrich their foods, many of which are still used to this day? Who would have thought that the wok – a Chinese invention – would become such an essential tool in the kitchens of Southeast Asian countries? Or that Arab-Muslim merchants would not only introduce rosewater and essence but also the vibrant chicken biryani bedecked with rose petals (page 54) that can form part of a wedding feast today in India, Pakistan and Malaysia? Or that the humble pandan leaf, with all its grassy, floral notes, would become an integral part of the now-famed Hainanese chicken rice that is practically the national dish of Singapore, and yet is never seen in the rice dishes of Hainan Island in China?

Then there's Malacca, the port city in Malaysia where, since the 15th century, southern Chinese and Indians from Tamil Nadu settled. The men from these communities married local women and, over time, formed syncretic societies with distinct customs, manners of dress and food styles. Today, the Chinese-Malay group is known as Peranakans, while the Indian-Malay group is called Chitty. As would be expected, these groups adopted the Malay language and, to this day, they speak a form of creolised Malay.

The food of the Peranakans is fascinating. The women, called Nyonya or Nonya, cloistered in their rarefied world of sewing and domesticity, are formidable cooks. Their prowess in the culinary arts is so well regarded that matchmakers could tell their cooking ability by the rhythm of the mortar and pestle they were using. Confined to their homes until they were married, they developed a hybridised cuisine that is creative, fragrant and elegant.

Best described as a mixture of Chinese and Malay with Thai and Indonesian overtones, their food is a delicious display of unexpected flavours and fresh herbs like mint, coriander (cilantro), Vietnamese mint and laksa leaf often grace the table along with the finely shredded leaves of makrut limes. Anyone who has enjoyed pork satay (page 132), which is based on the famous Malay dish, will appreciate the ingenuity of Nyonya cooks: it's served with an utterly memorable peanut sauce laden with pineapple. But for this single dish to exist at all, it's taken hundreds of years of migration, trade and custom. Across Asia, it's a similar story.

Globalisation has also of course introduced new ideas, techniques and ingredients to Asia that are changing the food scene there at lightning pace. Young chefs and cooks like Zor Tan in Singapore's Restaurant Born and Garima Arora of Restaurant Gaa in Bangkok are approaching the foods of their respective culinary heritage with unbridled flair and intelligence. So Western techniques may marry local ingredients like betel leaf and daikon or ingredients from the West such as Jerusalem artichokes and Spanish Ibérico pork may be given the Asian touch with traditional flavours. On paper, all these exciting developments perhaps sound hard to comprehend but the age of the internet is changing the food world so rapidly that it is almost hard to keep up. Certainly, it is fun, unique and surprising.

WELCOME TO MY COOKING CLASS

When I wrote my first cookbook, *Hong Kong Food City,* I closed my cooking school so that I could spend several months in that city to research and write. I returned with thoughts of revamping my cooking school in the country. The vision was to create a space that was environmentally friendly and sustainable so I could emulate my mother's garden in Malaysia. She knew almost instinctively what to grow: in her tropical garden, she had mango and papaya trees; she'd pick wing beans from the fence and

turn them into a simple stir-fry; she'd harvest sweet potatoes to toss with rice or make her own pickles from her bounty.

I wanted to create a school where I could pick the resources from my garden and the region and turn them into Asian dishes that were wholesome as well as delicious. Perhaps it was destiny that I found myself in bucolic Trentham, a tiny country town best known for its excellent potatoes and rich volcanic soil. Despite its size, Trentham is an amazing food destination, boasting an incredible organic bakery, an elegant French-inspired restaurant called Du Fermier, a truffière and a saffron farm. It was in this context that I reopened my cooking school focusing on the foods of Asia – which might include Singapore chilli crab, truffle dumplings and beef rendang – but with contemporary riffs, tied to the here and now, to my garden and to me.

This cookbook is an Asian cookbook, but one written and cooked with fresh eyes. I love my Asian heritage but I also love my life in Australia. The foods I've cooked and eaten in Malaysia are part of me. Eating a meat pie or a sausage roll is also part of me. I straddle the Asian world as much as the Western world. While the soul of my cooking lies very much in Asia, in particular Southeast Asia, there are techniques and ingredients in this book from the West that ensure the dishes in it are not only a joy to eat but also a pleasure to cook.

> The recipes I have chosen to share with you range in influence from Korea and Japan, to the many regions of China, south to Vietnam and Thailand, into Malaysia with its many cuisines, and Singapore, Indonesia and India.

Together, they reveal similarities between the different cuisines but also demonstrate their differences and their personalities. If there's a key thread, though, it's that they're utterly delicious and hopefully will expand your cooking repertoire. To make things a little easier, I've included icons that indicate what main cooking method each recipe contains, in case you are on the hunt for something to do with your new steamer basket, or just want something that comes together quickly.

- Wok
- Frying pan
- Saucepan
- Steamer
- Oven
- Grill
- Fast recipe (less than 30 minutes)

I encourage you to take shortcuts, be adventurous and experiment. After all, my life as a cook has always been inspired by what I find in the garden and in my pantry, or an idea plucked from my head that challenges tradition and embraces originality. Most times I will opt for the latter but I never entirely reject the former.

Among more contemporary flourishes there are also everyday dishes from across Asia. This book has grown substantially since its inception, and it could have continued to grow almost indefinitely. But what you have before you are the dishes I love to cook and eat. Some are simple, requiring no more than a few ingredients and less than half an hour to prepare, while others are meant for occasions when you have a bit more time.

I hope these recipes and essays convey the rich culinary traditions of Asia and that they are not only a source of inspiration but also a prompt to embark on your own journey of discovery among the infinite variety of a fascinating continent. Along the way, it is my fervent hope this book will be a dedicated companion to enjoy. And to cook with!

TONY TAN

MY ASIAN KITCHEN

AGAR AGAR   Also called agar, or kanten in Japan, this setting agent is extracted from members of the red algae family. It is usually sold in powdered form or in bundles of long crinkly strands. One teaspoon of the powdered variety will set about 320 millilitres (1 fl oz) of liquid. Always add powdered agar agar to cold water to mix, before adding to boiling water to dissolve. Store away from sunlight in airtight containers, and consider it a vegan substitute for gelatine.

BAMBOO SHOOT   Consumed all over Asia, bamboo shoots are much loved in East Asian and Southeast Asian cooking. They are sold canned, vacuum-packed, frozen and dried. I've tried fresh bamboo shoots, too, which taste sweeter and crunchier than commercial ones, but they must be parboiled to remove the hydrocyanic acid before eating. Wonderfully versatile, bamboo shoots may be stir-fried, braised and tossed in salads. They are harvested twice annually – in spring and winter – and while used interchangeably, connoisseurs prefer the more subtle winter shoot. Of the thousands of bamboo species found in the wild, only some 100 varieties are edible.

BEAN SHOOTS AND SPROUTS   More nutritious than beans, these delicious shoots are full of vitamins and are sold in every Asian country and now in supermarkets in the West. However, they have been receiving some bad press and I think it has a lot to do with bad handling and improper storage. In Asian countries, bean shoots are made from soybeans and mung beans; these are sold sparkling fresh and always cooked before consumption. More finicky Asian cooks tend to nip off the tops and bottoms of bean shoots – not only for visual beauty but also their crunchy eatability. In Malaysia, one of the legendary bean shoot dishes is stir-fried with dried fish, though you can substitute tofu or meat for this quick stir-fry.

BEANCURD   Commonly known as tofu in the West, beancurd is made by coagulating heated soy milk with gypsum (calcium sulfate) or nigari (a mineral-rich salt-making byproduct) and left to set in containers of various sizes. Once the whey is drained, the curd can be made extra soft (like junket), soft (silken), firm (regular) and extra firm. Protein-rich, tofu is also sold smoked, spiced and flavoured. Meanwhile, tofu puffs, which are fantastic in laksa and braised dishes, are made with fresh firm tofu cubes that are deep-fried until they turn springy or spongy.

Beancurd sticks and sheets (yuba), on the other hand, are made by heating soy milk and lifting off the skin that forms on the surface as it simmers gently; like regular milk forms a skin when it is simmered gently, soy milk does the same. From here it's either dried (and sometimes rolled up) or it's eaten immediately with soy sauce and almost any condiment, like ginger and spring onion or wasabi.

Cubes of tofu can also be fermented to make a few byproducts like stinky tofu (chou doufu), hairy tofu (mao doufu) and preserved tofu (dou fu ru or nam yue). The last is particularly invaluable in marinades, for instance in making char siu, and will lend umami-rich flavours to simple stir-fries. Smelling like a mature cheese, there are many kinds of dou fu ru, though the more common ones are the white variety sold in glass jars and brined with or without chilli, and the red variety, made with red-yeast rice. Both varieties may be used interchangeably, though white is preferred for congee. You'll see that I've also used the red variety for a cheesecake (page 315), and it's not uncommon in pastries. Either kind will keep for months in the fridge.

BELACAN (SHRIMP PASTE)	Pronounced 'belachan' in Malaysia and Singapore, shrimp paste is made with the *Acetes* species of small shrimp, also called geragau in Malaysia and rebon or trasi in Indonesia. These krill-like shrimp are mashed and mixed with salt, then left to ferment in the sun until the mixture is funky and pungent for cooking. A cottage industry, shrimp paste is sold in blocks and must be roasted or baked in foil in the oven before use to avoid contamination. Also known as kapi in Thailand and Cambodia, mam tom in Vietnam and bagoong in the Philippines, shrimp paste is indispensable in several Southeast Asian dishes. It also pops up in Cantonese cuisine and southern Chinese cooking, though very little is written about its use. This umami-packed condiment is fantastic in stir-fries, curries and soups, although it is best to use it sparingly unless you're used to its funkiness. Pounded with chillies and often dressed with lime juice, shrimp paste sambal – called sambal belacan – is beloved in Southeast Asia. Once a packet of belacan is opened, store it in airtight jars in the fridge. Note that I've seen some people confuse shrimp paste with shrimp sauce or salted fermented shrimp, a condiment also made with krill-like shrimp, called saeujeot in Korean, cincalok in Malaysia and hom ha in Hong Kong (China). This umami-rich ingredient adds depth and complexity to dishes, though it can be eaten on its own as a condiment with lime juice and chillies.
BLACK SOYBEANS	These beans are used for making douchi, the fermented, semi-solid black beans used in so many dishes in Chinese restaurants. Full of flavour, these umami bombs are not only great in Chinese cooking, they are also fantastic in pasta and steak sauces. They keep indefinitely stored in jars. My favourite brand is Double Rings.
BURDOCK ROOT	*See roots, corms and tubers.*
CANDLENUTS	Called buah keras in Malaysia and kemiri in Indonesia, these edible nuts are from the candlenut tree (*Aleurites moluccanus*) that is a native of Southeast Asia and Australia. The nuts are prized for their oil, which historically (as the name suggests) has been extracted for use as lamp oil. The nuts themselves taste slightly bitter raw and must be blended with spices, after which they lend a lovely creaminess to curries and stews. Sometimes hard to source, macadamia nuts are a good substitute. If you're not using candlenuts quickly, they're best kept in the freezer to prevent rancidity.
CARDAMOM	Often called the queen of spices, green cardamom (*Elettaria cardamomum*) is a joy to cook with. A member of the ginger family, it is indispensable in making garam masala, the 'hot' spice mix that makes Indian curries sing (see page 23). Always buy cardamom in the pod, and seek out those loaded with its distinctive sweet fragrance. Cardamom is not only fabulous in curries and rice dishes, but it is also wonderful in ice-creams (like the kulfi ice-cream on page 294) and in pastries. Black cardamom (*Amomum subulatum*) and white cardamom (*Amomum kravanh*) are sometimes called false cardamom because they are not as sweetly fragrant, although black cardamom is commonly used in Chinese cooking and white cardamom is used in Thai curries of Muslim origin.
CASHEW	Originally from South America, cashews are grown extensively in South Asia and Southeast Asia. The cashew fruit, sometimes called cashew apple, is orange-red in colour and the seed or nut is actually grown outside the fruit rather than in it. I used to eat the sweet-astringent fruit growing up in Malaysia. Cashew nuts are popular in stir-fries – one of the most popular Chinese dishes is chicken stir-fried with cashews, although you can substitute tofu for a vegan version. Another popular cashew dish is Sri Lankan spicy cashew curry (page 270). Back in Malaysia, meanwhile, we dry-fry raw cashews in warm salt in a wok over low-medium heat. When golden and roasted, the nuts are shaken in a metal sieve to remove the salt. Excellent as a beer snack.
CASSIA	*See cinnamon.*

CHILLI

It is hard to imagine Asian food without chilli, another ingredient from Central or South America brought back to Europe by the Spanish explorers in the 16th century. It was Portuguese traders who brought chilli (also spelled chili and chile) to Goa in India. From there, it spread to Sri Lanka, Malaysia and beyond. Interestingly, it was not the Portuguese seafarers who introduced this addictive fruit to fire the bellies of the Chinese in Sichuan and Hunan provinces, but apparently the Arab merchants who brought this spice via the Southern Silk Road. Regardless of its path, chilli is embraced with gusto in the spice-loving communities of the region. In the process, it has altered the cuisines of China, India, Korea and Southeast Asia forever.

The quantity of chilli use, however, varies from country to country and from region to region. Even in spice-rich India, the home of pepper, chilli's presence is dialled up in the south when compared with the tamer north. In Sichuan, chilli is the perfect partner for the mouth-tingling Sichuan pepper, and these two spices rule over any other ingredient on the plate. In Korea, chilli – in the form of gochugaru – is indispensable in kimchi.

Although newer varieties of chillies have been introduced to Asia relatively recently, two types of chilli remain the most popular – the cayenne and the birdseye. The degree of piquancy of these two chillies varies substantially depending on weather and growing conditions. The best test to check on the level of capsaicin (the chemical compound in chilli that gives you the rush of pain and ecstasy) is to cut off a slice and taste it. If it's mild, add more chillies to what you're cooking, and less if it is spicy hot.

It's worth noting that in Asia chillies are consumed both fresh and dried. Generally green or young chillies have a grassy nose; turning red when mature, they take on a fruitier quality. Fresh chillies have multiple uses: they can be fermented; sliced and mixed into soy or fish sauce as a dip; lend pep to stir-fries; or be blended with other ingredients to make spice pastes. Dried chillies are either sold whole, flaked or ground. Two popular Asian dried ground chillies are Indian Kashmiri and Korean gochugaru. Both are vibrant red but, in my opinion, each has its own qualities and they shouldn't be used interchangeably.

CHINESE SAUSAGE

Chinese sausage is the broad umbrella term for many types of sausage from several regions in China as well as Southeast Asia and beyond. These are wind-dried and sometimes smoked. The most common sausages in the West, however, are Cantonese, made with pork or chicken and spices and known as lap cheong or lup cheong. You can also find sausages made with duck liver, called yun cheong.

Usually sold in pairs in vacuum packs, lap cheong must be cooked before eating. Chinese cooks tend to serve these sweet and savoury sausages over steamed rice for a quick meal or in fried rice as well as stir-fries. While Cantonese sausages are readily available in Asian grocers, look for frozen Taiwanese pork sausages made with red yeast rice powder – they are super-delicious.

CINNAMON

Much has been written about the similarities of cinnamon and cassia. Along with perhaps half a dozen members of the same family known as *Cinnamomum*, cinnamon and cassia provide products more or less of the same cinnamon flavour but true cinnamon, native to Sri Lanka, is sweeter and more gentle. In contrast, cassia, from China and Vietnam, tends to be more pungent and distinctive.

Cinnamon is harvested by peeling off the outer bark to reveal the softer inner bark of the cinnamon tree. The inner bark is then peeled and dried in the sun where it curls up to form quills. Once dried, the paler quills are packed one inside the other. Cassia bark is processed similarly, but it is the corky bark that is dried and sold. In the US, most of the ground cassia bark is sold as cinnamon, but in Australia and the UK, this practice is illegal. Cassia works well in Chinese five-spice powder, master stocks and Southeast Asian curries. Cinnamon is preferred for desserts, cakes, pastries and pilafs.

CITRUS

The citrus family is huge, and while there is consensus that several of these refreshing fruits are from Asia, there are still wild varieties in that continent waiting to be domesticated or identified. Some varieties are used for juice, while others are valued for their skins and leaves. The common lime (*Citrus aurantifolia*), also called Mexican or Key lime, originated in Malaysia. Its refreshing acidity is used in chilli sauces and to pep up curries, either in the sauce or as wedges for squeezing. Makrut lime, aka kaffir lime, is used for its skin and leaves – although the juice can also be used – and is common in Thai as well as Nyonya dishes.

Calamansi limes, from the Philippines, are less common in the West, but you'll see the juice squeezed over food across Southeast Asia to highlight its incredible aroma. Also from the tropics and subtropics is pomelo, the sweet-sour giant of the citrus tribes, which is frequently used in Thai salads and, in this book, the Chinese prosperity toss (page 41). Two more varieties that are increasingly popular are the exquisite yuzu – great with roast chicken and seafood – from East Asia and the finger lime from Australia, the 'citrus caviar' now gracing upmarket tables internationally.

See also tangerine peel.

CLOVES

Even before the Dutch and Portuguese had a monopoly on this commodity from the fabled Spice Islands (the Moluccas), cloves had been used as a traditional medicine in China for thousands of years. To break the stranglehold, clove berries were smuggled by Frenchman Pierre Poivre to the Seychelles in the 18th century. Called ting xiang, meaning fragrant nails, by the Chinese, cloves are the buds of the clove plant. In China, they're used in making five-spice powder, while in Southeast Asia and India, cloves are used in moderation in curries, rice and spiced dishes. Always buy cloves from reputable merchants – there are a lot of adulterated ones sprinkled with artificial clove oil.

COCONUT

Imagine the worlds of Southeast Asian and Indian food – not to mention the Pacific Islands – without coconut (*Cocos nucifera*). Considered the tree of life by many, coconut palms offer so much: their wood is used to build houses, and the leaves are bound tightly to make roofs; the husk is used for making mats and ropes; and the shells are used as kitchen utensils. When young, the soft, translucent flesh is a joy to eat on its own or mixed with other tropical fruit in iced drinks. Coconut water, packed with potassium, sodium and manganese, is now popularised as a natural electrolyte; it is also delicious in savoury Thai, Vietnamese and some Chinese dishes like chicken soup cooked with herbs.

Coconut milk and cream, meanwhile, is made by grating the flesh of mature coconuts and pressing it. There is some confusion about the difference between coconut cream and coconut milk in the West. In Malaysia and Singapore, the first press or squeeze of grated coconut is called pati santan, meaning it is what we understand as coconut cream. Coconut milk is then made with the addition of water, resulting in what's known as santan, which is commonly the first addition to curries. Once the desired consistency is achieved with coconut milk, coconut cream is then added for the rich finish. As fresh coconut cream and milk are basically non-existent in the West, canned or UHT versions are the best substitutes – just avoid those sold in solid blocks or in powdered form. Southeast Asian desserts, like sticky rice with mango or the nutty black sticky rice are also made with coconut milk.

Over the last decade or so, freshly grated frozen coconut has become available in Asian grocers, and this has been a boon for cooks. If you can't find it, you can replace it with desiccated coconut, which can be reconstituted by being soaked in water for 15 minutes.

Finally, there's coconut oil. Virgin oil is made from coconut cream; while it solidifies in cool climates, it does not in the tropics. Refined coconut oil is made from copra or dried coconut meat, and is rendered solid by hydrogenation.

CORIANDER

Native to southern Europe and the Middle East, fresh coriander (cilantro), including the roots and seeds, is used extensively in Asian cooking. The fresh herb is also used extensively in Mexican and South American cuisines. As a green, it delivers a freshness that's unsurpassed compared with other herbs. As such, it is used liberally in Chinese, Thai and Indian cooking. Strangely, though, it is not as popular in Sri Lanka, probably due to its scent, which resembles stink bugs (the word coriander comes from the Greek word koris, meaning bug).

Coriander seeds smell and taste totally different from the plant. Green coriander seeds, or immature seeds, are a treat for pickling, while mature coriander seeds are brown and taste sweet, aromatic and vaguely citrusy, especially when you pick your own. Coriander seeds are a principal ingredient in Indian, Malay and Indonesian spice blends.

CUMIN

A member of the *Umbelliferae* family, cumin is one of the most important spices not only in Asian cooking but also in Middle Eastern, African and Latin American food. Its unique flavour is hard to put into words, though its distinctive aroma is considered spicy and warm rather than hot. This aroma is especially evident when it is heated in oil. Cumin is also an essential ingredient in many spice blends in India and Malaysia. When combined with tamarind and black pepper, it lends a glorious complexity to a duck dish called itik golek (page 183). Note that although cumin seeds and caraway seeds look similar (and were often substituted for each other in historical cookbooks due to errors in translation), the two are not interchangeable and have different flavour profiles.

CURRY LEAF

One of the most beautiful aromatic herbs, the curry leaf, is from the curry tree (*Murraya koenigii*), native to the subtropical forests of the Himalayan foothills. Its spread, however, is extensive throughout India and Southeast Asia. I've even successfully grown my own in my greenhouse in cool-climate Victoria. Curry leaf's flavour and fragrance has been described as a marriage between lemongrass, anise and roasted nuts, but none of the descriptions do this magical plant justice. If you have not used these leaves before, always buy fresh and never dried or frozen; they're incomparable.

When curry leaves are included in a recipe, they're almost always the first ingredient added to heated oil in which the dish is to be cooked. Once the leaves sizzle in the oil, watch out – the leaves then start to pop and the fragrance is ethereal. While the curry leaf is indispensable in South Indian and Sri Lankan cooking, Malaysians have taken to it like a duck to water. It has a natural affinity with green chillies and an easy dish of scrambled egg (page 110) is a fine example of what this spice can bring to even the simplest of preparations.

CURRY POWDER

See spice blends, and my essay Spice Histories, Pastes and Powders on page 136.

DAIKON

See roots, corms and tubers.

DASHI

Packed with umami, dashi (meaning stock) is one of the most elegant stocks from Japan. Traditionally made with kombu (or konbu) – dried kelp – and bonito flakes (katsuobushi), it's not difficult to prepare, although like all things delicious, it pays to buy the highest quality ingredients for this distinctly Japanese flavour that underscores so many of the nation's dishes. There are countless varieties of dashi, such as those made with shiitake mushrooms and anchovies.

While it is near impossible to find dried, smoked sticks of bonito from which the flakes are shaved, bonito flakes are readily available in Japanese and Asian supermarkets. Good-quality dried kombu should have a whitish powder on the surface; it's this powder that holds the flavour of the kelp, the essence of umami. If there's any sand or grit on the kombu, wipe it with a damp cloth, but never wash it. It's also essential to remove the kombu from the pot before the water comes to a boil, otherwise it'll impart a bitter taste. Nowadays, instant dashi is readily available, though it is wise to make this all-encompassing stock yourself to truly understand Japanese cuisine.

DILL	A member of the parsley family, this feathery ancient herb (*Anethum graveolens*), most likely originates from Southwest Asia. It is a favourite in Scandinavian and Iranian cooking, but its use is rather sporadic in Indian, Bangladeshi and Southeast Asian cuisines. It does, however, seem to pop up in certain northern Chinese dishes such as pork and cabbage dumplings with dill, and in Hui (Chinese Muslim) cuisine bao and lamb dishes. I have eaten dill in Laos, where it is used in several fish dishes including steamed fish fillets wrapped in banana leaves called mok pa. Then there's a North Vietnamese dish called cha ca la vong, which features dill and fish. At my cooking school I use dill with zucchini to make dumplings (page 99).
DOUBANJIANG	This chilli bean paste is one of the key ingredients in Sichuanese cooking. Made with broad beans (or sometimes soybeans), flour, chillies, salt and 'spices', and left to ferment naturally, it is indispensable for dishes like mapo tofu and fish-fragrant eggplant. Depending on the age of this complex umami-rich paste, the colour ranges from bright red to reddish brown. Several brands exist in the market; some are made to cater to milder palates or Cantonese cooking, but Sichuanese cooks always look out for those from Pixian district. Unfortunately, none of them are labelled in English but look for the words 'China Time-honoured Brand' on the jar, which is the Chinese equivalent to DOC.
DRIED SEAFOOD	Similar to Italy, Portugal and Spain with their salted cod, Asian countries dry all sorts of seafood because during the monsoons and the winter months, fishermen cannot set out to sea to fish. Consequently, drying is one of the oldest and simplest methods of preserving fish in Asia, to the point that some communities prefer dried over fresh seafood for certain dishes. For instance, one of the most well-known preserved fish dishes in Sri Lanka is Maldive fish sambal, made with dried, flaked tuna called Maldive fish, dried chillies, cinnamon, roasted coconut, fried shallots and cardamom. Back on the east coast of Peninsular Malaysia, fishermen cook anchovies, aka ikan bilis, in brine and then sun-dry them on palm mats for use in all sorts of dishes, including nasi lemak (page 52).
DUMPLINGS	Called jiaozi in Mandarin, dumplings take many forms including what is known as dim sum (meaning touch or dot your heart), served in Cantonese yum cha restaurants. They are delicate and small, and steamed, fried or deep-fried. Traditional dumplings are typically made with wheat flour; however, Cantonese and other southern Chinese dim sum/dumpling masters make them with all types of flour, which may include wheat starch, corn or rice flour. Most dumplings are filled with minced pork or prawns, though modern ones use fillings such as abalone, duck or truffles. Dumplings in the form of dim sum are usually eaten at lunchtime but, as society changes, they are now offered at dinnertime in Hong Kong (China) just as tapas are eaten in Spain. High-end, innovative dumpling restaurants are increasingly common in Singapore and Hong Kong (China) and it is worth the trip there just to sample them.
FENNEL	Another one of the 'ancient' herbs, fennel has been used as a herb and spice since time immemorial. In Asian cooking, the seeds lend an earthy, sweet anise or licorice flavour to Indian and Southeast Asian curries and Chinese master stock. Strangely, the fronds are not used as a herb, although I have used them in dumplings and salads for complexity.
FENUGREEK	Fenugreek (*Trigonella foenum-graecum*) is used both as a green and a spice. Its seeds should be cooked slowly to release a 'curry' aroma or they will taste bitter. Although fenugreek is used in some Southeast Asian dishes, like the famed trader's rice or nasi dagang of Malaysia, the spice is more popular with the Indian diaspora. Aloo methi, one of the traditional Indian dishes with potato, is cooked with fenugreek leaves.

FISH SAUCE

Like the soy sauces of East Asia, fish sauce is vital to Thai, Khmer and Vietnamese cooking. It is made by placing small anchovies and whole fish in large vats (traditionally wooden), filling them with salt and leaving them to ferment naturally. After a year or two, a beautiful amber-coloured liquid is drained into barrels, then bottled. This is commonly called the first press, known for its complex umami flavours – look out for the word 'nhi' on bottles of Vietnamese fish sauce, which indicates this quality.

Fish sauce is wonderfully versatile. It can be used as the dominant flavour in certain dishes, but it also melds beautifully with other ingredients to act as an unobtrusive but complex note. The best fish sauce comes from Phu Quoc in Vietnam. Avoid fish sauces with additives.

FIVE-SPICE

Of Chinese origin, and used in just about every regional Chinese cuisine, five-spice powder is traditionally made with cassia bark, star anise, fennel seeds, cloves and Sichuan pepper, with star anise and cassia bark being the dominant flavours. There are, however, variations that include nutmeg, dried mandarin peel, licorice and ginger. Before mass-produced five-spice, Chinese herbal shops would make five-spice blends for individual preferences. I can still remember that my mother preferred cassia bark in her braised-duck dishes. This mixture is also often used with char siu, poultry and beancurd dishes, and I have also used it with rabbit and quail. Apparently five-spice powder represents the five elements of Chinese cosmology, namely fire, earth, metal, wood and water. The best commercial five-spice powder in Australia is Deer Brand from Vietnam.

FLOURS AND STARCHES

The topic of flour in Asia is vast. Depending on the country and its usage, flours can be made with acorns, arrowroot, barley, buckwheat, chestnuts, chickpeas (garbanzos), corn, millet, mung beans (green gram), potatoes, sweet potatoes, soybeans, sorghum and even water chestnuts. For instance, beige-coloured acorn flour is made into jelly in Korea, arrowroot (*Maranta arundinacea*) – not to be confused with Chinese arrowroot (*Sagittaria trifolia*) – is favoured in many countries as a clear thickener, while sweet potato flour is made into noodles as well as giving fried chicken that extra crunch.

Since this is a major topic, I have decided to focus on wheat flour and how it is used to make rotis, bao and noodles, and when combined with other starches, to make a range of Chinese delicacies. For instance, wheat starch (not wheat flour) combined with tapioca starch makes dumplings that look translucent with what's commonly known as crystal pastry. When strong wheat flour is made into a dough, rested for a period, then washed with water to remove the starch, the rubbery residue is pure gluten called seitan (page 272), which is used in Buddhist vegetarian cookery. As to why, you wonder, bao buns are fluffy, it is because most wheat grown in China is softer than what's grown in Australia and the US. To make bao and Chinese noodles in the West, it is best to use cake (strong) flour.

GARAM MASALA

Meaning hot spices, garam masala has many regional variations and every home has its family recipe. It is added towards the end of the cooking process. Packaged garam masala is a pale imitation of homemade blends. Many recipes call for black cumin or shah zeera, aka royal cumin, which is often confused with nigella seeds. My recipe uses regular cumin to avoid this confusion. Some cooks dry-roast the spices separately before grinding them to a powder, but I don't.

1 tablespoon green cardamom seeds
5 cm (2 inch) stick cinnamon, broken into bits
1 teaspoon whole cloves
1 teaspoon black peppercorns
1 teaspoon cumin
½ teaspoon grated nutmeg

Except for the nutmeg, place all the ingredients in a spice or coffee grinder and blitz for 30 to 40 seconds to a fine powder, then mix in the nutmeg. Store in an airtight container. I keep mine in the fridge.

See also my essay Spice Histories, Pastes and Powders on page 136.

GHEE

Ghee, meaning 'clarified butter' in Hindi and Urdu, is used extensively in Indian cooking and can be heated to a higher temperature than butter without burning. To make ghee, heat a block of butter gently in a saucepan. The milk solids will form on top, then sink. You can then gently skim the foam from the top, before slowly pouring the clarified butter into a jar, leaving the milk solids behind.

GINGER (AND ITS FAMILY)

The ginger (*Zingiberaceae*) family is fascinating; among its stars are cardamom, galangal and turmeric. However, ginger remains the superstar. Cultivated for thousands of years, ginger is thought to be from Southeast Asia, though none is found in the wild. When young, this rhizome is tender, with pink-tinged tips, and is often pickled (page 282) to accompany Japanese sushi and Chinese meals. Fresh mature ginger, with its stronger flavour, is preferred for curries and stir-fries. While avoided by the Brahmins, ginger and garlic paste are frequently used bases in Indian dishes.

Turmeric, with its warm tone and sunshine colour, is another important ingredient and, in most cases, fresh is preferred. Galangal, the tough sister of turmeric and ginger with a medicinal and earthy flavour, is another must in Southeast Asian food. Without it, Thai and the cuisines of the Malay archipelago would feel soulless. Imagine rendang (page 119), for example, without galangal.

Lesser-known members of the ginger family are sand ginger (*Kaempferia galanga*), fingerroot or Chinese keys (*Boesenbergia rotunda*), and torch ginger flower (*Etlingera elatior*). About the size of the first joint of a finger, sand ginger – or kencur in Indonesian or cekur in Bahasa Malaysia – is commonly sold dried, though I have seen fresh sand ginger in Australia. Its peppery aroma is the backbone of Balinese food and its leaves are used in salads.

Fingerroot, also called krachai in Thai, resembles a cluster of keys or fingers with thin, brown skin. Its earthy camphor-like aroma is frequently used in Thai jungle curries. It is sold frozen or brined in jars in Australia and the West.

Torch ginger flower, known as bunga kantan in Malaysia, is often sold frozen, though these young buds with an elusive, lemony fragrance pop up at select florists in Australia and the US when in season. I love it in asam laksa (page 38) and in salads.

HOISIN SAUCE

A Cantonese invention, this umami-rich sauce is made with fermented soybeans, salt, sugar, garlic and chillies; some brands add vinegar, along with wheat flour to thicken it. This reddish-brown sauce is used as a dip, sometimes diluted with Shaoxing rice wine, and as a marinade for barbecued meats. It keeps indefinitely if refrigerated.

JAGGERY

See palm sugar.

LEAFY GREENS	Due to the growing appetite for healthy food and the desire for more diversity in the vegetable world, people are increasingly turning to so-called 'Asian' greens. But bear in mind that the leafy greens in East Asia are markedly different to those in West Asia. The list here is not exhaustive, merely a sampler of what is now likely available at your neighbourhood Asian greengrocer and supermarket.
	Leafy greens, especially those of the brassica family, also known as cruciferous vegetables, are numerous. These include gai lan (commonly called Chinese broccoli), wombok or Chinese cabbage or napa cabbage, choy sum, buk choy, gai choy, mizuma, tatsoi and komatsuna (a cross between Chinese cabbage and Japanese turnip). All bear a hint of mustard flavour and are marvellous in stir-fries, soups and salads.
	Lesser known are Malabar or Ceylon spinach (much appreciated for its mucilaginous quality), amaranth (commonly called bayam in Bahasa) and water spinach (known as kangkong in Southeast Asia and ong choy or kung xin cai in China), which are almost always stir-fried with garlic and sometimes with belacan or with fish sauce. Seasonal garland chrysanthemum, with its distinctive floral flavour, is a favourite with the Chinese, Korean and Japanese in soups and side dishes. Celtuce or stem lettuce, with crisp stems, is having its moment in the sun among Western chefs.
	If you have access to pennywort, a Sri Lankan salad of gotu kola with grated coconut is delicious. Asian basil (*Ocimum spp*), such as anise basil (commonly known as Thai basil), lemon basil and holy basil are featured in Thai, Vietnamese and Malaysian dishes. Perilla leaves are used in Vietnam, Japan and Korea, but strangely not in China. Another example of the fact that even in Asia there are regional preferences.
LEMONGRASS	It is hard to imagine Southeast Asian cooking without lemongrass. It's a member of a grass family of which, among more than 50 species, only two are cultivated for culinary and medicinal purposes. The first variety of lemongrass is *Cymbopogon citratus* and it is used extensively in Southeast Asian cooking. The second is *Cymbopogon flexuosus* and it is used in Sri Lankan and South Indian cooking. Both varieties can be used interchangeably and are prized for their zesty, lemony flavour due to the presence of citral, the compound also present in lemon rind. Some cookbook authors suggest that lemongrass can be replaced with lemon rind in Asian dishes, but I am not convinced. Imagine adding lemon rind to beef rendang (page 119) or to a Thai spice paste – the scent is different and it will most certainly affect the integrity of Southeast and South Asian cooking. In short, lemongrass is irreplaceable.
	Easy to grow in the tropics, lemongrass can still be grown in colder climes, but needs protection from frosts. Only the bulbous ends or stems (where most of the flavour is concentrated) are used in cooking – once the outer layers are peeled, the stems can be crushed and added to stews and soups, sliced paper thin for salads and sambals or ground to a fine powder and used in a range of spice pastes.
LOTUS ROOT	*See roots, corms and tubers.*
MACE	*See nutmeg.*
MELONS, GOURDS AND SQUASHES	Of all the melons and gourds from the Asian continent, only a few have made it to the mainstream markets. I suspect this has something to do with poor information – most people I've spoken to think they are bland or boring. But if you go to areas with Asian communities, you'll find varieties like winter melon, fuzzy melon (so named due to the 'hair' on it when young), angled loofah, chayote, snake gourd and bottle gourd. Like the zucchini, these gourds may not have distinctive flavours, but they readily absorb the flavours of other ingredients. Happily, the Japanese kabocha and the slender Asian eggplant are well received (the *Solanum* family is complex and fascinating – I've tasted a sour eggplant in Sarawak). Bitter melons and gourds in this group are still not popular, but their antiviral and antibacterial properties may convince some.

MIRIN	*See rice wine.*
MUSHROOMS	An important protein, especially for vegetarians, mushrooms have always been much esteemed in just about every Asian cuisine, considered by many Asian cultures as a gift from the gods, especially the reishi or lingzhi mushroom (which is associated with longevity and physical potency). Mushroom cultivation of several varieties is huge in Asia. Some common varieties sold fresh in Australia and beyond are enoki, shiitake, oyster, shimeji and black fungus. In Southeast Asia, fresh paddy-straw mushrooms are also common. In China, Japan and Korea, there is a long tradition of foraging wild fungi and the prized mushrooms are porcini, morels, matsutake or pine mushroom (*Tricholoma matsutake*) and chanterelles. Note that the pine mushroom or saffron milk cap (*Lactarius deliciosus*) is different to the pine mushroom found in East Asia. Cooking with mushrooms is a joy. My go-to dish is a quick stir-fry of mixed mushrooms with garlic and rice noodles with a splash of soy or vegetarian oyster sauce.
MUSTARD SEEDS	A member of the brassica family, mustard seeds, especially the brown variety, are used extensively in the cuisines of the Indian subcontinent. They are one of the first ingredients to be popped into hot oil for the seeds to release their pungent nutty fragrance. While their appearance as a spice is barely noted in other Asian cuisines, they are made into a dip in northern Chinese cooking. However, mustard seeds are also used for making oil. The 'extra virgin' mustard oil used in Indian cooking has a sharp, pungent aroma because it has a compound similar to wasabi, whereas the same oil made elsewhere does not.
NOODLES	*See my essay The Story of Noodles on page 34.*
NUTMEG	Along with pepper and cloves, nutmeg is one of the legendary spices that virtually changed the history of Southeast Asian nations, and it is much coveted as a spice in Europe. The Portuguese were the first to arrive in the Moluccas, the home of nutmeg, in 1514, thereby gaining a monopoly over the lucrative spice trade, with nutmeg worth more than gold in the 1500s. The Dutch arrived a century later and wrested control of the spice trade. It was also in the 17th century that the British and French arrived in Southeast Asia and these Western powers gradually colonised the emerging nations of the region. Once found only on the Molucca Islands to the east of Indonesia, nutmeg is a drupe or fruit. In Europe, especially Italy, it is popular in savoury as well as sweet dishes. In Indonesia, India and Malaysia, this fragrant spice is grated into spice blends and its aril, known as mace, is added at the end of cooking for its scent. In Penang and Indonesia, the fruit is sliced to make nutmeg juice and it is also candied to make manisan pala, meaning candied nutmeg.
OSMANTHUS	Not much has been written about this tiny edible creamy-white-to-orange flower – it is relatively unknown, except by those with Chinese heritage. Called gui hua (in Mandarin) and fragrant olive, osmanthus's original home is East Asia. If you visit Hangzhou in the autumn, the sweet, apricotty scent of these pinhead-sized flowers will charm you. Traditionally, the dried flowers are infused in tea and baijiu, the alcoholic spirit made with sorghum or rice. It is also made into syrups and used to flavour all manner of sweet things. I've combined it with honey in my savoury duck (page 173). Will it be the next big thing like pandan leaf? Time will tell.
OYSTER SAUCE	Created by a fortunate stroke of serendipity by Lee Kum Sheung in 1888, oyster sauce is a relatively recent creation. While the original recipe is a secret guarded by the descendants of Mr Lee and now the owners of Lee Kum Kee, you can make your own oyster sauce by simmering oysters with salt, sugar and soy sauce and thickening it with cornflour. Discard the spent oysters and store the reserved sauce in the refrigerator for up to a week as no preservative is added.

PALM SUGAR

The world of palm sugar is complex and interesting. Basically, the ones you find in most Asian grocers are made with coconut nectar or palmyra palm nectar. There is, however, a third palm sugar made from the sap that flows from the 'stem' of a harvested nipah fruit. This nectar or sap is cooked down slowly until the desired consistency is achieved. It is then poured into moulds and packaged for sale.

Generally, palm sugar from the palmyra palm is from Thailand and Vietnam; palm sugar from Malaysia and Indonesia is made from coconut. Unfortunately, most palm sugar in the West has cane sugar (ranging from 20 to 70 per cent) added. As a guide, the more you pay, the better the quality and the less cane sugar. If you come across gula apong, this is the sugar made from the nipah palm or mangrove palm, which grows wild in tropical Asia. Like the palm sugar made from coconut nectar, it tastes caramelly and slightly salty, with a faint hint of corn.

Even though it looks light brown and unrefined, jaggery from India is made with cane sugar.

PANDAN LEAF

Called the vanilla of the East, pandan leaf (*Pandanus amaryllifolius*) – also known as pandanus leaf and screwpine leaf – is an important ingredient in all Southeast Asian countries as well as in Sri Lanka. It is used to perfume savoury and sweet dishes. On the nose the scent is grassy with hints of coconut and almond, but when it is combined with rice or used in curries, its fragrance is unique and floral. In fact, it lifts the dish to another level of deliciousness.

The juice is also pounded from the leaves to extract the vivid green colouring that tints and flavours cakes and sweet delicacies such as the iconic onde onde (page 308) and chiffon cake (page 316). Most Asian grocers stock frozen and dried pandan leaves, but I strongly recommend trying to find fresh leaves. Dried pandan leaf is, in my opinion, a poor substitute for fresh but if fresh leaf is not available, it is wise to use more of the dried to capture the elusive fragrance. Once you have identified this exotic aroma, you'll know it is another culinary marker of Southeast Asian food.

PEPPER

Before chillies made it to the shores of Asia, pepper was king. While it has been usurped by chilli for heat, there are still times when pepper is used as the star. One such instance is in a dish of duck simmered with tamarind, coconut milk and black pepper. Called itik golek (page 183) in Bahasa Malaysia, this dish is not only delectable but it's a reminder that pepper still has a dominant place in the spice world.

PLUM SAUCE

A Chinese contribution to the world of gastronomy, plum sauce is easy to make. It is often teamed with roast duck and fried dishes like spring rolls and fish cakes. Chinese plum sauce is made with yellow-fleshed plum, but any plum is good. Here is my go-to recipe:

½ cup (110 g) white sugar, or to taste
½ cup (125 ml) vinegar
2 thin slices ginger, finely chopped
1 clove garlic, finely chopped
1 stick cinnamon
1 star anise
500 g (17½ oz) seeded plums or nectarines, roughly chopped
Salt, to taste
1 teaspoon chilli powder (optional)

Put all the ingredients and ½ cup (125 ml) water in a saucepan and simmer gently until the plums have softened. Remove the star anise and cinnamon. Blend to a smooth sauce. Keep refrigerated for up to a week.

RICE

In Asia, rice is the staff of life. Cultivated for more than 8000 years, rice is so revered that there are rice deities found in various Asian cultures. In Japan, rice is not only a symbol of harmony but it is used, either as grain or as sake, as a ritual offering to the ancestors. If you are in Asia, the traditional greeting is 'have you eaten rice yet?'

Generally, there are two types of rice. The first is long-grain, which includes basmati and jasmine. When cooked, basmati rice releases a fragrance that suits Indian food, while jasmine rice is an all-rounder, meaning it goes well with all Asian food. These both tend to be fluffy with separated grains when cooked.

The second category of rice is short- or medium-grain. This is the rice preferred in Korea and Japan and to some extent in China. Slightly sticky and plump, this rice is particularly suited for eating with chopsticks.

There is also another type of rice with a high amount of amylopectin (a kind of starch), which is sticky or sweet or glutinous rice. It is essentially used for making sweet puddings and rice wine, and is available in both white and black forms. Shaoxing rice wine, mirin and sake are made with fermented rice.

ROOTS, CORMS AND TUBERS

In all the areas of Asia that are near the coast, vegetables are grown in and around water. Lotus root, water chestnuts, daikon and burdock root are frequently eaten for their crunch and texture.

Lotus roots are the tubers of lotus flowers, and are high in fibre and have a unique taste. Fresh and frozen lotus is great in stir-fries, and also for chips, especially drizzled lightly with honey and chilli powder.

Fresh water chestnuts are hard to find in Australia, but if you have a pond or are into aquaponics, water chestnuts are easy to grow. A corm, they are delicious, fresh and sweet. Canned water chestnuts are readily available but I prefer frozen ones in stir-fries and dumplings.

Daikon is a popular vegetable in India, Japan, Korea, China and Southeast Asia. It is a member of the radish family and it comes in various shapes and sizes. Wonderfully versatile, it can be pickled for the likes of Japanese takuan and Korean danmuji. It is delicious in a simple stir-fry with green chillies, onions, garlic and curry leaves.

Burdock root is slightly bitter, with dark-brown skin and white flesh, and it is much appreciated as a delicacy in Japan and Korea. Not often seen in markets, it is very nutritious. It is called gobo in Japan, ueong in Korean and niu bang in Mandarin. It is usually shredded and cooked with soy, sake and mirin.

ROSE WATER

In Malaysia, Singapore and Indonesia, rose water is a staple in Malay and Indian communities. Originating in Persia and made from distilled rose petals, its enduring quality has much to do with its sensuous appeal and refined fragrance. It's used sparingly in drinks like falooda, and in Middle Eastern confectionary such as baklava and knafeh – timeless offerings that are lovely reminders that good things survive through time. Rose water also elevates many savoury foods and I have included it in a biryani (page 54).

SAGO

Sago is a tropical palm, and its starch is made into the slippery pearls that are popular in Southeast Asian sweet drinks and puddings. However, the 'sago' pearls sold in Asian grocers are now mostly made with tapioca or cassava. These pearls or balls are fun to drink, and are having their moment in the sun with iced tea and milk or coconut milk, often called bubble teas or boba.

SAFFRON

One of the costliest and most painstakingly harvested spices in the world, the saffron crocus (*Crocus sativus L.*) thrives in Kashmir in India. Said to be from Iran originally, saffron is also grown in China and Japan but, strangely, is used for medicinal purposes rather than culinary. This luminous ingredient sparkles like sunshine in many Indian dishes. While there is some confusion about how saffron came to India, most writers agree that Iranians spread it across the continent. A note of caution: should you be sold cheap saffron in Asia, it is turmeric. Saffron is grown near where I live in Trentham, and I celebrate this precious spice in the biryani on page 54.

SALT

As old as time, salt (sodium chloride) is indispensable in cooking. Of course, it can be divisive in some quarters, but salt is essential in our diet because not only does it enhance the flavour of our foods, it is also important for body functions such as nerve health, fluid balance and prevention of muscle cramps. While much has been written about salt from the West – such as Maldon sea salt, French fleur de sel, Hawaiian salt and Murray River salt – very little is known about salt from Asia apart from Himalayan salt.

However, there are some unique Asian salts to consider. One is moshio salt from Japan; it is made with seaweed added. Another to consider is asin tibuok from the Philippines made by the Boholano people; the seawater is filtered through ashes, which gives it a mild smoky flavour.

Origins aside, have you ever found that some salts taste saltier than others? This is because salt is made up of crystals and the density of each crystal affects the 'saltiness' of the salt. This is why I prefer to specify 'pinch of salt, or to taste' in my recipes. Additionally, salt intake has a lot to do with personal preference. My golden rule is this: you can always add more salt if you find a dish bland but you can't take it out!

There is another reason to consider how you're using salt. Many Asian food cultures use soy sauce, fish sauce, shrimp paste, fermented fish, miso and so on. All these ingredients are made with salt – and some brands use more salt and others less. My advice is to check the salt level of whichever sauce or condiment you're using and adjust the seasoning to taste.

SAMBAL

Many cultures use a relish as an accompaniment, and sambal plays that role in Indonesia, Malaysia and Singapore. Sambals can be cooked or uncooked, and most are made with chillies, though there are several that are gentler but still whet the palate. A ubiquitous sambal enjoyed in the three maritime countries is belacan (Malaysia and Singapore) or trasi (Indonesia), made with pounded chillies and roasted shrimp paste. Some other typical sambals are made with tomatoes, mango, coconut, durian, belimbing buloh (a member of the star fruit family) or lemongrass. There are also sambals in Thailand and Sri Lanka; in Thailand they are called nam prik and in Sri Lanka, sambol.

SESAME SEEDS, PASTE AND OIL

Another essential ingredient for the foods of China, Japan and Korea, sesame seeds were probably introduced to China from Iran centuries ago. The white, black or brown seeds are often scattered on pastries or ground to a powder for desserts. Like tahini (from the Arabic word for 'crush'), which is so popular in the Levant, Chinese roasted sesame paste, called zhi ma jiang, is used with noodles, cold dishes and flatbreads. Sesame oil (either regular or roasted) is used for frying, and roasted sesame oil is also used sparingly to drizzle over a finished dish. Beware: some sesame oils are mixed with vegetable oil so select the best available from Japan or Korea. My favourite is from Penang and the brand is Ghee Hiang.

SHALLOTS

Shallots (eschalots), spring onions (scallions), onions, garlic, leek and garlic chives are all part of the massive allium family. Although onions are used in Southeast Asian cooking, the shallot is preferred for its sweeter flavour. They are delicious pickled, and in Vietnam, Thailand, Malaysia, Singapore, Indonesia, Brunei and the Philippines, shallots are sliced thinly and deep-fried to use as a condiment for both savoury and sweet dishes. Called bawang goreng in Indonesia and Malaysia, these golden crispy shallots are sprinkled on noodles and curries, while in Thailand, they are used on a dessert called kanom mo kaeng thua, made with palm sugar, coconut milk and mung beans.

Asian shallots are tiny – some varieties aren't much bigger than a cumquat or a teaspoon – compared with those grown in Australia and the West, so don't be surprised if you come across a cookbook from Asia calling for 15 shallots where usually you'd expect five. For this cookbook, I've used Australian or Western shallots. They should weigh approximately 50 grams (1¾ ounces) each.

SICHUAN PEPPER

As the name suggests, this fragrant, citrusy berry is from Sichuan province but is also found growing in neighbouring provinces. Called hua jiao in Mandarin, meaning 'flower pepper', it comes in two varieties; red Sichuan pepper is stronger-tasting and green Sichuan pepper is more floral. Both induce a tingling sensation that numbs the lips and creates something of a 'buzzy' feeling, like eating a mouthful of pop rocks. Combined with chillies, it creates a 'mala' sensation, which means it is numbing and hot on the palate like when you eat mapo tofu. The Sichuan pepper imported to Australia varies in quality; always buy the best and freeze any left over. In the US, The Mala Market are the best suppliers of premium Sichuan pepper.

SOY SAUCE AND SOYBEAN PRODUCTS

Without soy sauce, there would be no Chinese, Japanese or Korean food as we know it. Typically made with cooked soybeans, wheat flour and a rice culture, the mixture is left to ferment in brine for months before the sauce is removed to make light soy sauce. Dark soy sauce ferments longer, which affects both the taste and colour. Avoid buying cheap soy sauce as some brands add monosodium glutamate and yeast products to enhance the flavour, skipping the long process of fermentation that gives good soy sauce its rich and complex flavour. Always look for the words 'naturally fermented' on the label. If you have coeliac disease, look for tamari soy sauce that is made with rice koji.

It's interesting to note that cooked soybeans fermented with different moulds (a common one is *Aspergillus oryzae*) are made into all sorts of products, like Japanese miso and Korean doenjang. In Singapore, Malaysia and Indonesia, a similar product, called taucheo (from the Hokkien dialect) contains whole fermented soybeans blended to a paste. While their flavours vary, they can be used interchangeably. Soybeans are also sometimes added to a sauce called sweet bean sauce (tian mian jiang) from northern China, which is mainly used as a dip or in stir-fries.

See also beancurd, tempeh.

SPICES

See my essay Spice Histories, Pastes and Powders on page 136.

STAR ANISE

Originating from southern China and Vietnam, star anise (*Illicium verum*), with its aniseed flavour, is one of the major spices used in Chinese cooking. It comes from an evergreen tree, which I saw for the first time in north Vietnam. Cultivated for its perfume and medicinal properties, star anise is now used globally as a culinary spice. It complements tangerine peel and cassia beautifully in poultry, beef and fish dishes (see page 242) and it is indispensable in pho, the much-loved Vietnamese soup. Always buy whole star anise, never star anise powder – the essential flavour dissipates as soon as the packet is opened.

STOCKS

See my essay Superior Stocks on page 162.

TAHINI	*See sesame.*
TAMARIND	It is hard to imagine the foods of India and Southeast Asia without this sweet and sour fruit, grown extensively in tropical regions. I can still remember picking these brown pods off the tamarind tree and sucking on the sweet-sour pulp, spitting out the fibre and flat seeds. The process of manually dehulling and deseeding tamarind was once laborious, but modern technology has changed this. The fruit is used in both sweet and savoury dishes like tamarind pork (page 158). Commercial tamarind is mainly sold in block form, while ready-made purées have preservatives. To make purée from a block, break off a piece and soak it in a little hot water. Leave it to soften, then massage until it reaches a purée consistency. Discard any solids and it's ready for cooking.
TANGERINE PEEL	Tangerine is a type of mandarin orange that is more tart than sweet. Only the dried form of the peel is typically used as a spice; the Chinese call it chenpi, meaning aged tangerine peel. It is often used with Sichuan pepper and star anise to make savoury dishes. It is also used in red bean soup, a common Chinese dessert. The best dried tangerine peel comes from Xinhui in Guangdong province, though it is rather expensive. While it may be hard to find quality as good as that from Xinhui, it is easy to make yourself during the citrus season. The peel of tangerines and mandarins can be left to dry naturally and stored in an airtight container.
TEMPEH	An ingredient from Indonesia, tempeh is made with cooked soybeans inoculated with a mould called *Rhizopus oligosporus*. It is left to ferment, and after a day or so, a whitish web of mycelium forms, which binds the soybeans together. Tempeh is incredibly nutritious, has a nutty flavour, and works well in various cooking styles such as stir-fries, soups, stews and sauces. Tempeh is vegan and vegetarian friendly, and is a good substitute for most of the meat, poultry and seafood recipes in this book.
TOFU	*See beancurd.*
VINEGAR	The world of Asian vinegars is fascinating and intriguing. While vinegars in the West are usually made from wine, barley or apple, in East Asia they are typically made with rice, though other grains like sorghum and barley are sometimes included. Some vinegar producers also add flavourings like shiso and spices. In Southeast Asia, especially in the Philippines, vinegars are made from the sap of coconut palm and nipa palm as well as sugarcane juice. Regardless of what grain or juice is used, the process is basically the same two steps. First, alcohol is made by combining a yeast with grain or juice. The yeast converts the sugars in the grain or juice into ethanol. Then the bacteria convert the ethanol into acetic acid, giving vinegar its sharp tang. Everyday vinegars lack depth and character, which is not to say they are bad, but rather that they have not been aged, or they are not made using the artisanal method. For instance, genuine balsamic vinegar from Modena takes 12 years to mature and at least 25 to be the finest, called vecchio. China's vinegar history goes back some 1400 years and it includes four legendary vinegars: the most famous globally is Zhenjiang (Chinkiang) black vinegar, and two of the other well-known brands are Hengshun and Gold Plum. The next is Sichuan Baoning vinegar. Then there is Shanxi vinegar followed by Fujian Yongchun Monascus (red) vinegar. Some of these vinegars are aged for three years, and all the way to several decades. They have widely different flavour profiles and some are great for dumplings, while others are delicious with lamb and beef. One final tip: Asian vinegars are milder. If you are using Western vinegar in Asian dishes, it is best to dilute it.
XO SAUCE	XO originates from Hong Kong (China) and both Spring Moon and Fook Lam Moon restaurants there are connected to its origins. I have a recipe for it (see page 231) which has been adapted by chefs around the world and explains the history further.

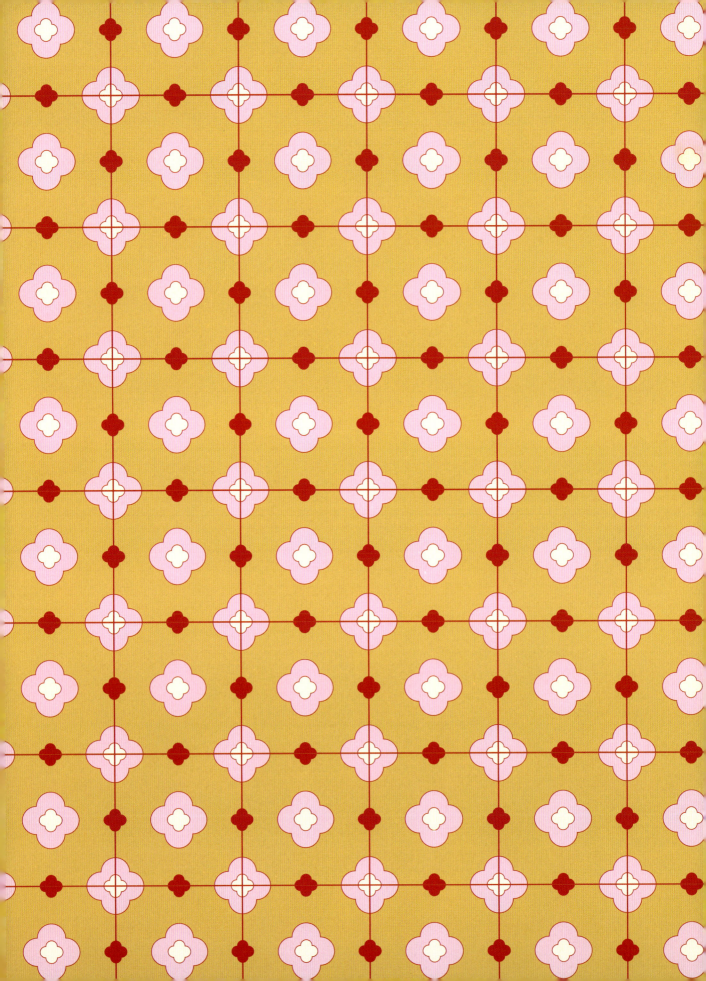

NOODLES AND RICE

THE STORY OF NOODLES

There's no doubt about it – noodles are popular, delicious and easy to cook. But there are still lots of people who are confused or daunted by the array of noodles on offer in Asian grocery stores. I must admit that sometimes I'm one of them! But I'm equally as excited by the range of noodles because I know they are like blank canvases; depending on the variety of noodle, you can make any dish that has stood the test of time or one that's modern and creative. Let's explore the enormous variety of noodles on offer before we get down to their finer points.

> Generally, Asian noodles are made from two grains – wheat or rice.

Wheat noodles can be made from wheat flour and water. Like pasta, they can also include eggs. Finally, wheat noodles can also be made with the addition of kansui, alkaline salts (sodium carbonate and potassium carbonate), sold in Asian supermarkets. Noodles made with kansui are firm and pleasantly chewy, and they look yellowish in colour because of the reaction between the flour and the salts. Ramen noodles and wonton noodles are made with kansui because alkaline noodles maintain their texture even when served in broth – a key feature.

Much has been written about kansui (also labelled as lye water) in noodles because in large quantities it's considered toxic, but minute quantities have been used since time immemorial, and I really think there's been an overreaction to this chemical compound in noodles. Besides, it has been used in making pretzels and for nixtamalising corn to enhance flavour and nutrition.

Making wheat noodles is simple, especially if you have a pasta machine. As you would with pasta, combine flour with water or beaten eggs and some salt, then knead the dough to develop the gluten strands. Resting the dough is essential to allow the gluten to relax, then you can roll it into sheets and cut it into strands of noodles. Making wheat noodles by hand isn't difficult either. After the usual resting time, my sister would use a long rolling pin to roll the dough into a thin sheet before folding it onto itself to create four or five layers, then cutting it into strands with a knife.

Rice noodles, on the other hand, are made with rice flour and tapioca flour or cornflour. There are two main ways of making them. For rice vermicelli, the flours must be cooked with water to a sticky batter, transferred to an extruder, such as a potato ricer, and gently extruded into boiling water. As soon as the noodles float to the surface, they're scooped out with a spider and plunged into iced water to stop the cooking process, after which they can be dried or used fresh. Flat rice sheets, such as those used for ho fun noodles, are made through a process where the rice flour and tapioca or cornflour is mixed with water before being poured onto sheets and steamed. The steamed rice sheet is then cut into noodles before drying.

Apart from wheat and rice, you've got soba noodles, especially popular in Japan, which are made with buckwheat flour and prized for their nutritional properties and distinctive nutty and earthy flavours. These silky noodles are usually served cold or in soups, though they are also perfect for stir-fries. I have to say that after a global search for premium organic buckwheat and wheat flour, I've discovered that Hakubaku, a Japanese company in Ballarat, a rural city in Victoria, is producing one of the best commercially available soba noodles.

Another common style is mung bean noodles. Also called cellophane, glass or bean thread noodles, they are semi-transparent when dry but turn glass-like and have an appealingly slippery texture when cooked. Usually made of mung bean flour (though there are imitators produced from pea flour and sweet potato flour), these noodles are sold dried and require soaking in water to soften before cutting. They are tasteless, but absorb the flavours of whatever ingredients they are cooked in. Ants climbing a tree (see my version on page 50), the glorious and legendary Sichuan dish, uses these delectable noodles. An easy-to-make cold noodle dish from Yunnan province (page 62) is also made with mung bean flour.

What other noodles are on offer? There are noodles made with konjac (*Amorphophallus konjac*), known as shirataki in Japanese. Sold in packets, they're bouncy and crunchy and are traditionally used in Japanese hot pot dishes such as sukiyaki. There are also the Korean sweet potato noodles called dangmyeon, which are delicious stir-fried in japchae. Then there are noodles made from soybeans, arrowroot or fermented corn.

Finally, there are flavoured noodles, such as the pastas with added spinach, saffron or beetroot for visual appeal and flavour. Chinese noodle-makers add dried shrimp roe and even scallops to their noodles to elevate the eating experience.

It's impossible to cover every strand of noodle and the dishes that spring from each in this book, but it's significant to recognise just how important noodles are – they're deeply rooted in Asia's culinary consciousness and are the source of much debate and the focus of many celebrations. The Chinese, for instance, eat noodles because they symbolise long life. It's for this reason that I've included the crunchy rice noodles for yee sang, the 'prosperity toss' in this chapter (see page 41).

I have also included traditional Chinese recipes, such as zhajiang noodles (page 61), that I've enjoyed in Hong Kong, and a version of ants climbing a tree (page 50) that I've shared in Chengdu. From Malaysia and Singapore, there's the ever-popular char kway teow (page 37), a decadent curry laksa I learnt from my sister (page 42), a divine tamarind-laced asam laksa showered with tropical herbs (page 38), comforting stir-fried Hokkien noodles (page 63), and a hauntingly delicious hae mee (page 59). And if you love Japanese food, there's a clean-tasting soba noodle dish with seafood (page 58).

To complete this ensemble, I've included a dish of stir-fried squid-ink noodles with lap cheong (page 39) and another from my restless mind – pan-fried fish with glass noodles perfumed with saffron (page 48), the ultimate in noodle luxury.

Rice and wheat noodles are obviously the most popular in Asia. The wonderful thing is they come in various shapes and textures; some are thin and long, while others are flat and eaten somewhat al dente like pasta. Some will hold well in rich, heavy sauces, while others are content with a whisper of a refined broth. As a diehard noodlehead, I invariably have in my pantry wheat noodles from India called seviyan, pad Thai noodles from Thailand, wonton noodles from Hong Kong (China) and Malaysian laksa noodles. While some of these are not interchangeable in some dishes, a lot of them are. If truth be known, the story of noodles spans the full culinary spectrum. Pull one strand and it inevitably leads to another.

CHAR KWAY TEOW

SERVES 2 | 4

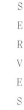

Its origin may be in Fujian province, but in Malaysia and Singapore this saucy, charred-noodle dish has taken on something of a cult status. Consumed by noodle lovers at all hours, it bears all the characteristics of Chinese cooking – softness, crunch, sweetness and saltiness – and it definitely helps that it's both economical and a cinch to make. All you need is a hot wok or frying pan or and the rest will take care of itself. Traditionally, blood cockles are featured but I have decided to omit these on account of their dubious freshness in Australia. With a glass of ice-cold beer, char kway teow always reminds me of warm tropical nights and sparkling seas.

Pound the sliced chillies to a paste (see note) with a mortar and pestle. Cut the rice noodle sheets into 1 cm (½ inch) strips and separate gently. If there is too much oil on the noodles, pour hot water over them. (In Australia, most fresh rice noodle sheets are sold refrigerated with oil used liberally to prevent the sheets from sticking.) Drain immediately in a colander and loosen with chopsticks to prevent sticking. Alternatively, you can microwave the noodles for about 2 minutes to soften.

Heat the oil in a wok over medium-high heat. Add the pounded chilli and the garlic, stir-fry for just 10 seconds – chillies burn easily – then add the daikon, lap cheong and noodles and toss until combined.

Push the noodles to one side, then pour the eggs into the centre. Bring the noodles back to the middle and stir-fry with the eggs for 2–3 minutes or until cooked through and everything is steaming and nicely charred.

Add the prawns, along with the dark and light soy sauces, bean shoots and garlic chives and stir-fry for about 3 minutes until the prawns are cooked and everything is well combined. Season to taste and serve immediately.

✖ Using sambal oelek is a good substitute for blending dried chillies.

Already-cut freshly made rice noodles are now sold in many Asian grocers. If these are not available, use refrigerated prepack noodles. Bring to room temperature before using; they are brittle when cold. Dried ho fun noodles work well, too.

Lap cheong (Chinese pork sausages) are sold in plastic packets in Asian grocers. If you can't find lap cheong, crisp-fried spicy chorizo is fantastic as an alternative.

For thick dark soy sauce, look for a Malaysian brand called Cheong Chan, or the Indonesian ABC kecap asin (asin meaning salt).

- 3–4 dried red chillies (see note), or to taste, softened in hot water, then sliced
- 500 g (1 lb 2 oz) fresh flat rice noodle sheets (see note)
- 2½ tablespoons neutral oil
- 2 garlic cloves, finely chopped
- 2 tablespoons dried daikon (white radish), very finely chopped
- 2 lap cheong (Chinese sausage), sliced thinly (see note)
- 2 eggs, beaten
- 200 g (7 oz) green prawns, peeled and deveined, tails removed
- 2 teaspoons thick dark soy sauce (kecap asin; see note)
- 1–2 tablespoons light soy sauce
- 2 handfuls bean shoots
- 30 g (1 oz) garlic chives, cut into 2.5 cm (1 inch) lengths
- Salt and white pepper, to taste

SERVES 6

ASAM LAKSA

If there's one Malaysian dish that beats rendang and char kway teow in my estimation, it's asam laksa. A rice-noodle soup flavoured with a heady fish broth made with tamarind and tropical spices, and topped with flaked fish and masses of tropical herbs, torch ginger flower, pineapple and cucumber, asam laksa has won the hearts and palates of Malaysians and visitors alike.

Arguably the most famous street food in Penang and northern Malaysia, its name is derived from the Malay word for tamarind – asam, the main souring agent used for the soup – though the dried pieces of a tropical Malaysian fruit, *Garcinia atroviridis* – called asam keping or asam gelugor – are usually added to enhance the tangy flavour. These key ingredients complement strong-tasting fish, such as wolf herring or chub mackerel, the preferred choice for making this dish.

It's a simple dish to make: just cook the fish with Vietnamese mint and galangal, then add ground spices to the fish stock. While the noodles are cooking, flake the fish into the stock. Then it's just a matter of serving the noodles, pouring the hot stock over the top and finishing it all with herbs, greens, pineapple and, if you can get your hands on it, a spoonful of hae ko, the molasses-like black shrimp paste, for extra funk and richness.

---

1 kg (2 lb 4 oz) whole fish (such as bream or snapper; see note)
3 slices asam keping (optional)
4 Vietnamese mint sprigs
4 slices galangal
150 g (5½ oz) tamarind pulp
1 tablespoon sugar, or to taste
1 teaspoon salt, or to taste
400 g (14 oz) dried laksa noodles, soaked in water until soft, then drained (see note)

SPICE PASTE
5 shallots (eschalots), sliced
4 dried red chillies, soaked in hot water and squeezed dry
4 fresh long red chillies, chopped
2 lemongrass stalks (white part only), sliced
2 tablespoons chopped galangal
2.5 cm (1 inch) fresh turmeric or 1 teaspoon ground turmeric
1 teaspoon belacan (shrimp paste)

TOPPINGS
½ pineapple, peeled and cut into thin strips
1 Lebanese cucumber, seeds removed, cut into thin strips
1 onion, thinly sliced
5 iceberg lettuce leaves, finely sliced
1 bunch of mint, leaves picked
1 bunch of Vietnamese mint, leaves picked
1 ginger flower (torch ginger; optional), thinly sliced (see note)
2–3 long red chillies, seeds removed and thinly sliced
1 tablespoon hae ko (black shrimp paste; optional), diluted in a little hot water (see note)

Place the fish in a large saucepan with the asam keping, Vietnamese mint and galangal, and cover with 2 litres (8 cups) water. Bring to the boil, then reduce the heat to medium and simmer until the fish is cooked through (the flesh should flake away easily from the bone).

Remove the fish from the saucepan, allow to cool, then flake the meat from the bones; discard the skin and bones.

Strain the fish stock into a clean saucepan and return the flaked fish to the stock.

Mix the tamarind pulp with 1 cup (250 ml) hot water. Mash the soaked tamarind with your fingers to extract as much pulp from the seeds as possible, then strain the mixture into a bowl. Pour the strained tamarind juice into the stock, discarding the solids.

For the spice paste, blend all the ingredients in a food processor or blender until finely chopped into a paste.

Add the spice paste to the fish stock along with the salt and sugar, adjusting to taste. Bring to a simmer and cook, stirring occasionally, for 20–30 minutes or until the flavours are rich and rounded.

When you're ready to serve, cook the soaked noodles in a saucepan of boiling water for 5–7 minutes. Drain well, then divide among bowls. Ladle the soup over the noodles and top with garnishes. Serve hot.

✖ Dried laksa rice noodles are found in Asian grocers. Thick rice noodles are a good substitute.

The recipe uses a whole fish. If you use fillets, reduce to 500 g (1 lb 2 oz).

Ginger flower (torch ginger) is sometimes sold fresh at florists, and is sold frozen in select Asian grocers. In Bahasa Malaysia, it is called bunga kantan.

Hae ko is also called petis udang and otak udang in Malaysia.

STIR-FRIED SQUID INK NOODLES WITH PRAWNS, LAP CHEONG AND TOMATO

SERVES 2–4

I once had some leftover squid-ink pasta and decided to spin it into noodles, adding them to a stir-fry with some seafood and chillies. I was feeling smug about it, thinking it was pretty original, until I saw similar recipes by Neil Perry and Christine Manfield. Great minds?

Squid ink is fabulous eating, but a lot of people tend to feel squeamish about it on account of its black colour. Serve it with something white or red and it should be more attractive to many. Squid ink is now easy to find; it's sold at gourmet delicatessens and fishmongers. Keep in mind that udon or Hokkien noodles are (almost) just as good if you don't feel like making squid-ink noodles from scratch. Or you could always pick up some fresh squid-ink pasta from a delicatessen or gourmet food shop if you can find it.

For the noodles, sift the flour onto a clean bench and make a well in the centre. Add the egg, squid ink, oil and salt, mix the dough by hand to bring it together, then knead gently until smooth and not sticky. Wrap in plastic wrap and leave at room temperature for 30 minutes to rest.

Set up a pasta machine and dust it well with flour. Cut the dough in half, dust with flour, then roll one half through the pasta machine (keep the other half covered), starting at the widest setting and reducing the settings notch by notch until the thinnest setting, dusting with flour as you go. Pass through the cutter of your pasta machine, or slice lengthways into fine strips with a sharp knife. Repeat with the remaining dough.

Cook the noodles in plenty of salted water until al dente. Drain well and toss with a little oil if you aren't using them immediately.

Heat a large, deep frying pan over high heat, add the oil, swirl to coat, then add the lap cheong, garlic, chilli, coriander (with the roots) and prawns, and stir-fry over high heat for 2–3 minutes until the prawns just turn pink. Transfer to a plate.

Return the pan to the heat and add the noodles along with the chicken stock and fish and oyster sauces. Simmer for 30 seconds to 1 minute, then return the lap cheong mixture to the pan along with the tomatoes. Toss well and adjust the seasoning to taste. Divide among bowls, top with coriander and serve with lemon wedges.

2 tablespoons olive oil
2 lap cheong (Chinese sausage), sliced (see note page 37)
2 garlic cloves, chopped
1 long red chilli, minced
1 coriander (cilantro) sprig, roots finely chopped, plus extra chopped coriander to serve
250 g (9 oz) green prawns, peeled and deveined
1 cup (250 ml) chicken stock
1 tablespoon fish sauce
1 tablespoon oyster sauce
1 cup (150 g) sliced cherry tomatoes
Salt and white pepper, to taste
Lemon wedges, to serve

SQUID-INK NOODLES
1⅔ cups (250 g) strong flour, plus extra for dusting
2 eggs, plus 2 egg yolks, lightly beaten
2 teaspoons squid ink, mixed with 1–2 tablespoons water to dissolve
1 tablespoon olive oil, plus extra for greasing
Good pinch of salt, or to taste

PROSPERITY TOSS
YEE SANG

SERVES 4–6

Salads, as we know them in the West, are not often associated with Chinese food; however, the practice of serving cold dishes in the form of starters has been common since the Spring and Autumn Period (770–476BCE). This trend is still popular in Beijing and Shanghai, but it has not caught on with many southern Chinese. Interestingly, when the Chinese migrated to Singapore and Malaysia, it became common to offer a salad of raw fish to diners during Chinese New Year. That said, the origin of this dish is rather murky. Some writers suggest it was created by a Cantonese chef in Seremban, a town in Malaysia. Others credit its origins to Singapore's Chinese chefs. The facts are these: it only became popular in the 1960s and it was not created in China. Called 'yu sheng' in Mandarin and 'yee sang' in Cantonese, this dish is consumed with great gusto because it is considered to be auspicious to toss and mix all the ingredients together ('lou hei' meaning 'tossing prosperity') during Chinese New Year. Consequently, the dish is referred to as prosperity toss.

Although rice vermicelli is not used in the original raw fish salad, this version is a favourite with my family. Noodles are, after all, a must-eat dish during birthdays and celebrations. The original dish uses plum sauce, but it's too sweet in my opinion. I've put my spin on it by creating the dressing below instead.

For the dressing, combine all the ingredients in a screw-top jar, and shake well to combine. (Alternatively, whisk them together in a bowl.)

Heat 8–10 cm (3–4 inch) oil in a wok or heavy-based saucepan and set up a plate with paper towel on it, ready to drain. When the oil is hot (bubbles should form around a wooden chopstick when it's dipped in) add the vermicelli in batches, deep-frying until crisp and puffed (only a matter of seconds). Remove the vermicelli with tongs or chopsticks and drain on the paper towel. Repeat with the remaining vermicelli.

To serve, place the noodles on a platter. Arrange the carrot, daikon, pickled leeks, gingers, spring onion and pomelo around and over the crisp vermicelli. Toss the makrut lime leaves with the fish and spread it over the top. Pour the dressing over the fish and sprinkle the peanuts and sesame seeds on top.

Serve immediately, encouraging diners to mix the salad with chopsticks to ensure good fortune.

Neutral oil, for deep-frying
120 g (4¼ oz) dried rice vermicelli
100 g (3½ oz) carrot, cut into fine matchsticks
100 g (3½ oz) daikon (white radish)
2 tablespoons pickled baby leeks (optional), finely chopped
1 tablespoon pickled ginger, chopped
2 tablespoons preserved sweet ginger, chopped
1 cup (50 g) spring onion (scallions), finely sliced
2 segments fresh pomelo (optional), shredded by hand
3 makrut lime leaves, cut into thin slices
500 g (1 lb 2 oz) sashimi-grade salmon or ocean trout, thinly sliced
2 tablespoons peanuts, chopped
1 tablespoon sesame seeds, roasted

DRESSING
¼ cup (60 ml) mirin
1 tablespoon Shaoxing wine
2 tablespoons light soy sauce
1 tablespoon neutral oil
Pinch of Chinese five-spice powder
Dash of sesame oil, approximately ¼ teaspoon

SERVES 3 | 4

LAKSA LEMAK

Invariably called laksa throughout Malaysia and Singapore, there are almost as many versions of this favourite as there are cooks. To the south of the country, laksa means a spicy noodle soup enriched with coconut milk and topped with a range of ingredients, ranging from bean sprouts and shredded chicken to fish cakes and fried beancurd. Some writers claim the origin of laksa lemak is the state of Melaka (Malacca), but this is questionable. Some cooks insist on using only fresh, thick, rice noodles called laksa noodles, but it is not really necessary.

This laksa recipe is the coconut-milk version, which as far as I know belongs to the southern style. It's a recipe shared with me by my sister Quee Wah, who was a great curry laksa cook.

½ cup (125 ml) neutral oil
800 ml (28 fl oz) chicken stock
400 ml (14 fl oz) tinned or fresh coconut milk
1 tablespoon caster (superfine) sugar
6 square fried beancurd puffs, soaked in hot water then squeezed to remove excess water, cut in half diagonally
150 g (5½ oz) small green prawns, peeled and deveined
500 g (1 lb 2 oz) fresh thick rice noodles or Hokkien wheat noodles
150 g (5½ oz) bean sprouts, blanched and refreshed in cold water
1 chicken breast (about 250 g/9 oz), steamed or poached, then shredded
Salt, to taste
Coriander (cilantro) sprigs or hot mint leaves (see note), to serve

SPICE PASTE

2 fat lemongrass stalks, tough outer leaves removed and tied into a knot, white part of stalks finely chopped
2 garlic cloves
2 cm (¾ inch) piece fresh turmeric, finely chopped
2.5 cm (1 inch) galangal, finely chopped
6 candlenuts, crushed
1 onion or 150 g (5½ oz) shallots (eschalots), chopped
6–10 long red chillies, thinly sliced
1 tablespoon (about 15 g/½ oz) belacan (shrimp paste), roasted (see note)
3 cm (1¼ inch) piece ginger, finely chopped

For the spice paste, add the chopped lemongrass to a food processor (reserve the tied leaves) with the remaining ingredients and blend to a fine paste, adding a little water if necessary.

Heat the oil in a large saucepan over medium heat, add the spice paste and stir-fry for 5–10 minutes or until fragrant.

Add the chicken stock, coconut milk, sugar and tied lemongrass leaves and bring slowly to the boil. Add the fried bean puffs, then reduce the heat to low and simmer, stirring occasionally, for 15–20 minutes. Add the prawns, and poach for 1–2 minutes. Season to taste with salt.

When you're ready to serve, scald the noodles in a saucepan of boiling water for 2 minutes, drain and divide among deep soup bowls with the bean sprouts, chicken, prawns and beancurd. Pour the hot stock on top and finish with coriander or hot mint.

✖ Although known as hot mint, this herb does not belong to the mint family. It has been reclassified from *Polygonum odoratum* to *Persicaria odorata*. Cookbooks also use names such as Vietnamese mint and laksa leaf. It is the same thing.

To roast belacan, wrap it in foil and bake at 120°C (250°F) for 20–30 minutes.

FRIED RICE WITH CHICKEN, SALTED FISH AND BEAN SHOOTS

SERVES 2–4

When I was a child, my mother would often stretch the family meal with steamed salted fish and minced pork to be served over rice. Sometimes she would stretch the rice further by frying it with bits of salted fish. Though it's satisfying and full of wok-fragrance, we considered salted-fish fried rice as rather plebeian, but now it's chic to serve this humble family dish in some upmarket restaurants.

Heat a wok or a large frying pan over high heat. Add 2 tablespoons oil, swirl to coat, then add the salted fish and stir-fry until crisp and golden (about 1–2 minutes). Transfer to a plate and return the wok to the heat.

Add the chicken to the wok and stir-fry for 1–2 minutes until it turns white. Transfer to the plate with the salted fish and return the wok to the heat again.

Add the remaining oil, pour in the eggs and fry, swirling them around until just set. Add the rice and stir-fry for 2 minutes, making sure the grains are separate and breaking up the eggs as you go.

Add the spring onion and return the salted fish and chicken to the wok, toss to combine, cook for a further 2–3 minutes, then add the bean sprouts, soy sauce and salt and pepper and stir-fry for another minute or until heated through. Serve at once.

✖ One of the best salted fish is made from mackerel. A product of Thailand, it is sold in refrigerated counters sealed in plastic wrap, most often at Thai grocers. Sometimes, I have substituted baccalà and, while it tastes somewhat different, it's still delicious.

4 tablespoons neutral oil
30 g (1 oz) salted fish (see note), or to taste, skin removed, lightly rinsed in water
100 g (3½ oz) chicken (any cut), cut into 1 cm (½ inch) pieces
2 eggs, beaten with a pinch of salt
400 g (14 oz) cooked medium-grain white rice (preferably day-old), grains separated
½ cup (60 g) thinly sliced spring onions (scallions)
1 cup (115 g) bean sprouts, tails removed and cut into sections
1 tablespoon light soy sauce
Salt and white pepper, to taste

CANTONESE FRIED RICE

SERVES 2–4

The Chinese love fried rice, and it also happens to be one of the best ways of using up leftover rice. After all, the best fried rice is usually made with leftover rice because the grains separate more readily after a night in the fridge, giving a more even and appealing result. Fried rice is one of the most consistently rewarding meals because, like risotto, there are so many variations, but it pays to follow the recipe – it's the little things that make the difference.

100 ml (3½ fl oz) neutral oil
2 lap cheong (Chinese sausage), cut into small cubes (see page 37)
2 eggs, lightly beaten, mixed with ¼ teaspoon salt
500 g (1 lb 2 oz) cooked medium-grain white rice (preferably day-old), grains separated
120 g (4¼ oz) green prawns, peeled, deveined and chopped
3 spring onions (scallions), finely chopped
½ teaspoon sesame oil
2 teaspoons light soy sauce
Salt and freshly ground pepper, to taste

Heat a wok or large frying pan over high heat. Add 2 tablespoons oil, swirl to coat, then add the lap cheong and stir-fry until just crisp. Transfer to a plate.

Add the remaining oil, then pour in the eggs and fry, swirling them around until just set. Add the rice and stir-fry for 1–2 minutes, making sure the grains are separated and breaking up the egg as you go. Add the prawns and spring onions, return the lap cheong to the wok, and stir-fry for another 1–2 minutes until the prawns are just cooked and have changed colour. Add the sesame oil and soy sauce down the side of the wok, add salt and pepper to taste, and stir-fry for another minute. Serve at once.

✿ If you find rice is consumed in bigger quantities, you may need to offer an extra 100 g (3½ oz) of cooked rice per person and adjust the rest of the ingredients accordingly. In this case you may need a larger wok to fry the rice perfectly. The heat source is of vital importance to yield a superior product.

CHINESE OLIVE FRIED RICE

Serves 6–8

This recipe is based loosely on a Teochew (Chiu Chow) dish. Chinese olives have the same shape as European and Middle Eastern olives but otherwise are wholly different, coming from a tropical fruit called *Canarium album*. They are usually used as a preserve, and are sold whole or shredded, the latter often mixed with pickled mustard greens. It is often used as a condiment to have with congee. I've given it a whirl in fried rice here, where it adds something a little different to the usual. Different brands of Chinese olives contain more salt, so adjust the seasoning carefully and taste as you go.

Heat a wok or large frying pan over high heat. Add 2 tablespoons oil, swirl to coat, then add the olives and prawns and stir-fry until the prawns are pink (about 30 seconds). Transfer to a plate, wipe the wok clean and return to the heat.

Add the remaining oil, pour in the egg and fry, swirling around until just set. Add the rice and stir-fry for 1 minute, making sure the grains are separated and breaking up the egg as you go. Add the spring onions and return the olive-prawn mixture to the wok, toss to combine and cook for a minute to heat everything together, then add the sesame oil, soy sauce, salt and pepper, and stir-fry for another minute. Serve hot.

✖ If your diners like to eat extra fried rice, you can add 100 g (3½ oz) of cooked rice per person and adjust the rest of the ingredients accordingly. In this case you may need a larger wok to fry the rice perfectly. The heat source is of vital importance to yield a superior product.

5 tablespoons neutral oil
¼ cup (50 g) Chinese chopped olives mixed with mustard greens (see above)
150 g (5½ oz) green prawns, peeled and deveined, chopped
1 egg, lightly beaten and mixed with ¼ teaspoon salt
500 g (1 lb 2 oz) cooked medium-grain white rice (preferably day-old), grains separated
3 tablespoons thinly sliced spring onion (scallions)
1 teaspoon sesame oil
2 teaspoons light soy sauce
Salt and freshly ground white pepper, to taste

SERVES 2–4

FRIED RICE WITH PINEAPPLE
KHAO PAD SAPPAROT

Fried rice in Asia is what risotto is to the West: it comes in hundreds of guises and it always pleases just about any diner. The following recipe from Thailand is intriguing because I have seen it in Vietnam as well as in China's Yunnan province (although black glutinous rice is used instead). You can use chicken, prawns, chicken liver or any ingredient that catches your imagination. And, if you really want to go all out, you can do as some restaurants do and serve it in a hollowed-out pineapple.

- ¼ cup (60 ml) camellia tea oil (from health-food shops), or any neutral oil, plus an extra tablespoon
- 2 lap cheong (Chinese sausage), diced (see note page 37)
- 2 garlic cloves, finely chopped
- 2–3 tablespoons finely chopped onion, to taste
- 1 teaspoon curry powder
- 3 large prawns (about 130 g/4½ oz total), peeled, deveined and chopped
- 1 egg, lightly beaten
- Large pinch of white sugar
- 2 tablespoons soy sauce
- 3 cups (about 550 g/1 lb 3 oz) cooked medium-grain white rice (preferably day-old), grains separated
- ½ cup (80 g) diced pineapple
- 1 firm tomato, coarsely chopped
- 1 spring onion (scallion), thinly sliced
- 1 coriander (cilantro) sprig, chopped

Heat a wok or large frying pan over medium-high heat. Add the ¼ cup oil, swirl to coat, then add the lap cheong and stir-fry for 1 minute or until just crisp. Transfer to a plate, reserving the oil in the wok.

Reduce the heat to medium, add the garlic and stir-fry until fragrant and just beginning to colour (about 30 seconds). Add the onion and curry powder and cook, stirring constantly, until fragrant, then add the prawns and stir-fry for 2 minutes until almost cooked through. Push all to the side.

Add an extra tablespoon of oil and pour in the egg, scramble for a minute, then add the sugar and soy sauce, and immediately stir in the cooked rice.

Stir until well coated and the grains are nicely separated and starting to pop, then add the pineapple, tomato and crisp lap cheong, reduce the heat to low and mix gently until hot.

When everything is hot, add the spring onion and toss it through. Serve sprinkled with coriander.

GLASS NOODLES WITH PAN-FRIED FISH AND SAFFRON BROTH

SERVES 2–4

Glass noodles, or mung bean vermicelli, are often teamed with seafood in Chinese, Thai and Vietnamese cuisines. They can be super-rustic or super-sophisticated, with crushed salted duck egg yolk presented as a garnish. Saffron – or xi hong hua – was used in medieval China but not so much in present-day Chinese cooking. But since I now live in Trentham, where saffron is grown at Trentham Fields, I'm using it in this delicious dish.

¼ cup (60 ml) neutral oil
3 spring onions (scallions), thinly sliced
2 shallots (eschalots), finely chopped
1 tablespoon finely chopped ginger
2 garlic cloves, finely chopped
125 g (4½ oz) glass noodles, soaked in hot water until soft, then drained and cut into 15 cm (6 inch) lengths
½ teaspoon saffron threads, soaked in ¼ cup (60 ml) chicken stock
3 cups (750 ml) chicken stock, plus ¼ cup (60 ml) (see note)
Pinch of caster (superfine) sugar
1 tablespoon light soy sauce, or to taste
6 snapper fillets, skin on and pin-boned
Finely grated zest of 2 lemons (or to taste)
2 tablespoons thinly sliced chives or coriander (cilantro)

Heat a wok or large frying pan over high heat. Add 1 tablespoon oil, swirl to coat, then add the spring onions. Stir-fry for 30 seconds, then add the shallots, ginger and garlic, and stir-fry for 30 seconds to 1 minute until golden and fragrant.

Add the glass noodles, saffron and chicken stock, bring to the boil, then add the sugar and soy sauce. Leave to simmer until the liquid is slightly thickened and the sugar is dissolved (about 5 minutes).

At the same time, heat the remaining oil in a frying pan over medium-high heat. Season the fish with salt on both sides, then fry skin-side down for 2–3 minutes until crisp. Flip and cook for another 2–3 minutes until just cooked through.

To serve, transfer the noodles to a platter, top with the fish fillets and finish with the lemon zest and chives.

✖ You need very good stock to make this dish sing (see page 162–63).

JEWELLED-RICE CONGEE WITH SWEETCORN AND WHITEBAIT FRITTERS

SERVES 2–4

Recently, packets of rice mixed with adzuki beans, pearl barley, mung beans, lotus seeds, black urid beans, glutinous rice, millet and wheat have surfaced in some Asian grocers. They are the latest congee mixture and, apparently, the craze in China.

As you may know, congee is comfort food eaten for breakfasts and suppers. It can be simple or elaborate, with garnishes ranging from pickles, preserved duck eggs, salted fish, fermented beancurd and so on. It can be cooked in water or chicken stock (I even came across a stock made with Yunnan ham). Try this with whitebait fritters, a New Zealand tradition of all things, and if you're not already in love with congee, you might just be converted.

Rinse the rice mixture, cover with plenty of water and leave to soak for 1 hour or preferably overnight. Strain through a fine sieve.

Place the corn cob in a saucepan and add 2 cups (500 ml) chicken stock. Bring to the boil and cook until tender (about 15 minutes). Shave the kernels off the cob with a sharp knife.

Place the soaked rice mixture in a large saucepan, pour in the remaining stock and add the salt and oil. Bring to the boil, add the corn kernels, then reduce the heat to low and simmer, partially covered with a lid, stirring regularly to prevent sticking, for about 2 hours or until soft, creamy and slightly runny. Turn off the heat and cover tightly.

For the whitebait fritters, place the whitebait in a colander to remove excess moisture. Sift the flour into a bowl, add the egg, sesame oil and a dash of water, and whisk to a smooth batter.

Add the whitebait, spring onion and coriander, season to taste, and toss to coat.

Heat a tablespoon of oil in a non-stick frying pan over medium heat. Place a large spoonful of the fritter mixture into the pan and spread it evenly. Fry until the underside is nicely browned, about 3–4 minutes, then flip and do the same on the other side. Repeat with the remaining mixture.

Serve bowls of the congee with a splash of soy sauce and sesame oil and the accompaniments of your choice, with a whitebait fritter on the side.

✖ Remember rice absorbs liquid readily – you may have to add more. Wheat and barley take a little longer to cook so if some of the other grains turn mushy, don't worry – it's meant to be creamy.

If fresh whitebait is not available, frozen whitebait works a treat, too.

1 cup (220 g) mixed rice grains (see introduction and note)
1 sweetcorn cob
3 litres (12 cups) golden or regular chicken stock
Large pinch of salt, or to taste
2 tablespoons neutral oil
Soy sauce and sesame oil, to serve

WHITEBAIT FRITTERS
500 g (1 lb 2 oz) fresh whitebait (from select fishmongers; see note)
2 tablespoons self-raising flour
2 eggs, beaten
1 teaspoon sesame oil
1 spring onion (scallion), thinly sliced
1 large sprig fresh coriander (cilantro), finely chopped
Salt and white pepper, to taste

ACCOMPANIMENTS OF YOUR CHOICE
3 spring onions (scallions), thinly sliced
Crisp-fried shallots
Deep-fried crisp anchovies
Finely chopped salted radish
Cooked salted duck egg, cut into small pieces
Chopped chillies

SERVES 2–4

GLASS NOODLES WITH MINCED PORK, SHIITAKE AND GARLIC CHIVES

This is my version of a famous Yunnan dish often called 'ants climbing a tree' noodles. It is made with minced meat, often pork, but whatever mince you use it's the way the meat clings to the noodles as you lift them that gives it the rather poetic name.

I'm using mung bean noodles (also called cellophane or bean thread noodles) for this recipe, but any kind of noodle is fine, such as thin rice or wheat noodles. You just need to adjust the timing for the noodles to cook through.

3–4 dried shiitake mushrooms
250 g (9 oz) minced pork
1 tablespoon Shaoxing wine
1–2 tablespoons doubanjiang (chilli bean paste)
1 teaspoon cornflour (cornstarch)
200 g (7 oz) dried mung bean noodles (see note)
¼ cup (60 ml) neutral oil
1–2 long red chillies, seeds removed, thinly sliced
½ cup (125 ml) chicken stock, plus an extra ½ cup (125 ml) as needed
½ teaspoon caster (superfine) sugar
Salt and white pepper, to taste
Light or dark soy sauce, to taste
1 cup (125 g) chopped garlic chives (2 cm/¾ inch pieces)

Soak the dried mushrooms in hot water for 20 minutes. Drain and squeeze out excess water, discard the stems, then cut the caps into fine dice.

Add the pork, Shaoxing, doubanjiang and cornflour to a bowl, mix well to combine, and leave for 15 minutes to marinate.

Place the noodles in a bowl, pour cold water over the top and soak for 10 minutes or until tender. Drain well.

Heat the oil in a wok, add the mushrooms and chilli and stir-fry until fragrant (1–2 minutes). Add the marinated pork and stir-fry for 2-3 minutes, breaking up the meat as you fry so there are no lumps, then add the noodles along with the stock, sugar, salt and pepper and soy sauce, adjusting to taste.

Cook, stirring now and then, until most of the liquid has been absorbed. If the noodles are absorbing liquid too quickly, add another ½ cup (125 ml) stock. Stir in the garlic chives just before serving.

✖ Mung bean/glass/bean thread noodles may be soaked in hot water briefly but must be used immediately, as they have a tendency to turn mushy if left too long.

NASI LEMAK

SERVES 6

This delectable one-plate meal is as much a hawker favourite as it is a festive offering throughout Malaysia, Singapore and Indonesia. I must admit I have a weakness for this most delicious dish. Several versions exist, some more elaborate than others (including those offered with beef rendang, like this one), but the key features are the fabulous rich rice and a fiery sambal usually made with dried chillies with the occasional fresh chilli tossed in for that vibrant colour.

The secret ingredient in this sambal is ikan bilis – dried anchovies. The recipe may look long and appear complicated but, once you break down the components, it's actually quite straightforward. And trust me, when you taste it, it's certainly worth all the effort.

- 2 cups (400 g) Thai jasmine rice, washed thoroughly and drained
- 2 cups (500 ml) coconut milk
- Pinch of salt
- 2 pandan leaves
- 1 lemongrass stalk (white part only), bruised
- 15 g (½ oz) ginger, cut into julienne

SAMBAL IKAN BILIS
- 30 g (1 oz) long dried chillies, bases snipped and soaked in hot water
- 3 fresh long red chillies, or to taste, chopped
- 2–3 shallots (eschalots; about 100 g), chopped
- 2 garlic cloves, chopped
- 10 g (¼ oz) dried ikan bilis (dried anchovies), rinsed
- ½–1 teaspoon belacan (shrimp paste), roasted, to taste (see note page 42)
- ½ cup (125 ml) neutral oil
- 1 small red onion, sliced
- 2–3 tablespoon tamarind concentrate, to taste
- 1 tablespoon caster (superfine) sugar
- Salt, to taste

ACCOMPANIMENTS
- ¼ cup (35 g) roasted peanuts
- Beef rendang (see page 119)
- 30 g (1 oz) ikan bilis (dried anchovies), deep-fried in oil until crisp
- 3 hard-boiled eggs, halved
- 1 small cucumber, thinly sliced

Put the rice in a saucepan or rice cooker with the coconut milk, salt, pandan, lemongrass and ginger. Add enough water so it reaches 3.5 cm (1½ inches) above the level of the rice. Cook, covered with a lid, on medium heat (or according to the manufacturer's instructions if you're using a rice cooker) until all the liquid is absorbed. Reduce the heat to low and continue to steam with the lid on for another 10 minutes. Remove from the heat, fluff up with a fork and set aside, covered.

Meanwhile, for the sambal ikan bilis, blend the soaked and fresh chillies, shallot, garlic, ikan bilis and belacan in a food processor to a smooth paste. Heat the oil in a wok or frying pan over medium heat, add the paste and fry until aromatic or the oil floats to the surface, then add the onion, tamarind, sugar and salt, adjusting to taste. Reduce the heat to low and let it bubble away, stirring regularly, for 10 minutes until the chillies have been cooked out and it reaches a thickish sauce consistency, adding a little water if the sambal is cooking too quickly. Taste it and adjust the seasoning if needed.

To serve, put the rice in the centre of individual serving plates, scatter some peanuts over it and surround it with beef rendang, ikan bilis, egg, sliced cucumber and sambal ikan bilis.

TRADERS' RICE

NASI DAGANG

SERVES 2 | 4

I can still remember eating my first traders' rice in the local market in my hometown. Wrapped in banana leaf, the rice still warm and topped with a piece of skipjack tuna simmered in an aromatic coconut gulai (curry), it was a revelation.

Emblematic of the east coast of the Malay Peninsula, nasi dagang – the name means traders' rice – is a composite dish where the rice is the star. Making the rice perfectly requires some skill and patience, however, since it combines jasmine and glutinous rice that has to be soaked and then steamed until partially tender before it is sprinkled with fenugreek seeds. Coconut milk is added before it is returned to the steamer to render the rice soft and fragrant.

The dish is always served with ikan tongkol, a member of the skipjack tuna family, but I have regularly used mackerel or snapper. Traditionally the fish is cooked with asam keping – sun-dried slices of *Garcinia atroviridis*, a sour fruit native to Southeast Asia. I have at times tossed in lime peel or rice vinegar in its place without missing the flavour.

The recipe looks long, but it's actually easy to make if you start it a day ahead. It truly is delicious, and I urge you to go for it.

For the rice, combine the jasmine and glutinous rice, then rinse until the water runs clear. Cover the rice with water and leave to soak overnight.

The next day, drain the rice, transfer to a cake tin or a steamer basket lined with baking paper and steam, covered, over a wok of boiling water, for 25 minutes until tender.

Stir the salt into the coconut milk, then remove the rice from the steamer, and stir in the seasoned coconut milk and fenugreek seeds. Return to the steamer and steam for another 15–20 minutes (topping up water as needed) until the rice is fluffy with distinct grains. Gently fold in the shallots and ginger and keep warm.

Place the fish, asam keping and salt in a saucepan. Cover with water and bring to a gentle boil. Simmer for 5 minutes, then turn off the heat. Leave to steep for 15–20 minutes until the fish is cooked through and the stock is aromatic. Transfer the fish to a bowl and strain the stock into a container. Discard the asam keping.

For the spice paste, place the soaked and fresh chillies, garlic, shallots, ginger and galangal with ½ cup (125 ml) water in a blender or food processor and blend to a fine paste. Heat the oil in a saucepan, add the paste and cook, stirring, over medium heat until fragrant (about 10 minutes). Add the ground spices and continue to fry, stirring, for 3–5 minutes until incorporated.

Stir in 2 cups (500 ml) reserved fish stock, then add the coconut cream and sugar. Leave to bubble gently for 10 minutes, then add the cooked fish to warm through. Season to taste and serve with the rice.

✖ Trader's rice is usually served for breakfast. However, you can serve it as a light lunch with a salad or a pickle (page 281 or 284).

600 g (1 lb 5 oz) mackerel or snapper cutlets, skin on
5–7 pieces asam keping, to taste (see above)
1 teaspoon salt
4 long green chillies
4 long red chillies
1 lemongrass stalk (white part only), halved lengthways
1 cup (250 ml) coconut cream, or to taste
2–3 teaspoons gula melaka or dark brown sugar, to taste

RICE

200 g (7 oz) jasmine rice
100 g (3½ oz) glutinous rice
Good pinch of salt
1½ cups (375 ml) coconut milk
1 teaspoon fenugreek seeds
2–3 shallots (eschalots), thinly sliced
3 cm (1¼ inch) piece (about 15 g) ginger, julienned

SPICE PASTE

12 dried chillies, bases snipped and soaked in hot water until soft, chopped
4 long red chillies, chopped
3 garlic cloves, chopped
2 shallots (eschalots), chopped
5 cm (2 inch) piece (25 g) ginger, chopped
3 cm (1¼ inch) piece galangal, chopped
½ cup (125 ml) neutral oil
1 teaspoon belacan (shrimp paste)
1 teaspoon ground cumin
1 tablespoon ground fennel seeds
1 tablespoon ground coriander

ROSE-SCENTED CHICKEN BIRYANI
NASI BIRYANI

As a kid growing up in Malaysia, I attended Muslim weddings where chicken biryani formed part of the feast. Lavish and elegant, especially when it is presented on exquisite trays adorned with fried nuts, herbs and edible silver leaf, it really is one of the most beautiful one-plate dishes I've ever eaten.

No one knows for certain when biryani came to Southeast Asia. Some writers believe it landed with Arab traders, while others say that it arrived via India. But there is no doubt that biryani originated in Iran, since in Persian, 'birinj biriyan' means fried rice.

Regardless of the path it took, in Southeast Asia it has taken on different personalities and permutations compared with its Indian and Iranian cousins.

While certain ingredients, such as ghee and yoghurt, reflect its forebears, the cooking method differs. Instead of cooking rice and meat together as in certain parts of India, the local way of cooking this aromatic dish is to cook the meat and rice separately before it is assembled.

Traditionally, this extremely popular rice dish is tinted yellow with food colouring. Since I live in Trentham, where saffron is grown, I'm adding it for colour and flavour, as well as rosewater (pandan leaf is a great alternative) to give this dish even more lift.

Start this recipe a day ahead to marinate the chicken.

- 1 kg (2 lb 4 oz) boned chicken pieces (with or without skin)
- 1 teaspoon chilli powder
- ½ teaspoon ground turmeric
- Large pinch of salt
- 2 onions, thinly sliced
- 2 tablespoons ginger
- 5 garlic cloves, chopped
- 2 cups (500 ml) neutral oil
- 5 shallots (eschalots), thinly sliced
- 1 cup (155 g) raw cashews
- 1 tablespoon ghee
- 5 green cardamom pods
- 3 cm (1¼ inch) cinnamon stick
- 5 cloves
- 1 star anise
- 3 tomatoes, finely chopped
- 1 cup (260 g) Greek yoghurt
- 1 teaspoon salt

Place the chicken in a large zip-lock bag, add the chilli powder, turmeric and the salt. Seal bag, massage well to coat, then refrigerate overnight to marinate.

For the spice paste, blend all the ingredients with ½ cup (125 ml) water until smooth. Refrigerate until needed. You can also do this a day ahead.

The next day, blend the onion, ginger and garlic with ½ cup (125 ml) water to a coarse paste and set aside.

Heat the oil in a wok or large saucepan over medium-high heat. Add the shallots, reduce the heat to medium and fry, stirring, for 8–10 minutes until golden brown. Remove with a slotted spoon and drain on paper towel. Add the cashews to the same oil and fry, stirring occasionally, for 3–4 minutes until golden. Remove and drain on paper towel. Reserve both to serve.

Chopped coriander (cilantro), unsprayed rose petals and Indian gold leaf (optional), to serve

SPICE PASTE
- 1 tablespoon ground coriander
- 1 tablespoon ground cumin
- 1 teaspoon ground cardamom
- 1 tablespoon chilli powder
- 1 teaspoon freshly grated nutmeg
- 1 tablespoon garam masala (page 23)

RICE
- 2½ tablespoons melted ghee
- 3 cm (1¼ inch) cinnamon stick
- 5 cardamom pods, bruised
- 4 cloves
- 1 teaspoon salt
- 1 teaspoon rosewater
- 4 cups (800 g) basmati rice, washed and drained
- 1 cup (250 ml) evaporated milk
- ½ teaspoon saffron threads, steeped in 1 tablespoon water

Remove 1½ cups (375 ml) oil and reserve for another use (see note), leaving the remainder in the wok. Add the ghee, swirl until hot and melted, then add the cardamom, cinnamon, cloves and star anise. Let the spices bloom in the oil and ghee for 2 minutes, then add the onion-ginger-garlic paste and stir-fry for 3–5 minutes until fragrant and lightly coloured.

Add the spice paste and continue to stir-fry over medium heat for 4–5 minutes until the oil separates and you can really smell the spices.

Add the chicken, stir-fry fry over medium heat for 1–2 minutes, then stir in the tomatoes and yoghurt. Reduce the heat to low and simmer, stirring occasionally to prevent sticking, for 20–25 minutes until the sauce is reduced slightly and the chicken is cooked through. Season with salt and keep warm.

Meanwhile, for the rice, heat the ghee with 2 tablespoons reserved aromatic oil in a large saucepan over medium heat (or use a rice cooker). Add the cinnamon, cardamom, cloves and salt and cook, stirring, for 1 minute or until fragrant.

Add the rice and rose essence and stir until the rice is coated with the aromatic oil. Stir in 1.25 litres (5 cups) water and the evaporated milk and bring to the boil. Reduce the heat to medium and simmer until the liquid is mostly evaporated and small holes appear on the surface. Reduce the heat to low, cover with a lid, leaving a small gap, and cook for a further 15–17 minutes until the rice is tender. Turn off the heat and stir in the saffron.

Fluff up the rice with a spatula and spoon two-thirds of it onto a large platter. Spoon the chicken over the rice, then spoon another layer of rice over the chicken. Sprinkle with the crisp-fried shallots and cashews, and top with coriander, rose petals and gold leaf to serve.

✻ The aromatic oil used for frying shallots and cashews is precious. Use it for other dishes such as fried greens or vegetables (pages 255 and 259).

SOBA NOODLES WITH SEAFOOD

I ate this lovely dish at The Ritz-Carlton in Singapore years ago. It was so delicious that the flavour – rich with soy, bonito flakes and oyster sauce, and fragrant from celery leaves – has remained with me ever since.

I was lucky enough to find the recipe in a cookbook called *Asian Tapas* written by Christophe Megel, former chef of Singapore's Ritz-Carlton. This recipe, which is light, clean and perfect for summer, is adapted from that cookbook.

30 mussels, scrubbed, or 18 green prawns, shells on
300 g (10½ oz) dried soba noodles
¾ cup (110 g) sliced sun-dried tomatoes
¾ cup (170 g) chopped silken tofu (2 cm/¾ inch dice)
1 long red chilli, minced
⅓ cup (10 g) celery leaves or coriander (cilantro) leaves, to serve

DRESSING
2 tablespoons oyster sauce
2 tablespoons light soy sauce
2 tablespoons katsuobushi (bonito flakes)
¼ cup (60 ml) rice vinegar

Place the mussels in a steamer set over a wok or saucepan of boiling water and steam for 2 minutes or until all have opened. Drain and set aside to cool before removing the mussels from the shells and debearding them. If you're using prawns, cook them in boiling salted water for 2 minutes or until the shells turn pink. Drain and shell the prawns, halve them lengthways, then devein them.

Cook the soba noodles in a saucepan of boiling salted water for about 5–7 minutes or until soft. Drain briefly, then plunge the noodles into iced water to cool. Drain well.

For the dressing, combine the ingredients and ½ cup (125 ml) water in a small saucepan. Bring to the boil, cook for 20 seconds, then remove from the heat and strain into a bowl, discarding the solids.

Transfer the soba to a serving platter, add the mussels or prawns, sun-dried tomatoes, tofu and chilli, pour the dressing over and toss gently. Serve topped with celery leaves.

HAE MEE
PORK AND PRAWN NOODLE SOUP

If you haven't had this dish before, you're in for a treat. A noodle soup made with prawn shells and your choice of chicken or pork bones, this is one of those soulful dishes that grabs your attention immediately and keeps it right there until the last drop.

Popularised by Penang hawkers, its ancestry is Fujian, even though I'm told it's a pale imitation compared to the Penang version. Punchy, aromatic and extremely moreish, it's not difficult to make, though you'll need to peel your own prawns to give you shells for the umami-rich stock. In case you're in a pinch and only have prawn meat, it always pays to keep some prawn shells in the freezer, adding to them each time you use some. If you love prawns and noodle soup, this is one to make again and again.

For the stock, place the bones and the pork or chicken in a large saucepan, cover with 3 litres (12 cups) water and bring to the boil, skimming the surface to remove any impurities. Reduce the heat to medium and simmer for 20 minutes until the pork is cooked through. Remove and cut into bite-sized pieces (if you're using a chicken, after cooking, cut it into pieces through the bone with a cleaver or the heel of a sharp, heavy knife).

Add the peppercorns, ginger and ikan bilis to the stock and leave to simmer gently for another 40 minutes until deeply flavoured. Strain the stock through a fine sieve into a clean saucepan, discarding the solids.

For the spice paste, blend the ingredients to a paste in a food processor or blender.

Heat the oil in a large saucepan over medium-high heat, add the spice paste and fry, stirring, for 3–4 minutes until fragrant. Add the reserved prawn heads and shells, stir until the shells turn red, then add the stock, along with the soy sauce and sugar. Simmer for 30 minutes. Taste and adjust seasoning with sugar, salt and pepper.

At this stage, you can either strain the prawn soup or leave as is for a more concentrated flavour.

Bring another saucepan of salted water to the boil, add the prawns and cook for 3–4 minutes until pink, then remove. Drop in the bean sprouts briefly to blanch them, then remove. Then add the noodles and simmer to refresh them for 3–5 minutes if working in two batches or 8–10 minutes if all at once, then drain.

Divide the noodles among bowls along with the prawns, bean sprouts, pork (or chicken), water spinach and eggs, and pour the hot strained stock over the top. Top with fried shallots and garlic chives to serve.

SERVES 6

100 ml (3½ fl oz) neutral oil
700 g (1 lb 9 oz) green prawns, peeled and deveined, heads and shells reserved
1 tablespoon light soy sauce
1–2 teaspoons caster (superfine) sugar, or to taste
Salt and white pepper, to taste
1 cup (115 g) bean sprouts
1 kg (2 lb 4 oz) Hokkien or rice noodles
Small bunch of water spinach (kangkong or ong choy)
3 boiled eggs, peeled and halved
3 tablespoons crisp-fried shallots
Crisp-fried shallots and ¾ cup (90 g) chopped garlic chives, to serve

STOCK
1 kg (2 lb 4 oz) pork bones or chicken frames
250 g (9 oz) pork fillet or belly or chicken Maryland (thigh, with drumstick attached)
1 teaspoon black peppercorns
2 slices ginger
30 g (1 oz) ikan bilis (dried anchovies)

SPICE PASTE
10 dried chillies, soaked in hot water until soft, chopped
1 onion, finely chopped
2 garlic cloves, minced
1 teaspoon belacan (shrimp paste)

CHINESE BOLOGNESE

ZHAJIANG MIAN

SERVES 2–4

This one-plate meal, featuring noodles tossed in a delicious meat sauce and topped with shredded cucumber, should be called Beijing minced pork with brown bean sauce, but that doesn't sound particularly enticing, so I prefer to call it Chinese Bolognese. It's not quite as popular as Bolognese is in Australia, but give it time.

It calls for brown bean sauce, made from fermented soybeans and wheat flour, which is available in jars. In Cantonese, it's known as mo si jeung (in Mandarin it's tian mian jiang). Look for the Pun Chun brand; if you can't find it, substitute miso.

I have also included a recipe for making wheat noodles with eggs. If you've got a pasta machine, it's a straightforward process that'll make this dish all the more enticing, so it's well worth a go.

2 tablespoons brown bean sauce
1 tablespoon hoisin sauce
1 tablespoon Shaoxing wine
1½ cups (375 ml) chicken stock
⅓ cup (80 ml) neutral oil
5 spring onions (scallions) whites and greens separated, finely chopped
2 large garlic cloves, minced
300 g (10½ oz) minced pork
1 teaspoon caster (superfine) sugar, or to taste
Salt and white pepper, to taste
500 g (1 lb 2 oz) wheat noodles (see below) or fresh Shanghai or Tianjin noodles
1 cucumber, shredded

Combine the brown bean sauce, hoisin sauce, Shaoxing and chicken stock and mix well.

Heat a wok over high heat, add the oil, the white part of the spring onion and the garlic, and stir-fry for 20 seconds until softened. Add the minced pork, stir-fry until the meat changes colour and breaks up, then add the sauce-stock mixture, reduce the heat to medium and simmer for 5–10 minutes until reduced. Season with the sugar, salt and pepper, adjusting to taste. (You can also add another cup of chicken stock if you prefer a runnier consistency.)

Meanwhile, cook the noodles in a saucepan of boiling water for 3–4 minutes. Drain, rinse off excess starch if necessary, then divide among bowls.

Ladle the meat sauce over the noodles and top with cucumber and spring onion tops to serve.

✖ Shanghai noodles tend to stick. A small quantity of oil tossed through will stop this, especially if you are cooking them way ahead of serving.

WHEAT NOODLES

3⅓ cups (500 g) flour, preferably cake flour, plus extra for dusting
Salt, to taste
3 eggs, beaten
100–250 ml (3½–9 fl oz) water, depending on how soft you like the noodles

Place the flour in a large bowl and make a well in the centre. Add the salt, eggs and water, gently mix everything together, then turn out onto a clean bench and knead for 10 minutes or until smooth. Wrap in plastic wrap and set aside for 30 minutes to rest.

Cut the dough in half, dust with flour, then roll one half through a pasta machine (keep the other half covered), starting at the widest setting and reducing the settings notch by notch until the second-thinnest setting, or thinnest if you prefer them extra fine. Pass through the cutter, or slice lengthways into noodles and repeat with the remaining dough. Dust with flour to prevent sticking and keep covered in the fridge until ready to cook.

SERVES 2–4

SPICY MUNG BEAN NOODLE SALAD
LIANG FEN

This wonderful homemade noodle salad is especially popular during the hot summer months in China's Yunnan province, and ever since I introduced it into my cooking class, it's been equally popular with my students. Served with a range of toppings, it's not only aromatic and spicy, but it's great for vegetarians, too, though you could include meat or seafood if you like.

Traditionally, this salad is made from a dark-coloured pure chickpea flour, but as this is not commonly sold in the West, I've used mung bean flour instead. Homemade mung bean noodles require practice but, once you have mastered the technique, they're very easy to make. You'll need a large plastic tray around 28 x 36 cm (11 x 14 inches) – this helps to prevent the dough from sticking. If you want to try this dish but don't have time to make the noodles, in a pinch you can use wheat or rice noodles.

½ cup (70 g) roasted peanuts, lightly crushed
Chopped coriander (cilantro) or mint, to serve

MUNG BEAN NOODLES
60 g (2¼ oz) mung bean flour (see note)
150 ml (5 fl oz) cold water

DRESSING
1 teaspoon caster (superfine) sugar, or to taste
Good pinch of salt, or to taste
1 tablespoon light soy sauce
1 tablespoon Chinkiang vinegar
2 teaspoons sesame oil
⅓ cup (80 ml) neutral oil
2 spring onions (scallions) finely minced
30 g (1 oz) ginger, minced
1 tablespoon roasted sesame seeds
1–2 teaspoons dried chilli flakes
1 teaspoon roasted Sichuan pepper powder

Place the mung bean flour in a bowl, add the cold water and whisk thoroughly to combine. Set aside and bring 2 cups (500 ml) water to the boil in a saucepan. As soon as it comes to the boil, whisk the mung bean flour mixture again, then pour it into the saucepan of boiling water in a steady stream, whisking vigorously until it becomes a translucent, starchy mass.

Tip the dough into a large, ungreased plastic tray. Working quickly, tip the tray in all directions to spread dough all over the tray until it is evenly spread. Leave to cool at room temperature, then refrigerate until chilled (about half an hour).

Meanwhile, for the dressing, whisk the sugar and salt into the soy and vinegar in a large bowl until dissolved. Add the remaining ingredients and stir to combine.

When you're ready to serve, roll the mung bean dough up lengthways to form a sausage. Cut into thin noodles, toss with dressing and top with crushed peanuts and coriander.

✺ Mung bean flour is from Thailand and it is sold as mung bean starch under the label Pine Brand. This can be hard to find in the UK, but Chinese brands may be available. In Mandarin, mung bean starch is called lu dou fen, and in Cantonese it's called luk dau fun.

STIR-FRIED VEGETARIAN HOKKIEN NOODLES

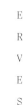

Hokkien noodles, the popular Chinese wheat noodles originally from Fujian province, are extremely versatile, equally at home in stir-fries or soup-based dishes. Below is one of my innumerable vegetarian versions.

Soak the dried mushrooms in 1 cup (250 ml) hot water for 20 minutes. Drain and squeeze out excess water (reserve the soaking liquid), discard the stems, then cut the caps into small dice.

Heat the oil in a wok or large frying pan over high heat. Add the onion and garlic and stir-fry for a few seconds or until the garlic turns golden, then add the mushrooms, carrot and tofu and stir-fry for another minute until the carrots are softened and everything is well combined.

Push the vegetables and tofu to the side of the wok, then add the noodles. Stir-fry for 1–2 minutes, then add the light and dark soy sauce, oyster sauce, Shaoxing and reserved mushroom soaking liquid.

Cover with a lid and, once the stock comes to the boil, add the mustard greens. Season with salt and pepper, mix well and serve hot.

✽ Vegetarian oyster sauce is sometimes sold as imitation oyster sauce in Chinese grocers.

If you find the stock is evaporating before the noodles are fully cooked, add a little water.

- 6 dried shiitake mushrooms
- ¼ cup (60 ml) neutral oil
- 1 small onion, thinly sliced
- 2 garlic cloves, finely chopped
- 1 small carrot (about 100 g) sliced
- 250 g (9 oz) firm tofu, cut into 2 cm (¾ inch) cubes
- 500 g (1 lb 2 oz) Hokkien noodles
- 1 tablespoon light soy sauce
- 1 teaspoon dark soy sauce
- 1 tablespoon vegetarian oyster sauce (see note)
- 1 tablespoon Shaoxing wine
- 180 g (6 oz) Chinese mustard greens, cut into bite-sized pieces
- Salt and white pepper, to taste

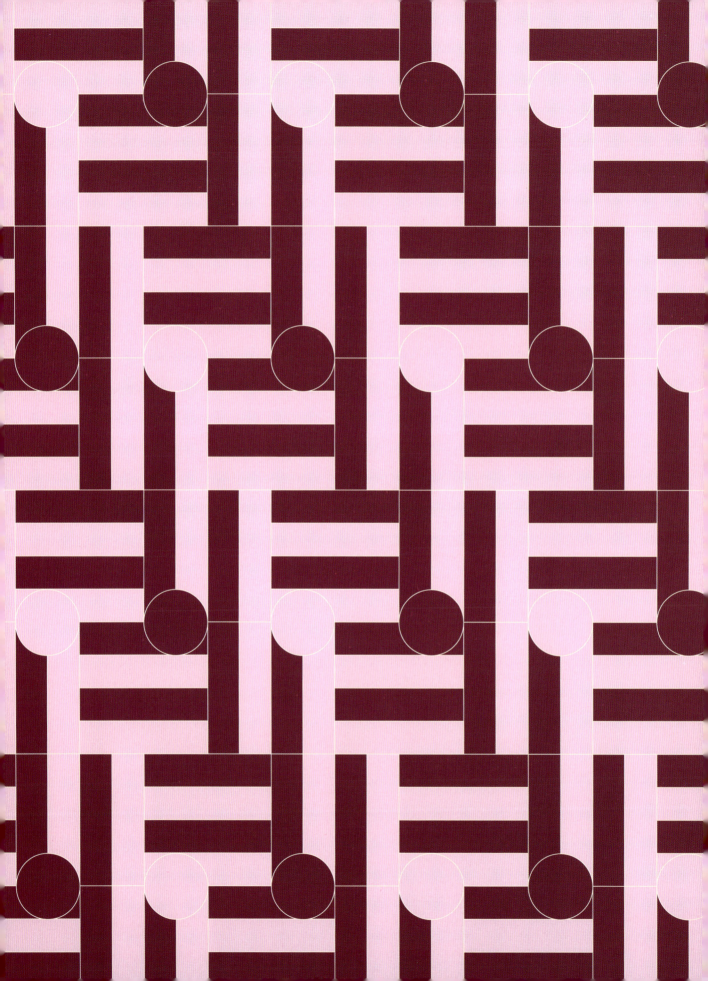

DIM SUM, DUMPLINGS, BUNS AND SNACKS

MUSHROOM DUMPLINGS WITH CURRY OIL

SERVES 6–8

This is a dish I created some years ago when a vegetarian friend dropped by unexpectedly for dinner. In my panic, I chopped up some mushrooms, fried them with aromats, chilled the mix, then folded it into dumplings. Once I pulled them out of the water, I tossed them with some fragrant curry oil I'd made earlier and the rest is history. The mushroom stuffing also works perfectly with a firm cheese such as a good cheddar, or firm beancurd, which you can add to the mix.

24 wonton wrappers

MUSHROOM DUMPLING FILLING
5 dried shiitake mushrooms
2 tablespoons olive oil
1 tablespoon unsalted butter
2 garlic cloves, minced
2 shallots (eschalots), finely minced
1 teaspoon minced ginger
1 long red chilli, finely chopped
1 sprig thyme, leaves picked, plus extra leaves to serve
600 g (1 lb 5 oz) button mushrooms, chopped
1 teaspoon porcini powder
Salt and white pepper, to taste

CURRY OIL
¾ cup (180 ml) neutral oil
2 tablespoons curry powder
1 teaspoon minced ginger

For the filling, soak the mushrooms in hot water for 20 minutes. Drain and squeeze out excess water, discard the stems, then cut the caps into fine dice.

Heat the oil with the butter in a frying pan over medium heat, swirling to melt the butter, then add the garlic and shallots and fry until translucent. Add the ginger and chilli, then add the thyme, button mushrooms and diced shiitake mushrooms and cook, stirring occasionally, until most of the juices released from the mushrooms have evaporated. Stir in the porcini powder, season with salt and pepper and transfer to a bowl to cool.

Meanwhile, for the curry oil, add all the ingredients to a small saucepan over medium heat and stir until fragrant. Season to taste with salt. Remove from the heat and leave until needed.

To make the dumplings, lay out 8 wonton wrappers on a bench. Put about 1 teaspoon of the mushroom filling in the centre of each wrapper. Brush a little water along the edges of the wrapper, then fold one corner over the filling to the opposite corner to form a triangle, pressing the edges together to seal. Repeat with the remaining wrappers and filling.

Poach the dumplings, in batches, in plenty of boiling salted water until they float to the surface. Remove with a slotted spoon and toss gently with the curry oil. Serve hot, topped with extra thyme leaves.

PEARL BALLS

MAKES 25–30

This famous stuffed-rice entrée is said to be from Hunan province, a major rice-growing area in China, and is very popular in Malaysia and Singapore. The glutinous rice grains that form the coating take on a pearl-like quality when steamed, hence the name. Although soy sauce is the usual accompaniment, I like to serve pearl balls with a Sichuan-style dipping sauce, which brings more spice and fragrance to the mix. Start this recipe at least four hours ahead to soak the rice.

1½ cups (300 g) glutinous or sweet rice

PEARL-BALL FILLING
5 dried shiitake mushrooms
450 g (1 lb) minced pork
100 g (3½ oz) water chestnuts, chopped
1 small carrot (about 70 g/2½ oz), very finely chopped
2 spring onions (scallions), finely chopped
1½ tablespoons very finely chopped ginger
2 tablespoons light soy sauce, plus extra for dipping
1 tablespoon Shaoxing wine
1 tablespoon sesame oil
2 tablespoons cornflour (cornstarch)
Salt and white pepper, to taste

SICHUAN-STYLE DIPPING SAUCE
⅓ cup (80 ml) light soy sauce
1 tablespoon Chinkiang vinegar
1 teaspoon chilli oil
1 garlic clove, minced
1 tablespoon finely chopped spring onion (scallions)
1 tablespoon finely chopped coriander (cilantro)

Wash and drain the rice to remove any dust. Cover with water and soak overnight or for at least 4 hours. Drain well and transfer to a baking tray.

For the filling, soak the dried mushrooms in hot water for 20 minutes. Drain and squeeze out excess water, discard the stems, then cut the caps into small dice.

Combine the mushrooms, pork, water chestnuts, carrot, spring onions and ginger in a bowl, then add the soy sauce, Shaoxing, sesame oil, cornflour and salt and pepper. Stir well to combine.

Form into little balls with your hands, each about 20 g (¾ oz), then roll them in the rice to coat evenly, pressing lightly to ensure the rice sticks to the balls.

Place the balls well apart in steamer baskets lined with greaseproof paper. Cover and steam over simmering water in a wok for 25 minutes or until the rice grains soften.

For the Sichuan-style dipping sauce, combine the ingredients in a bowl and use as required.

Serve the pearl balls with the Sichuan-style dipping sauce.

LAMB DUMPLINGS, XI'AN STYLE

MAKES 30

I first ate these dumplings when I went to see the terracotta warriors in Xi'an years ago. At that time, I didn't know there were many Chinese Muslims in that city and that their dumplings were made with lamb or chicken. This is my take on their sensational dumplings, using wonton wrappers instead of the heavier northern-style dumpling wrapper.

For the filling, sprinkle the salt onto the shredded cabbage in a bowl, mix well and set aside for 15 minutes. Rinse off the salt under running water, then squeeze the cabbage with a tea towel to remove excess liquid. Return the cabbage to a large bowl, add the remaining ingredients and stir in one direction to combine.

Working with one wrapper at a time, place a teaspoonful of lamb filling in the centre of the wrapper. Brush a little water along the edges of the wrapper, then fold one corner over the filling to the opposite corner to form a triangle, pressing the edges together to seal. Repeat until all the filling is used.

To fry the dumplings, heat ¼ cup (60 ml) of oil in a non-stick frying pan over high heat and arrange the dumplings in the frying pan to cover the surface.

Cook for 2–3 minutes, then add ½ cup (125 ml) water to the pan, reduce the heat to medium, then cover with a lid and simmer until most of the water has evaporated. (If it is evaporating too quickly, add 1–2 tablespoons water to give the dumplings time to cook through.) Uncover, raise the temperature to medium-high and cook for another minute or until the bottoms are brown and crisp.

Repeat with any remaining dumplings, or freeze raw dumplings for later.

Transfer to a serving plate and serve hot with the dipping sauce of your choice, though it's best to enjoy them with one made with chillies and Sichuan pepper.

360 g (12¾ oz) packet square wonton wrappers (about 36)
Neutral oil, for frying
2 spring onions (scallions), finely chopped
Dipping sauce, to serve

FILLING
2 teaspoons salt
200 g (7 oz) wombok (Chinese cabbage), finely shredded
300 g (10½ oz) minced lamb, preferably 70% lean and 30% fat
1 tablespoon finely chopped ginger
½ teaspoon Chinese five-spice powder
1 teaspoon freshly ground cumin seeds
1 teaspoon white pepper
1 tablespoon light soy sauce
½ teaspoon caster (superfine) sugar
1 teaspoon oyster sauce
1 tablespoon sesame oil
2 teaspoons Shaoxing wine
2 coriander sprigs, finely chopped
1 egg

CHICKEN AND PRAWN WINDMILL DUMPLINGS

GAI HA GAO

MAKES 24 | 30

This delicious dumpling is a salute to the master dim sum chefs of the cities in Shanghai, Hong Kong and Singapore. The dough, the most traditional and widely used dumpling dough, is a favourite with dim sum masters because it can be shaped and sculpted without too much effort. The dough itself uses two different kinds of flour: tapioca flour and wheat starch. Wheat starch (called tang meen fun in Cantonese) is what remains of wheat flour when the wheat's protein is removed to make gluten.

Traditionally these thin wrappers are shaped by using the flat side of an oiled cleaver but, since this dough can feel rather soft and strange to make if it's your first time, I've also offered a cheat's method to help you get the hang of it.

For the filling, combine all the ingredients in a large bowl and mix well. Cover and refrigerate until needed.

For the dumpling wrappers, add the wheat starch, tapioca flour and salt to a bowl and mix well. Pour in the boiling water all at once and stir quickly with a pair of chopsticks to incorporate the flour. Add the oil and continue to stir until a ball forms. Turn the hot dough onto a lightly floured surface and knead by hand until the dough is smooth and pliable. Wrap tightly in plastic wrap and leave at room temperature for 10 minutes to rest.

Before working with the dough, lightly oil the work surface. Roll the dough into a long cylinder and cut in two. Cover one cylinder with a hot, damp tea towel or place it in plastic wrap while you cut the other cylinder into 2.5 cm (1 inch) pieces (you should have about 10–12 pieces). It is best to make these wrappers in multiples of five, keeping the remaining pieces under a damp tea towel or in plastic, because you want the dough to remain soft and pliable.

Working with one piece of dough at a time, roll out the dough with a well-oiled cleaver or a rolling pin to form 9–10 cm (3½–4 inch) discs (if you're using a rolling pin, roll the dough out between two sheets of oiled plastic wrap).

Place a wrapper on your palm and spoon 2 teaspoons of the filling onto the centre. Then, with your thumb and forefinger, gather opposite ends of the wrapper and fold together, pinching in the middle. To form a windmill shape, with your other hand, push the exposed corners into the centre. Pinch the edges to seal. Cover the dumplings as you go to prevent them drying out, and repeat with remaining dough and filling.

Place the dumplings in steamer baskets lined with silicon or baking paper studded with holes, then cover and steam over simmering water in a wok, for 6–8 minutes or until translucent. Serve with your choice of soy sauce, Chinkiang vinegar or chilli sauce.

✖ Bamboo pith is a fungus that grows in bamboo forests and is sold dried in packets at Chinese and Asian grocers – it's called juk saang in Cantonese.

Light soy sauce, Chinkiang vinegar or chilli sauce, to serve

GAI HA GAO FILLING

200 g (7 oz) peeled green prawns, chopped
200 g (7 oz) minced chicken
50 g (1¾ oz) carrots, finely diced
50 g (1¾ oz) tinned or frozen bamboo shoots, finely diced
5 pieces dried bamboo pith, soaked in water until soft, then drained and diced (see note)
2 tablespoons coriander (cilantro) leaves, chopped
1 tablespoon ginger, finely chopped
½ egg white, lightly beaten
1 teaspoon sesame oil
1 tablespoon light soy sauce
1 teaspoon cornflour (cornstarch)
Pinch of caster (superfine) sugar (optional)
Salt and white pepper, to taste

DUMPLING WRAPPERS

⅔ cup (125 g) wheat starch
⅔ cup (120 g) tapioca flour, plus extra for dusting
Pinch of salt
300 ml (10½ fl oz) boiling water
1 tablespoon neutral oil, plus extra for greasing

DEEP-FRIED GLUTINOUS RICE DUMPLINGS
HUM SUI GOK

MAKES 12 | 15

These deep-fried savoury dumplings, filled with pork and dried shrimp, are made with glutinous rice flour and wheat starch, which makes them pleasantly chewy. As for the fillings, some chefs prefer bamboo shoots while others add preserved daikon. If you choose the latter, it adds extra depth; it is sold as preserved turnip in Chinese grocers.

Neutral oil, for deep-frying
Chilli sauce, to serve (optional)

HUM SUI GOK FILLING
2 dried shiitake mushrooms
2 tablespoons neutral oil
125 g (4½ oz) minced pork
125 g (4½ oz) char siu (barbecued pork, from Chinese barbecue shops, or see page 93), finely diced
1 tablespoon finely chopped spring onion (scallion)
20 g (¾ oz) dried shrimp, soaked in cold water for 10–15 minutes, drained and finely chopped
2 tablespoons finely chopped tinned or frozen bamboo shoots or preserved daikon (white radish)
2–3 tablespoons chicken stock or water
1 tablespoon light soy sauce
Dash of dark soy sauce
½ teaspoon caster (superfine) sugar
1 tablespoon Shaoxing wine
Pinch of Chinese five-spice powder
Salt and white pepper, to taste
1 tablespoon cornflour (cornstarch), mixed with 2 tablespoons water

HUM SUI GOK DOUGH
1½ cups (250 g) glutinous rice flour
⅓ cup (60 g) wheat starch (see introduction page 71)
2 tablespoons lard or vegetable shortening, melted
1 tablespoon caster (superfine) sugar
Pinch of salt, or to taste
1 cup (250 ml) boiling water

For the filling, soak the dried mushrooms in hot water for 20 minutes. Drain and squeeze out excess water, discard the stems, then cut the caps into fine dice.

Heat a wok over high heat and add the oil. Once the oil is shimmering, add the minced pork, char siu and spring onion. Swish around until partially cooked, about 1–2 minutes, then stir in the shrimp, bamboo shoots and diced mushroom. Add the chicken stock, light and dark soy sauce, sugar, Shaoxing, five-spice and salt and pepper, bring to the boil, then add the cornflour slurry and stir until thickened. Remove from the wok, allow to cool, then cover and chill until needed.

For the hum sui gok dough, combine the glutinous rice flour and wheat starch in a bowl. Add the melted lard, sugar and salt, then pour in three-quarters of the boiling water and stir to form a dough. (If there's some dry flour remaining, add the rest of the water.) Working quickly, knead until smooth. Roll the dough into a sausage and cut into 12–15 pieces (50–60 g/2 oz each).

Roll out each piece of dough with a rolling pin to make discs 7 cm (2¾ inches) in diameter. Spoon 2 teaspoons of filling into the centre of each and fold the edges together to seal.

Heat a deep-fryer or a large saucepan filled with neutral oil to 160°C (315°F; bubbles should form around a wooden chopstick when it's dipped in). Deep-fry the dumplings for 14–15 minutes until they float to the top and turn golden. Remove with a slotted spoon and drain on paper towel. Serve hot or warm with your choice of accompaniment – I suggest chilli sauce.

✣ If the oil is getting hotter than 170°C (325°F) while you're deep-frying, add a couple of tablespoons of cold oil to maintain the temperature.

STEAMED CHICKEN BAO
GAI BAO

MAKES 10 | 12

Chinese steamed buns – bao – are always popular at yum cha sessions and come filled with all sorts of stuffings, including a more unconventional one I tried recently filled with jackfruit in hoisin sauce. This chicken bao is an evergreen crowd-pleaser, and it's especially great for kids who tend to have less adventurous palates. The following recipe uses low-gluten Chinese flour called bao flour for the dough; you can always use cake flour – just keep in mind that the result will be a little heavier.

First, make the dough. Put all the dough ingredients and ½ cup (125 ml) water in a bowl, mix well, then turn out onto a lightly floured surface and knead for 5 minutes. Return dough to a lightly oiled bowl, cover with plastic wrap and leave at room temperature to rest for 30 minutes.

Meanwhile, cut out 15 squares of baking paper measuring 6 cm (2½ inches).

For the filling, soak the dried mushrooms in hot water for 20 minutes. Drain and squeeze out excess water, discard the stems, then cut the caps into fine dice.

Place the mushrooms in a bowl with remaining ingredients and mix well. Fry a tiny piece of the filling in oil in a small frying pan to check for correct seasoning, then adjust it to taste. Place the filling in the fridge, covered, for 30 minutes to chill.

To make the bao, roll the dough into a long sausage about 2 cm (¾ inch) thick, then cut it into 20 equal pieces. Place a piece of dough on a floured surface and flatten it with your palm. With a rolling pin, roll it into a disc about 10 cm (4 inches) in diameter. Put a tablespoon of filling in the centre of the dough, then gather the edges to enclose the filling, pinching and twisting the top slightly. Transfer to a square of baking paper and repeat with the remaining dough and filing.

Place the bao in the steamer on the squares of paper in a steamer set over a wok of simmering water, leaving a little space between each for expansion, for about 8–10 minutes or until well fluffed up. Serve hot.

GAI BAO DOUGH
- 2 cups (300 g) bao flour or cake flour, plus extra for dusting
- ⅓ cup (70 g) caster (superfine) sugar
- 1½ tablespoons baking powder
- 1 tablespoon melted lard or neutral oil, plus extra for greasing

GAI BAO FILLING
- 5 dried shiitake mushrooms
- 300 g (10½ oz) boned, skinless chicken thighs, cut into 1 cm (½ inch) pieces
- 150 g (5½ oz) water chestnuts, diced
- 2 spring onions (scallions), thinly sliced
- 1–2 tablespoons very finely chopped ginger
- 1 tablespoon Shaoxing wine
- 1 teaspoon sesame oil
- Dash of neutral oil
- 2 teaspoons cornflour (cornstarch)
- 1 teaspoon caster (superfine) sugar
- 1 teaspoon salt, or to taste
- White pepper, to taste

RICE ROLLS WITH PORK AND WOOD-EAR MUSHROOMS
BANH CUON

SERVES 6–8

This is the Vietnamese equivalent of cheong fun, the Cantonese fresh rice roll served at yum cha, but I think banh cuon tastes better, hence its inclusion in this chapter. In essence, it's a piece of freshly steamed rice wrapper or crêpe stuffed with a filling of pork or prawns or both.

The traditional method of making this deliciously tender rice roll is to steam it on a piece of calico stretched tightly over the top of a pot of simmering water. The roll is covered with a lid and it is left until it's cooked, then rolled up. If you don't have a steamer, you can still make this in a non-stick pan, but the result is perhaps not as delicate.

If you are not going to make the crêpe wrappers, you can use rice paper and deep-fry the rolls, in which case they are called cha gio, but note that the filling traditionally features additional chopped glass noodles and beaten egg.

Crisp-fried shallots, thinly sliced spring onions (shallots) and chopped coriander (cilantro), to serve

BANH CUON BATTER
1½ cups (240 g) rice flour
½ cup (90 g) potato flour
3 cups (750 ml) water
Pinch of salt
1 tablespoon neutral oil, plus extra for greasing (including up to ½ cup/125 ml more if you're not using the steamer method)

BANH CUON FILLING
2 tablespoons neutral oil
3 shallots (eschalots), finely chopped
½ cup finely chopped onion
1 small garlic clove, minced (optional)
1 dried wood-ear mushroom, soaked in hot water to reconstitute for 15 minutes, chewy centres removed, finely shredded (it should yield about ½ cup/125 ml)
300 g (10½ oz) minced pork
1 cup (175 g) finely diced jicama or water chestnuts
1 teaspoon fish sauce
½ teaspoon caster (superfine) sugar
Salt and white pepper, to taste

For the batter, combine all the ingredients in a bowl. Whisk until smooth, cover and set aside at room temperature for 30 minutes to rest.

For the filling, heat the oil in a frying pan over medium heat. Add the shallots, stir for 10 seconds, then add the onion, garlic and wood-ear mushrooms and cook until the onion is soft and translucent (about 3 minutes). Add the pork, jicama, fish sauce, sugar and salt and pepper. Continue to cook, breaking up the pork as you go, for 3–4 minutes until it's cooked through. Transfer to a bowl and leave to cool.

To make the wrappers, oil a baking tray. If you're using a steamer, have a steamer set up with a piece of calico stretched across it and secured with a rubber band, and set it over boiling water. Alternatively, have a small non-stick frying pan with ½ cup (125 ml) oil at the ready.

If you're using the steamer, stir the batter well and, with a small ladle, spoon about 3 tablespoons of batter onto the centre of the calico.

With the bottom of the ladle, quickly spread the batter out to form a thin disc of about 15 cm (6 inches) in diameter. Cover with a lid and steam for about 1 minute until the batter is translucent and crêpe-like. Uncover and, holding a thin spatula at a 45-degree angle, gently lift the side of the wrapper and lift it carefully onto the oiled tray.

Let the wrapper cool for 20 seconds, then place 2 teaspoons of filling in the centre and roll it up into a small roll, tucking in the edges. Repeat with the remaining batter and filling. Since the rice batter settles quickly, remember to stir it every time you make a wrapper. At no time should you stack the wrapper. Once you've established a rhythm it's much easier, but it is better to work with another person if you are in a hurry.

If you are using a non-stick pan, heat ½ teaspoon oil over low-medium heat, then add 3 tablespoons of batter. If it sizzles, reduce the heat. Cover with a lid and leave to steam for about 40 seconds – it is ready when it pulls away from the sides. Slide it onto the oiled baking sheet and fill after 20 seconds as opposite. Remember to wait a minute between crêpes to allow the pan to get back to heat.

Serve with crisp-fried shallots, thinly sliced spring onions and chopped coriander, with nuoc cham (see below) for dipping.

NUOC CHAM
⅓ cup (80 ml) lime or lemon juice
1 tablespoon rice vinegar (optional)
¼ cup (55 g) caster (superfine) sugar
⅔ cup (170 ml) lukewarm water
5–6 tablespoons fish sauce
2–3 birdseye chillies, finely chopped
2 garlic cloves, finely chopped (optional)

Combine the lime juice, vinegar, sugar and water in a bowl and stir to dissolve the sugar. Taste and adjust the flavour to your liking. Add the fish sauce and adjust to taste again. Add the chilli and garlic, if you'd like to use it – some cooks leave it out with banh cuon.

THAI DUCK CURRY DUMPLINGS

MAKES 20

This dumpling came about by accident. I had leftover duck curry in the fridge one day and, because it was slightly gelatinous, I thought I could add extra gelatine to make the sauce thicker, then stuff it into dumplings. I put teaspoonfuls of the curry into gow gee wrappers, then poached them. It was a hit with friends. Foie gras shavings are a marvellous topping for this dumpling.

For the filling, add the red curry paste and half the coconut cream to a saucepan and stir constantly over medium heat until fragrant. Stir in the duck meat, then add the remaining ingredients, except for the gelatine. Simmer for 10 minutes. Meanwhile, soften the gelatine leaves in a little cold water.

Squeeze out excess water from the gelatine, then stir it into the hot curry until dissolved. Remove the curry from the heat, cool, then refrigerate for 6 hours or until set.

Meanwhile, for the curry sauce, combine the coconut milk, curry paste, palm sugar and fish sauce in a saucepan and bring to a gentle boil, stirring occasionally. Add the lime leaves and paprika, then check the seasoning and add a little salt if you think it needs it. Keep warm.

Place the gow gee wrappers on a clean surface. Spoon 1 teaspoon filling on one half of each wrapper, brush the opposite edge with water and fold over to form a half moon. Pinch the edges together to seal.

Poach the dumplings, in batches, in boiling salted water until they float to the surface. Remove with a slotted spoon and serve immediately with a spoonful of the curry sauce and extra sliced lime leaves. You can use the rest of the sauce as a dipping sauce.

20 gow gee wrappers

DUCK CURRY FILLING
2 tablespoons red curry paste, or to taste
½ cup (125 ml) coconut cream
500 g (1 lb 2 oz) Chinese roast duck meat, minced by hand
½ cup (125 ml) coconut milk
2 makrut lime leaves, finely shredded
100 g bamboo shoots or water chestnuts, finely diced
2 tablespoons fish sauce
2 teaspoons palm sugar (or jaggery), grated
2 gelatine leaves

CURRY SAUCE
2 cups (500 ml) thin coconut milk
2–4 teaspoons red curry paste, to taste
1 teaspoon grated palm sugar (or jaggery)
1 tablespoon fish sauce
3 makrut lime leaves, thinly sliced, plus extra to serve
½ teaspoon paprika
Pinch of salt, or to taste

MAKES 24

CHIU CHOW DUMPLINGS

These sensational dumplings are called Chiu Chow fun gor in dim sum restaurants. Interestingly, because they originate from the Teochew (Chiu Chow) people, they are not often served in Cantonese dim sum houses.

SAUCE FOR FILLING
1 tablespoon light soy sauce
1 tablespoon Shaoxing wine
1 teaspoon oyster sauce
½ teaspoon caster (superfine) sugar
Dash of sesame oil
Salt and white pepper, to taste
1 teaspoon tapioca flour, mixed with 3 tablespoons water

FILLING
15 g (½ oz) dried shiitake mushrooms
2 tablespoons neutral oil
100 g (3½ oz) minced pork
50 g (1¾ oz) preserved daikon (chai poh), rinsed and finely chopped
50 g (1¾ oz) dried shrimp, soaked in hot water for 10–15 minutes, rinsed, drained and finely chopped
2 shallots (eschalots), finely chopped
2–3 spring onions (scallions), finely chopped
50 g (1¾ oz) roasted peanuts, coarsely chopped
30 g (1 oz) garlic chives, cut into 1 cm (½ inch) lengths

DUMPLING WRAPPERS
⅔ cup (125 g) wheat starch, plus extra for dusting
⅔ cup (120 g) tapioca flour
Pinch of salt
1 tablespoon neutral oil
300 ml (10½ fl oz) boiling water

Add all the sauce ingredients to a bowl and stir to combine.

For the filling, soak the dried mushrooms in hot water for 20 minutes. Drain and squeeze out excess water, discard the stems, then cut the caps into fine dice.

Heat the oil in a wok over medium heat, add the pork, daikon, dried shrimp, shallots and mushrooms and stir-fry until fragrant. Add the sauce, stir to coat, then once the sauce begins to thicken, add the spring onions, peanuts and garlic chives. Transfer to a plate or bowl and leave to cool.

For the dumpling wrappers, place the wheat starch, tapioca flour and salt in a bowl and mix well. Add the oil to the boiling water, then pour it into the flour mixture all at once, stirring quickly with a pair of chopsticks until a ball forms.

Turn out the hot dough onto a lightly floured surface and knead until a smooth and pliable dough forms. Cut the dough in half, roll each half into a 4.5 cm (1¾ inch) cylinder and wrap tightly in plastic wrap. Leave for 10 minutes to rest.

Lightly brush a clean surface with neutral oil. Cut the dough into 2.5 cm (1 inch) pieces (you should end up with 10–12 pieces from each cylinder). It is best to make these wrappers in multiples of five, keeping the remaining pieces under a damp tea towel or in plastic to help keep the dough soft and pliable.

Working with one piece of dough at a time, roll out the dough with a well-oiled cleaver or a rolling pin into discs 9–10 cm (3½–4 inch) in diameter.

Place a wrapper on your palm and spoon 2 teaspoons of the filling in the centre. Dampen the edges with water and, with your fingers, gather the edges of the wrapper to form a half-moon. Cover the dumplings with a damp tea towel as you go to prevent them drying out, and repeat with the remaining dough and filling.

Place the dumplings, about 3 cm (1¼ inches) apart, in steamer baskets lined with baking paper. Steam over simmering water for 6–8 minutes until translucent. Serve with soy sauce, Chinkiang vinegar or chilli sauce.

PORK AND CHINESE CABBAGE DUMPLINGS
SHUIJIAO

MAKES 30

Another member of the northern Chinese dumpling (jiaozi) family, shuijiao means 'water dumplings'. Plump and full-flavoured, they're typically eaten during the cold winter months and during Chinese New Year. Pork and Chinese cabbage are classic fillings, although you can substitute lamb, beef or fish. As for the sauce, shuijiao are often dipped in a tangy soy sauce laced with chilli oil, which is why in some dim sum palaces, such as Hutong in Hong Kong, they're sometimes called Sichuan dumplings. The jellied chicken stock (which is made from 500–700 g/ 1 lb 1 oz–1 lb 9 oz chicken feet and bones, boiled in a stockpot for an hour or so) adds additional umami-rich mouthfeel, but you can use regular chicken stock.

30 gyoza wrappers (or see below for homemade dumpling skins)

SHUIJIAO FILLING
2 cups (150 g) lightly packed finely shredded Chinese cabbage
1 teaspoon salt
350 g (12 oz) minced pork (around 70% lean meat and 30% fat – ask your butcher to do this for you)
⅓ cup (100 g) jellied chicken stock (see introduction)
1½ tablespoons finely chopped ginger
1 tablespoon light soy sauce
1 tablespoon Shaoxing wine
1 tablespoon neutral oil
2 teaspoons sesame oil
Salt and white pepper, to taste

DUMPLING SKINS – JIAOZI PIO
300 g (2 cups) plain (all-purpose) flour, plus extra for dusting
Pinch of salt
¾ cup (185 ml) just-boiled water

If making the dumpling skins, combine the flour and salt in a bowl. Make a well in the centre and, with a pair of chopsticks or a wooden spoon, stir in the just-boiled water steadily. If it's still very lumpy, add extra water by the teaspoon. If it's very wet, add flour by the tablespoon. Transfer to a lightly floured bench and knead for 2 minutes until smooth and pliable. Place in a plastic bag and rest at room temperature for at least 15 minutes while you make the filling.

For the filling, put the shredded cabbage in a bowl and toss with the teaspoon of salt. Leave for about 15 minutes to allow the salt to draw excess moisture from the cabbage. Drain in a colander and flush with water. Drain again and squeeze moisture from the cabbage in a clean tea towel over the sink. You should have about ¾ cup (180 ml) firmly packed cabbage.

Transfer the cabbage to a bowl, add the remaining filling ingredients and mix thoroughly. Fry a tiny piece of the filling in oil in a small frying pan to check for correct seasoning, then adjust it to taste. Cover with plastic wrap and leave for 15 minutes to rest.

To form the dumpling skins, turn out the dough onto a lightly floured bench. Cut it in half and return half to the bag to prevent it from drying while you work with the other half. Roll the dough into a cylinder and cut the dough into pieces. Weigh each piece to around 15–20 g (½–¾ oz) if you want to be precise, then flatten each with your hand before using a small rolling pin to roll them into discs 9 cm (3½ inch) in diameter, dusting each one with flour as you go to prevent sticking and keeping covered under slightly damp tea towels. Repeat with the remaining dough.

To fold the dumplings, hold a wrapper in your palm and place 1 tablespoon of filling in the wrapper, slightly off centre. Press and shape the dough around the filling, then dampen edges, bring them together and pleat them on one side only, keeping the back edge flat. Set the dumpling on a bench and fold in the ends if they stick out. Transfer the dumpling to a baking tray lined with baking paper. Repeat until the filling and wrappers are used up.

SOY DIPPING SAUCE
⅓ cup (80 ml) light soy sauce
2 tablespoons Chinkiang vinegar or red rice vinegar
1–3 teaspoons chilli oil, or to taste
1 tablespoon thinly sliced ginger
1 teaspoon minced garlic
1 teaspoon dried chilli flakes

DUMPLING LACE (OPTIONAL)
⅔ cup (100 g) flour
¼ cup (60 ml) neutral oil

To boil the dumplings, half-fill a large saucepan with water seasoned with a pinch of salt and bring to the boil. Add half the dumplings and gently swirl them around to prevent them from sticking. Cook until they float to the surface, then remove with a slotted spoon and keep warm while you cook the remaining batch.

Alternatively, if you want to fry these dumplings rather than boil them, heat a non-stick pan containing a thin film of neutral oil.

If making the lace batter, whisk the flour, oil and 550 ml (19 fl oz) water together in a bowl.

Arrange the dumplings, pleat-side up, in the frying pan. Cook for about 3 minutes, then, if using, pour ½ cup (125 ml) lace batter into the pan.

Reduce the heat to medium-low, cover with a lid and simmer until most of the water has evaporated and the dumplings are almost cooked through. (If it seems like it's evaporating too fast, add 1–2 tablespoons extra water to give the filling time to cook through.) Remove the lid, increase the heat to medium-high and cook for another minute or so until the bottoms are golden and crisp.

Meanwhile, for the soy dipping sauce, stir all the ingredients together.

Serve the dumplings with the soy dipping sauce.

If not using the lace, simply wait until the oil is warm, then add the dumplings, making sure they are not sticking together. Leave to cook undisturbed for 3-5 minutes. Add warm water, then bring to the boil, and cover for about 2 minutes until the bases are crisp and the dumplings are easily removed from the pan.

THE RIGHT OIL FOR THE TASK

I've often been asked in my cooking classes what oil I use. My response is that depends on what I'm cooking. Historically and well before globalisation, countries in the more northern parts of Asia tended to use animal fats as well as soybean oil and rapeseed oil. In Southeast Asia, the Thais traditionally used coconut oil and lard, and I gather it may have been the same in Vietnam. In Malaysia, Singapore and Indonesia, coconut oil is traditional, while in India mustard oil is favoured in the east and in Bengal, while coconut and sesame oil (aka gingelly) are popular in the south. Ghee (clarified butter) is also used, especially in desserts. These are just some of the oils that were consumed before other oils from different parts of the world entered the food scene in Asia.

While I can't be definitive about when peanuts entered Asia, according to some experts, it was the Portuguese and Spanish who brought them to the continent in the 17th century. Much valued for its high smoke point and flavour, peanut oil became popular with chefs and cooks in China and Southeast Asia over time.

The next oil to enter the Asian market was palm oil. From West Africa, it was introduced to Indonesia by the Dutch in the 1840s and to Malaysia by the British in the 1870s. It rapidly became the oil of choice in the region.

What do I use? I stir-fry regularly because this cooking technique is fast and fuel efficient, so I typically go for an oil that has a high smoke point.

Traditionally, oils from fruits such as olives, and seeds, like sesame and peanuts (really a legume) are extracted either by mechanical pressing or by crushing at a particular temperature. When cold-pressed and bottled immediately, these oils are called unrefined or virgin oils and are best used for drizzling or cooking on low heat.

To increase the smoke point of an oil (which simply refers to the temperature at which an oil begins to shimmer and smoke), producers use industrial methods such as high-temperature heating and bleaching to remove impurities (minerals and flavours) to make neutral or refined oils. As an example, the smoke point of refined peanut oil is approximately 210°C (410°F), while rice bran oil is 232°C (450°F). Even though refined peanut oil has a high smoke point, and most of the allergenic proteins are removed, I tend to avoid using it just in case someone has an anaphylactic reaction in a cooking class. In its place, I use grapeseed oil due to its similarly high smoke point. Light green in colour, it's an oil with a neutral flavour that works very well in Asian dishes.

> I favour grapeseed oil for stir-frying, while I tend to go for rice bran oil for deep-frying. Studies have also shown both these oils to be effective in lowering cholesterol due to their high levels of vitamin E.

In the recipes in this book, recommend simply a 'neutral oil', so you can use whatever you have on hand. Grapeseed and rice bran oils would be useful ones to have in your pantry.

Much as I would love to write more about the health benefits of various fruit, seed and nut oils, it is beyond the scope of this essay. I would, however, suggest you read the labels of the various vegetable oils you can buy. Vegetable oil is commonly mentioned in Asian cookbooks to distinguish it from lard and other animal fats. It usually includes soybean oil, sunflower oil, palm oil and canola oil. While some vegetable oils are great for cooking, others are less positive because they may contain genetically modified seeds either to improve oil quality or to increase tolerance to herbicides.

Like many of us who are concerned with heart disease, diabetes and obesity, I tend to avoid certain oils and fats. But when I need to enhance the flavours of dishes from a particular region in Asia, I don't hesitate to cook with the traditional oils used there. For instance, I like to mix coconut oil with grapeseed oil to highlight a dish from Bali or from the East Coast of Malaysia where I come from. Instead of butter, I also like to use lard in some Chinese pastries for its crumbly, 'short' consistency. Interestingly, lard has had a resurgence due to its health benefits.

Three last points. First, regardless of what oil you cook with, it's wise not to reuse the oil from deep-fried foods because it may be rancid at best and harmful to your health if it has oxidised. Second, roasted sesame oil is never used in stir-fries. Like Korean perilla oil, roasted sesame oil is used as a flavour enhancer or a condiment added towards the end of cooking a dish. Finally, trans fats, or trans fatty acids, are products of oils and fats altered through hydrogenation. These commercially produced solid fats are sometimes used in making pastry dough and for deep-frying but can cause heart disease and a host of illnesses, so I avoid using them at all times.

HAR GOW

PRAWN DUMPLINGS

A yum cha classic consisting of translucent dough filled with sweet prawn meat, har gow is a dumpling that demonstrates the mastery of dim sum chefs. The trick is that the dough must be prepared as close to the cooking time as possible, otherwise the dumplings will either split or not be as translucent as you'd like when steamed. Knead the dough as soon as it's cool enough to handle: the boiling water must reach every bit of the wheat starch and tapioca flour when it's still hot. This is one dumpling where the dough can't be made ahead of time and refrigerated, so it's best to make the filling well ahead of steaming, or you can also fill the dumplings and freeze them, before steaming them straight from the freezer. You can buy har gow moulds, though the result will not be as beautiful.

SERVES 6–8

Soy sauce or dipping sauce, to serve

HAR GOW FILLING
250 g (9 oz) peeled prawns, chopped
3 tablespoons finely chopped bamboo shoots
3 tablespoons diced water chestnuts
1 teaspoon sesame oil
½ teaspoon light soy sauce
½ egg white, lightly beaten
1 tablespoon cornflour (cornstarch)
¼ teaspoon salt, or to taste
Pinch of white pepper, or to taste

WHEAT STARCH DOUGH
¾ cup (130 g) wheat starch
1⅓ cups (170 g) tapioca flour or cornflour (cornstarch)
Pinch of salt
300 ml (10½ fl oz) boiling water
1 teaspoon neutral oil, plus extra for greasing

To make the filling, place all the ingredients in a bowl and mix well. Fry a tiny piece of the filling in oil in a small frying pan to check for correct seasoning, then adjust it to taste. Place the mixture in the fridge, covered, until required.

To make the wheat starch dough, combine the wheat starch, tapioca flour and salt in a bowl and mix well. Pour in the boiling water all at once and stir quickly with a pair of chopsticks to incorporate the flour. Add the oil and continue to mix. The consistency should be like a biscuit mix: dry and slightly crumbly. Continue mixing until the dough is cool enough to handle, then knead with your hand in the bowl until it begins to come together. Remove from the bowl and knead lightly on the bench for a few more minutes until it is shiny and smooth. Cut the dough in half and place both halves in separate plastic bags. Cool for about 30 minutes on the bench before use.

When you're ready to make the wrappers, lightly oil the surface of your bench. Roll each piece of dough into a thin sausage – about 2.5 cm (1 inch) wide – then cut each sausage into segments about 2.5 cm (1 inch) long. Roll each segment into a small ball. Press down on each ball with the palm of your hand, then roll out with a rolling pin to form a round dumpling skin of about 8 cm (3 inch) in diameter. (Traditionally, a dim sum chef uses their cleaver to form these round skins, but a rolling pin is just as useful for beginners.)

To fill the dumplings, place 1 teaspoon of filling into the centre of each wrapper and fold the skin in half, forming a half-moon shape. (It is best to make these wrappers in multiples of five, keeping the remaining pieces under a damp tea towel or in plastic wrap because you want the dough to remain soft and pliable.) Holding a dumpling securely with your left hand, begin to pleat with your right hand. Continue to pleat until the dumpling is completely closed. Tap the sealed edge with your thumb or knuckle to give the dumpling its har gow crescent shape (see opposite). Place in a steaming basket and cover with a slightly damp tea towel. Repeat with the remaining filling and wrappers.

Steam for 5–7 minutes until translucent and cooked through. Serve with soy sauce or a dipping sauce of your choice.

TAIWAN PEPPER BUNS
HU JIAO BING

MAKES 12

Made with minced pork or beef, hu jiao bing's dominant flavour is black pepper, hence its name, although other Chinese ingredients – including five-spice and rice wine – also play an integral part in this amazing street food. Apparently this famous bun, which some writers have compared to a pastie on steroids due to its full flavour, comes from the city of Fuzhou in China's Fujian province. The filling uses gelatinised stock, which makes the buns extra juicy, but it's an optional addition. Start this recipe a day ahead to make the pastry.

HU JIAO BING FILLING
500 g (1 lb 2 oz) minced pork
3 teaspoons freshly ground black pepper
2 tablespoons crisp-fried shallots
2 tablespoons Shaoxing wine
1 teaspoon sesame oil
1 teaspoon finely chopped ginger
1 tablespoon light soy sauce
2 teaspoons white pepper
1 teaspoon Sichuan pepper
1 teaspoon Chinese five-spice powder
1 teaspoon caster (superfine) sugar
100 ml (3½ fl oz) chicken stock or water (warmed if you're adding the gelatine)
2 gelatine leaves (I use McKenzie; optional – see above)
2–3 spring onions (scallions), finely chopped

YEAST PASTRY
2¼ teaspoons or 1 sachet (7 g) dried yeast
30 g (1 oz) caster (superfine) sugar
2⅔ cups (400 g) plain (all-purpose) flour, plus extra for dusting
50 g (1¾ oz) lard
Big pinch of salt, or to taste
Neutral oil, for greasing

GLAZE
2 tablespoons honey
½ cup (125 ml) hot water
50 g (1¾ oz) sesame seeds

To make the filling, combine all the ingredients in a bowl and mix well. If you'd like to add the gelatine, melt the leaves in the warmed stock or water, leave to cool, then mix into the filling. Refrigerate until chilled. (This can be prepared a day ahead.)

For the yeast pastry, combine the yeast with the sugar and 2 tablespoons of warm water, stir to dissolve and stand at room temperature until frothy. Sift the flour into a large bowl, add the yeast mixture, then add 1 cup (250 ml) water, the lard and the salt and stir until combined. Turn the dough out onto a lightly floured surface and knead until smooth. Transfer the dough to a lightly oiled bowl and brush the surface with oil. Cover and refrigerate overnight.

The next day, make the glaze by dissolving the honey in the hot water. Place the sesame seeds in a bowl and divide the filling into 12 equal portions. Preheat the oven to 200°C (400°F).

Roll the pastry into a sausage on a lightly floured surface and cut it into 12 equal pieces. Roll each into a disc 10 cm (4 inch) in diameter, leave to rest for 10 minutes, then place a ball of filling into the centre of a disc. Mould it into a bun, sealing the pastry underneath. Repeat with the remaining dough and filling.

Brush the buns with the glaze, then dip the tops of the buns into the sesame seeds until well coated. Spread on a baking tray lined with baking paper, then bake for 25–30 minutes, turning the tray halfway through cooking, until golden. Rest for 5 minutes and serve hot.

CRISP BEANCURD SKIN DUMPLINGS
FU PEI GUEN

MAKES 12 | 20

This Cantonese dumpling uses the thin beancurd skin that is sold in Chinese grocers as the wrapping. Beancurd skin (also known as yuba in Japanese) is nutritious and easy to work with, but you need to find the soft, pliable variety – the only way to tell is to touch it to test how soft it is. Typically, Japanese yuba is thicker than Chinese fu pei. One more thing to note is that it burns easily, so it is best not to cook the dumplings too quickly or you'll find that the filling is still raw by the time the wrapper is cooked.

For the filling, combine all the ingredients in a bowl and mix well. Cover and leave to marinate for 20 minutes.

Spoon 2 tablespoons of the filling onto a piece of beancurd skin. Smear the edges of the beancurd with beaten egg and fold it over to form a roll. Repeat until all the mixture is used. (You may cover and refrigerate the dumplings at this point for up to 2 hours.)

Heat 2.5 cm (1 inch) oil in a frying pan over low-medium heat until shimmering, and shallow-fry the dumplings until the filling is cooked through and the skin crisp. Drain well on paper towel and serve with your choice of chilli sauce, Chinkiang vinegar, soy or Worcestershire sauce.

✖ You can also deep-fry the dumplings but take care, as they brown quickly.

Beancurd sheets vary in size, so you may need to adjust the quantity.

2 sheets of dried beancurd skin (fu pei), cut into 10 cm (4 inch) squares (see note)
1 egg, beaten
Neutral oil, for shallow-frying
Chilli sauce, Chinkiang vinegar, soy or Worcestershire sauce, to serve

FU PEI GUEN FILLING
200 g (7 oz) minced pork
200 g (7 oz) prawn meat, cut into 1 cm (½ inch) dice
80 g (2¾ oz) char siu (barbecued pork, from Chinese barbecue shops, or see page 93), cut into 1 cm (½ inch) dice
50 g (1¾ oz) water chestnuts, diced
30 g (1 oz) garlic chives, finely chopped
1 spring onion (scallion), finely chopped
Salt and white pepper, to taste
Pinch of sugar
2 teaspoons sesame oil
2 teaspoons Shaoxing wine
1 tablespoon cornflour (cornstarch) or tapioca flour

XIAO LONG BAO
SOUP DUMPLINGS

MAKES 30 | 40

Made famous by Nanxiang tea house in Shanghai, these dumplings can be a devil to make. But once you know the secrets behind them and that they require practice – and patience – you'll find that suddenly it isn't difficult at all. Keep at it!

Three preparations in this recipe can be made in advance, then all of it put together when it's time to fold the dumplings: the gelatinous 'soup'; the filling; and the pastry. In fact, most restaurants make the gelatinous filling a day or two ahead to save time, and some even freeze it. Once the dumplings are made, they can also be frozen before being cooked straight from the freezer.

As for the dumpling skin – the fiddly bit – the pastry must be thin, but strong enough to hold the filling. As such, it's best to use a medium-strength flour with enough gluten to give it some elasticity, but not a bread flour, which will make the skin tough.

GELATINISED 'SOUP'
500 g (1 lb 2 oz) pork skin (ask your butcher)
2 spring onions (scallions), cut into 10 cm (4 inch) lengths
5 thin slices of ginger
150 ml (5 fl oz) Shaoxing wine
Salt and white pepper, to taste
1 tablespoon powdered gelatine (optional; only used if the soup doesn't set)

Traditionally, a xiao long bao is part of the tang bao (soup dumpling school). It's offered in just about every part of China including Hong Kong, where it's called sui gao. The soup is made with pork skin and bones and in some restaurants Yunnan ham as well. Some restaurants also use trotters, chicken bones and chicken feet to create the sticky feel of the soup. This version stays simple, with pork skin the key gelatinising element. Start this part of the recipe a day (or at least 4 hours) ahead of making the rest so the soup can set.

Place the pork skin in a saucepan with enough water to cover. Bring to the boil, boil for 2 minutes, then tip off the water and wash the skin under cold running water. Slice off any fat and return the skin to a clean saucepan.

Add the spring onions, ginger, Shaoxing and 1.5 litres (6 cups) water. Bring to the boil, reduce the heat to low, cover with a lid and simmer gently for 1½ hours or until the skin is very soft.

Drain the pork skin (reserving the liquid), roughly chop it, season with salt and pepper, then place it in a blender and strain the liquid over the top. Whizz until mushy, then strain through a fine sieve into a deep baking tray, discarding the solids. Season to taste, then check that the soup has set properly by spreading a tablespoon on a saucer and placing it in the freezer. It should solidify in a minute or two; if it doesn't, return the mixture to a saucepan, bring to a simmer and whisk in a tablespoon of powdered gelatine, then repeat the process.

Cover the soup with plastic wrap, then chill until set – about 2 hours or preferably overnight. Once the jelly is set, chop it into very fine pieces. Keep refrigerated until needed.

PORK FILLING
10 g (¼ oz) spring onion (scallion; white part only), chopped, plus ½ cup (60 g) thinly sliced
20 g (¾ oz) ginger, chopped
500 g (1 lb 2 oz) finely minced pork, with at least 15–20% fat (and preferably from a female pig)
1 tablespoon light soy sauce
Pinch of caster (superfine) sugar, or to taste
Pinch of salt, or to taste
2 teaspoons sesame oil
Neutral oil, for frying

A traditional xiao long bao is filled with pork, although you can make a more luxurious version with the addition of picked crabmeat and roe. In either case, the best pork filling is hand-chopped so that a little texture remains. Blend the 10 g (¼ oz) spring onion (white part) with the ginger and 100 ml (3½ fl oz) water (or pound them together with a mortar and pestle) until blitzed finely. Strain through a fine sieve, reserving the juice and discarding the solids.

Place the minced pork, soy sauce, sugar, salt and sesame oil in a bowl and mix to combine well. Add the ginger–spring onion juice bit by bit, stirring in a clockwise direction until incorporated. Add the gelatinised soup (see opposite) and the ½ cup spring onion, stirring in the same direction until well combined. Fry a tiny piece of the filling in oil in a small frying pan to check for correct seasoning, then adjust it to taste. Cover and chill until required.

XIAO LONG BAO DOUGH
1⅔ cups (250 g) plain (all-purpose) flour, plus extra for dusting
A couple of drops of neutral oil

Making this dough is similar to making an English hot-water pastry in that the dough is 'cooked'. Most recipes call for a mixture of boiling water with cold water added, but as long as the water temperature is 80–85°C (175–185°F), the recipe should work. I'd even go so far as to call it fail-safe, except it is advisable to knead and relax the dough after the initial 'cooking'.

Place the flour in a bowl and make a well in the centre. Bring ½ cup (125 ml) water and the oil to the boil in a small saucepan. Remove from the heat and let the temperature drop to 80–85°C (175–185°F), then pour it into the flour all at once, stirring it quickly with a spatula or chopsticks until combined. If the dough is still dry, add another teaspoon or two of hot water; if it's too wet, add another tablespoon of flour.

Turn out onto a lightly floured surface and knead for 5 minutes or until pliable. Cover or wrap in plastic wrap and set aside for 10 minutes for the dough to relax, then knead it for another 5 minutes. Dust lightly with flour, wrap in plastic wrap and leave to rest for 20 minutes or until required.

XIAO LONG BAO DIPPING SAUCE
1 cup (250 ml) red rice vinegar or Chinkiang vinegar
50 g (1¾ oz) finely shredded ginger

For the dipping sauce, mix the 2 ingredients and set aside until required.

To make the dumplings, halve the dough, keeping one half wrapped in plastic wrap while you work on the other. Roll the first half of dough into a long sausage on a lightly floured bench and cut it into 15–18 g (½ oz) pieces. Dust each piece lightly with flour and roll into a disc 7 cm (2¾ inch) in diameter, making sure the centre is just a little thicker.

Working with one disc at a time, spoon 2 teaspoons of filling into the centre, then pleat to form a dumpling by placing your thumb at the top of the filling and pinching anti-clockwise until the dough is completely sealed. Repeat with the remaining dough and filling.

Place the dumplings in steamer baskets lined with baking paper. Steam for 10–12 minutes (depending on size) until cooked. The gelatinised soup will liquify as it cooks.

Serve at once, with the xiao long bao dipping sauce. Just don't eat them too quickly, since the insides can be boiling hot.

MAKES 12

SQUID-INK POTSTICKERS

You may not find squid-ink potstickers in run-of-the-mill dim sum restaurants but, as some of you may know, the Chinese food scene — particularly Cantonese — in cities such as Hong Kong and Singapore is changing rapidly. If you love the savoury and briny flavours of squid ink, these dumplings are worth all your effort. If you can't find squid ink, you can skip this ingredient and proceed with making the dumpling dough.

Neutral oil, for frying
Chilli sauce, to serve

SEAFOOD FILLING
300 g (10½ oz) prawn meat, cut into 1 cm (½ inch) dice
150 g (5½ oz) scallops (without roe), cut into 0.5 cm (¼ inch) dice
50 g (1¾ oz) water chestnuts
2 tablespoons finely chopped ginger
1 teaspoon sesame oil
1 tablespoon light soy sauce
1 tablespoon crisp-fried shallots
2 tablespoons coriander (cilantro), finely chopped
2 makrut lime leaves, thinly sliced
¼ teaspoon caster (superfine) sugar
¼ teaspoon salt

SQUID-INK DUMPLING DOUGH
2⅔ cups (400 g) plain (all-purpose) flour
2 sachets (8 g) squid ink (see note)
½ teaspoon salt

For the filling, combine all the ingredients in a bowl and mix well. Cover with plastic wrap and refrigerate for 30 minutes to chill.

For the squid-ink dumpling dough, pour the flour into a bowl and make a well in the centre. Combine the squid ink with 300 ml (10½ fl oz) water and salt in a small saucepan and bring to the boil. Remove from the heat, cool for 30 seconds, then pour into the flour. Mix well to combine, then turn out onto the bench and knead for 5 minutes until soft and pliable. Cover with a damp tea towel and leave to rest at room temperature for 30 minutes.

To make the dumplings, roll the dough out with a rolling pin to 2 mm (1/16 inch) thick, then cut out rounds with a 9 cm (3½ inch) ring cutter. Place 1 tablespoon of filling in the centre of each wrapper, then fold them in half, but don't seal them firmly. Pinch the front edge to form about eight pleats, then seal well to form a crescent shape.

To cook the dumplings, heat 2 tablespoons of neutral oil in a non-stick frying pan over medium-high heat. When the oil is hot, add the dumplings (the size of your pan determines the number of dumplings), making sure they don't touch each other. Fry for 1 minute, or until the base is just beginning to crisp, then add ⅓ cup (80 ml) water and immediately cover with a lid. Reduce the heat to medium and leave to steam for 4–5 minutes or until the water has evaporated. Uncover and continue to cook until the dumplings have formed a crust on the bottom (about 3–5 minutes). Remove with a spatula and serve immediately with chilli sauce.

✵ Uncooked dumplings may be frozen for 2 weeks, and can be cooked straight from the freezer.

Squid ink is available from select delis, fishmongers or online.

STEAMED PORK BUNS WITH FERMENTED BLACK BEANS AND CHILLI

MAKES 10–12

This is my take on Cantonese pork buns and those featured in David Chang's book *Momofuku*. The recipe appears long but it's a cinch to make. Just remember to marinate the pork overnight and roast it on the day you are making the buns. It really is delicious eating and totally different to what you would be served in a yum cha restaurant.

If you do not wish to make the dough from scratch, you can buy ready-mixed bun flour from Chinese and Vietnamese grocers.

Chinkiang vinegar, to serve

BAO FILLING
2 tablespoons neutral oil
1 small onion, diced
1 tablespoon finely chopped garlic
1 tablespoon finely chopped ginger
5 tablespoons finely sliced spring onions (scallions)
2 long red chillies, or to taste, finely chopped
3 tablespoons fermented black beans, lightly rinsed and chopped
300 g (10½ oz) char siu (barbecued pork, from Chinese barbecue shops, or see opposite) coarsely diced
1 tablespoon Shaoxing wine
1 tablespoon light soy sauce
Pinch of caster (superfine) sugar, or to taste
150 ml (5 fl oz) chicken stock or water
1 tablespoon cornflour (cornstarch), mixed with a little water

BAO DOUGH
60 g (2¼ oz) caster (superfine) sugar
1 cup (250 ml) lukewarm water
1½ teaspoons dried yeast
430 g (15¼ oz) cake flour, plus extra for dusting
3 teaspoons baking powder
2 tablespoons neutral oil, plus extra for greasing
Pinch of salt

To make the filling, heat the oil in a wok over medium heat. Fry the onion until soft but not coloured. Add the garlic, ginger, spring onions and chilli and fry until fragrant. Spoon half the mixture into a bowl to use as a dip.

Add the black beans, diced pork and Shaoxing to the wok and stir-fry for 30 seconds. Reduce the heat and add the soy sauce, sugar and stock or water. Cook for about 2 minutes, then stir in the cornflour slurry until the filling begins to thicken. Remove from the heat and transfer the filling to a shallow dish. Cool to room temperature, then chill in the fridge until required. (The filling may be made a day ahead.)

To make the dough, dissolve the sugar in the lukewarm water, then stir in the yeast and set aside in a draught-free place for 10 minutes or until foamy.

Sift the flour and baking powder into a bowl. Make a well in the centre and add the yeast mixture, oil and salt. Stir with a wooden spoon until combined. Turn the dough out onto a lightly floured surface and knead for 8–10 minutes until soft and pliable.

Place the dough in a lightly oiled bowl, turn to coat evenly with the oil, then cover with a tea towel or plastic wrap. Set aside until doubled in size (1–2 hours or up to 4 hours on a cold day).

Cut out 20 squares of baking paper, each 7 cm (2¾ inch). Punch down the dough and turn out onto a lightly floured bench. Cut the dough in half and cover one piece with a tea towel. Roll the other piece into a cylinder and cut it into 10 equal pieces. Roll each piece into a ball, then flatten it into a circle 12 cm (4½ inch) in diameter.

Hold a round of dough in your cupped hand and spoon 1 tablespoon of the chilled filling into the centre. Gather the dough around the filling, then pinch the edges together to form a bun and gently twist to seal. Place the bao on a piece of baking paper. Repeat with the remaining dough and filling.

Cover the bao with a tea towel and set aside until they have risen sightly (about 30–60 minutes).

Steam the buns in batches in a covered steamer over a saucepan of boiling water until puffed and cooked through (12–15 minutes). Serve hot with the reserved onion mixture combined with Chinkiang vinegar as a dip.

CHAR SIU
BARBECUED PORK

MAKES 500 G (1 LB 2 OZ)

This is my take on the traditional Cantonese char siu – the marinade is different from those found in Chinese cookbooks. The quantity below is more than you need to make the steamed pork buns opposite or the pastries over the page, but enjoy the bonus – add it to hot noodles or a quick stir-fry, or use it in the pastries on page 94.

Cut the pork lengthways into 4 × 2.5 cm (1½ × 1 inch) strips. Place in a bowl.

Mix all the marinade ingredients in a bowl, then pour the mixture over the pork. Coat well and leave to marinate for at least 2 hours or preferably overnight – but no longer.

Preheat the oven to 240°C (475°F). Arrange the pork on a wire rack over a roasting tin filled with boiling water.

Roast for 20–30 minutes or until the pork is just cooked and nicely charred. Baste the pork with the marinade two or three times during cooking and turn it over once or twice. Leave the pork to cool. It will keep in the fridge for 2 days, or it can be frozen.

500 g (1 lb 2 oz) pork neck

MARINADE
1 tablespoon caster (superfine) sugar
1 tablespoon light soy sauce
1 tablespoon Shaoxing wine
1 tablespoon honey
1 tablespoon mei kuei lu chiew (rose dew cooking wine) or brandy
2 cubes red fermented beancurd, mashed
2 garlic cloves, finely chopped
½ teaspoon Chinese five spice powder

CHAR SIU SOU
FLAKY BARBECUE PORK PASTRIES

MAKES 20

Many of us know of steamed barbecue pork bao and other steamed delicacies at yum cha joints, but, unless you're a dim sum regular, chances are haven't heard of a school of baked pastries that are equally delicious. Among them, char siu sou stands out. The juxtaposition of the flavourful sweet-savoury char siu filling and the light and crisp lard pastry is remarkable. It is calorific, but by advice is to throw caution to the wind and enjoy this sinful delight.

The method for the dough here is very similar to making puff pastry, but it's more straightforward because it uses lard or shortening, which is more manageable than a solid block of butter. It's best to make this recipe over two days.

Beaten egg yolk, for brushing
Sesame seeds, for sprinkling

CHAR SIU SOU FILLING
2 tablespoons neutral oil
1 small onion, diced
300 g (10½ oz) char siu (barbecued pork, from Chinese barbecue shops, or see page 93), diced
1 tablespoon Shaoxing wine
1 tablespoon oyster sauce
1 tablespoon hoisin sauce
1 tablespoon light soy sauce
½ teaspoon sesame oil
1 teaspoon caster (superfine) sugar
150 ml (5 fl oz) chicken stock or water
2 tablespoons cornflour (cornstarch), mixed with a little water

WATER DOUGH
1¼ cups (180 g) plain (all-purpose) flour, plus extra for dusting
1 teaspoon caster (superfine) sugar
Pinch of salt
¼ cup (60 g) chopped lard or shortening

OIL DOUGH
½ cup (75 g) plain (all-purpose) flour
⅓ cup (90 g) lard or vegetable shortening, chopped

First, make the filling. Heat the oil in a wok over medium heat, add the onion and fry until soft but not coloured. Add the char siu and Shaoxing, stir-fry for 30 seconds, then reduce the heat to low and add the oyster sauce, hoisin, soy sauce, sesame oil, sugar and stock or water. Cook, stirring, for about 2 minutes, then stir in the cornflour slurry and stir until thickened. Transfer to a shallow dish, cool to room temperature, then chill for at least 4 hours or overnight.

For the water dough, combine the flour, sugar and salt in a food processor. Pulse for 20 seconds, then add the lard. Process for 1 minute or until a coarse meal forms. Transfer to a bowl, add 75 ml (2¼ fl oz) water and mix to combine, adding another teaspoon of water if required, until it forms a shaggy mass. Knead for 2–3 minutes, dust lightly with flour, then wrap in plastic wrap and rest for 30 minutes.

For the oil dough, combine the flour and lard in a bowl and mix with your hands until the mixture forms a homogenous mass. Set aside.

To assemble, on a lightly floured surface, roll the water dough and oil dough separately into two sausages, then divide each into 10 equal portions.

Roll each piece of water dough into a disc large enough to wrap each piece of oil dough, then place a piece of oil dough on each round of water dough, wrap them up and roll them into a ball. Flatten a ball with a rolling pin, roll it into a rectangle about 14 cm (5½ inches) long and 8 cm (3¼ inches) wide, then roll the dough up like a roulade and turn it 90 degrees. Roll it out flat again and repeat the turning and rolling two more times. Finally, roll the dough into a 7–8 cm (2¾–3¼ inch) square, add 2 teaspoons of char siu filling in the centre, and fold the dough into a triangle to seal. Repeat with remaining dough and filling until you've made all the pastries.

Brush the top of the pastries with beaten egg yolk and sprinkle them with sesame seeds. Bake in a 180°C (350°F) oven for 25–30 minutes until golden. Transfer to a wire rack to cool and serve either warm or at room temperature.

MAKES 30

POTSTICKER DUMPLINGS
WOR TIP

Of Shanghainese origin, these potsticker dumplings are known as wor tip in Cantonese and guo tie in Mandarin, which translates as 'pot' and 'stick'. No one knows their provenance for certain, but it is said that one day a cook of the emperor was making dumplings and forgot them on the stove. They burned, and he was forced to present them to the emperor, claiming they were a new invention. Needless to say, they've become immensely popular everywhere from Beijing to yum cha and dumpling houses across the world. The accompanying dipping sauce, a combination of light soy and red rice vinegar, is special, too. Red rice vinegar is traditional, and tastes more delicate than Chinkiang (black) vinegar.

I've given the method for making the wrappers here, but you can also buy pure-wheat round Chinese wrappers from Asian grocers if you want to skip that step. If you are making several batches at once, it's a good idea to keep them warm in a hot oven.

Neutral oil, for shallow-frying

WOR TIP FILLING
3⅓ cups (250 g) finely shredded wombok (Chinese cabbage)
1 teaspoon salt
250 g (9 oz) minced pork
2 tablespoons minced ginger
1 spring onion (scallion), finely chopped
2 teaspoons light soy sauce
1 tablespoon Shaoxing wine
½ teaspoon caster (superfine) sugar
1 tablespoon sesame oil
1 tablespoon cornflour (cornstarch)

DUMPLING WRAPPERS
2 cups (300 g) plain (all-purpose) flour, plus extra for dusting
Pinch of salt
200–220 ml (7–7¾ fl oz) boiling water

LACE BATTER (OPTIONAL)
⅔ cups (100 g) plain (all-purpose) flour
¼ cup (60 ml) neutral oil
Pinch of salt, or to taste

SOY-VINEGAR DIPPING SAUCE
½ cup (125 ml) light soy sauce
½ cup (125 ml) red rice vinegar

OR

VINEGAR-GINGER DIPPING SAUCE
1 cup (250 ml) red rice vinegar
3 tablespoons finely shredded ginger

For the filling, put the shredded cabbage in a bowl and toss with the salt. Leave for about 15 minutes to allow the salt to draw excess moisture from the cabbage. Drain in a colander and flush with water. Drain again and squeeze moisture from the cabbage in a clean tea towel over the sink. You should have about 2 cups of cabbage. Combine the cabbage with the remaining filling ingredients, mix well and refrigerate for 2 hours.

For the dumpling wrappers, place the flour and salt in a large bowl. Let the boiling water cool for 10 seconds, then add it to the flour, stirring rapidly with chopsticks to combine. Once the mix is cool enough to handle, knead it for 10 minutes or until smooth. Form the dough into two sausages. Dust lightly with flour and wrap loosely in a plastic bag. Leave for 20 minutes to rest.

Working with one sausage at a time, cut into 14–16 pieces (about 16 grams/½ oz each). On a lightly floured board, roll out each piece with a rolling pin to a round 10 cm (4 inch) in diameter. Spread 1 scant tablespoon of filling into the centre of a wrapper. Brush the edge of the wrapper with water, then fold into a half-moon shape, pleating as you seal it. Press one side of the dumpling against the side of your hand to flatten it slightly and create the classic pot-sticker shape. Repeat with the remaining dough and filling, always keeping the unused dough covered so it remains soft and pliable.

For the lace batter, whisk all the ingredients together along with 600 ml (21 fl oz) water in a bowl. When you're ready to cook, heat about 3 tablespoons of oil in a frying pan over high heat. Arrange the dumplings, pleat-side up, in the frying pan. Cook for about 3 minutes, then pour ½ cup (125 ml) water or lace batter into the pan. Reduce the heat to medium-low, cover with a lid and simmer until most of the liquid has evaporated and the dumplings are almost cooked through. (If it seems like it's evaporating too fast, add 1–2 tablespoons water to give the filling time to cook through.) Remove the lid, increase the heat to medium-high and cook for another minute or so until the bottoms are golden and crisp.

Serve hot with dipping sauce. For either dipping sauce, combine the ingredients in a bowl and mix well.

STEAMED PORK SPARE-RIBS
JING PAI KWAT

SERVES 8–10

This simple yet sophisticated dish reflects the essence of Cantonese and southern Chinese cooking, and is a must-order on yum cha menus. Pork spare-ribs are steamed into submission after being marinated in garlic, chillies, ginger and salted or fermented black beans – four ingredients that form a seasoning that is very typical of the style of cooking in southern China.

Salted or fermented black beans (dow see in Cantonese) are black beans preserved in salt and spices. The beans, which are sold in plastic bags or small, round cardboard containers and keep indefinitely, are quite pungent and should be used sparingly. Although some cookbooks suggest not to rinse them in water, I find some brands far too salty, so I prefer to take the edge off a little.

Toss the spare-ribs with baking soda in a bowl, rubbing to coat. Set aside for 30 minutes to tenderise. Rinse thoroughly, then pat dry with paper towel.

Combine the chilli, garlic, black beans, light and dark soy sauce, sugar, Shaoxing, cornflour and ginger in a bowl and mix well. Add the spare-ribs, turn to coat and refrigerate for at least an hour or overnight to marinate.

When ready to serve, divide among individual dishes or place them in a central dish for steaming. Place the dish or dishes on a steaming rack in a steamer set over boiling water. Cover and steam for 20–30 minutes or until cooked through – use a fork to test if you like. Serve immediately topped with spring onion.

✽ It is best to steam the spare-ribs in a single layer. As a variation, add some dried mandarin peel. In Malaysia, I use fresh green papaya juice and leaves to tenderise the meat, but since these aren't readily available in Australia, when here I use baking soda, which does the same trick – it raises the pH level of the surface, hence not allowing the proteins to bond together.

- 500 g (1 lb 2 oz) pork spare-ribs, cut through the bone into 2 cm (¾ inch) bite-sized pieces
- 2 teaspoons bicarbonate of soda (baking soda)
- 1 long red chilli, finely chopped
- 3 garlic cloves, finely chopped
- 1 tablespoon salted black beans (see above), rinsed and chopped
- 1 tablespoon light soy sauce
- 1 teaspoon dark soy sauce
- 1 teaspoon caster (superfine) sugar
- 2 teaspoons Shaoxing wine
- 2 teaspoons cornflour (cornstarch)
- 1 cm (½ inch) piece ginger, minced
- 1 spring onion (scallion), thinly sliced on an angle, to serve

ZUCCHINI DUMPLINGS

25 | 30 MAKES

T L

Using dill in dumplings and buns is pretty common in northern China. Perhaps this has something to do with historical trade along the Silk Road.

That said, while the first time I ate dumplings with dill was when I was in Beijing a few decades ago, the next time I recall eating them was at Shandong Mama, a storied restaurant with a cult following tucked into a Chinatown arcade in central Melbourne. They're known for their mackerel dumplings, but this recipe is inspired by another hit on their menu: the vegetarian dumplings stuffed with zucchini and mushrooms and flavoured with dill.

First, make the filling. Grate the zucchini on the large side of a box grater into a bowl. Add the salt, toss well, then leave for about 20 minutes to allow the salt to draw excess moisture from the zucchini. Place the zucchini in a clean tea towel and squeeze out as much water as possible.

Meanwhile, soak the dried mushrooms in hot water for 20 minutes. Drain and squeeze out excess water, discard the stems, then cut the caps into fine dice.

Toss the zucchini and mushroom with the remaining ingredients to combine well, and season to taste with salt and pepper.

For the dumpling wrappers, place the flour and salt in a large bowl. Let the boiling water cool for 10 seconds, then add it to the flour, stirring it rapidly with chopsticks to combine. Once the mix is cool enough to handle, knead it for 10 minutes or until smooth.

Form the dough into two sausages. Dust lightly with flour and wrap loosely in a plastic bag. Leave at room temperature for 20 minutes to rest.

Working with one sausage at a time, cut it into 12–15 pieces (12–14 g/¼–½ oz each). On a lightly floured board, roll out each piece with a rolling pin to a disc 12 cm (4½ inch) in diameter, preferably thinner at the edge and thicker in the centre.

Spoon a teaspoon of filling into the centre of a wrapper and gather the edges together. Pinch and form into a dumpling shape and repeat with the remaining wrappers and filling.

To cook the dumplings, bring a large saucepan of water to a rolling boil and drop in 8–10 dumplings. When the water comes back to the boil, pour in a cup (250 ml) of cold water and bring it back to the boil again. Once the dumplings float on the surface, they are done (about another 5 minutes). Transfer the dumplings to serving bowls with a slotted spoon. Serve immediately with dipping sauce (see below).

For either dipping sauce, combine the ingredients in a bowl and mix well.

✖ You can also fry the dumplings in a frying pan.

800 g (1 lb 12 oz) zucchini (courgette)
1 scant teaspoon salt, plus extra to taste
25 g (1 oz) dried shiitake mushrooms
½ bunch of dill, finely chopped
1 spring onion, finely chopped
2 × 1.5 cm (½ inch) cubes fermented beancurd, or to taste
1 teaspoon light soy sauce, or to taste
1 tablespoon neutral oil
2 teaspoons sesame oil
White pepper, to taste

DUMPLING WRAPPERS
2 cups (300 g) plain (all-purpose) flour, plus extra for dusting
Pinch of salt
200–220 ml (¾ cup) boiling water

SOY-VINEGAR DIPPING SAUCE
½ cup (125 ml) light soy sauce
½ cup (125 ml) red rice vinegar

OR

VINEGAR-GINGER DIPPING SAUCE
1 cup (250 ml) red rice vinegar
3 tablespoons finely shredded ginger

SERVES 8

CHAWANMUSHI WITH SHELLFISH OIL AND CRAB MEAT

T

I adore the Japanese steamed savoury custard known as chawanmushi. It's simply delicious, especially if you make your own dashi. As a concept, steamed egg is popular with Koreans as well, while the Chinese call this dish jing shui dan. It's simple to make, but a flawless steamed egg custard must be cooked over gentle heat for it to shine. This is humble cooking, but I've taken this dish in a more sophisticated direction with the addition of shellfish oil (made at least a day ahead) and crab meat.

DASHI
1 piece kombu
50 g (1¾ oz) katsuobushi (dried bonito flakes, available from Japanese grocers)

CUSTARD
8 eggs
3 teaspoons Japanese light soy sauce (Kikkoman's usukuchi is best)
1 tablespoon sake or mirin
Pinch of caster (superfine) sugar
Pinch of salt, or to taste

TOPPINGS
150 g (5½ oz) cooked crabmeat
1 tablespoon grapeseed oil
8 tablespoons shellfish oil (see opposite)
2 tablespoons thinly sliced chives
Salt and white pepper, to taste

For the dashi, pour 1.5 litres (6 cups) water into a saucepan, add the kombu and bring to just under the boil. Remove the kombu, then add the katsuobushi and remove from the heat. Leave to cool and, once the flakes start to sink, strain through a fine sieve.

Meanwhile, for the custard, break the eggs into a bowl and, with a fork, beat gently, trying to avoid making bubbles. Add the remaining ingredients and 1.2 litres (40 fl oz) dashi and stir to combine. Strain through a fine sieve into a jug, then pour the mixture into 8 × 150 ml (5 fl oz) individual bowls or ramekins. Cover each with a lid, if you have them, or with plastic wrap, then place them in a steamer over a saucepan of simmering water on low-medium heat for 10–15 minutes or until just set.

Before serving, quickly flash the crabmeat in a frying pan over medium heat with a tablespoon of grapeseed oil and a pinch of salt and pepper until warmed through. Keep warm.

To serve, spoon a tablespoon of shellfish oil over each chawanmushi, add a dollop of crabmeat and garnish with chives.

✖ These light and delicious custards may be cooked in a bain-marie in the oven at 120°C (250°F) if a steamer is not available. If you don't want to take the extra step of making your own dashi, one packet of instant dashi is sufficient for 600 ml (20 fl oz) water. Dashi keeps for 3 days in the refrigerator.

SHELLFISH OIL

2 cups (500 ml) neutral oil
Heads and shells from 1 kg (2 lb 4 oz) raw prawns
1 small onion, cut into 1 cm (½ inch) dice
1 small carrot, cut into 1 cm (½ inch) dice
½ celery stalk, cut into 1 cm (½ inch) dice
1 leek (white part only), finely chopped
½ fennel bulb, chopped
2 large dried red chillies (optional), roughly chopped
1 tomato, chopped
1 tablespoon tomato paste (concentrated purée)
1 teaspoon black peppercorns
1 star anise
1 dried bay leaf
2 thyme sprigs
1 tablespoon brandy

Heat half the oil in a large, heavy-based saucepan over high heat, then add the prawn heads and shells. Fry until the shells are red and glossy (about 3–4 minutes).

Add the onion, carrot, celery, leek, fennel and chilli and sauté for about 10 minutes or until the vegetables are tender.

Add the remaining ingredients, including the remaining oil, reduce the heat to as low as it goes and cook gently for 2 hours until the flavour is infused into the oil. Remove from the heat, cool, then refrigerate overnight to steep.

The next day, strain the oil through a muslin-lined fine sieve, discarding the solids. Store in a sealed sterilised jar in the fridge.

✖ If you don't have time to make it, shellfish oil is sometimes sold at delicatessens.

SPRING ONION PANCAKES
CHUNG YEW BING

This is one of northern China's best-known snacks. Traditionally made with lard or duck fat but nowadays more often made with neutral oil, the typical technique is to pan-fry the spring onion pancakes, but many restaurants in Australia tend to deep-fry them which, in my opinion, is never as good. They appear rather difficult to make on account of the hot-water method but it is no different to making choux pastry. In Beijing, locals eat these at any time of the day.

Sift the flour and salt into a large bowl. Add the lard to a saucepan, pour in 220 ml (7¾ fl oz) water and bring to the boil, stirring to combine. Pour the boiling lard and water into the flour and mix well to combine.

While the dough is still hot, tip it out onto a clean bench and knead for 5 minutes until smooth and elastic. Return the dough to the bowl and leave for 30–45 minutes to allow the gluten to relax.

Roll the dough into a sausage on a lightly floured bench, then divide it into 20–24 equal pieces.

With a small rolling pin, roll out a piece to a round 12 cm (4½ inch) in diameter, brush with sesame oil, stopping just before the edges, then scatter it with a little spring onion.

Lift up the side of the dough nearest to you and roll it up into a thin cigar, pinching the ends to seal. Flatten it slightly, then roll up the dough again from one end to the other like a snail.

Repeat with the remaining dough, sesame oil and spring onion, cover with a clean tea towel and rest for 20 minutes.

Flatten the discs with your hand, then roll out each piece into a disc 10 cm (4 inch) in diameter (don't worry if the surface breaks), dusting lightly with flour if it's sticking. Cover again, and leave for 10 minutes to rest.

Heat a frying pan over medium heat, add 2 tablespoons oil and fry for 2–3 minutes on each side until crisp and golden brown in spots. Repeat with the remaining dough. You may have to wipe the frying pan with clean paper towels if too much flour is used to dust the pancakes. Serve hot.

- 1⅔ cups (250 g) plain (all-purpose) flour, plus extra for dusting
- 1 teaspoon salt
- 2 tablespoons lard
- 3–4 teaspoons sesame oil
- 3 spring onions (scallions), thinly sliced
- 200 ml (7 fl oz) neutral oil, for frying

ROTI JOHN

SERVES 4

This street food of minced beef or chicken with eggs slathered on French bread and fried is popular in Indonesia, Brunei, Singapore and Malaysia. This simple and delicious sandwich made its debut back in the 1960s when there was a British naval base in Singapore. Apparently, while the soldiers were stationed in Singapore, they would stop at a stall selling bread and omelettes. According to legend, as the stallholder saw all British soldiers as more or less the same, he would ask them this question: 'Roti, John?' Every British serviceman was referred to as John. Regardless of its origin, it really is a joy to eat. I'm surprised it hasn't caught on in the West.

⅓ cup (80 ml) neutral oil or ghee
1 large onion, finely chopped
1 tablespoon finely chopped lemongrass
1 garlic clove, minced
1–2 tablespoons meat curry powder (such as Alagappa, or Cap Burung Nuri)
½–1 teaspoon chilli powder
½ teaspoon ground turmeric
1 teaspoon garam masala (page 23)
500 g (1 lb 2 oz) finely minced beef, lamb or chicken
Salt and white pepper, to taste
4 eggs
2 tablespoons chopped Vietnamese mint
1 baguette, cut into 4 equal pieces
Softened butter, for brushing
Coriander (cilantro) sprigs, to serve
Chilli sauce and tomato sauce, to serve

Heat a wok over medium-high heat, then add 2 tablespoons of oil. Once it's shimmering, add the onion, lemongrass and garlic and stir-fry until the onion turns translucent.

Meanwhile, mix the curry powder, chilli, turmeric and garam masala with enough water to make a paste. Add to the wok and cook for 2–3 minutes, stirring constantly.

Add the meat and cook, stirring now and then, until it is well coloured and the moisture has evaporated. Season to taste with salt and pepper, and add enough water to cover the meat. Bring to the boil, then reduce to a simmer and cook until all the liquid is absorbed. Leave to cool.

Beat the eggs in a large bowl, then add the cooled meat mixture and stir to combine.

Cut each piece of baguette in two lengthways (but not all the way through) and open them up.

Generously grease a large non-stick frying pan with the remaining oil, heat over medium-high heat, then add a large dollop of the omelette mixture and cook for 1–2 minutes, stirring and tossing until softly set. Open out a cut baguette and place it on top of the omelette in the pan, crust-side up, pressing gently so the omelette sticks to it. Cook until the omelette is firm, brushing some butter on top of the baguette as it sets.

Remove the baguette and omelette with a spatula and fold together to form a sandwich. Top with coriander and serve with a mix of some chilli sauce and tomato sauce, to your taste.

MAKES 12

ROTI CANAI

Even though the root of this flaky bread is south Indian, there's no denying that Malaysia and Singapore have made roti canai (pronounced cha-nye) their own. Traditionally made with nothing more than flour, water and ghee along with some salt and sugar, roti canai is a flatbread that came with the Malayalis and the Tamils to Penang and British Malaya at the turn of the 20th century. At that time, it was probably called roti prata, the term currently used in Singapore, or roti parotta, as it's known in Kerala (the Malayalis from Kerala are well known for this roti).

Apparently, roti canai made its debut in Mamak (Indian-Muslim) hawker stalls and neighbourhood coffee shops in Penang and Singapore. Soon after, around the 1920s, it was firmly established throughout the country. When this unleavened bread made the transition to being called roti canai, however, is unknown, although the fact it is no longer made strictly by the Mamaks has something to do with this; Malay cooks have embraced this delicious staple as their own, so while roti is still the Hindi word, canai is a Malay word meaning to knead and to stretch. In short, it has become Malaysianised.

It's unique among flatbreads and, in the hands of a professional roti canai maker, the process is pure theatre. After all, how many flatbreads have you seen flung into the air, and then stretched to paper-thin layers before being folded and fried on a hot griddle? Obviously, the difference between a pedestrian roti and one made by a skilled artisan is enormous.

A well-made roti canai is a thing of beauty. It should be light, soft and buttery on the inside and slightly crunchy and flaky with tanned heat spots on the outside. It ought to break away into shards with just enough resistance to prove the dough is properly made and rested. As with a good loaf of bread, handmade roti canai is best. It is only excellent freshly made; avoid pre-made ones at all cost, as they turn soggy and limp shortly after cooking.

Although it is best enjoyed at breakfast with a lentil curry or on its own, this addictive flatbread has several incarnations. It is delectable with egg, when it's known as roti telur, as a light lunch and as a dessert, known as roti pisang, filled with melted soft banana.

There are a few things to note that should give you a better result. First, you'll need flour with at least 11 per cent wheat protein to make the dough stretchable and strong enough to prevent tearing. Adding sugar lends flavour and helps to caramelise the bread, which is why you also find recipes using condensed milk. Flipping roti canai in the air requires patience and practice – if that's failing you, you can always stretch it as though you were making strudel. Finally, when you're folding roti canai, trapping air is the key to creating the layers, so be sure to give this stage attention.

1 cup (250 ml) neutral oil
Melted ghee or clarified butter, for cooking

DOUGH
3⅓ cups (500 g) plain (all-purpose) flour
Salt, to taste
3 teaspoons caster (superfine) sugar, or to taste
60–70 ml (2–2¼ fl oz) milk
1 egg, lightly beaten
1 tablespoon neutral oil

For the dough, combine all the ingredients in a food processor, add ¾ cup (185 ml) water, and blend until everything comes together in a ball. (Or, combine the flour, salt and sugar into a bowl, make a well in the centre, then add the milk, egg, oil and ¾ cup/185 ml water and stir to combine.) Turn out onto a clean bench and knead the dough by hand for about 10 minutes until pliable and shiny.

At this stage, if you're not in a hurry, rest the dough in a bowl for 20 minutes, covering it with a slightly damp tea towel.

Roll the dough into a long sausage, divide it into 12 even pieces, then roll each piece into a ball.

Pour ½ cup (125 ml) of the oil into a bowl and place the balls of dough into the oil, coating them well to help prevent sticking. Cover the dough with a clean tea towel or plastic wrap and leave at room temperature to rest for at least 1 hour, but preferably overnight.

When you're ready to cook, lightly oil your hands, then roll each ball of dough into a round 20 cm (8 inch) in diameter on an oiled bench.

If you want to flip it like a professional, put your right hand under the dough and your left hand over it (if you are right-handed). Grab the dough and, in a circular motion, flip the dough from right to left, making sure it doesn't fold over itself as it lands.

Grab the stretched disc again, and continue to flip it until you have a sufficiently wafer-thin dough that you can see through. Dab lightly with melted ghee, then fold the right edge into the centre, followed by the left edge. Now fold the side closest to you towards the centre, then the top side, folding it like an envelope.

Alternatively, once you've made the dough into a disc, stretch it out with your hands like you're making strudel dough. Once it is paper-thin, brush lightly with melted ghee and fold as above. Another method is to loosely coil the dough into a sausage, then, starting from one end, turn it around on itself until it becomes a round, coiled disc. Flatten this disc with a rolling pin to about 15 cm (6 inches) in diameter.

To cook the roti, heat a roti pan (tawa) or a griddle, coat the surface with ghee and cook the roti one at a time, flipping over a couple of times, until golden and crisp on both sides (3-5 minutes). Serve at once, and continue until all the rotis are done.

MAKES 10 | 12

ROTI JALA

In Bahasa Malaysia, roti means bread and jala means a net. Roti jala, however, doesn't mean 'bread in the form of a net' but rather it is a descriptive term for these appealing lace pancakes. Visually lovely, roti jala is immensely popular during festivals such as Hari Raya, the feast day after the Muslim fasting month. The lacy appearance of the pancake is due to a special brass container with three to five spouts attached either to the side or at the base, which is used to spread the batter onto a special pan called a tawa. If you have neither, a squeeze bottle and a non-stick pan will do the job. Roti jala is great with curries with lots of gravy, as it mops up the sauce beautifully; try it with a curry such as my curry kapitan (page 197).

- 3⅓ cups (500 g) plain (all-purpose) flour, sifted
- 2 cups (500 ml) coconut milk or fresh milk
- 2 eggs
- 1 teaspoon ground turmeric
- 1 tablespoon neutral oil, plus extra for greasing
- Pinch of salt, or to taste

Tip the sifted flour into a food processor, add the coconut milk, eggs, turmeric, oil and salt, adjusting to taste, and blend until smooth. Pour into a jug and leave to rest at room temperature for 20 minutes.

Heat a tawa (roti pan) or non-stick frying pan over medium heat and swipe a little oil over the surface. Pour 200 ml (¾ cup) pancake batter into the roti jala container (or a squeeze bottle). With a quick circular motion, pour the mixture from a height of 10–15 cm (4–6 inches) thinly over the pan in a lattice pattern and cook gently for 1–2 minutes until cooked through but still soft, then flip it over and cook for a further 30 seconds. Once the pancake is cooked, gently fold over into a triangle with a spatula and transfer to a plate. Repeat with the remaining batter.

✖ If there are spouts at the bottom of your container, it's a good idea to have a bowl ready to collect the batter while making each pancake. As roti jala moulds can be near impossible to find, a plastic sauce container does the job just as well.

TOP HATS
KUIH PIE TEE

MAKES 35–40

Unless you're from Malaysia or Singapore, or have friends from there, chances are you have never heard of these morsels of deliciousness. An elegant contribution from the southern school of Peranakan cooking, this elegant delicacy's origin is clouded in mystery. A prominent Baba writer, Ong Jin Teong, suggests that kuih pie tee is a Singaporean invention because it was called Syonanto pie when the Japanese occupied the island during the Second World War. To compound this obscurity, the Peranakan community in Malacca call it 'top hat', as it resembles an inverted hat worn by British gentlemen in the 18th century. As a result, it's suggested that the name pie tee is a derivative of the British pastie.

Regardless of its provenance, this dainty party snack is a must-make because it really is divine; it might just take you to a patio in the tropics with sarong-clad people walking by. It consists of two parts: a delicate, crisp pastry shell and an umami-packed filling made with jicama, pork or seafood or both. It does require a pie tee mould, but these are now sold online, so they are easy to acquire.

To make the filling, heat the oil in a wok over medium-high heat. Add the shallot and stir-fry until aromatic, then add the dried shrimp and stir-fry for a minute before adding the carrot, jicama and bamboo shoot. Stir-fry for 2 minutes until softened, then add the stock, oyster sauce, sugar and salt and pepper to taste. Bring to the boil, reduce the heat to low, and leave to simmer gently, covered, until the whole thing is slightly soft and deeply savoury (about 20 minutes). Transfer to a plate and leave to cool.

For the pastry shells, combine the flours and salt in a bowl. Add the beaten egg and 200 ml (7 fl oz) water, mix well to combine, then strain through a sieve. Set aside for 30 minutes to rest.

Now for the fun part. Put the batter in a smallish bowl. Add enough oil for deep-frying to a saucepan (the oil should reach just slightly above the height of the pie tee mould). If you have a clip-on thermometer, attach it to the side of the saucepan. Dip the pie tee mould in the oil, leaving it there until the oil reaches 170–180°C (325–350°F).

Remove the mould, shake off excess oil, then dip it into the batter to cover just below the rim. Shake off excess batter, then transfer the mould to the oil, shaking or bobbing it gently until the batter begins to set. As soon as it does, ease it off the mould with a satay stick or chopsticks, then leave it to cook for 2–3 minutes or until golden brown. Transfer to paper towel to drain, and repeat to use up all the batter.

As you continue to make the pastry shells, your batter will thicken, so add a teaspoon of water from time to time, stirring to dilute. Your first few pastry shells will break and look like nothing on Earth. Have patience! Once you've done your practice run, the rest will be a walk in the park. Just remember to maintain the temperature and stir the batter every now and then.

To assemble, fill your pastry shells with the filling and finish with a flourish of toppings.

---

2 tablespoons neutral oil
1 shallot (eschalot), finely chopped
2 garlic cloves, finely chopped
50 g (1¾ oz) dried shrimp, soaked in warm water for 10–15 minutes, drained and finely chopped
100 g (3½ oz) carrot, grated
300 g (10½ oz) jicama or water chestnuts, grated
100 g (3½ oz) bamboo shoots, finely chopped
1 cup (250 ml) prawn or chicken stock
1 tablespoon oyster sauce, or to taste
½ teaspoon caster (superfine) sugar
Salt and white pepper, to taste
Crisp-fried shallots, finely sliced spring onions (scallions), cooked crab meat or prawns, and chilli sauce, to serve (optional)

PASTRY SHELLS
50 g (1¾ oz) rice flour
50 g (1¾ oz) plain (all-purpose) flour
30 g (1 oz) cornflour (cornstarch)
Pinch of salt
1 egg, beaten
Neutral oil, for deep-frying

SERVES 2–3

SCRAMBLED EGGS WITH CURRY LEAVES AND GREEN CHILLIES

Inspired by the foods of south India, this scrambled egg has been my companion ever since I was a kid growing up in Malaysia; my Indian 'aunty' – she was a neighbour – would make it for me whenever I was hungry. Flavoured with fresh curry leaves and green chillies, it is fabulous as a light lunch or as part of a meal to eat with roti or pilaf. To this basic recipe, you can add fresh prawns or crab meat for a more substantial meal.

4–5 large eggs
Salt and white pepper, to taste
2 tablespoons ghee
1 sprig curry leaves, coarsely chopped
2 long green chillies, or to taste, thinly sliced
1–2 teaspoons ginger, minced
½ small onion, thinly sliced
¼ teaspoon ground turmeric
2 small tomatoes, diced
2 spring onions (scallions), finely sliced
Coriander (cilantro) sprigs, to serve
Chapatti, roti, rice or a salad, to serve

Beat the eggs lightly in a bowl and season with salt and pepper.

Heat a large frying pan over medium-high heat. Add the ghee and, once it's shimmering, add the curry leaves, green chilli and ginger (be careful; curry leaves can spit) and stir-fry for 30 seconds until the curry leaves are crisp.

Add the onion and turmeric and stir-fry for another 2 minutes or until the onion is soft, then add the tomatoes and spring onions and stir-fry for 2–3 minutes until softened.

Pour the eggs into the hot pan, reduce the heat to medium-low and, with a spatula, gently pull the edges towards the centre. As the eggs start to set (they should be creamy and just set), fold them carefully over each other and slide them onto a warm plate.

Top with coriander and serve with chapatti, roti or rice or a salad.

MAKES 20

PEANUT CRACKERS
REMPEYEK KACANG

If you happen to be in Southeast Asia, you'll notice the locals are inveterate snackers, and there's a profusion of hawker foods that you'll find on just about any street. One of these snacks is peanut crackers, or crisps, called rempeyek kacang. Made with peanuts and a rice batter, these crunchy, savoury deep-fried snacks are flavoured with a host of spices, though none of them are chilli hot.

Originally from Indonesia, rempeyek or peyek is also popular in Malaysia and Singapore. These flat discs of deliciousness are quick and easy to make once you get the hang of it. They make great beer snacks, too.

This recipe uses peanuts, but other nuts such as pinenuts, chopped cashews and slivered almonds can be just as good. I've also even eaten rempeyek topped with tiny shrimp and anchovies. Experiment!

- 1½ cups (250 g) rice flour
- 30 g tapioca or sago starch
- 1 egg
- ¼ cup (60 ml) coconut milk
- 4 makrut lime leaves, finely shredded
- 1 teaspoon cumin seeds
- ½ teaspoon ground coriander
- Salt, to taste
- Neutral oil, for deep-frying
- 150 g (5½ oz) roasted or fried peanuts (see note)

Combine the rice flour, tapioca starch, egg, coconut milk and 1¼ cups (310 ml) water in a large bowl and whisk until smooth. Add the makrut lime leaves, cumin and coriander seeds, season to taste with salt, and stir well to combine.

Heat 8 cm (3 inch) oil in a wok to 180°C (350°F; bubbles should form around a wooden chopstick when it's dipped in). If you have a wok spatula (wok chan; see note), put it in the wok to heat. Ladle a scant ¼ cup (60 ml) of stirred batter onto the wok spatula and sprinkle some peanuts on top. Leave it to cook in the oil and it should slowly detach from the spatula in 2–3 minutes.

When it begins to turn light golden, flip the cracker over. Cook for another minute, then use a slotted spoon to transfer the cracker to paper towel. Leave to drain. Repeat until all the batter is used.

✖ Roasted peanuts are readily available from supermarkets. But if you are using raw peanuts, they should take about 10 minutes (depending on size) if you fry them over medium heat. Remember, peanuts burn easily and they will continue to cook while they are hot.

Remember to stir the batter to maintain consistency. If your batter is too runny or thin, add 1 tablespoon of rice flour at a time to thicken it. If the batter is too thick, add 1–2 tablespoons of water.

If you don't have a wok spatula or turner, just use a ladle to make free-form crackers. It will still taste delicious.

KAYA

COCONUT JAM

MAKES 800 ML (28 FL OZ) OR 3 CUPS

Kaya is a Malaysian and Singaporean kopitiam (coffee house) staple. It is also popular in parts of Indonesia, the Philippines and Thailand. Also called coconut jam, kaya is made with eggs, sugar, coconut milk and pandan leaves. The best kaya must be smooth and satiny; like lemon curd, it must never be granular. For this reason it's best to make it over a double-boiler and not to let the water come to the boil because the kaya can curdle, especially if the base of your bowl touches the boiling water; cook it over barely simmering water. Although it's not difficult to make, it does require patience because there is a lot of stirring involved. When the temperature of the kaya reaches 76°C (168°F), it is cooked.

This Hainanese kaya recipe is a tribute to my sister Quee Wah. I still remember the hot afternoons when she made kaya under a tree with the air filled with wood smoke as she stirred the kaya mixture over a massive wok. I also remember she strained the beaten eggs before starting, which gives a silkier result.

400 ml (14 fl oz) coconut cream or coconut milk
3 pandan leaves, knotted (see note)
8 eggs
180–300 g (6–10½ oz) caster (superfine) sugar (to taste)

CARAMEL
50 g (1¾ oz) caster (superfine) sugar
1 tablespoon unsalted butter
Pinch of salt

Pour the coconut cream into a saucepan, add the pandan leaves and place over low heat just to warm it. Set aside.

Crack the eggs into a bowl, add the sugar, and beat gently to combine. Strain the egg mixture into a heatproof bowl, pour in the warm coconut cream, along with the pandan leaf, and stir well with a spatula or whisk to combine.

Set the bowl over a saucepan of gently simmering water (don't let the base of the bowl touch the water) and stir continuously until the sugar is completely dissolved. Continue to stir frequently for 25–30 minutes until the mixture reaches 76°C (168°F), or until it coats the back of a spoon, and it leaves a line when you run your finger through it. Remove from heat.

For the caramel, place the sugar in a small saucepan over medium-high heat and cook, without stirring, until caramelised (2–3 minutes). Add the butter and salt (be careful; hot caramel will spit), stir to combine, then add the caramel to the bowl of coconut cream.

Place the bowl back over simmering water and stir continuously until the caramel is completely blended (3–5 minutes). Remove from the heat and cool to room temperature, stirring occasionally. Remove the pandan leaves, then pour the kaya into sterilised jars and refrigerate. This will keep for 2–3 weeks. Spread it on toast, or I'm even partial to spreading it on a sponge cake or handing it out as a gift.

✖ You can use as many as 10 eggs if you prefer a thicker kaya; coconut cream makes for a thicker kaya, while coconut milk creates a runnier kaya; once you're more confident, you can cook it directly over the heat instead of using a double-boiler but always with a low flame; finally, if you have a Thermomix, it makes great kaya. Use only the best coconut milk or cream – many brands sold here contain water – and your kaya will be as good as it can be.

Although pandan leaves give kaya its distinctive flavour, you can use anything else that takes your fancy, such as vanilla. Sugar is a personal thing, so if you like sweet kaya, then add 300 g (10½ oz). Since I don't have a sweet tooth, I use 180 g (6 oz) and just 50 grams (3 oz) for the caramel.

MAKES 12

SESAME DOUGHNUT WITH CUSTARD AND CHOCOLATE
JIN DEUI

Sesame doughnuts or sesame balls (known as jin deui in Cantonese) are a kind of Chinese ball-shaped fried pastry made with glutinous rice flour and traditionally filled with lotus or red-bean paste. This version is made with a custard filling – a delicious influence from Hong Kong – while the glutinous rice flour gives the dough its signature viscosity and chew.

The custard filling needs to be made first so it can chill and set, so it's best to start this recipe a day ahead.

50 g (1¾ oz) dark chocolate buttons, crushed
50 g (1¾ oz) sesame seeds
Neutral oil, for deep-frying

CUSTARD FILLING
2 small eggs, beaten
60 g (2¼ oz) butter, melted
2½ tablespoons milk
80 g (2¾ oz) caster (superfine) sugar
40 g (1½ oz) condensed milk
20 g (¾ oz) plain (all-purpose) flour, plus extra for dusting
12 g (¼ oz) custard powder

DOUGH
180 g (6½ oz) glutinous rice flour, plus extra for dusting
¼ cup (60 ml) boiling water
60 g (2¼ oz) caster (superfine) sugar
Pinch of salt

To make the custard filling, combine all the ingredients along with 1 tablespoon of water in a heatproof bowl and stir over a saucepan of gently simmering water until it's thick enough to coat the back of a spoon. Cover the surface directly with plastic wrap to prevent a skin forming and refrigerate until set and well chilled. Scoop out the custard onto a lightly floured bench and roll it into a log. Divide it into 12 equal portions, about 30 g (1 oz) each, cover and refrigerate until needed.

To make the dough, combine 60 g (2¼ oz) glutinous rice flour with boiling water in a bowl, and mix to combine. Add the sugar and mix well to form a soft dough. Rest for 5 minutes.

Meanwhile, combine the remaining glutinous rice flour, 70 ml (2¼ oz) of room-temperature water and salt in a large bowl and mix well. Add the cooked glutinous rice and mix well until combined. Transfer the dough to a lightly floured surface and knead until smooth and pliable. Form into a ball, dust it lightly with glutinous flour, then wrap in plastic wrap to stop it from drying out. Leave at room temperature for 30 minutes to rest.

To make the doughnuts, form the dough into a log and divide it into 12 equal portions. With your hands, flatten each portion into a disc 6–7 cm (2½–2¾ inch) in diameter, making sure the edges are thinner than the centre. Place one portion of custard in the centre, followed by a teaspoon of chocolate, then form the dough around the filling into a ball. Dust liberally with sesame seeds and set aside. Repeat with remaining ingredients.

Half-fill a wok or saucepan with oil and heat it to 160°C (320°F) over medium-high heat (bubbles should form around a wooden chopstick when it's dipped in). Add 4–5 doughnuts at a time, reduce the heat to low and deep-fry, rotating them with a slotted spoon so they cook evenly and don't stick, for 8–10 minutes until the doughnuts expand and begin to float. During this time, the temperature should have dropped to about 140°C (275°F).

Increase the heat so the temperature reaches 180°C (350°F) and cook for 3–5 minutes or until golden. Drain on paper towel, skim the sesame seeds off the oil and repeat with remaining doughnuts. Serve hot.

EGG TART

DAN TAT

SERVES 8 | 10

In Hong Kong, the egg tarts – generally speaking – are made with short pastry, while those in Macau, the former Portuguese colony, are made with puff pastry, and the filling includes a touch of cornflour. This egg tart, made with a short pastry and some cornflour in the custard, is a fusion of Hong Kong and Macanese versions, and differs from those you see so often at yum cha in that it's baked as one large tart that's then cut into slices to serve.

As a variation, adding a handful of dates onto the baked crust before pouring on the custard will offer a different dimension.

EGG TART CUSTARD
2 cups (500 ml) milk (see note)
1 cup (250 ml) pure cream
1 vanilla bean, split, seeds scraped
Pinch of salt
120 g (4¼ oz) caster (superfine) sugar
1 egg, plus 4 egg yolks
50 g (1¾ oz) cornflour (cornstarch)

EGG TART PASTRY
¼ cup (60 ml) milk
1 egg
210 g (7½ oz) plain (all-purpose) flour
30 g (1 oz) caster (superfine) sugar
Pinch of salt
180 g (6½ oz) unsalted butter, cut into 1 cm (½ inch) dice and chilled

For the pastry, beat the milk together with the egg and set aside. Combine the flour, sugar and salt in a food processor and pulse briefly to combine. Add the butter and pulse again until the mixture resembles pea-sized crumbs. With the motor running, stream in the milk-egg mixture until a dough begins to form, but hasn't yet formed into a ball. Turn out the dough and shape into a disc. Wrap tightly in plastic wrap and refrigerate for at least 30 minutes to rest and chill.

Grease a 23 cm (9 inch) loose-bottomed tart tin and line it with baking paper. Roll the pastry out to a round 40 cm (16 inch) in diameter and about 5 mm (¼ inch) thick. Line the tin with the pastry, wrapping it over the rim so that it won't slump during baking. Refrigerate for 1 hour to rest.

Preheat oven to 180°C (350°F). Line the pastry with foil and fill it with baking weights, then blind-bake for 20 minutes. Remove the foil and weights and bake for another 5 minutes until the base is pale golden. Leave to cool at room temperature while you make the custard.

To make the custard, bring the milk, cream, vanilla pod (reserve the seeds) and salt to simmering point in a saucepan. Meanwhile, combine the sugar, egg and yolks, cornflour and vanilla seeds in a bowl and whisk until smooth. Add ½ cup (125 ml) of the warm milk to the sugar-egg mixture, whisking it in to temper before whisking in the remainder. Return the saucepan to medium heat and cook, stirring continuously, until the custard thickens and begins to bubble. Transfer to a bowl and place a sheet of plastic wrap directly on the custard to prevent a skin forming. Leave to cool.

To cook the tart, heat the oven to 220°C (425°F). Stir the cooled custard until smooth, then pour it into the crust. Level the top with a spatula and bake for 40–45 minutes until the surface is mostly dark brown, rotating the tart as needed for even browning. Cool, trim any overlapping pastry, then cut into slices to serve.

✖ If you'd like a softer custard, use 3 cups (750 ml) of milk instead of 2 cups (500 ml).

MEAT

BEEF RENDANG

SERVES 6

Possibly the most magnificent Indonesian culinary export, beef rendang is the contribution of the Minangkabau people from West Sumatra, of which Padang is the capital. Properly cooked, this dish – first mentioned around the 1550s – is fit for a king, which is why it is served on festive occasions.

Traditionally, rendang must be dry – the coconut-based sauce is heavily reduced by long, slow cooking so it eventually 'fries' the meat. The result is succulent, richly complex and delicious, whether it's made, as is common, with water buffalo or beef, chicken, lamb or even jackfruit. If you are served rendang with some residual sauce, it is a variant called 'kalio' – calling it a curry is a mistake Western food writers often make.

Combine the lemongrass, ginger and galangal in a food processor and blend to a fine paste. Add the onion, chilli and garlic and blend again until a coarse paste forms.

Heat the oil in a heavy-based saucepan over medium heat, add the paste and fry, stirring, for about 8–10 minutes, or until the oil separates into a gorgeous red.

Add the beef and fry, turning occasionally, until lightly browned all over (5–6 minutes).

Add the coconut and fry for another minute, then add the coconut milk, sugar and 2 cups (500 ml) water. Bring to the boil, stirring frequently to prevent curdling, then reduce the heat to low and leave to bubble gently, stirring now and then, until the beef is tender and the coconut milk much reduced (about 1.5–2 hours).

Once the coconut milk is beginning to turn to oil, remove the beef from the saucepan. Continue to stir the sauce (be careful; it will spit) until it is almost evaporated and almost dry, about 5–10 minutes. Return the beef to the saucepan, stir gently, season to taste with salt and serve with rice.

---

2 lemongrass stalks (white part only), finely chopped
3 cm (1¼ inch) piece ginger (about 30 g/1 oz), peeled and chopped
4–5 thin slices fresh galangal (about 20 g/¾ oz), peeled and finely chopped
1 large onion, or 6 shallots (eschalots), finely chopped
6–10 long red chillies, coarsely chopped
5 garlic cloves
⅓ cup (80 ml) neutral oil
700 g (1 lb 9 oz) beef oyster blade, cut into 5 cm (2 inch) cubes
35 g (1¼ oz) desiccated coconut, dry-fried in a pan until golden brown
2 cups (500 ml) coconut milk
1 teaspoon caster (superfine) sugar
Salt, to taste

MAKES 6 | 8

ALICE'S ULTIMATE MEAT PATTIES

This homestyle dish is from my dear friend Alice Yong, a food writer in Malaysia and an arbiter of taste. Passed down from her mother, it is based on a dish of steamed egg with meat (known as jing soi dan in Cantonese) that's similar to chawanmushi. Instead of steaming it, however, she decided to fry it with spring onions, oyster sauce and sesame oil. It is a joy to eat with rice but it's fantastic with bread, too, where it turns into something like a meat pattie sandwich.

The dish may appear deceptively simple, but some patience is necessary during the cooking process as the heat has to be moderated when the patties are being fried; otherwise, they may burn on the outside while remaining raw inside.

4 large eggs
300 g (10½ oz) minced pork (or, use minced chicken or beef)
2 tablespoons chopped spring onion (scallion)
1 tablespoon oyster sauce
¼ teaspoon white pepper
1 teaspoon sesame oil
½ teaspoon salt
Neutral oil, for frying
Condiments and rice, bread or buns of choice, to serve

Crack the eggs into a large bowl and whisk them gently. Add the minced pork and spring onion, mix well, then add the oyster sauce, pepper, sesame oil and salt and mix well.

Heat a tablespoon of oil in a frying pan over high heat. Once it's hot, lower the heat to medium-high and add 2 tablespoons of the pork mixture, spreading it like a thinnish omelette. Cook for 2–3 minutes, then, with a spatula, fold it into a half-moon patty. Be careful when flipping as oil may splatter.

Cook for 1–2 minutes on each side until golden brown, then transfer to paper towel to drain.

Repeat, adding more oil as necessary, until the mixture is used up. Serve with your favourite chilli sauce, tomato sauce or with wasabi mayonnaise and perhaps with rice or bread or buns.

MY FAMILY'S BEEF BRISKET

SERVES 4

My sister and brother-in-law used to run a coffee shop, commonly known as a kopitiam, in Malaysia and Singapore. Their eatery in Malaysia was in a sawmill overlooking the Kuantan River. Locals would flock there for their beef brisket and curry laksa. I have inherited this delicious brisket recipe from them, and it is pretty easy to make. You need pickled mustard greens, but they're readily available in Asian grocers. Do seek them out – they'll give the dish real oomph. This is traditionally eaten with noodles but it's fabulous with rice, too, and since this is a soupy dish, sometimes I even eat it on its own, especially when the weather's cold.

Put the beef in a saucepan and cover with water. Bring to the boil, reduce to a simmer and cook for 5 minutes. Remove with a slotted spoon and rinse under cold water. Rinse the saucepan.

Wrap the cumin, fennel seeds, cinnamon, star anise and peppercorns in muslin and tie into a bag with kitchen string. Heat the oil in a large, heavy-based saucepan over medium-high heat and fry the ginger until it begins to turn golden. Now add the garlic and fry for another 1–2 minutes.

Add the brisket, soy sauce, sugar or beef cube and the bag of spices and cover with the stock. Bring to the boil, then reduce the heat to low and simmer gently, partially covered, until beef is fork tender (about 2 hours). Season with salt and pepper.

Remove the beef with a slotted spoon, then, when cool enough to handle, slice it and divide it among soup bowls. Add the pickled mustard greens, then ladle the hot broth over the top. Scatter with celery leaves and coriander. Serve with fresh chopped chilli, chilli sauce and rice or noodles.

✖ The original recipe includes tripe. If you wish to add tripe, cook it for 3 hours but remove the beef brisket after 2 hours.

1 kg (2 lb 4 oz) beef brisket, trimmed
1 tablespoon cumin seeds
1 tablespoon fennel seeds
1 × 8 cm (3¼ inch) cinnamon stick
3 star anise
1 tablespoon white peppercorns, crushed
1 tablespoon neutral oil
2 tablespoons chopped ginger
2 whole garlic bulbs, peeled and lightly crushed
2 tablespoons light soy sauce or fish sauce
1 teaspoon caster (superfine) sugar or 1 beef stock cube
3 litres (105 fl oz) chicken stock or water
Pinch of salt and white pepper, or to taste
300 g (10½ oz) pickled mustard greens, sliced
1 cup (20 g) loosely packed Chinese or regular celery leaves
1 cup (30 g) loosely packed coriander (cilantro)
Sliced long red chilli, to serve
Chilli sauce and rice or noodles, to serve

BALINESE DRY-SPICED SHREDDED BEEF
BALINESE SERUNDING

SERVES 6–8

If you have eaten meat floss before – the Chinese dried meat that looks like cotton or wool – serunding is a coarser version of this popular treat. It's teased apart by hand and if cooked properly, beef serunding will keep for a couple of weeks. It can also be made with chicken or coconut. Packed with flavour, it is very similar to the serunding enjoyed in Malaysia and absolutely worth the effort. Although you can use any cut of meat, because it requires shredding by hand I use topside, which doesn't have lots of gristle or tendon. This dish is often eaten at room temperature.

1 kg (2 lb 4 oz) beef topside, cut into 4 steaks
1 lemongrass stalk, bruised
7 garlic cloves, peeled
2 teaspoons coriander seeds, crushed
2–3 fresh red long chillies, chopped
2 tablespoons minced galangal
1 tablespoon minced ginger
4 cloves
2 teaspoons black peppercorns, ground
1 teaspoon shrimp paste
¼ cup (60 ml) neutral oil
2 tablespoons dark coconut or palm sugar
Salt, to taste
2 tablespoons lime juice

Add the beef to a pot with the lemongrass, add a scant amount of salt and cover with water. Bring to the boil, skimming any impurities that rise to the surface, then reduce the heat to low and simmer for an hour or until the meat is very tender. Remove beef and leave to cool. Discard the liquid (or you may wish to retain it for a soup). Once it's cool enough to handle, shred by hand with the grain to form fine threads of beef about the width of a wooden skewer.

Add the garlic, coriander seeds, chilli, galangal, ginger, cloves, peppercorns and shrimp paste to a food processor and blend to a coarse paste.

Heat the oil in a large frying pan over medium heat. Add the spice paste and fry, stirring, until fragrant (about 5 minutes). Add the sugar, followed by the beef, then season with salt to taste and fry, stirring occasionally, until the sugar has melted and the meat is dry and well coated with the spices, about 5–8 minutes, or until the meat is dry. Squeeze in the lime juice, and serve with rice or in a sandwich with tomato or cucumber.

THAI GRILLED BEEF SALAD
YAM NEUR

Extremely popular for its hot, sour and spicy flavours, Thai beef salad needs little introduction. I don't remember exactly when I first tasted this feisty number – it was probably cooked by my sister Quee Wah's Thai daughter-in-law – but I always gravitate to it whenever I feel like something that'll whet my appetite in the most fiery but delicious way.

In Thailand, the chilli sauce is called seua rong hai, meaning crying tiger, a reference to the sauce's incendiary nature. Tone down the chilli heat if you like, but do try this salad – it's the perfect starter for a quick meal cooked on the grill.

Toss the beef with the soy sauce and a turn or two of black pepper and leave to marinate while you prepare the other ingredients.

While the beef is marinating, dry-roast the rice in a wok or frying pan over medium-high heat until golden brown (3–5 minutes). Remove from the heat and set aside. When the rice is cool, transfer it to a spice grinder and grind it to a fine powder, or pound with a mortar and pestle.

For the chilli sauce, combine all the ingredients in a bowl and check seasoning – it should taste hot, sour and salty – adjusting it to taste.

Drain the beef, pat it dry and heat a barbecue or a char-grill pan with a dash of oil to high heat. Grill the beef, turning once, for 5 minutes for medium-rare, or until cooked to your liking. Rest for 5 minutes, then thinly slice.

Toss with cucumber and herbs and scatter with roasted rice powder to serve.

✖ Roasted rice powder is sold at Asian grocers, but it's easy to make. I like to roast ½ cup (80 g) glutinous rice (or any raw rice) until golden and nutty and store it in an airtight jar, then grinding it to a powder as I need it.

250 g (9 oz) beef fillet, excess fat trimmed
2 tablespoons light soy sauce
Freshly ground black pepper
1 tablespoon glutinous rice
Neutral oil, for grilling
1 small cucumber, seeds removed, sliced
Handful of fresh coriander (cilantro)
Handful of mint leaves
1 tablespoon sawtooth coriander (culantro; optional), thinly sliced

CHILLI SAUCE
1–2 teaspoons dry-roasted chilli powder or 3–4 red birdseye chillies, minced
Pinch of caster (superfine) sugar (optional)
1 tablespoon thinly sliced spring onion (scallion)
2 tablespoons lime juice
2 tablespoons fish sauce, or to taste

SERVES 6–8

EGGPLANT WITH MINCED PORK

This is a homestyle dish not often seen in restaurants, but if you're in Singapore and come across a stall at a food court that serves cze-cha (literally meaning 'cook fry') dishes, you're likely to spot it being offered. It's particularly popular among office workers.

It's a dish that relies on the salt and umami of preserved soybeans. You'll find them in Asian grocers, but some brands can be very salty, so be attentive with how much salt you add to the dish.

½ cup (125 ml) neutral oil, plus extra as needed
600 g (1 lb 5 oz) eggplant (aubergine), cut into 3 cm (1¼ inch) pieces
150 g (5½ oz) shallots (eschalots) or 1 small onion, thinly sliced
3 teaspoons minced garlic
3 teaspoons minced ginger
1 tablespoon preserved soybeans, mashed (see above)
1 teaspoon chilli powder, or to taste
250 g (9 oz) minced pork or prawns
2 teaspoons caster (superfine) sugar
1 tablespoon fish sauce, or to taste
Salt and white pepper, to taste
Chopped coriander (cilantro), crisp-fried shallots and thinly sliced long red chilli, to serve

Heat the oil in a wok over high heat until shimmering, then fry the eggplant a few pieces at a time, turning occasionally, for 5–6 minutes or until soft. Drain and set aside.

In the same oil (you may need to add about 2 tablespoons, as the eggplant tends to absorb oil easily), fry the shallots, stirring occasionally, until golden. Add the garlic and ginger followed by the soybean, chilli powder and minced pork and stir-fry, breaking up the mince with a metal spatula, until the mince is nicely browned, well separated and the flavours absorbed.

Sprinkle the mixture with a splash of water, return the eggplant to the wok, then add the sugar and fish sauce. Turn down the heat to medium-low and cook, stirring, for another 3 minutes to allow the flavours to mingle. Season to taste with salt and pepper and add chopped coriander.

Serve at once, topped with fried shallots and chilli.

BEEF SALAD WITH ROASTED BEETROOT, PRESERVED LEMON AND HERB DRESSING

SERVES 6

This dish is loosely based on Thai grilled beef salad (page 125) but given my personal touch. It combines sweet–sour elements (tamarind not only adds a distinctive flavour but also tenderises the beef) and some interesting ingredients to create the wow factor.

I don't remember exactly where I got the recipe – probably from a food magazine. But since I grow my own beetroot and preserve my own lemons and cumquats, this is a salad I serve regularly. You can replace the Chinkiang vinegar in the roasted beetroot with balsamic if you prefer. And you can always omit the beetroot and replace it with tomato.

---

80 g (2¾ oz) tamarind pulp
140 g (5 oz) honey
700 g (1 lb 9 oz) beef fillet, fat trimmed
1 teaspoon cumin powder
Salt and white pepper, to taste
¼ cup (60 ml) grapeseed oil
1 long red chilli, seeds removed, julienned
Handful of fresh coriander (cilantro) leaves or rocket (arugula) leaves, to serve

ROASTED BEETROOT
¼ cup (60 ml) olive oil
6 small beetroot
2 tablespoons honey
2 tablespoons Chinkiang vinegar
Handful of fresh thyme, leaves picked
3 oranges, segmented
1 tablespoon finely chopped preserved lemon skins or candied cumquats
1 large makrut lime leaf, finely shredded

GREEN HERB SAUCE
1½ cups (375 ml) extra-virgin olive oil
1 large garlic clove, crushed
1–2 birdseye chillies, to taste, chopped
2 anchovy fillets
2 tablespoons Dijon mustard
30 g (1 oz) sultanas, soaked in warm water for 5 minutes, drained
30 g (1 oz) capers, rinsed
6½ cups (150 g) flat-leaf parsley leaves
5 cups (100 g) mint leaves
3⅓ cups (100 g) basil leaves
Juice of 1 lemon, or to taste
1 tablespoon Chinkiang vinegar
Salt and white pepper, to taste

Place the tamarind pulp in a bowl and cover with 2 cups (500 ml) warm water. Soak for 20 minutes, then, with your fingers, mash and squeeze the tamarind to extract as much juice as possible. Pour the juice through a sieve into a container large enough to hold the beef, discard the pulp and mix the juice with the honey. Place the beef in the container, toss to coat in the tamarind-honey mixture, then cover and refrigerate for 12 hours, turning once or twice.

Meanwhile, for the roasted beetroot, heat the oven to 180°C (350°F). Line a baking tray with foil, leaving plenty overhanging, drizzle the foil with oil, then place the beetroot on top, drizzle with honey and vinegar and sprinkle with thyme. Fold the foil over the beetroot to form a neat parcel and bake for 40 minutes or until beetroot are tender. Cool, then peel and cut into segments. Combine the beetroot, oranges, preserved lemon and lime leaves, adding any baking juices.

For the green herb sauce, add the oil, garlic, chillies, anchovies, mustard, sultanas, capers and herbs to a food processor and blend to a purée. Add the lemon juice, vinegar and 100 ml (3½ fl oz) warm water. Season to taste with salt and pepper and blend again to combine. Pass through a fine sieve, pressing a spoon against the sieve to extract as much flavour as possible.

Drain the beef, pat it dry and season with cumin, salt and pepper. Heat a barbecue or a char-grill pan with a dash of oil to high heat. Drizzle beef with oil, then grill, turning once, for 3–4 minutes each side for medium-rare, or until cooked to your liking. Rest in a warm place for 15 minutes, then slice thinly.

Combine the sliced beef with the roasted beetroot. Toss gently, then add the green herb sauce a little at a time, adjusting to taste (you won't need all the dressing). Add the chilli and coriander and toss together to serve.

PORK CHOP BUN, MACANESE STYLE
JU PA BAO

MAKES 5

Katsu sandos are everywhere these days, but if you go to Macau, you'll find the ju pa bao, the delicious and easy-to-make Macanese–Canto equivalent of this sandwich. Juicy, crunchy and seasoned with rice wine, five-spice and other secret ingredients, the ju pa bao is apparently the descendant of the lauded bifana, the Portuguese bread roll filled with pork cutlet.

A street food, the ju pa bao may be topped with cheese and egg like a steak sandwich at some places, while others serve it with a Portuguese bread roll. This is my version of this fantastic sando. You can substitute chicken chop as an alternative. Either way, be warned: it's addictive!

Combine all the marinade ingredients in a bowl. Slice the pork into 5 × 100 g (3½ oz) pieces, add to the bowl and marinate for at least 20 minutes, or ideally overnight in the fridge.

When you're ready to serve, bring the pork back to room temperature, place a large frying pan over medium heat and add the lard and butter. Once the lard and butter are melted and hot, remove the pork slices from the marinade, shaking off any excess, and add to the pan. Fry on one side until golden, about 5 minutes, then flip the pork and add the remaining marinade. Cook for another 2–3 minutes or until just cooked through.

Meanwhile, grill the bread rolls to your preference (I usually do this in a cast-iron grill pan). Smear with butter or with some of the pork glaze from the pan and add a slice of pork. Serve hot with mustard.

✖ If you place the pork in the freezer for 1 hour – or until just firm enough to still be sliced – this helps to slice it more easily.

- 500 g (1 lb 2 oz) pork cutlet or chop (see note)
- 2 tablespoons lard or neutral oil
- 2 tablespoons unsalted butter, plus extra to serve
- 5 crusty white bread rolls or 10 slices white bread
- Mustard, to serve

MARINADE
- ½ cup (125 ml) Shaoxing wine
- ¼ cup (60 ml) light soy sauce
- 2 garlic cloves, coarsely chopped
- 1 tablespoon Worcestershire sauce
- 1 teaspoon English mustard, plus extra to serve
- 1 teaspoon caster (superfine) sugar, or to taste
- 1 teaspoon Chinese five-spice powder
- ½ teaspoon white pepper
- 1 tablespoon cornflour (cornstarch)

XINJIANG LAMB SKEWERS

YANG ROU CHUANR

SERVES 4 | 6

If you haven't eaten Xinjiang lamb skewers before, you're in for a treat. Called yang rou chuanr in Mandarin, this contribution from the Uyghurs is a must-make if you love lamb. This recipe is from chef Tina Li of Dainty Sichuan restaurant in Melbourne. She says the secret lies in roasting and grinding the cumin and Sichuan pepper for the distinctive scent and flavour. She also adds some water to the marinade and binds it with potato flour – this helps the lamb stay juicy.

It's best to start this recipe a day ahead for the marinade to work its magic, although, at a pinch, 20 minutes will do the trick. Her recipe also uses a Chinese-Muslim spice powder called 13 fragrances (shi san xiang in Mandarin). It contains dried mandarin peel, resurrection lily rhizome and female ginseng, among other things. Once opened, the oils in this spice dissipate so it should be used quickly.

For a deluxe version, chef Li serves her lamb skewers with a topping but if you're time poor, the skewers are great with chopped tomato or cucumber and fresh coriander.

LAMB AND MARINADE
½ teaspoon salt
Pinch of caster (superfine) sugar
400 g (14 oz) boneless lamb shoulder or leg, cut into 2 cm (¾ inch) cubes
2 teaspoons soy sauce
1 teaspoon Xinjiang spice mix or 13 fragrances, plus extra to taste
1 teaspoon ground cumin
2 teaspoons chilli powder, dry-roasted
2 teaspoons potato flour
1 tablespoon neutral oil, plus extra for brushing
8–12 bamboo skewers, soaked in water for 30 minutes

TOPPING
2 tablespoons neutral oil
1 garlic clove, finely chopped
1 tablespoon ginger, finely chopped
¼ diced red capsicum (pepper)
¼ diced green capsicum (pepper)
¼ small red onion, diced
1 tablespoon chilli oil
Pinch of ground Sichuan pepper
Pinch of ground cumin
Salt, to taste

Combine the salt and sugar with the lamb, tossing to coat. Add the soy sauce, mix again, then add ¼ cup (60 ml) water and mix thoroughly. Add the Xinjiiang spice, cumin, chilli powder, potato flour and oil and toss to coat. Leave to marinate for 20 minutes, or overnight in the fridge.

Thread 3–5 lamb pieces onto each skewer. When you're ready to cook, heat a barbecue or grill pan to high, brush the lamb skewers lightly with oil and arrange on the grill. Cook, turning the skewers as each side begins to char, for 2–3 minutes or until cooked to your liking. If you like, you can sprinkle the skewers with a little Xinjiang spice mix as you go. Remove and keep warm.

For the topping, heat the oil in a wok over medium-high heat, add the garlic, ginger, capsicum and onion and stir-fry until fragrant.

Add the chilli oil, Sichuan pepper and cumin and season to taste with salt. Stir-fry another 30 seconds, then drizzle over the warm lamb skewers to serve.

✖ I like to serve the lamb on its own. However, it is delicious to eat with spring onion pancakes (see page 103).

MAKES 25–30

NYONYA PORK SATAY

If there's one dish that's most recognisable from Southeast Asia, it's satay. The superstar of Southeast Asian street food, these skewers of barbecued meats are incredibly delicious served hot off the grill. Infused with smoke, satay is so popular it's even served in first- and business-class cabins of the region's carriers, such as Singapore and Malaysia Airlines.

The home of satay is Indonesia (where it's spelt sate), but no one can pinpoint exactly when it appeared. Some writers believe it arrived with Arab spice traders who barbecued their meats on skewers for shawarma. Others consider its etymology to be derived from the Hokkien words 'sa teh', meaning three pieces. In the absence of historical evidence, I'm inclined to think this is pure conjecture.

Whatever the provenance, the variations of sate in Indonesia are pretty mind-boggling. Sate buntel, for instance, is made with minced goat and wrapped in caul fat to resemble a fat sausage. In Bali, minced seafood mixed with grated coconut and spices is moulded around stalks of lemongrass to create sate lilit.

Although there are scores of varieties of sate in Indonesia, the most popular is the version served with peanut sauce. In Malaysia, satay fans flock to the town of Kajang for some of the best in the country. According to my Malaysian friend and food writer Alice Yong, it was a Javanese satay vendor, Tasmin Sakiban, who pioneered the satay business in this town in 1917. Not long after, other Javanese satay sellers materialised and the town became synonymous with this glorious dish.

I don't remember exactly when I first had this Nyonya pork satay, but I do recall eating it in Penang and the surprise of finding pineapple in the heavenly peanut sauce. While there are quicker versions of this classic and relatively easy-to-make dish, it pays to give yourself a couple of days to make this dish really sing.

The secret to a great satay lies in the marinade and the peanut sauce. While it's easy to buy the marinade to infuse the meat, making your own spice paste is far superior. As for the satay sauce, while it's tempting to use commercial peanut butter, it's best to roast your own peanuts to create that elusive peanutty fragrance to complement the charry scent of the meat.

Other than relating this short story on satay's provenance and prominence as well as its secrets, my advice is to make it. It's perfect for summer and fun to make. Get your barbecue fired up and when the scents of your delicious skewers get going, they will take you straight back to the beaches or streets of Southeast Asia. And don't forget to crack open that beer!

500 g (1 lb 2 oz) pork neck, sliced into 3 cm (1¼ inch) pieces, each weighing no more than 10 g (¼ oz)
25–30 bamboo skewers
1 lemongrass stalk, lightly bruised
½ cup (125 ml) neutral oil mixed with ½ cup (125 ml) coconut milk
Chopped cucumber, to serve
Chopped pineapple, to serve

MARINADE
1 large lemongrass stalk (white part only), finely chopped
1 thin slice galangal
2 cm (¾ inch) piece ginger, chopped
1 tablespoon coriander powder
1 teaspoon cumin powder
1 teaspoon turmeric powder
1 teaspoon chilli powder, or to taste
2 garlic cloves, peeled
3 shallots (eschalots) or 1 small onion (about 100 g), chopped
1 tablespoon sugar, or to taste
1 teaspoon salt

PINEAPPLE SATAY SAUCE
1 tablespoon tamarind pulp (40 g)
100 ml (3½ fl oz) neutral oil
200 g (7 oz) peanuts, skinned and dry-roasted
¾ cup (200 g) crushed, drained pineapple
1 cup (250 ml) coconut milk
1 tablespoon palm sugar (or jaggery), or to taste
Pinch of salt, or to taste

SATAY SPICE PASTE
6–8 dried long red chillies, soaked in hot water until soft, drained and chopped
4 shallots (eschalots), sliced
2 garlic cloves, chopped
2.5 cm (1 inch) piece fresh turmeric or 1 teaspoon ground turmeric
2.5 cm (1 inch) piece galangal, chopped
2 lemongrass stalks (white part only), chopped
1 teaspoon belacan (shrimp paste)

For the marinade, blend all the ingredients to a fine paste in a food processor (or pound with a mortar and pestle).

Toss the pork with the marinade to coat and refrigerate for at least 6 hours, or preferably overnight, to marinate.

Meanwhile, soak the skewers in water for at least 1 hour and start the satay sauce. Place the tamarind pulp in a bowl and cover with 2 cups (500 ml) warm water. Soak for 20 minutes, then, with your fingers, mash and squeeze the tamarind to extract as much juice as possible.

Meanwhile, for the satay spice paste, blend all the ingredients to a fine paste in a food processor (or pound with a mortar and pestle).

For the sauce, heat the neutral oil in a saucepan over medium heat, add the spice paste and fry, stirring, until aromatic (about 5 minutes). Add the strained tamarind water, peanuts, pineapple, coconut milk and sugar and season to taste with salt, mix thoroughly, then slowly bring to the boil. Reduce the sauce to a simmer, and stirring frequently to prevent burning, cook gently for 15–20 minutes or until the oil rises to the surface. Keep at room temperature if you're serving immediately, or refrigerate and bring back to room temperature to serve.

When you're ready to cook, thread 4–5 pieces of pork onto each skewer. Heat a barbecue or grill pan to high heat. Grill the skewers, using the bruised tip of the lemongrass to brush the skewers with the coconut-infused oil constantly to allow the meat to take on the coconut milk flavours. Turn the skewers regularly to prevent the meat from burning until just a little charred and just cooked through but still moist (2–3 minutes each side).

Serve hot with satay sauce, cucumber and pineapple.

SPICE HISTORIES, PASTES AND POWDERS

This is a story about spices and early migration, and how nostalgia for familiar foods has pollinated the world we know today. It is also a story about how local tastes have married with foreign ingredients to produce the spice blends we love.

Long before the arrival of European missionaries and conquerors to South and Southeast Asia, Indian and Arab traders were already plying the sea routes aboard ships laden with pepper, nutmeg and cloves. Along the way, these traders settled in various ports, such as Malacca in Malaysia in the 15th century. At that time, Malacca was known as the gateway to the Spice Islands (Moluccas), with an estimated population of around 40,000, comprising ethnic Malays, Javanese, Buginese, Chinese, Persians, Arabs and Tamil Muslims.

While these traders were waiting for the trade/monsoon winds to change to carry them home, they settled in this cosmopolitan hub and introduced not only the spices and dishes of their homelands, but also their religious beliefs and cultures. From the Arab countries came cumin, coriander, saffron and Islam; and from India, pepper, cinnamon, Buddhism and Hinduism. From the Chinese, it was star anise, tea and Taoism.

While we do not know exactly what foods were consumed in Malacca during that period, we know for certain that the cooking of Southeast Asia has benefited greatly from spices such as cumin, fennel, cardamom and mustard seeds – ingredients introduced from India and the Middle East. We can also deduce from the names of dishes where they come from. For instance, one of the most celebrated dishes in Malaysia and Singapore, biryani, comes from the Persian word 'berenj', which means rice. Another dish, the much-loved meat-filled layered pancake called murtabak, comes from the Arabic word 'mutabbaq', meaning 'folded.'

It was also towards the end of the 15th century that Portuguese seafarers, in order to break the duopoly of the lucrative spice trade controlled by the Venetians and the Arabs, rounded the Cape of Good Hope and landed on India's Malabar Coast. They conquered Goa and, under direction from the king of Portugal, set sail for Malacca, which in 1511 surrendered to the Portuguese. With the fall of Malacca, the control of the fabled spice trade slipped from the hands of the Arabs to the Europeans.

Although the Portuguese dominated the spice trade from Goa to Macau for more than a century, other European powers, motivated by spice, had entered the race to get to Asia. In 1492, for example, with the blessing of King Ferdinand and Queen Isabella of Spain, Christopher Columbus sailed westward to find a route to the fabled riches of Asia, leading to the discovery of the Americas.

While Columbus did not get to Asia, he brought back chillies, tomatoes and other ingredients that are now relevant to Asian cooking. Equally, spices that were once exclusive to Asia are now grown in the Caribbean and the tropical parts of South America.

Fast-forward to the 17th century, when French, Dutch and British interest in Asia reached fever pitch and the annexation of spice-growing countries gradually occurred. The Dutch East India Company, formed in 1602, colonised Indonesia and in the process ousted the Portuguese from the Spice Islands. The British East India Company, established in 1600, eventually controlled all of India through conquests and treaties, and from there Penang and Singapore. Although there were Chettis and Jawi Peranakan (Tamil Muslims who married local women) who settled in Malacca and on the Malay Peninsula, it was during the British Period (1786 to 1957) that Indian workers – mainly from South India – came to Malaysia in large numbers and with them we have the arrival of curry.

While we know the British colonials developed a penchant for curries, especially in the form of curry tiffin lunches, it was South Indians, in particular Tamils, who in their craving for spicy foods, introduced so called 'curry' dishes to Malaysia and beyond. While curry is taken to mean anything that is cooked with spices, this is not quite right. The word does not even exist in any of the Indian languages. Apparently, it comes from the Tamil word meaning gravy or sauces. And yet this word is used nowadays with gay abandon to describe almost anything cooked with spices. Perhaps this has something to do with the lack of understanding of the nuances and complexity of foods cooked with spices. In any event, spice blends with the name curry are here to stay.

In Asia, the blending of spices is taken so seriously it is akin to an art form – highly creative, individual and regional. A spice blend is created not only from local ingredients but also from historical and cultural influences. For instance, Thailand's fabled massaman curry paste (gaeng massaman) is derived from Muslim influences – the name is probably from the archaic term 'mussulman' to describe Muslims.

Over in Indonesia and Malaysia, spice pastes are called bumbu and rempah respectively. Despite some similarities with Malaysian rempah in the sense that ginger, galangal, lemongrass and candlenuts are used, Indonesian bumbu is an eye-opening and exciting range of spice pastes because of the country's sheer size and regional variations. Some spice blends, called bumbu dasar, consist simply of shallots, garlic, galangal, candlenuts and coriander, while others are more elaborate, like the Balinese base genep.

Interestingly, the sizeable Indian population in Malaysia and Singapore not only introduced the foods and spices of their homeland but their curry powders have merged with local rempah. The result is the creation of robust and spectacularly delicious spice dishes. Some of these are called gulais, meaning stews, while others are simply called curries, which goes to show the impact of Indian food in this part of the world. For instance, the classic chicken curry, kari ayam, uses South Indian curry powder along with lemongrass, the occasional local makrut lime leaf and star anise for a result that's not only sublime, but markedly different to curries in India.

It goes without saying that India's contribution to spices and spice blends has enriched the world. Equally, though, the spice pastes (gaeng) of Thailand, the rempah of Malaysia, the kroeung of Cambodia and the thuna paha of Sri Lanka, spices undoubtedly offer an intoxicating and endless adventure in cooking.

Several dishes use spice pastes in this book. Some are complex, like massaman (page 139), and others are simple, like sambal belacan (page 261), the chilli and shrimp paste condiment eaten in some Southeast Asian countries. An important aspect of cooking with spice blends is never to allow them to burn, but to gently coax the heady flavours from them.

Generally, I cook my spice paste with a generous splash of neutral oil, frying it over medium heat until the moisture has evaporated and the oil is infused with the aroma of the spices. Some cooks use the term 'when the oil separates' to describe this stage.

MACANESE BEEF 'CURRY' WITH DAIKON

SERVES 6

When the Portuguese colonised Goa and Malacca, they adopted spiced dishes and carried these with them to Macau. This delicious curry made with daikon is a good example, combining both Southeast Asian and Chinese influences.

Traditionally this recipe uses beef tendons, but since they can be hard to source, I've recommended oyster blade instead. The recipe is adapted from Abraham Conlon, Adrienne Lo and Hugh Amano's cookbook The Adventures of Fat Rice.

- 1 kg (2 lb 4 oz) oyster blade beef, cut into 3–4 cm (1¼–1½ inch) dice
- 2 small onions, chopped
- 5 garlic cloves, chopped
- 5 cm (2 inch) piece ginger, chopped
- 2 tablespoons neutral oil
- 2 tablespoons hot curry powder
- 1 tablespoon white wine vinegar
- 2 litres (8 cups) chicken stock or water
- 1 small daikon (white radish; about 250 g/9 fl oz), peeled and cut into 2 cm (¾ in) dice
- 1 bunch of radish, quartered, for garnish (optional)
- Steamed rice or bread, to serve
- Pinch of salt, to taste

MARINADE
- 2 tablespoons Shaoxing wine
- 1 tablespoon soy sauce
- 1 tablespoon curry powder

For the marinade, combine all the ingredients in a bowl.

Add the beef to the marinade, toss to coat, and set aside for 20 minutes to marinate.

Place the onions, garlic and ginger in a food processor and blend to a coarse paste. Heat the oil in a large saucepan over medium-high heat, then add the onion mixture and cook, stirring, until it starts to caramelise (5–7 minutes).

Add the beef and cook, turning occasionally, until just browned (about 2 minutes). Mix the hot curry powder with the vinegar, then add it to the saucepan, stirring, for 5–6 minutes until fragrant (add a splash of stock if it's catching on the bottom).

Pour in the stock, stir well, then bring to the boil. Reduce the heat to low, cover with a lid and simmer, stirring occasionally, for 1.5 hours or until fork tender, adding the daikon halfway through cooking.

Remove the beef and daikon from the saucepan and set aside. Increase the heat to high and simmer rapidly until the curry is reduced to a sauce consistency (about 15 minutes). Check seasoning and adjust it with salt to taste, then return the beef and daikon and stir just to warm through.

Top with chopped radish and serve with steamed rice or bread.

MASSAMAN CURRY OF BEEF
GAENG MASSAMAN

Serves 6–8

Because gaeng massaman is considered one of the most complex and time-consuming curries to make, rich with sweet-spicy flavours of cinnamon, cloves, cardamom, mace and nutmeg against a backdrop of dried chillies, historically it's been a special-occasion curry often served at weddings. Along with the spices, the inclusion of potatoes, peanuts and tamarind suggests it may be of Indian origin, but Thai food scholar and chef David Thompson suggests its origin could be Persian. Another school of thought is that it's a dish from southern Thailand, where there are many Thai Muslims. I like to think it's the latter, because the beef is simmered until deeply tender, a method much loved by the Malays. The Malays also love to simmer meat with spices.

Beef is the preferred meat here, though just about any meat or seafood may be used. The quantities for the chillies can be adjusted according to your heat preference, and you can remove the seeds if you like. This dish is beautiful accompanied by rice and some pickled ginger or salted duck eggs. If necessary you can balance the flavours with hints of lime juice, sugar and fish sauce.

For the massaman curry paste, combine all the ingredients in a wok and dry-roast over medium-low heat until charred, softened and fragrant (about 3 minutes), adding a little water if the ingredients start burning. Remove from wok, cool, then blend to a smooth paste in a food processor.

For the spice mix, combine the ingredients in a wok with a splash of water and dry-roast over medium heat until very fragrant (about 2 minutes). Cool, then finely grind in a spice grinder.

Stir the spice mix into the curry paste, season to taste with salt, and store in an airtight container in the refrigerator until required.

Place the beef in a stock pot with the coconut milk, cassia bark, cardamom pods and bay leaves. Bring to the boil, then reduce the heat to medium and simmer until the meat is almost tender (1–2 hours), adding a little water during the braising if the liquid is reducing too quickly.

Add the potatoes and peanuts and simmer for 10 minutes.

Mix the tamarind pulp with 1 cup (250 ml) hot water. Mash the soaked tamarind with your fingers to extract as much pulp from the seeds as possible, then strain into a bowl.

Bring the coconut cream to a gentle boil in a small saucepan. Cook, stirring constantly, until fragrant and oily specks appear on the surface (6–10 minutes). Add 2–3 tablespoons massaman paste and continue to cook, stirring to prevent burning and adding some of the braising liquid if it's reducing too quickly, for 2–3 minutes or until fragrant. Stir in the palm sugar and fish sauce, followed by the tamarind water, then add this mixture to the pot with the beef.

Add the onion, then simmer for 5 minutes until well combined. Season to taste until the sweet, sour and salty elements are balanced.

✤ The curry paste makes about 1½ cups (375 ml), enough to have plenty left over for next time.

- 1 kg (2 lb 4 oz) gravy beef or chuck steak, cut into 4 cm (1½ inch) cubes
- 1.25 litres (5 cups) coconut milk
- 3 cm (1¼ inch) piece cassia bark
- 4 cardamom pods, crushed
- 3 bay leaves
- 3–5 medium potatoes, quartered
- 2 tablespoons roasted peanuts, crushed
- ¼ cup (60 ml) tamarind pulp
- 1 cup (250 ml) coconut cream
- 2 tablespoons palm sugar (or jaggery), or to taste
- ¼ cup (60 ml) fish sauce
- 1 large onion, cut into wedges

MASSAMAN CURRY PASTE
- 6–10 dried long red chillies, soaked in water until soft, drained then chopped
- 5–10 dried small red chillies, soaked in water until soft, drained then chopped
- 6 shallots (eschalots), chopped
- 6 garlic cloves
- 1 tablespoon minced galangal
- 1 stalk lemongrass (white part only), thinly sliced
- 3 coriander (cilantro) roots, scraped clean and chopped

SPICE MIX
- 2 tablespoons coriander seeds
- 1 teaspoon cumin seeds
- 1 teaspoon mace
- 2 cm (¾ inch) piece cassia bark
- 5 cloves
- ½ teaspoon white peppercorns
- ¼ teaspoon cardamom seeds
- 1 teaspoon salt, or to taste

BEEF FILLET WITH SICHUAN SAUCE

SERVES 4

This recipe is inspired by a dish at Flower Drum, Melbourne's temple of Cantonese cuisine, in which steak is served with a mild Sichuan sauce. I suppose it's a dish that draws on the tastes of the restaurant's both Chinese and Australian clientele. I have upped the ante by treading a more traditional Sichuan path, meaning that it's hot. You may wish to tone it down.

Feel free to make the sauce ahead and warm it through again while you're frying the steak. And don't stop with beef: lamb and chicken are equally appealing. If you can't find doubanjiang, you can use gochujang in a pinch.

Season the steaks with salt and pepper and brush lightly with oil. Heat a wok over high heat and add the 2 teaspoons of oil. When the wok is smoking, add the steaks and fry, turning – depending on the thickness of the steaks and your preference, this may take anything from 3–6 minutes per side. Remove from heat and rest, wrapped loosely in foil, while you prepare the sauce.

Clean the wok and return it to the heat. For the Sichuan sauce, add the oil, then, when it's just smoking, add the spring onions and toss for 30 seconds until softened.

Reduce the heat to medium, then add the garlic, followed by the doubanjiang and sichuan pepper. Stir-fry for 30 seconds, then add the stock and soy sauce. Bring to the boil, then add the sugar and salt, adjusting to taste. Stir in the cornflour mix to thicken (about 30 seconds).

Slice the steaks, transfer to plates, spoon Sichuan sauce over the top and serve with stir-fried greens and steamed rice.

2 × 250 g (9 oz) fillet steaks
Salt and black pepper, to taste
2 teaspoons neutral oil, plus extra for brushing
Stir-fried greens and steamed rice, to serve

SICHUAN SAUCE
1 tablespoon neutral oil
2 spring onions (scallions) finely sliced
2 garlic cloves, finely chopped
2 tablespoons (55 g) doubanjiang (chilli bean paste)
1 teaspoon ground sichuan pepper (optional)
1 cup (250 ml) chicken stock
1 tablespoon light soy sauce
Pinch of caster (superfine) sugar
Good pinch of salt, to taste
1 teaspoon cornflour (cornstarch) or potato flour, mixed with 2 tablespoons water

PENANG NYONYA BRAISED PORK
HONG BAK

SERVES 6

The fondness for braised dishes among the Baba and Nyonya communities is due to their Hokkien ancestry. Their food is a mixture of Chinese-Malay-Indonesian influences. Over some 600 years, they have created their own cooking style, though some dishes have retained their Malay or Chinese heritage. Traditionally, soy sauces and preserved soybeans are common ingredients in braised meats, but the addition of local spices, such as coriander and aromatic ginger (*Kaempferia galanga*), is a departure from Hokkien flavours. Aromatic ginger is a distinctive fragrant rhizome called sar keong in Cantonese, and it is often used by that community in chicken dishes. Within the Baba community, the tender leaves are also used in ulam rice salad.

This recipe is the Penang version of the Malacca and Singapore babi chin. It is remarkably simple to make, but the flavours are absolutely outstanding. Partnered with a refreshing, tangy salad or kerabu, it is the perfect dish on a hot summer's day. Once you've tried it with pork, give it a go with duck or chicken, which are fine substitutes.

2½ tablespoons neutral oil
500 g (1 lb 2 oz) pork belly or pork shoulder, skin on, cut into 5 cm (2 inch) cubes
2 teaspoons caster (superfine) sugar
2 cups (500 ml) chicken stock or water
Salt, to taste
Thinly sliced spring onions and sambal belacan (page 261), to serve

SPICE PASTE
100 g (3½ oz) shallots (eschalots), or 1 onion
3 garlic cloves, peeled
2.5 cm (1 inch) piece frozen aromatic ginger or 1 teaspoon ground aromatic ginger (see note)
2 tablespoons coriander seeds, dry-roasted and ground
1–1½ tablespoons salted or preserved soybeans (taucheo)
1 teaspoon ground white pepper

For the spice paste, blend all the ingredients in a food processor to a fine paste.

Heat the oil in a wok over medium heat, add the spice paste and fry, stirring, until fragrant. Add the pork and stir-fry, tossing, until seared, then add a teaspoon of sugar and stir-fry for another minute.

Add the stock and the remaining sugar and season with salt. Simmer, stirring now and then, until the meat is tender and the sauce nicely syrupy (about 45 minutes–1 hour). If the liquid is reducing too quickly, add a little water. Top with spring onions and serve with your favourite sambal belacan.

✖ Some preserved soybeans are very salty and it is best to give them a quick rinse under cold water before blending with the other ingredients. Aromatic ginger is often sold in dried form in Western countries, although I have bought it frozen at times.

VIETNAMESE SHAKING BEEF

BO LUC LAC

SERVES 4 | 6

Like a great steak and onions, this fast and easy Vietnamese beef recipe is another of my go-to dishes when I need to knock up something quickly. Its name had always mystified me until my dear Vietnamese friend, Quang, explained that it's a sort of onomatopoeia for the shaking sound of the beef as it is cooked in the wok. Some writers claim the dish to be of Vietnamese–Chinese provenance, while others believe it is a purely French technique of cooking beef. Regardless of its origin, this dish is a winner. The pickled bean sprouts are optional – you could also serve the beef with some sliced cucumber, a mixed salad or stir-fried water spinach.

300 g (10½ oz) beef fillet, cut into 2 cm (¾ inch) cubes
2 tablespoons neutral oil
1 garlic clove, crushed
1 small onion (optional), thinly sliced
2 teaspoons caster (superfine) sugar
2 spring onions (scallions) thinly sliced

PICKLED BEAN SPROUTS
½ cup (125 ml) rice vinegar
1 tablespoon salt
500 g (1 lb 2 oz) bean sprouts

MARINADE
1 teaspoon fish sauce or soy sauce, or to taste
1 teaspoon oyster sauce (optional)
1 tablespoon rice wine
Pinch of caster (superfine) sugar
Pinch of salt, or to taste
Generous pinch black pepper

For the pickled bean sprouts, combine the vinegar and salt with 4 cups (1 litre) water in a saucepan and bring to the boil. Set aside to cool until it reaches room temperature.

Pour the brine solution over the bean sprouts and leave to marinate for at least 1 hour. (Drain before serving.)

Combine the marinade ingredients in a bowl. Stir in the beef cubes and leave to marinate for an hour.

Heat the oil in a wok over medium-high heat. Add the garlic and onion, if using, and toss until just softened and fragrant.

Stir in the beef and continue cooking, shaking the pan vigorously until the beef is done to your liking (3–7 minutes). Halfway through cooking, sprinkle the sugar over the beef so it melts and caramelises with the pan juices.

Serve immediately garnished with the spring onion and with the drained pickled bean sprouts on the side.

✖ The pickled bean sprouts are best eaten on the day they are made.

BEEF WITH MANDARIN PEEL

A delightful mix of hot, spicy, savoury and slightly sweet flavours enlivened with dried mandarin peel (also known as tangerine peel), this easy-going dish bears all the hallmarks of Hunan-Sichuan cooking. Although the two provinces lay claim to this gorgeous dish, it has morphed to incorporate other Chinese cooking styles. A Cantonese version I ate recently in Hong Kong recently tones down the fiery chilli sauce. This recipe is adapted from Yan-Kit's *Classic Chinese Cookbook*.

20 g (¾ oz) dried mandarin peel (see note) or pared peel of 1 orange
500 g (1 lb 2 oz) beef rump, cut into thick slices (about 3 cm/1¼ inches)
⅓ cup (80 ml) neutral oil
2.5 cm (1 inch) piece (about 25 g/1 oz) ginger, shredded
6 spring onions (scallions), white and green parts separated, sliced
1 tablespoon Shaoxing wine
2–3 tablespoons Sichuan chilli sauce or sambal oelek
1 teaspoon cornflour (cornstarch), mixed with 2 tablespoons water

MARINADE
2 teaspoons light soy sauce
2 teaspoons dark soy sauce
2 teaspoons Shaoxing wine
½ teaspoon Chinese five-spice powder
1 teaspoon caster (superfine) sugar
1½ teaspoons cornflour (cornstarch)
Good pinch of salt, or to taste
1 dried red chilli, seeds removed, chopped
1 tablespoon chilli oil

Soak the mandarin peel in cold water for about 2 hours or until soft. Drain and slice into thin strips, about 5 mm (¼ inch) wide. (Or, if using orange peel, bring a saucepan of water to the boil, add the orange peel and boil for 5 minutes. Drain and rinse in cold water, then cut into thin strips, similar to the mandarin.)

For the marinade, add the dark and light soy sauces, Shaoxing, five-spice, sugar and cornflour to a bowl with the salt, add 1 tablespoon of water and mix well. Mix in the chopped chilli, then add the beef and toss to coat. Refrigerate for 1 hour to marinate, then stir in the chilli oil.

Heat a wok over high heat until smoking. Add the oil, swirl it around once or twice, then add the ginger and white part of the spring onions. Let it sizzle for 20 seconds, then add the citrus peel. Stir-fry for a few seconds, then add the beef and continue stir-frying for 1–2 minutes until the wok returns to heat again.

Splash in the Shaoxing and stir, then once the sizzling dies down, add the chilli sauce. Cover, reduce the heat to low, then stir-fry for another 1–2 minutes until the citrus flavours permeate the beef.

Dribble the cornflour slurry in with the beef and stir as the sauce thickens. Add the green spring onion, and serve at once.

✖ You can buy dried mandarin at Asian grocers. To make your own, peel a few mandarins and either use a dehydrator, or hang the peels near a window with plenty of air circulating for a few weeks to dry out. Store in an airtight container – they should last up to a year.

STIR-FRIED LAMB WITH SPRING ONIONS AND STEAMED BUNS
CONG PAO YANG ROU

SERVES 2–4

Lamb is considered a warming meat and northern Chinese love eating it to ward off the winter cold. This famous Beijing dish was traditionally eaten in winter and spring but now it is common year round. Some experts believe this dish is handed down from the Mongolians, while others say it was introduced by Chinese Muslims. Fittingly, there are several versions – some even add cumin seeds.

The success of this dish lies in cutting the lamb into paper-thin slices and cooking it with masses of leeks (tender young leeks are best) or spring onions to lend the dish its distinctive fragrance.

This is perfect served with rice, but northern Chinese folk prefer the fluffy buns known as mantou. Steamed rather than baked, mantou are simple to make but, like all breads, take time; you'll find the recipe below, but you'll also find mantou in Chinese grocers, if you'd like to skip ahead.

For the steamed buns, pour the water into a large bowl, add the dried yeast and sugar and stir well. Stand in a warm place for about 15 minutes or until foamy.

Put the flour and salt in a food processor and, with the machine running, pour the yeast mixture through the feed tube in a steady stream. A ball will form in about 10 seconds. If it doesn't, add another tablespoon of water. Turn the dough out onto a floured surface and knead for 3–5 minutes until smooth.

Transfer the dough to a lightly oiled bowl, cover with a damp tea towel and leave in a warm place for about 1.5 hours or until it has doubled in size. Gently knock back the dough and tip it onto a lightly floured surface. Knead for about 5 minutes, then form it into a long sausage and cut it into 12 pieces. Shape into balls, then place each ball on a 5 cm (2 inch) square of baking paper.

Place the buns on their paper squares in large steaming baskets, leaving a gap between. Cover and leave to rise again (about 20 minutes). Steam over simmering water for 12–15 minutes or until cooked through (to test, insert a satay stick into a bun – if it comes out clean, the buns are done). Leave the lid slightly ajar for 5 minutes to stop the buns from collapsing.

For the marinade, mix all the ingredients well in a bowl. Add the lamb to the marinade, toss to coat, and leave for 30 minutes to marinate.

For the sauce, mix together all the ingredients to combine well.

When you're ready to serve, heat a wok over high heat until smoking, add the oil and swirl it around once or twice. Add the garlic and ginger, let sizzle for 10 seconds or until they're just taking on colour, then immediately add the lamb. Stir-fry, tossing rapidly, for 20–30 seconds or until the lamb is partially cooked and slightly charred. Pour in the sauce and stir to mix through.

Add the spring onions and stir-fry until the whole mixture has absorbed most of the sauce. Check and adjust the seasoning and sprinkle in sesame oil if required. Serve with steamed buns.

✤ Mantou can be frozen and steamed again to serve. It is also sold frozen in Asian grocers.

---

350 g (12 oz) lamb fillet, fat trimmed and sliced into paper-thin pieces
⅓ cup (80 ml) neutral oil
2 garlic cloves, thinly sliced
3–4 thin slices ginger
250 g (9 oz) spring onions (about 8), cut into 5 cm (2 inch) lengths
Sesame oil, to serve

MANTOU
¾ cup (185 ml) tepid (30°C/85°F) water
1 teaspoon dried yeast
1 tablespoon caster (superfine) sugar
2 cups (300 g) plain (all-purpose) flour
¼ teaspoon salt
Neutral oil, for greasing

MARINADE
1 tablespoon light soy sauce
1 tablespoon Shaoxing wine
1 teaspoon caster (superfine) sugar
Salt and a few generous turns of pepper

SAUCE
2 teaspoons dark soy sauce
2 teaspoon Shaoxing wine
1 teaspoon sesame oil
2 teaspoons Chinkiang vinegar (optional)

BEEF COOKED IN SWEET SOY SAUCE
SEMUR

Serves 8–10

Originally of Dutch origin but adapted into its current, spiced form by Indonesians, beef semur is also enjoyed by Singaporeans and Malaysians, especially the Eurasian community. Although this is typically presented purely as a meat dish, some add eggs, potatoes and tomatoes to this mildly spiced, vinegared dish. Brisket, chuck steak and stewing beef (shin or silverside) are all well suited to the slow simmering here.

¼ cup (60 ml) neutral oil
2 large onions, quartered
4 garlic cloves, crushed
1 kg (2 lb 4 oz) stewing beef, cut into 4 cm (1½ inches) cubes
5 cm (2 inch) piece cinnamon
4 star anise
10 cloves
4 cardamom pods
2 slices ginger (or galangal)
100 ml (3½ oz) kecap manis (sweet soy sauce)
2 tablespoons light soy sauce
1 tablespoon distilled white vinegar (or coconut vinegar)
Pinch of caster (superfine) sugar, or to taste
2 litres (8 cups) beef stock or water
4 potatoes, peeled and cut into large pieces
4 carrots, peeled and cut into chunks
2 tomatoes, quartered
3 makrut limes leaves, finely shredded
1 long red chilli, thinly sliced
Crisp-fried shallots, to serve

Heat the oil in a saucepan over medium-high heat, add the onion and garlic and cook, stirring occasionally, until golden (8–10 minutes).

Add the beef, cinnamon, star anise, cloves, cardamom and ginger and fry, stirring occasionally, until fragrant and the beef is sealed. Add the kecap manis, soy sauce, vinegar and sugar, adjusting the sweetness to taste. Cover with the stock, bring to the boil, then reduce to a simmer and cook until beef is tender (1–1.5 hours, depending on the cut).

Add the potatoes and carrots and simmer until tender and the liquid has reduced to sauce consistency (15–20 minutes). Stir in the tomatoes, simmer until warmed through, then check the seasoning, adjusting to taste.

Serve with rice, topped with makrut lime, chilli and fried shallots.

✖ As salt levels vary in different brands of soy sauces, it pays to add salt just before serving. Chicken, pork and beancurd are good alternatives to the beef.

BRAISED PORK BELLY WITH SOY SAUCE
NYONYA TAU YU BAK

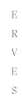

SERVES 4–6

This popular rustic dish reminds me of Dongpo pork, the braised pork from Hangzhou in China made famous by the 11th-century poet-scholar it was named after. Called tau yu bak by the Hokkien people, (tau yu means 'soy sauce' and bak means 'cooked in meat'), it is one of my mother's favourite dishes, and it is also much-loved by the Peranakan community. Though it's rarely on restaurant menus, one of the best versions I've had recently was at Tek Sen, a super-casual eatery in Penang. A cinch to make, it tastes even better if served a day or so after it's cooked.

Traditionally, pork belly is preferred, though any other meat may be used. There are many versions and the recipe below is my family's version. Others add firm beancurd, called taukwa, and boiled eggs, while others pop in five-spice powder and star anise for extra kick.

Heat the oil in a large, heavy-based saucepan over medium heat. Add the garlic and lemongrass and stir until the garlic is lightly golden, (1–2 minutes). Add the sugar and cook until caramelised (1 minute).

Add the pork, stir well to coat, then add the dark and light soy sauces and stir-fry for 1 minute. Add the water, then increase heat and bring to the boil, skimming off any impurities that rise to the surface. Reduce the heat to low-medium, cover with a lid and simmer gently until the meat is fork tender and the sauce is syrupy (1–1.5 hours).

Adjust seasoning with pepper and salt and adding soy and sugar as desired.

Dish onto a serving plate, discard lemongrass and garnish with spring onions or fried shallots. Serve with steamed rice and sambal belacan mixed with lime juice (optional).

✖ If you don't like the porky smell, blanch the sliced pieces in boiling water and then rinse in cold water. Lemongrass is not traditionally added, but it certainly lends depth and flavour to this homestyle dish.

- 2 tablespoons neutral oil
- 7 garlic cloves, crushed
- 1 lemongrass stalk (white part only)
- 3 teaspoons caster (superfine) sugar, or to taste
- 600 g (1 lb 5 oz) pork belly, cut into 5 cm (2 inch) cubes
- 1 tablespoon dark soy sauce
- 2 teaspoons light soy sauce
- 3 cups (750 ml) water
- ½ teaspoon freshly cracked black pepper
- Good pinch of salt, or to taste
- Handful of sliced spring onions (scallions) or crisp-fried shallots, steamed rice, and sambal belacan mixed with lime juice (optional; see page 261), to serve

SERVES 4 | 6

BRAISED LAMB WITH BEANCURD STICKS AND TANGERINE PEEL

FOO JOOK YEONG YUK BO

When the weather turns cool, one of the traditional dishes I think of is this slow-cooked lamb with beancurd sticks flavoured with tangerine peel, a dish I grew up eating during the monsoon months in Malaysia. Not only is this dish deeply comforting, it's also easy to put together.

If you haven't used beancurd sticks before, they're worth seeking out in Chinese grocers because they're wonderfully textural and very nutritious. Their role here is not only to lend body but also a different mouthfeel to the tender lamb. Traditionally, the dish uses lamb flap or lamb breast, but lamb shoulder is just as delicious.

1 kg (2 lb 4 oz) lamb shoulder, cut into 4 cm (1½ inch) cubes
2 tablespoons neutral oil, plus extra for deep-frying
3 dried beancurd sticks
3 spring onions (scallions), green and white parts separated, cut into 3 cm (1¼ inch) lengths
2 garlic cloves, chopped
5 slices ginger
2 star anise
2 cubes red fermented beancurd, or to taste, mashed (see note page 248)
2 tablespoons Shaoxing wine
1 teaspoon caster (superfine) sugar
1 piece dried tangerine peel, soaked in warm water and torn into small pieces
1 cup (250 g) bamboo shoots, cut into 2 cm (¾ inch) dice
1 tablespoon oyster sauce
3 cups (750 ml) chicken stock or water
10 water chestnuts or 1 carrot, cut into chunks
Salt and white pepper, to taste
1 teaspoon cornflour (cornstarch) mixed with 1 tablespoon water
½ teaspoon sesame oil
Coriander sprigs and steamed rice, to serve

MARINADE
1 tablespoon Shaoxing wine
2 teaspoons ginger juice (see note)
½ teaspoon Chinese five-spice powder
1 teaspoon light soy sauce
½ teaspoon sesame oil
Freshly ground white pepper, to taste

Place the lamb in a bowl and add the marinade ingredients. Mix thoroughly and leave to marinate for 1–2 hours.

Half-fill a wok with oil and heat to 170°C (325°F). Break the beancurd sticks into thirds and quickly deep-fry them until they are puffed up but not browned (2–3 minutes). Remove with a slotted spoon, drain on a wire, then place in a bowl. Pour boiling water over the fried sticks to cover, then cover with a plate and leave for 20–30 minutes to soften. Drain, then squeeze out excess liquid. Cut into bite-sized pieces of about 5 cm (2 inches).

Drain oil from the wok, wipe it clean, then place over medium-high heat. Add 2 tablespoons oil, swirl once or twice, then add the white part of the spring onion along with the garlic and ginger and fry, tossing occasionally, until golden (1–2 minutes).

Add the star anise and red fermented beancurd, stir-fry for a few seconds, then add the lamb and stir-fry until sealed (2–3 minutes). Add Shaoxing, sugar, tangerine peel, bamboo shoots, oyster sauce and drained beancurd sticks. Stir-fry for 30 seconds, then add the stock.

Transfer contents to a large saucepan and check all the ingredients are covered with stock. If not, add some more. Bring to a simmer, then cook, stirring occasionally, for 1–1.5 hours or until the lamb is juicy and tender. Add water chestnuts and simmer for 5–8 minutes, ensuring some crunch remains, and the sauce has reduced by half overall.

Season to taste, then stir in the cornflour slurry until incorporated and add the sesame oil.

Top with coriander sprigs and serve with steamed rice.

✖ I like to enjoy the lamb with some crisp stir-fried greens or a salad of garland chrysanthemum and some chopped chillies. If you like, you can also add a dipping sauce made with a couple of cubes of mashed fermented beancurd, sesame oil, water and a pinch of sugar to taste.

Ginger juice can be made by squeezing 30 g (1 oz) of grated ginger through a muslin or a cheesecloth.

SICHUAN TWICE-COOKED PORK
HUI GUO ROU

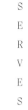

One of the most famous dishes from Sichuan province, twice-cooked pork is a favourite with many Chinese families that evokes nostalgia among Sichuanese living abroad. Meaning 'back to the pot meat' because the pork is first boiled and then stir-fried with a medley of flavours, it's a simple dish to prepare, even if it is cooked twice.

The traditional cut for this dish is pork belly with the skin on, and the recipe usually calls for tender Chinese leeks, but I've also enjoyed the dish cooked with green and red capsicums, which I've included here. Whatever you choose, the dish should be bright red due to the chillies that are blended into the doubanjiang, but it is a matter of aesthetics rather than necessity – just make sure it's packed with hot, pungent flavours.

Put the pork belly, skin and all, in a large pot of boiling water. Simmer over moderate heat for 20–25 minutes, depending on the thickness of the pork, until cooked but still firm. Remove, allow to cool, then refrigerate for 2 hours to firm up further. Once chilled, either remove the skin or keep it on (the skin will give it crunch, which adds texture – including it is a matter of personal preference), and slice the pork into 2 mm (1/16 inch) pieces with a sharp knife.

Heat a wok over medium heat and add 1 tablespoon of oil. Add the leek and stir-fry for 1 minute, adding a pinch of salt as you go. Transfer to a plate and keep in a warm place.

Add the remaining oil, along with the chilli oil, to the hot wok, then add the pork slices. Stir-fry for about 2 minutes until slightly crisp.

Push the pork to one side of the wok, then add the green and red capsicums, as well as the dried chillies and stir-fry for 20 seconds. Add the sauce ingredients, and simmer for 2 minutes or until the sauce is reduced.

Season to taste, return the leek to the wok, toss for another 20 seconds, then serve immediately.

400 g (14 oz) pork belly, skin on
2 tablespoons neutral oil
½ large leek, thinly sliced on the diagonal
1 tablespoon chilli oil
½ small green capsicum (pepper), seeds removed, sliced
½ small red capsicum (pepper), seeds removed, sliced
½ cup (15 g) small dried red chillies
Salt and white pepper, to taste

SAUCE
½ cup (125 ml) chicken stock
1½ tablespoons doubanjiang (chilli bean paste)
1 tablespoon fermented black beans, rinsed and lightly mashed (optional)
2 teaspoons sweet bean paste (tian mian jiang) or hoisin sauce (optional)
1 teaspoon dark soy sauce
1 teaspoon caster (superfine) sugar

ROAST LAMB WITH SAFFRON AND TANDOORI SPICES

Serves 8

I'm told this lamb dish originates from the kitchens of the Mughals. Lamb is usually marinated with yoghurt (a natural tenderiser), lots of ginger and garlic plus a host of warm spices, then baked in a tandoor or clay oven, but it works well in a regular oven, too.
I like to offer the lamb cooked medium to medium-rare, but the choice is yours here, too. Instead of serving it with rice, you can try it with couscous or roti.

For the marinade, put the yoghurt and cream in a bowl and mix well. In a food processor or mortar and pestle, blitz or grind the garlic and ginger with the salt and a splash of the lemon juice to a fine paste. Add this to the yoghurt mixture with the remaining ingredients and the rest of the lemon juice and mix well.

Prick the lamb all over with a skewer to allow the marinade to penetrate, then rub the marinade all over the lamb, roll up and tie with butcher's string to re-form the shape of the leg. Cover and refrigerate for at least 3 hours, or overnight, to marinate.

Bring the lamb back to room temperature and preheat the oven to 220°C (430°F). Place the lamb on a wire rack set in a baking dish and place in the oven to roast.

After 45 minutes, test the lamb at its thickest point by slipping in a metal skewer. Leave it in place for 1 minute, then touch it against your lower lip. If it feels quite hot and the juices that run from the pierced spot are rosy-pink, then the lamb is medium-rare. If the skewer is faintly warm and the juices are red, leave the lamb to roast another 10 minutes, then test again.

When cooked to your liking, remove to a warm spot to rest for at least 15 minutes. Carve and serve with your preferred grain and a simple salad.

1 leg of lamb, boneless, trimmed

MARINADE
1 cup (260 g) plain yoghurt
¼ cup (60 ml) single (pure) cream
2 tablespoons finely chopped garlic
2 tablespoons finely chopped ginger
1 teaspoon salt, or to taste
2 tablespoons lemon juice
Pinch of saffron threads, soaked in 1 tablespoon hot water
2 teaspoons chopped coriander
2 teaspoons garam masala (see page 23)
1 teaspoon chilli powder
1 teaspoon ground turmeric
1 teaspoon freshly ground black pepper

BALINESE ROAST PORK
BABI GULING – BE CELENG

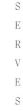

SERVES 6–8

One of the most delicious preparations from Hindu Bali, babi guling, or spit-roasted suckling pig, is a firm favourite for any visitor to the island. It's tender and sinfully delicious, with perfect crackling. Balinese suckling pigs are often roasted when they weigh between 10 and 20 kilograms (22 to 44 pounds), though nowadays most pigs used are between 30 and 40 kilos (66 to 88 pounds).

The traditional method of making this dish is to rub the cavity with a mixture of spices and sometimes tapioca leaves. The skin is then rubbed with turmeric juice before roasting. As this option of using a whole pig is not readily accessible to the home cook, I have come up with this version using belly pork. In fact, you can use just about any cut of pork with a good cap of skin for crackling.

Blend the turmeric with ½ cup (125 ml) water in a food processor or blender, then strain into a small bowl. Set aside.

Rub the pork belly all over with the salt, massaging it into the flesh and the skin, then set aside while you make the spice paste.

For the spice paste, blend all the ingredients in a food processor until well combined.

Place the pork belly skin-side down, then pack the meat side with the spice paste, spreading it to the edges and topping it with the lime and salam leaves. Roll up the pork belly and secure it with satay sticks or butcher's string. Brush the skin with the turmeric juice and leave at room temperature for another 30 minutes to marinate.

Preheat the oven to 200°C (400°F). Place the pork on a wire rack set over a baking tray and roast, basting two or three times, for 1.5 hours until the skin is crisp and the meat is cooked through (the juices should run clear when you pierce the thickest part with a skewer). Remove from the oven and rest for 10 minutes to allow the fat to settle.

Remove the satay sticks or string, then carve the meat into slices. Serve with pickles, a salad, and steamed rice.

✤ Salam leaves (*Syzygium polyanthum*) have an earthy, citrusy flavour. Bay leaves are often used instead but I'm not convinced – so if you can't find salam leaves, go without.

---

50 g (1¾ oz) fresh turmeric (or 1 tablespoon ground turmeric)
2.5 kg (5 lb 8 oz) piece pork belly
1½ tablespoons salt
5 makrut lime leaves, finely shredded
2 salam leaves (optional; see note)
Pickles, salad and steamed rice, to serve

SPICE PASTE
¾ cup (125 g) chopped shallots (eschalots)
8–15 birdseye chillies (to taste), chopped
5 large garlic cloves
2 large lemongrass stalks (white part only), chopped
2 tablespoons chopped ginger
2 tablespoons chopped fresh turmeric
1 tablespoon chopped galangal
1 teaspoon ground kencur (aromatic ginger; optional)
2 tablespoons coriander seeds, crushed
1 tablespoon black peppercorns, crushed
2 tablespoons neutral oil
1 teaspoon salt

TAMARIND PORK
BABI ASAM

SERVES 6–8

This braised dish is distinctly Nyonya – a cooking style born from the marriage between the Chinese and the Malays centuries ago – and doesn't exist in Malay cooking because pork isn't eaten, while the Chinese don't cook with spice pastes.

Although it's not complicated to prepare, it is nonetheless mouth-watering, with rich and complex flavours. Some like the dish packed with chillies, while others prefer it tart. Since I love sour flavours, I am more inclined to add a splash of lime juice just before serving. Traditionally, this is made with pork belly and spare ribs, but pork shoulder is just as good.

- 80 g (2¾ oz) tamarind pulp
- ⅓ cup (80 ml) neutral oil
- 2 tablespoons salted soybeans (taucheo; see note), mashed
- 2 tablespoons caster (superfine) sugar or palm sugar (jaggery)
- 1 kg (2 lb 3 oz) pork belly, cut into bite-sized pieces, or pork spare-ribs, cut through the bone into 6 cm (2½ inch) chunks
- 1 lemongrass stalk (white part only), bruised
- 5 long green chillies (or to taste; seeds removed if you like it milder), sliced
- 6 long red chillies (or to taste; seeds removed if you like it milder), sliced
- Salt, to taste
- 1 tablespoon lime juice, or to taste

SPICE PASTE
- 4 candlenuts
- 5 shallots (eschalots; about 250 g/9 oz)
- 4 fresh red chillies, chopped
- 3 garlic cloves, chopped
- ¼ cup (30 g) chopped galangal
- 1 teaspoon chopped fresh turmeric
- 2 teaspoons belacan (shrimp paste)

Place the tamarind pulp in a bowl and cover with 2 cups (500 ml) warm water. Soak for 20 minutes, then, with your fingers, mash and squeeze the tamarind to extract as much juice as possible.

For the spice paste, blend all the ingredients to a fine paste in a food processor (or pound with a mortar and pestle).

Heat the oil in a saucepan over low-medium heat, add the spice paste, and fry, stirring constantly, until golden and fragrant (about 10 minutes). Sprinkle with a little water if it is cooking too quickly and draw it away from the heat now and then to prevent it burning.

Increase the heat to high, add the salted soybeans and the sugar, stir-fry for another minute, then add the pork and lemongrass. Reduce the heat to medium and toss to seal the meat.

Strain the tamarind liquid through a sieve into the saucepan, bring to the boil, then reduce the heat to low and simmer until the pork is tender and the liquid is reduced to sauce consistency, about 1 hour, adding the chilli (reserving a tablespoon to serve) halfway through the cooking time.

Season to taste with salt and sugar, then remove from heat and stir in the lime juice. Serve with reserved chilli.

✖ Different brands of salted soybeans have more salt so be cautious when adding salt to the finished dish. If you have any ginger flower (torch ginger), you can also shred this and use it as a fragrant garnish.

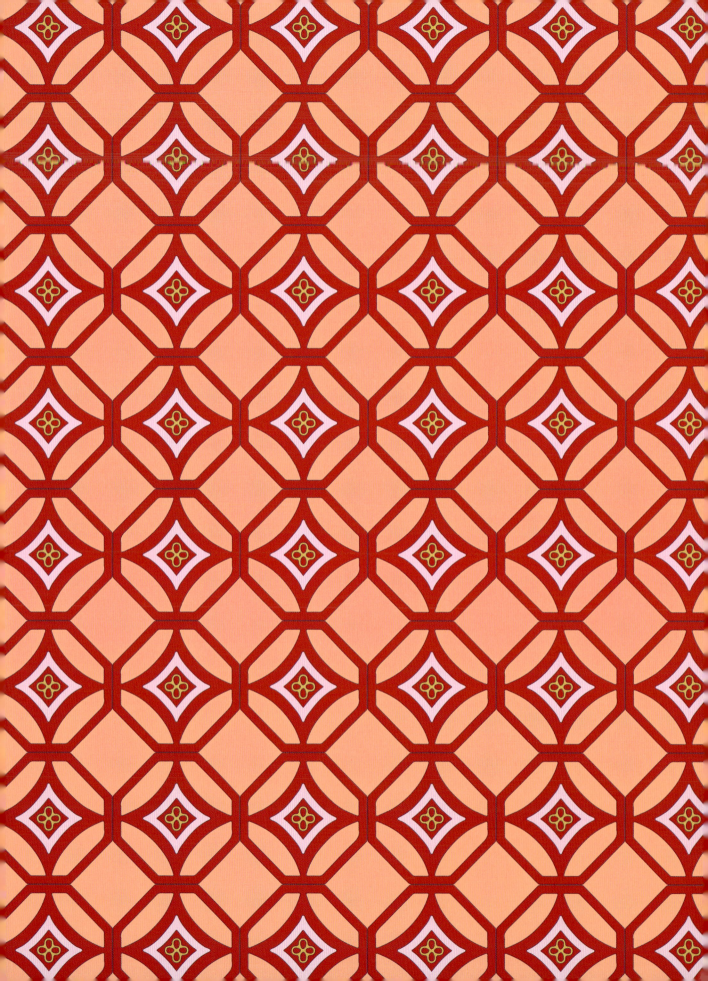

POULTRY

SUPERIOR STOCKS

Every time I write about stock, I can't help but think of my mother Lim Heng Keow, as her prowess in stock-making is so deeply ingrained in my consciousness. Her stocks consisted of nothing more than chicken bones (occasionally a few chicken feet), slices of ginger, spring onions and water. But she was fastidious. Skimming with the ease of a trained chef – although she never was one – she removed every molecule of fat and every impurity from the barely simmering liquid to yield a clear stock of exceptional flavour.

Why stock-making is so important in Asian culture is something I've often grappled with. After all, there are so many good commercially made stocks in Asian grocers, and you can find every imaginable Asian stock cube out there, typically packed with punchy monosodium glutamate thanks to Kikunae Ikeda, the Japanese chemist, who isolated this compound from kombu, or kelp. MSG is basically pure umami, often called the fifth taste, which the Japanese describe as 'the essence of deliciousness'.

But while MSG may have spread through Asia like a grass fire, and made its way into so many supermarket products in the West, stocks packed with MSG lack the beauty, complexity and subtlety of the properly made kind. Even in Japan, where MSG originated, there are plenty of cooks who will make dashi – the kombu-based stock, most often featuring dried bonito flakes, that forms part of the soul of Japanese cooking – from scratch. Properly made, this clear stock determines the success of a Japanese dish.

Koreans similarly have their own ingredients and methods of making stock. To me, Korean cooking is fascinating because there are so many different types of stocks or broths made solely with chicken, beef brisket and bones, dried anchovies or pork bones. Depending on the primary ingredient, flavourings like garlic, spring onions (scallions), daikon and dried kelp are included to lend different flavours to the stocks.

The Chinese also employ similar ingredients to make different stocks. Traditionally, Chinese cooks tend to combine two types of meat (usually chicken and pork) with spring onions and ginger to make everyday stock. Then there is superior stock – the kind you find at high-end Chinese restaurants. Filled with the characteristic collagen-rich or gelatinous quality of a refined stock, it is made with pork, chicken and the much-lauded Jinhua ham in Zhejiang province or Xuanwei ham from Yunnan. Sometimes dried scallops, abalone or duck are included for an extra umami kick.

> Exquisitely rich and clear, a fine superior stock is the calling card of a great chef or cook.

The other great thing about superior stock is this: it is perfectly achievable at home, and can be made with jamón or prosciutto in place of traditional Chinese hams.

I've found that throughout Asia, the differing flavours of stocks tend to have nearly as much to do with the locality as the whimsy of the cook. While Chinese cooks like to add a dash of rice wine, Vietnamese cooks like to perfume their broth with star anise, cassia bark and fish sauce. Thai, Malaysian and Singaporean cooks may include makrut lime leaves or lemongrass to enhance their stocks. Dried seafood is also a common addition throughout Asia. Some cooks use dried squid or cuttlefish, others may throw in a handful of dried shrimp or even dried oysters. The degree and nuance of flavourings, and the inclusion or exclusion of particular ingredients is then up to the individual.

Ultimately, stock-making in Asia is incredibly diverse, sophisticated and exciting. Well-made stocks bring balance, depth and vitality to soups, braises and many more preparations.

The best part is that stock-making is super-easy. All you need to make a fabulous stock is good-quality ingredients, then you can leave it to murmur gently on the stove while you attend to other things. When it's done, the stock you've made not only is an expression of your individuality but it also nourishes you with all the goodness that not even the best stock cube can ever offer. Please make some. I've included a few starting points here.

CHICKEN STOCK

For a general-purpose chicken stock with a gelatinous mouthfeel, I use a mix of chicken parts. Add about 2 kilograms of chicken parts (carcasses, wings, neck and feet) into a large stockpot and cover with cold water. Bring to the boil and reduce the heat to simmer for about 5 minutes. Tip the chicken parts into a large strainer and rinse under cold running water to remove the scum and wash out the stockpot. Return the chicken parts to the pot, and add 60 g (2 oz) coarsely chopped ginger and 3 spring onions (scallions), along with 2–3 dried shiitake mushrooms (optional). Bring to the boil, reduce the heat to a bare murmur and cook, uncovered and undisturbed for 2 hours. Strain through a fine strained or cheesecloth and discard the solids. Cool to room temperature, then refrigerate overnight. The next day, skim any solidified fat from the surface. Use within 2–3 days or freeze for up to 3 months.

CHINESE SUPERIOR STOCK

Rinse 500 g (1 lb 2 oz) pork bones, put them in a large bowl, cover with cold water and leave to soak for 1 hour. Drain the bones, rinse well and put in a large stockpot along with a quartered chicken (around 1.8 kg/4 lb). Cover with cold water and bring to the boil, then reduce the heat and simmer for about 10 minutes. Tip the chicken and bones into a colander and rinse well under running water. Rinse the stockpot. Put the chicken and bones along with 100 g (3½ oz) cured ham (jamón or prosciutto), 3 dried scallops (optional), 50 g (1¾ oz) bruised ginger, 2 spring onions (scallions), 2 whole white peppercorns and 2 tablespoons of rice wine in the stockpot and cover with plenty of cold water. Bring to the boil and immediately reduce the heat until the liquid is barely simmering. Cook, uncovered, for at least 4 hours, skimming off any impurities that rise to the surface. Set aside to cool. Skim any residual fat from the surface and strain the stock through a sieve lined with muslin (cheesecloth). Leave to cool completely, then refrigerate. The stock will keep refrigerated for 4–5 days, or can be frozen for up to 3 months.

VEGETABLE STOCK

Asian vegetable stocks vary greatly across Asia, but this version, which takes from a wide range of traditions, is one of my favourites. Heat 2 tablespoons of neutral oil in a large stockpot over high heat. Add the 2 small diced onions, 2 spring onions (scallions) and 60 g (2 oz) ginger – both coarsely chopped – and fry, stirring constantly to prevent burning, about 5 minutes. As soon as the vegetables have taken on a bit of caramelisation, add 500 g (1 lb 2 oz) carrots and 100 g (3½ oz) celery – both thinly sliced – as well as 30 g (1 oz) dried shiitake mushrooms, 1 teaspoon of black peppercorns, 1 crushed lemongrass stalk, 3 litres (100 fl oz) water and bring to the boil. Turn the heat down to low and simmer, uncovered for 2 hours. If water is evaporating too quickly, add another cup of water. Strain the stock into a large bowl and discard the solids. Leave to cool and keep in the fridge for 3 to 4 days or freeze for up to 3 months.

STIR-FRIED CHICKEN WITH GINGER AND WOOD-EAR MUSHROOMS
GAI PHAD KING

SERVES 4

Ginger is not often featured in Thai cooking, but in this recipe, ginger is the star. Super-easy, fast to make and incredibly delicious, this has become one of my go-to dishes, especially when young ginger is in season. The dish includes taucheo (salted soybean paste), a contribution from the Teochew community, who've been living in Thailand for centuries. Wood-ear mushrooms are added for crunch, but if you don't have access to them, use whatever mushrooms you like – it will not affect the integrity of the dish.

¼ cup (60 ml) neutral oil
2 cloves garlic, chopped
1 small onion, thinly sliced
400 g (14 oz) chicken breast, thinly sliced
100 g (3½ oz) ginger (preferably young ginger, see note), sliced into fine strips
2 long red chillies, sliced
1 cup (90 g) fresh wood-ear mushrooms, trimmed of woody stems and cut into pieces (or 15 g dried; see note)
1 tablespoon fish sauce
1 tablespoon soy sauce
1 tablespoon oyster sauce
1 teaspoon salted soybean paste or miso
½ cup (125 ml) chicken stock or water
2 spring onions (scallions), cut into 5 cm (2 inch) lengths
Salt and white pepper, to taste
Steamed rice, to serve

Heat the oil in a wok over medium-high heat. Add the garlic, stir-fry briefly until it begins to brown, then add the onion and chicken and continue to fry for 2–3 minutes until the chicken turns white.

Add the ginger, chilli and mushrooms, then the fish, soy and oyster sauces, followed by the bean paste. Mix well, then stir-fry for another minute before adding the chicken stock. Cook, stirring, for another minute, then add the spring onions, tossing to combine. Season to taste and serve with steamed rice.

✖ Wood-ear mushrooms are now sold fresh. If you're using dried, soak them in hot water for 20 minutes before use – 15 g (½ oz) dried will yield about 1 cup (250 ml) once reconstituted.

Young ginger is creamy in colour, with a pink blush on the tops. The skin should peel off easily. Look for it in Asian grocers.

ISAAN-STYLE GRILLED CHICKEN WINGS

GAI YANG

SERVES 8 | 10

Gai yang is a north-eastern Thai street food that is so delicious it's now found throughout Thailand. Often eaten with green papaya salad and sticky rice, this is the quintessential Issan meal.

The traditional recipe uses a whole chicken that's split open and flattened, rubbed with a marinade rich with ginger, lemongrass and coriander, then grilled over a moderate charcoal fire until fragrant. This is a beautiful way to make this dish, but I often make it like I've described here, with small chicken drumsticks or wings, which are excellent at cocktail parties. The chicken can be marinated overnight, which frees you up to make other dishes and leaves only the grilling at the very end.

For the chilli sauce, combine all the ingredients and 1 cup (250 ml) water in a saucepan. Place over medium-high heat, bring to a simmer and cook, stirring, until the liquid forms a thickish syrup. Season to taste with salt, stir well and transfer to a small bowl or jar (see note).

For the marinade, add ginger, lemongrass, coriander root and garlic to a food processor or mortar and blend or pound with a pestle until smooth. Transfer to a large bowl and add the remaining ingredients.

Add the chicken wings to the marinade, toss to coat, then refrigerate for 6 hours, or overnight, to marinate.

Heat a barbecue or a charcoal grill to low heat. Grill the wings slowly, turning occasionally, for 15 minutes or until charred and cooked through (see note). Serve with the chilli sauce and sticky rice.

✖ Chilli sauce will keep refrigerated for a week. You can also roast the chicken wings in a 180°C (350°F) oven.

2 kg (4 lb 8 oz) chicken wings
Sticky rice, to serve

CHILLI SAUCE

4 long red chillies, finely chopped
2 birdseye chillies, finely chopped
2 garlic cloves, finely chopped
2 coriander (cilantro) roots, finely chopped
80 g (2¾ oz) caster (superfine) sugar
2½ tablespoons white vinegar

MARINADE

2 tablespoons finely chopped ginger
2 tablespoons finely chopped lemongrass (white part only)
2 tablespoons finely chopped coriander root
4 garlic cloves, peeled
1 cup (250 ml) light soy sauce
2 teaspoons caster (superfine) sugar
1 tablespoon black pepper

DRUNKEN CHICKEN WITH SHAVED ICE
ZUI JI

SERVES 8–10

No one knows precisely when and where this classic dish originated. It's sometimes traced to Beijing, but more often to the Shanghai region. I have also come across references suggesting it goes back to the Tang Dynasty, but this claim seems rather dubious to me.

Because of its long pedigree, there are several versions of this delicious cold starter. The most common methods involve poaching or steaming a whole chicken, which is then given a cold bath before being steeped in Shaoxing wine for at least 5 hours (preferably overnight). Since good drunken chicken uses top-quality Shaoxing wine with a dash of rose dew wine (a distilled spirit made from sorghum and other grains and infused with rose petals), it would be rather silly to dispose of the heady, aromatic stock – traditionally, the broth is reserved for soups. Singaporean chef Jereme Leung ingeniously turned the stock into a shaved ice. This creative twist has transformed a classic into an exciting contemporary dish that's perfect for summer days.

1.5 kg (3 lb 5 oz) skin-on chicken thigh cutlets
1 cup (250 ml) Shaoxing wine
Pinch of salt
Spring onion curls, to garnish (optional)

MARINADE
1 cup (250 ml) Shaoxing wine or dry sherry
3 spring onions (scallions) cut into 5 cm (2 inch) lengths
5–8 ginger slices, about 2 mm (1/16 inch) thick
1 tablespoon dried goji berries, soaked in a bowl of water, plus extra to serve
2 star anise
2 teaspoons mei kuei lu chiew (rose dew cooking wine)
2 teaspoons salt
1 teaspoon caster (superfine) sugar, or to taste

Ask your butcher to bone the chicken thigh cutlets (or do it yourself).

Combine the marinade ingredients in a large bowl and mix well. Add the chicken thighs and marinate in the fridge for at least 5 hours (or preferably overnight).

Take the chicken out of the fridge to come to room temperature.

Combine the Shaoxing, salt and 8 cups (2 litres) water in a large saucepan and bring to the boil. Add the chicken and marinade and poach over medium-low heat for 10 minutes. Turn off the heat and leave to steep for another 15 minutes. Transfer the chicken to a deep container with just enough broth to cover it. Leave to cool completely.

Meanwhile, strain the remaining broth through a piece of muslin (cheesecloth) and leave to cool. Pour the broth into shallow trays and place in the freezer until firm, regularly breaking up the ice crystals with a fork until it looks like a granita.

To serve, cut the chicken into bite-sized slices and top with the shaved ice, a few goji berries, and wisps of spring onion, if using.

THE ART OF DUCK

I love duck. I can still remember the first time it crept into my consciousness. I must have been only five because we didn't have our own restaurant then. It was a hot, windless afternoon when my mother ordered wonton noodles with Cantonese roast duck from a street vendor. The skin glistened in the sun as I bit into the succulent dark meat all aglow with hints of star anise and honey. The sensation was pure magic. Since that day, my love affair with duck has remained unwavering and steadfast.

In the West, duck is considered a luxury and is often reserved for special occasions. It's also viewed by some people as intimidating to cook, since ducks have more subcutaneous fat and a thicker skin than other poultry. Many people in Asia think the same, but the truth is that duck is rather forgiving – it can be cooked in just about any manner, and it will still yield that unique flavour prized by the cognoscenti and duck lovers like me.

> That said, some of the more elaborate preparations are some of the most celebrated.

It's no secret, for example, that Peking duck is rather involved and complex. Obviously, this is a restaurant dish and, like many restaurant dishes that have stood the test of time, a great Peking duck requires excellent ingredients and a skilled chef. The best I've ever eaten is at Liqun Roast Duck Restaurant in Beijing, which uses fruit woods, like apricot and peach, to impart an elusive flavour. The best in Australia? It's still at Flower Drum in Melbourne: the duck meat is tender, the skin crisp like potato crisps and it's served wrapped in warm, paper-thin Chinese pancakes with a smear of hoisin sauce and refreshing blades of spring onion. The experience is stupendous.

It is possible for us mortals to make this legendary duck at home, and I've written about it extensively in my first book, *Hong Kong Food City*. In this book, I've included a couple of other Chinese duck recipes (every region in China has a famous duck dish) that are just as delicious. The Shanxi duck (page 190) looks difficult and technique-driven, but if you split the work over two days, it's a piece of cake. The other dish is called slow-cooked boned duck with fragrant stuffing. More on that later.

Beyond China, I've included several other equally delectable duck dishes, which shouldn't be intimidating to cook either. From Thailand, there's a red duck curry with lychee (page 175), perfumed with torn makrut lime leaves. From Malaysia, there's slow-cooked duck with cumin and black pepper (page 183), an intriguing dish that speaks to me of soulful cooking. Called itik golek, meaning 'rolled duck' due to the manner of turning the duck while cooking, it's a lovely braised dish, the long cooking allowing the scents of the spices to infuse the duck. I have a feeling this dish precedes the arrival of chillies as only black pepper is included to impart the gentle heat.

From both Singapore and Malaysia, there's duck flavoured with galangal and soy sauce (page 174). Called lor ark, this braised dish is not only effortless to prepare but it's also hauntingly delicious. Its ancestry is Teochew but apparently, barring the traditional add-ons like tofu and eggs, it's nothing like the version in China. Then from Bali, there's duck betutu (page 191), an insanely delicious ceremonial dish that's fit for the gods.

> By now you've probably deduced that I'm passionate about duck; that's why I've included so many magnificent and inspiring dishes.

But I'm no different from so many people with Asian background; I think we have an affinity with duck because it is etched into our gastronomic universe. Part of the reason is because our staple grain is rice. The synergy between duck and rice has existed for hundreds, if not thousands, of years. If you've been to Bali, you'll likely remember flocks of ducks being herded into paddy fields to feed on insects and frogs. This natural cycle is prevalent in just about every Asian country, and shows why duck is so valued, and not just for its meat and eggs.

At my cooking school, I teach participants how to cook duck creatively. One of the dishes is duck with fragrant osmanthus, a tiny flower native to East Asia used in teas, syrups and rice wines. I'm also growing this delicately scented flower because of how well it complements the flavour of duck. Also used to spike Chinese rose-dew wine (gin with floral botanicals is a great substitute), it has been a revelation.

Here's a story. When I first taught my riff on the legendary eight-treasure duck with fragrant stuffing in New Zealand, everyone loved it so much that it was nicknamed 'the duck that won a thousand hearts'. It's no surprise: flavoured with star anise, five-spice and dried mandarin peel, the stuffing is a knockout, and when it's sealed inside a boned duck, the aromatics permeate the meat and the result is nothing short of swoon-worthy. But here's the catch: you need to bone the duck. Consider it an opportunity to get to know your butcher better, or to practise your knife skills. Remember, when it emerges from the oven glistening with the colour of rich caramel and a lip-smacking scent, you've made the duck that won a thousand hearts and all that effort will have paid off. The recipe is on page 192.

One last piece of advice: never throw away the fat. It's liquid gold! I use duck fat not only for roasting potatoes, but also in stir-fries, especially if the fat has been infused with spices. It really is the gift that keeps on giving.

DUCK BREAST WITH SWEET OSMANTHUS SAUCE AND BABY BAMBOO SHOOTS

SERVES 8

Osmanthus – a tiny fragrant flower that blooms in clusters – is slowly becoming known in the West. Native to China, it's used in perfumes, teas and other preparations including Chinese liqueurs and confections. The liqueur – kuei hua chen jiew – is sometimes sold in better Asian grocers. This dish actually uses two 'wines'. The first is a spirit made with sorghum and infused with rose petals called mei kuei lu chiew. The second is the osmanthus liqueur but if you can't find it, use osmanthus jam or syrup, or even 2 tablespoons dried osmanthus flowers (available in Chinese grocers), combined with 1 tablespoon sugar and 2 tablespoons Shaoxing wine.

Combine the ingredients for the wine marinade in a bowl. Rub the marinade all over the duck. Cover and refrigerate for at least 4 hours or overnight.

Bring a pot of water to the boil and very quickly blanch the duck breasts, in two or three batches, until the skin contracts. Drain well and pat dry.

For the vinegar wash, melt the maltose with 2 cups (500 ml) water in a small saucepan over low heat. Add both vinegars.

Brush the duck breasts well with the vinegar wash to ensure an even coating. Hang the duck on skewers or metal hooks, making sure they do not touch. Use an electric fan to dry out the skin, or leave them in a well-ventilated spot for about 4 hours. (Alternatively, you can dry the duck breasts on wire cake racks, also ensuring they do not touch.)

Meanwhile, mix the sauce ingredients together in a saucepan. Gently cook over medium-low heat for 3–5 minutes for the flavours to develop. Check the seasoning and set aside. Keep warm.

Preheat the oven to 220°C (430°F). Heat 2 tablespoons of oil in a large frying pan or wok over medium-high heat and cook the duck breasts, skin-side first, for 6–8 minutes on each side, depending on size; do this in batches if necessary. Place the duck skin-side up on a wire rack and transfer to the oven for 3 minutes to finish cooking. Remove from the oven and rest the duck for another 5 minutes.

While the duck is resting, heat the remaining tablespoon of oil in a wok or frying pan over medium-high heat. Add the bamboo shoots and edamame and fry for 1 minute. Add the spring onion, chilli, stock and soy or oyster sauce. Bring to the boil, then season.

Slice the duck breasts and serve with the sauce and vegetable mixture.

✣ Baby bamboo shoots are sold cooked in sterilised packets and edamame are available frozen.

Instead of serving the edamame whole, you can purée them to serve as a delicious cream sauce.

8 duck breasts, skin on
3 tablespoons neutral oil
600 g (1 lb 5 oz) baby bamboo shoots
400 g (14 oz) edamame (young soybeans), boiled until soft, drained
1 spring onion (scallion), finely chopped
1 red chilli, seeded and finely chopped
2–3 tablespoons chicken stock or water
1 tablespoon light soy or oyster sauce
Salt and white pepper, to taste

WINE MARINADE
⅓ cup (80 ml) mei kuei lu chiew (rose dew cooking wine)
80 g (2¾ oz) ginger, chopped, pounded and squeezed for juice
2 garlic cloves, finely chopped
2 shallots, finely chopped
1 teaspoon Chinese five-spice powder
1 teaspoon bicarbonate of soda
Salt, to taste

VINEGAR WASH
125 g (4½ oz) maltose (from Asian grocers)
1 tablespoon red rice vinegar
100 ml (3½ fl oz) white rice vinegar

SAUCE
2 tablespoons hoisin sauce
2 tablespoons osmanthus liqueur
1½ cups (375 ml) chicken stock
2 tablespoons plum sauce
½ teaspoon ground Sichuan pepper
Dash of dark soy sauce
Salt and white pepper, to taste

TEOCHEW DUCK
LOR ARK

SERVES 4–6

The Teochew (Chiu Chow) are famous for their braised dishes, and one of the best examples of the genre is their braised duck. Known as lor ark in Singapore and Penang (lor means 'to braise' and ark means 'duck'), the robust and earthy flavour of this dish is so popular that Penang Nyonyas make this regularly at home. In essence, it is nothing but a marinated duck that is poached in a master stock, but the combination of the caramel and top quality Chinese five-spice makes all the difference. One of my favourite places to eat this dish was at Lim Seng Lee Duck Rice Restaurant Singapore. My version is easier and even more delicious.

1 × 2.4 kg (5 lb 5 oz) duck or 8 duck Marylands (thigh, with the drumstick attached)
½ teaspoon Chinese five-spice powder (top-quality)
Pinch of salt, or to taste
100 g (3½ oz) galangal, thinly sliced
3 tablespoons caster (superfine) sugar
3 large garlic cloves, bruised
2 star anise
5–8 cm (2–3¼ inch) piece cinnamon
1 tablespoon thick dark soy sauce (kecap asin; see note page 37)
2 tablespoons light soy sauce
6 hard-boiled eggs, peeled (optional)
Steamed rice or congee, to serve

CHILLI SAUCE
6 long red chillies
2 garlic cloves, peeled
100 ml (3½ fl oz) rice vinegar
Caster (superfine) sugar, to taste
Fine salt, to taste

For the chilli sauce, blend all the ingredients in a blender until smooth. Add a little water to dilute it if you find the flavours too strong or pungent.

TRADITIONAL METHOD

Clean and wipe the duck dry. Rub the Chinese five-spice and a pinch or two of salt over the skin and inside the cavity. Put 2 slices of galangal in the cavity and place in the refrigerator to marinate for at least an hour, or preferably overnight.

Spread the sugar over the base of a heavy-based pan large enough to hold the duck. Place over medium-high heat and when the sugar begins to caramelise, remove from heat immediately and add the garlic, star anise, cinnamon and 1 cup (250 ml) water (be careful; hot caramel will spit).

Add the remaining ingredients, lower the duck into the same pan and add enough water to cover. Bring to the boil, skimming any impurities that rise to the surface, then reduce to a simmer. Add eggs, if using, to simmer in the sauce for about 15 minutes, then remove the eggs and leave to cool.

Continue to simmer, basting every so often, for 1–1.5 hours or until the duck is tender and the sauce is syrupy. Remove the duck, then, when cool enough to handle, cut through the bone into bite-sized pieces. Transfer to a platter, halve the eggs and add to the platter, then pour some of the sauce over. Serve with chilli sauce and rice or congee.

MY METHOD

I use duck Marylands. Rub the five-spice and salt over the duck legs and put them in a baking dish. Cover and refrigerate overnight to marinate. When ready to cook, caramelise the sugar in a saucepan as above, adding the garlic, star anise, cinnamon and water following the same method. Add the remaining ingredients and another litre (4 cups) water, bring to the boil, then carefully pour the liquid over the duck legs, leaving the skin exposed above the surface. Bake in a 180°C (350°F) oven for 1.5–2 hours until the duck is tender and the skin crisp. Skim off the fat and place the tray over a flame to reduce until the sauce is syrupy. Season the sauce with salt to taste. Serve.

✖ You don't need the eggs in my method. Goose prepared this way is equally delicious.

THAI RED DUCK CURRY WITH LYCHEE

SERVES 4

The combination of red curry paste and Chinese roast duck is said to have originated in Bangkok, where large numbers of Chinese settled. The two ingredients combine beautifully in this aromatic dish, a staple of Thai cookery. Making your own curry paste can seem daunting, but it's a breeze with a food processor or a blender, and the results are far more rewarding and complex than using jarred paste. It also freezes well. While this recipe suggests duck, this curry is also excellent with white fish, chicken or tofu.

For the red curry paste, cut the dried chillies into 2 cm (¾ inch) pieces, then soak them in a bowl of warm water until softened. Drain, then chop finely. Finely grind the coriander seeds, cumin and peppercorns with a spice grinder or mortar and pestle. Add the chilli, spices and remaining ingredients to a food processor and blend to a smooth paste, adding a couple of tablespoons of water if necessary.

To make the curry, add the oil and coconut cream to a medium saucepan over medium heat and stir until the coconut cream splits (3–5 minutes). Add 3 tablespoons of red curry paste (you can freeze the rest) and stir until the paste takes on a deeper colour and is nicely fragrant (3–4 minutes).

Stir in the fish sauce and palm sugar, and stir for another minute, or until the pungency of the fish sauce and the sweetness of the sugar kicks in, then add the coconut milk. Increase heat to high, bring to the boil, then add the duck, eggplant, chillies and lime leaves. Simmer for another minute, then stir in the lychees and pineapple to warm through. Check the seasoning – the curry should taste spicy, hot and sweet, so adjust to taste with fish sauce and palm sugar as needed.

Serve curry with steamed rice and top with Thai basil leaves.

✱ To roast shrimp paste, wrap the preferred quantity in foil and place it in an oven at 120°C (250°F) for 10–15 minutes.

2 tablespoons vegetable or coconut oil
200 ml (7 fl oz) coconut cream
2 tablespoons fish sauce, or to taste
1 tablespoon shaved palm sugar, or to taste
350 ml (12 fl oz) coconut milk
½ Chinese roast duck, bones removed, cut into bite-sized pieces
2 apple eggplant (aubergine), sliced
1 handful pea eggplant
2 long red chillies, halved, seeds removed and sliced
4 makrut lime leaves
½ cup lychees (100 g), seeds removed
½ cup (80 g) chopped pineapple
Steamed rice and Thai basil leaves, to serve

RED CURRY PASTE
10–15 dried long red chillies
1 tablespoon coriander seeds, roasted
1 teaspoon cumin seeds, roasted
1 teaspoon white peppercorns
4 shallots (eschalots) or ½ red onion, chopped
6 garlic cloves, chopped
4 birdseye chillies (optional)
1 tablespoon galangal, chopped
1 lemongrass stalk (white part only), finely chopped
1 tablespoon coriander root, chopped
1 teaspoon shrimp paste, roasted (see note)
Pared zest of ½ makrut lime, chopped
1 teaspoon salt

GRILLED CHICKEN WITH SAVOURY COCONUT SAUCE
AYAM PERCIK

In Malaysia, the state of Kelantan on the north-east coast of the peninsula is best known for its beautiful beaches and laid-back lifestyle. Isolated from the rest of the country several decades ago, Kelantan is the most conservative state, although the food is anything but. Coconut milk reigns supreme and sugar takes on more than a cursory bow in dishes that feel vaguely Thai (the state was once part of Thailand).

More importantly, the state has created a dish that's both seductive and sublime: ayam percik. In Malay, 'percik' means to splash and is pronounced 'per chayk'. Ayam percik may not be as glamourous as the satays that grace the pointy end of Malaysia Airlines cabins, but it's just about the most fragrant chicken dish you'll ever come across.

Ayam percik (pictured on page 178) is cooked over coconut embers and its scent is enough to drive anyone crazy with hunger. It pops up at pasar malam (night markets) and roadside stalls and is nothing more than a marinated chicken grilled over an open fire. What sets it apart is the sauce that's used for basting the bird. Fragrant and smoky, the dish became so popular that it swept through the country like the proverbial wildfire and is now served at Kuala Lumpur's high-end restaurants.

The flavours and cooking technique have changed over the years. The sauce of the original Kelantan version is much sweeter and packed with lemongrass and coconut milk. Most cooks these days prefer a spicier twist to the original, adding cardamom, cloves and chillies and calling it ayam percik utara ('utara' means north). I have to say that I prefer this spicier version.

As with all simple recipes, it's the details that matter. For starters, it's best to butterfly the chicken for even grilling, even though street stalls traditionally offer barbecued legs wedged between bamboo sticks. Some vendors also cook the chicken legs in the sauce before grilling. This certainly speeds up the cooking process but I find it robs the dish of its soul.

There are two other factors to consider: you need to marinate the bird well ahead of grilling and you need to make a sauce that's not only creamy but also a little spicy and tangy, with none of the chilli heat. This is done by using candlenuts to thicken the sauce and an unusual ingredient called asam keping (or asam gelugor) to offset the sweetness of the sauce. Asam keping is a dried sour fruit of the mangosteen family. It's somewhat difficult to find; at a pinch, you can use tamarind. The recipe is quite flexible, so adjust the hot, spicy and sour notes to suit your palate.

Once you've made the sauce, the next step is to use some quality charcoal to 'perfume' the chicken with its subtle smoky aroma. In Malaysia, most cooks use coconut charcoal. In Australia, I prefer to use binchotan, the Japanese white charcoal made from oak. By all means use your electric grill or even roast the chicken in the oven, but it won't taste quite the same — nothing beats the flavour of chicken charred over flame. Once you've got the fire going, let it reduce to glowing embers before popping the chicken on. I like to give it a slow char over low–medium heat so the chicken remains succulent while still forming a crust with the help of frequent basting.

Just to gild the lily, ayam percik is served with nasi kerabu, an exquisite rice salad tinted blue with butterfly pea flower and packed with herbs and greens such as young cashew and turmeric leaves. These are difficult to source, but I've come up with a recipe that's pretty close to the real thing. I also like to serve it alongside a refreshing tomato and cucumber salad with a squeeze of lime and chopped fresh coriander. Sit back, grab a beer or a wine and enjoy your summer — and this great chicken. Happy days! Start this recipe a day ahead to marinate the chicken.

1 × 1.8 kg (4 lb) chicken
¼ cup (60 ml) neutral oil
2 lemongrass stalks (white part only), sliced
2 pieces asam keping (see note)
2 makrut lime leaves, plus extra to serve
2 cloves
3 cardamom pods
1 tablespoon sugar
400 ml (14 fl oz) coconut milk
Salt, to taste

MARINADE
1–2 teaspoons chilli powder, to taste
2 teaspoons ground turmeric
1 teaspoon caster (superfine) sugar
Salt, to taste

SPICE PASTE
8–10 dried chillies
4 candlenuts
3 garlic cloves, peeled
5 shallots, coarsely chopped
1 lemongrass stalks (white part only), thinly sliced
3 cm (1¼ inch) piece ginger, coarsely chopped
3 cm (1¼ inch) piece galangal, coarsely chopped
5 shallots (eschalots)

To butterfly the chicken, place it breast-side down and use a pair of poultry shears to cut along either side of the backbone. Open out the chicken, pressing down on the breastbone to flatten the bird. Cut through the cartilage from the neck end and, using your fingers, run along the sides of the breastbone and tease it out. Trim off and discard any fat. Wipe the chicken dry and make a few slashes on the thickest part of the legs and breasts.

Combine the marinade ingredients in a bowl. Sprinkle the marinade over the chicken, place it inside a large resealable plastic bag and seal. Massage well and place in the fridge to marinate overnight.

To make the spice paste, soak the chillies in hot water until soft, then drain, reserving the soaking liquid. Coarsely chop the chillies, then grind in a mortar and pestle with the remaining ingredients until a coarse paste forms, adding some reserved chilli-soaking liquid if necessary.

Heat the oil in a saucepan over medium–high heat. Add spice paste, sliced lemongrass, asam keping, lime leaves, cloves and cardamom and stir for 5–6 minutes until fragrant. Add the sugar, coconut milk and 1 cup (250 ml) water. Reduce the heat and simmer, stirring now and then, for 5–7 minutes until the sauce thickens slightly. Season, and discard the lemongrass. Leave the sauce to cool.

Take the chicken out of the fridge to come to room temperature. Brush off the marinade.

Prepare a charcoal grill for cooking. When the glowing coals have a light coating of ash, brush the grill with oil and add the chicken, skin-side down. Cook, basting with the sauce and turning occasionally, for 35–40 minutes until the chicken is nicely charred and the juices run clear – test by inserting a skewer into the thickest part. Rest for 10 minutes, then cut the chicken into pieces, garnish with makrut lime leaves, and serve with the salad below, or your favourite salad. Offer any leftover sauce to go with the chook.

✖ Asam keping, also called asam gelugor (*Garcinia atroviridis*), is a fruit belonging to the mangosteen family. It is sold sliced and dried in Asian grocers. It acts as a souring agent with none of the sweet undertones associated with tamarind, and won't cloud a soup or sauce. If you can't find it, lime juice will suffice.

Sugar in marinades burns easily, so watch carefully when grilling the chicken. If pressed, you can roast in a hot oven, basting regularly.

KERABU RICE SALAD
500 g (1 lb 2 oz) steamed medium-grain white rice
1 lemongrass stalk (white part only), thinly sliced
4 snake beans, thinly sliced
1 golden shallot, thinly sliced
1 small cucumber, seeded and cubed
4–5 tablespoons roasted desiccated coconut
10 mint leaves, thinly sliced
6 makrut lime leaves, thinly sliced
15 Thai basil leaves, thinly sliced
15 sprigs coriander leaves, picked
10 Vietnamese mint, finely sliced
Pinch of caster (superfine) sugar, or to taste
Pinch of salt, or to taste
Handful of shredded cabbage (optional)
Handful of bean sprouts (optional)

Combine all the ingredients, except the cabbage and bean sprouts, in a large bowl. Toss to combine, then season to taste and serve, topping with the cabbage and bean sprouts, if using.

CHICKEN WITH BLACK BEAN SAUCE

SERVES 2–4

This dish is a take on the ubiquitous chicken with black bean sauce you find in suburban Australian Chinese restaurants. This version, inspired partly by crisp-skinned pipa duck, is a more refined, luxurious spin featuring a boned whole chicken that's roasted before the sauce is drizzled over it. A dish to love for its sheer beauty, in every sense of the word.

1 × 1.8 kg (4 lb) chicken

MARINADE
¼ cup (60 ml) Shaoxing wine
80 g (2¾ oz) ginger, chopped and pounded to extract 2 tablespoons juice, juice strained
2 tablespoons neutral oil
1 tablespoon light soy sauce
½ teaspoon Chinese five-spice powder

BLACK BEAN SAUCE
1 tablespoon neutral oil
1 onion, finely diced
2 garlic cloves, finely chopped
1 red capsicum (pepper), finely diced
1 spring onion (scallion), thinly sliced, plus extra to serve
2 tablespoons fermented black beans, rinsed and lightly crushed
1 cup (250 ml) chicken stock
2 teaspoons light soy sauce
1 teaspoon dark soy sauce
1 teaspoon cornflour (cornstarch), mixed with 2 tablespoons water
Salt and white pepper, to taste

First, bone the chicken (or ask your butcher to do it for you). Turn the bird breast-side down, and cut along one side of the spine from neck to tail. With short, sharp strokes of your knife and keeping the knife close to the bone, separate the meat from the carcass, working towards the wing joint. Find the wishbone and remove. Find and cut through the ball-and-socket joint connecting the wing bone to the carcass, then continue cutting the meat away from the bone, working your way down to the leg. Find the joint connecting the leg bone to the carcass and cut through it. The wing, thigh joints and drumsticks should be separated from the carcass but still attached to the skin. Repeat with the other side, then gradually trim along the breastbone to remove the frame from the flesh. Cut off the wing tips, then holding a thigh bone from the flesh side, scrape the meat from the bone with the knife, then carefully cut through the tendons and knee joint. Repeat with the other leg. Discard frame, wing tips and thigh bones or save them to make stock.

For the marinade, combine all the ingredients in a bowl. Place the chicken in a baking tray, rub it all over with the marinade and leave it for 20 minutes to marinate. Meanwhile, preheat oven to 180°C (350°F).

Roast the chicken for 60–80 minutes or until the juices run clear when a thigh is pierced with a skewer.

While the chicken is roasting, make the black bean sauce. Heat a wok or frying pan over high heat until a drop of water evaporates within a second or two. Add the oil and onion, swirl it around until it softens, then add the garlic and capsicum. Stir-fry for 10 seconds, add spring onion and black beans, stir-fry for 10 more seconds, then add the chicken stock and the soy sauces and bring to the boil. Reduce the heat to medium and simmer for 8–10 minutes to allow the flavours to develop, adding more stock if it is reducing too quickly. When it reaches a light sauce consistency, stir in the cornflour slurry and season to taste. Remove from the heat and set aside until you're ready to serve.

Allow the chicken to rest for 5 minutes before cutting it into serving portions and arranging it on a platter. Add any roasting juices to the black bean sauce, warm if necessary, then drizzle the sauce over the chicken. Top with spring onion to serve.

BALINESE-STYLE ROAST SPATCHCOCK WITH GLUTINOUS RICE

SERVES 10

With a wonderful interplay between the richness of the coconut milk and perfume from the spices, this is a dish I consider to be fantastic eating. It incorporates Eastern ingredients and cooking techniques while accommodating Western sensibilities without compromising on flavour or integrity. The recipe looks long but it can be easily achieved if you break it over two days.

This dish is not found among traditional recipes but it is inspired by Southeast Asian flavours. The spice paste can be frozen to create other dishes using duck, quail and game. Kencur is aromatic ginger often sold in powdered form in Indonesian grocers. Spatchcocks (baby chickens) should be available at select butchers or poulterers. Start this recipe a day ahead to soak the rice for the stuffing. The flavour of these exquisite birds is even better if they are slowly roasted over a charcoal fire.

Neutral oil, for frying
2 cups (500 ml) coconut milk
10 spatchcocks (baby chickens), 400 g (14 oz) each, boned (see page 181)

RICE STUFFING
500 g (1 lb 2 oz) glutinous rice, soaked overnight
⅓ cup (80 ml) neutral oil
1 large onion, diced
1 tablespoon black peppercorns, crushed
½ cup (70 g) garlic, chopped
½ cup (25 g) coriander (cilantro) roots, chopped
1 teaspoon ground kencur (aromatic ginger)
Salt, to taste

SPICE PASTE
5–6 shallots (eschalots), about 220 g (7¾ oz), peeled
4 large garlic cloves, peeled
3 lemongrass stalks (white part only), thinly sliced
6 candlenuts, crushed
5 cm (2 inch) piece fresh turmeric, sliced (or 1½ teaspoons ground turmeric)
5 cm (2 inch) piece kencur root (or 1½ teaspoons ground kencur)
5 cm (2 inch) piece ginger, peeled
1 teaspoon black pepper
2 large red chillies
3 birdseye chillies
1 teaspoon coriander seeds
2 teaspoons shrimp paste
5 makrut lime leaves, thinly sliced
1 tablespoon salt, or to taste

For the rice stuffing, drain the soaked rice well and transfer to a cake tin, or a steamer basket lined with baking paper, and steam, covered, over a wok of boiling water for 20 minutes until tender, fluffing rice after 10 minutes so it cooks evenly. Transfer the rice to a large bowl and cool completely.

Heat the oil in a frying pan over medium-high heat. Fry the onion, crushed peppercorns, garlic, coriander roots and ground kencur until fragrant (about 5 minutes). Mix with the cooked rice and leave to cool.

For the spice paste, blend or grind the ingredients, except the lime leaves and salt, to form a smooth paste. Add the sliced lime leaves and salt and mix well.

Heat 3 tablespoons of oil in a frying pan over medium heat and fry the paste until golden and fragrant (about 5 minutes). Stir in the coconut milk and add more salt to taste. Leave the marinade to cool.

Rub the cavity and skin of the chickens using the spice paste as a marinade. (For optimum flavour, it's best to refrigerate the marinated birds for at least a couple of hours or overnight.

Preheat the oven to 180–190°C (350–375°F).

Spoon the cooled rice mixture into the birds' cavities. Use a wooden or metal skewer to secure the cavities.

Heat 2 tablespoons of oil in a frying pan over medium-high heat. Working in batches, sear the birds in the hot oil for 4–5 minutes. Transfer the chickens to a large baking tray, or use two if necessary. Roast, basting regularly, for 30–40 minutes depending on size, until the chickens are cooked through and the skin is crisp.

Pour any remaining marinade into a pan with 1 cup (250 ml) water and bring to the boil. Mix in any roasting juices and serve as a sauce with the chicken.

✤ For an attractive presentation, you can wrap the seared birds in banana leaves and generously coat with the leftover marinade before roasting. Serve the wrapped birds on individual plates and encourage diners to unwrap the leaves and enjoy the heavenly aroma.

SLOW-COOKED DUCK WITH CUMIN AND BLACK PEPPER
ITIK GOLEK

SERVES 2–4

If there's one dish that encapsulates the beauty of Malay food, this must be it. A deceptively simple recipe from Kedah state – near the Thai border – its beauty lies in its exquisite, savoury sauce made from nothing more than egg, potato, cumin, pepper, tamarind and fresh coconut milk. It is a dish served during festivals like Hari Raya. Not much is known about its origin, but I suspect that it predates the arrival of chilli. This recipe is from Zakiah Hanum, a friend who was not only a committed preserver of the traditional foods of Malaysia but also a custodian of Malay culture.

For the spice paste, grind the cumin finely with a spice grinder or a mortar and pestle, then coarsely grind the peppercorns. Add a tablespoon of water and stir to form a smooth paste. Combine the paste with the onion and garlic. Heat the oil in a saucepan over medium-high heat, stir in the spice paste and reduce the heat to medium. Fry, stirring frequently, until aromatic and the oil separates (7–8 minutes).

Add the egg and potato. Add salt to taste, then stir-fry for another minute. Transfer to a plate to cool. (Note: this step can be done a day ahead; just cover and refrigerate overnight.)

Remove any loose fat and giblets from the duck's cavity, and cut off the oil glands from the parson's nose. Rinse the duck, wiping the bird inside and out, then dry it with paper towel. Stuff the duck with half the spice mix and, if you like, secure the opening with a wooden or metal skewer, tied with string if necessary.

Place the tamarind pulp in a bowl and cover with 2 cups (500 ml) warm water. Soak for 20 minutes, then, with your fingers, mash and squeeze the tamarind to extract as much juice as possible. Strain and set aside.

Add the coconut milk, tamarind water, 800 ml (28 fl oz) water, the remaining spice mix and the salt to a saucepan large enough to hold the duck. Bring to the boil, stirring frequently, then lower the duck in, submerging it.

Bring back to the boil, then reduce the heat to low and simmer until the bird is tender (about 1.5 hours). Transfer the duck to a plate until cool enough to handle before pulling out the skewers, cutting the string and spooning out the stuffing. Preheat the oven to 200°C (400°F).

Add the stuffing to the saucepan, increase heat to low-medium and simmer for 10–15 minutes, stirring occasionally, until reduced to a sauce consistency.

Meanwhile, roast the duck for 10–15 minutes to crisp up the skin. Serve with sauce and rice or roti jala.

1 hard-boiled egg, finely chopped
1 small potato, boiled and crushed
1 × 2.5 kg (5 lb 8 oz) duck
100 g (3½ oz) tamarind pulp
1.2 litres (2 lb 10 fl oz) milk from 2 grated coconuts
1 teaspoon salt, or to taste
Steamed rice or roti jala (page 108), to serve

SPICE PASTE
55 g (2 oz) cumin seeds, roasted
3 tablespoons whole black peppercorns
1 onion, finely chopped
1 garlic bulb, peeled and finely chopped
¼ cup (60 ml) neutral oil

SERVES 4

ROAST STUFFED SPATCHCOCK WITH DAIKON

I've read volumes about the variety of edible mushrooms in France and Italy. In fact, I've made it a mission of mine to check out mushroom stands whenever I'm in Europe. But little did I know that Yunnan province has an abundance of mushrooms, too. On one misty morning in Kunming a few years ago, I was mesmerised by the sight of porcini, morels and chicken of the woods at a local market. 'How do locals eat them?' I asked my guide. The answer: in a stir-fry or soup. If that wasn't all that surprising, discovering that Yunnan exports these prized mushrooms to the food halls of Paris and Tokyo certainly was.

This recipe uses shiitake and porcini mushrooms – both found in China – stuffed into a boned chicken, which is then glazed with a traditional Chinese glaze. The result is similar to some of the Chinese-inspired roast chicken dishes I've found in Chinese American cookbooks, except this is more of a special-occasion dish on account of the fact the chicken is boned before it's stuffed. Try it with whatever mushrooms you can get your hands on.

4 spatchcocks (baby chickens), about 400 g/14 oz each, boned (see method on page 181)
Thinly sliced chives or chopped coriander, to serve
Spring onion oil (optional; see page 198), to serve

STUFFING
5 dried shiitake mushrooms
½ cup (10 g) dried porcini mushrooms
200 g (7 oz) steamed medium-grain white rice (about 70 g/2½ oz raw)
4 shallots (eschalots), finely chopped
3 spring onions (scallions) thinly sliced
3 garlic cloves, finely chopped
60 g (2¼ oz) ginger, finely chopped
1 tablespoon brandy or mei kuei lu chiew (rose dew cooking wine)
1 teaspoon Chinese five spice powder
Salt and white pepper, to taste

SAUCE
2 tablespoons neutral oil
6 garlic cloves, thinly sliced
3 shallots (eschalots), finely chopped
2 cups (500 ml) chicken stock
150 ml (5 fl oz) porcini soaking liquid (reserved from the stuffing)
100 ml (3½ fl oz) Shaoxing wine
2 tablespoons light soy sauce
1 teaspoon dark soy sauce
Splash of brandy
1 tablespoon butter
2 cups (350 g) daikon (white radish) diced, blanched and refreshed

For the stuffing, soak the dried mushrooms in two separate bowls of hot water for 20 minutes. Drain and squeeze out excess water (reserve the porcini water), discard the stems, then slice the caps thinly. Add the mushrooms to a bowl with the remaining ingredients, toss to combine, then with the spatchcocks skin-side down, divide the stuffing among the birds, laying it down the centre. Fold the flesh and skin over to cover, then seal the spatchcocks with skewers.

For the sauce, combine all the ingredients except for the daikon in a saucepan and bring to the boil. Reduce the heat to low, add the daikon and simmer for 5 minutes. Meanwhile, preheat the oven to 180°C (350°F).

Ladle some sauce over the spatchcocks to coat evenly, then place them on a wire rack, resting on their sides (wing-side down), set over a roasting pan. Roast for 30–40 minutes, ladling with more sauce every 10 minutes, until golden brown and cooked through.

Cut the spatchcock into serving pieces and serve with remaining sauce on top and spring onion oil, if using.

✿ Mei kuei lu chiew liquor, which translates as 'rose dew wine', is made with sorghum and rose petals.

BRAISED CHICKEN WITH LEMONGRASS
GA XAO XA OT

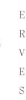

A classic and popular South Vietnamese dish that's loaded with flavour and simple to prepare. When I first ate this quick stir-fry in Ho Chi Minh City years ago, I was blown away by the simple presentation and sophisticated flavours. Who would have thought a combination of lemongrass, fish and sugar could be such an incredible bomb?

It has as many versions as there are cooks. Some use coconut water and turmeric, others do not, but all of them are great so long as the chicken pieces remain succulent and scrumptious. I prefer chicken thigh over breast here; if you do use chicken breast, just reduce the cooking time.

Combine minced lemongrass with garlic, chilli, fish sauce and sugar in a bowl. Add the chicken and mix well. Cover and refrigerate for 2 hours, or preferably overnight, to marinate.

Heat the oil in a wok over medium-high heat, and stir-fry the bruised lemongrass until fragrant and just beginning to brown. Add the marinated chicken and stir-fry for 3-5 minutes, or until the pieces are white and opaque.

Add the onion, soy sauce and ½ cup (125 ml) water, reduce the heat to low and simmer for 5–7 minutes until the liquid is reduced to a sauce consistency. Season to taste.

Transfer to a plate, scatter with Vietnamese mint or coriander and serve with steamed rice.

3 lemongrass stalks (white part only), 1 stalk minced, the other 2 bruised
3 garlic cloves, finely minced
1 long red chilli, seeds removed, finely chopped
2–3 tablespoons fish sauce, or to taste
1 tablespoon caster (superfine) sugar
500 g (1 lb 2 oz) boneless, skinless chicken thigh fillets, cut into bite-sized pieces
2 tablespoons neutral oil
1 onion, cut into wedges
1 teaspoon dark soy sauce
Salt and white pepper, to taste
Vietnamese mint or coriander (cilantro) leaves, to serve
Steamed rice, to serve

MY MOTHER'S ROAST CHICKEN

SERVES 4

There's a story behind this family favourite. Until we had our own restaurant, my mum worked as a cook for the British during the colonial period in Malaysia. She learnt to cook many things, including trifle, bread-and-butter pudding, cakes and this not-so-English roast chicken. I don't know when she added soy sauce to this dish, but I think it gives it a distinctive Chinese flair.

In fact, there's a whole genre of this style of cooking. If you're ever in Kuala Lumpur, Hainanese cooks still offer cross-cultural dishes at the Coliseum Café. In Hong Kong, it's called see yauh sai chan, meaning 'soy sauce Western'. I guess the process of cooks experimenting with flavours just never stops. Please try it. I know very well how delicious and comforting it is.

- 1 × 2 kg (4 lb 8 oz) chicken
- 3 garlic cloves, crushed, plus 1 whole garlic clove
- 2 onions, chopped
- 2–3 potatoes (Dutch cream or Desiree), peeled and cut into small chunks
- ¼ cup (60 ml) olive oil
- Salt and ground black pepper, to taste
- 1 large knob of butter
- ½ cup (125 ml) chicken stock, plus extra for deglazing
- Sharp green salad, to serve

MUSTARD GLAZE

- 1 tablespoon English mustard
- 2 tablespoons light soy sauce
- 1 teaspoon dark soy sauce
- 1 tablespoon Worcestershire sauce
- Pinch of sugar

Remove the chicken from the fridge 2 hours before cooking to come to room temperature. Heat oven to 220°C (425°F).

For the mustard glaze, place the ingredients in a bowl and mix well.

Place the chicken in a flameproof roasting pan and rub it all over with the crushed garlic. Slip the garlic clove into the cavity. Brush the chicken all over, including the cavity, with the mustard glaze.

Scatter the onion and potato around the chicken, drizzle the vegetables with olive oil and season with salt and pepper.

Pour the chicken stock into the roasting pan and smear the butter over the chicken. Roast on the centre rack of the oven for 20–25 minutes, basting with the juices halfway, then reduce oven temperature to 180°C (350°F), baste once more, and roast for another 35–40 minutes or until the juices run clear when a thigh is pierced with a skewer (or the internal temperature reaches 82°C/180°F).

Transfer chicken and vegetables to a plate and rest in a warm place for 10 minutes. Meanwhile, add a splash of stock or water to the roasting pan and bring to a simmer over high heat, scraping the base of the pan.

To serve, put the bird on a chopping board and cut off the legs. Cut the legs in half between the drumsticks and thighs, remove the wings, then remove the breasts. Cut the breasts into large slices, then arrange the chicken and the vegetables on a platter. Pour the roasting juices over the top and serve immediately with a zippy salad of cucumber and greens.

✖ In our family, this roast chicken is eaten with rice and chilli sauce or spiced salt and lime juice.

FRAGRANT DUCK, SHANXI STYLE
SHANXI YA

SERVES 6–8

I think everyone knows Peking duck or Cantonese roast duck, but I'm not sure many people have heard of Shanxi-style fragrant duck, an absolutely delicious recipe I found in *Chinese Home-style Cooking*, a cookbook published by China's Foreign Language Press. The duck is first marinated, then steamed until tender, before it is deep-fried to a rich mahogany colour.

It might look involved, but it is actually a cinch to make when you break the recipe into two days – one for marinating, the next for finishing it off. Serve it with the Sichuan pepper-salt dip, and you'll find yourself making this again and again.

1 × 2.2 (5 lb) kg duck
Neutral oil, for deep-frying
Steamed or baked mantou buns, to serve

MARINADE
⅓ cup (80 ml) Shaoxing wine
100 ml (3½ fl oz) light soy sauce
1¼ tablespoons ground Sichuan pepper
1 teaspoon ground star anise
½ teaspoon ground cloves
1 teaspoon ground cinnamon
2 tablespoons sweet bean sauce (fermented flour sauce – tian mian jiang)
2 spring onions (scallions), thinly sliced, plus extra to serve
1 tablespoon finely shredded ginger

SICHUAN PEPPER-SALT DIP
1 tablespoon Sichuan pepper
⅓ cup (40 g) sea salt

To make the Sichuan pepper-salt dip, heat a dry wok over medium heat and add the peppercorns. Toss for 30 seconds or until the peppercorns are fragrant and begin to pop. Transfer to a bowl. Return the wok to the heat and add the salt. Cook, stirring constantly, until it begins to turn golden. Add to the peppercorns, allow to cool, then grind in a spice grinder until a fine powder.

For the marinade, combine all the ingredients in a bowl and mix well.

Remove any loose fat and giblets from the duck's cavity and cut off the oil glands from the parson's nose. Wash the duck and wipe it dry, then rub the marinade all over the duck. Refrigerate for 4 hours, or preferably overnight, to marinate.

Place the duck in a heatproof dish and place in a large steamer set over a wok of boiling water. Cover and steam for 2 hours, topping up with hot water as needed, or until duck is tender.

Remove the duck, leave to cool and drain well, then wipe dry with paper towel and cut the duck in half through the bone lengthways.

Add oil to a depth of 5 cm (2 inches) to a wok or deep-fryer and heat it to 180°C (350°F). Carefully lower the duck into the hot oil skin-side up and deep-fry until golden (8–10 minutes; if you like, you can cut the duck in half lengthways, then split in two before frying, which will make it quicker). Remove, and drain on a wire rack or paper towels.

Cut the duck through the bone into bite-sized pieces and serve with the Sichuan pepper-salt dip and steamed or baked mantou.

BALINESE ROAST DUCK
BEBEK BETUTU

Duck (bebek in Balinese) is considered by the Balinese to be a symbol of wisdom because, like the turtle, it's able to survive on land and water. And bebek betutu (betutu meaning 'to roast meat') is considered a rather prestigious dish, for it is often served to and eaten by the Hindu priest. Traditionally the duck is wrapped in banana or cassava leaves and baked in a pit, though nowadays professional Balinese cooks use a wood-fired oven to achieve that distinctively smoked aroma.

Although not as famous as the Balinese suckling pig, duck betutu usually known by its Indonesian name, babi guling, and is a favourite with visitors and locals alike. Warung Agus restaurant in West Melbourne serves a fantastic quail betutu. Chicken is also a delicious alternative. Recipe courtesy of *The Serai* in Bali.

Remove any loose fat and giblets from the duck's cavity and cut off the oil glands from the parson's nose. Rinse the duck, wiping the bird inside and out, then dry it with paper towel.

For the spice paste, blend or grind all the ingredients, except the lime leaves and salt, to a smooth paste. Add the lime leaves and salt and mix well.

Rub the duck well inside and out with the spice paste, filling the cavity with the remainder. Secure the opening with a wooden or metal skewer.

Preheat the oven to 160°C (315°F). Wrap the duck with banana leaves or greaseproof paper and roast for 3 hours or until the juices run clear when a thigh is pierced with a skewer. Unwrap the duck, increase the oven temperature to 190°C (375°F), and roast for 20 minutes until nicely golden. (Alternatively, you can steam the duck, wrapped, for 1.5 hours, then roast it as above until crisp; just be sure to save any juices from steaming.)

Carve the duck as desired and serve with the sauce from the cavity and any roasting juices.

1 × 2 kg (4 lb 8 oz) duck (preferably the Pekin variety), or 6 duck Marylands
Banana leaves or greaseproof paper for wrapping

SPICE PASTE
5–6 shallots (eschalots, about 220 g/7¾ oz), peeled
4 large garlic cloves, peeled
3 lemongrass stalks, thinly sliced
6 candlenuts, crushed
5 cm (2 inch) piece fresh turmeric, sliced, or 1½ teaspoons ground turmeric
5 cm (2 inch) piece kencur root (aromatic ginger) or 1½ teaspoons ground kencur
5 cm (2 inch) piece ginger
1 teaspoon black peppercorns
2 long red chillies
3 birdseye chillies
1 teaspoon coriander seeds
2 teaspoons belacan (shrimp paste)
¼ cup (60 ml) neutral oil
5 makrut lime leaves, thinly sliced
1 tablespoon salt, or to taste

SERVES 8–10

SLOW-COOKED DUCK WITH FRAGRANT STUFFING — THE DUCK THAT WON 1000 HEARTS

Also known as eight-jewel stuffed duck, this recipe comes from Heong Sok, the chef at my family's restaurant in Malaysia. Although the Cantonese (chef Heong included) claim that this dish is their creation, in truth it is from the Eastern school. Yuan Mei, the 18th-century gourmet, has a detailed recipe from Hangzhou in his cookbook *Suiyuan Shidan*. Over the years, this celebrated presentation has remained a sentimental favourite with all Chinese. This is due partly to the superb flavour and the number eight, representing the eight Immortals of Taoism, the eight paths to happiness and the eight symbols of Buddha.

This recipe can appear daunting at first, but with care and organisation it's very achievable, and more than worth the effort. Here are a few pointers. It is best to split the task over two days. On the day before serving this duck, soak the rice and soak and trim the mushrooms. Retain the mushroom soaking water for the duck stock.

When it comes to boning the duck, the Chinese method would be to bone it from the neck. This method is called tunnel boning, and requires immense patience and skill. But you can always bone the duck from the back, then down to the breast. Refrigerate the boned duck, and make the stock with the bones. If you're using fresh chestnuts (dried chestnuts may be used if fresh are not available), split them or make an incision, then boil and skin them while the water is still warm.

On the following day, make the stuffing, cook it, cool it, then fill the duck and sew it up before frying and roasting it. This is a little break from tradition, in which the duck is deep-fried, then steamed until tender. But I think it's easier, and just as effective, to deep-fry the bird, then roast it.

Should you decide not to use glutinous rice, barley is a lovely substitute. As a variation, I use half black and half white glutinous rice for texture and interest. Remember to have a trussing needle and kitchen twine ready. Frozen peeled chestnuts are sold in Chinese grocers.

30 g (1 oz) dried shiitake mushrooms (about 6–8)
1 × 2.4 kg (5 lb 5 oz) duck
Splash of Shaoxing wine
1 teaspoon Yuen Chun brand thick black soy sauce, or any thick dark soy sauce (kecap asin; see page 37)
1 teaspoon caster (superfine) sugar, plus extra to taste
1 cup (250 ml) neutral oil (if you plan to sear the duck before roasting)
1 star anise
Splash of light soy sauce
1 tablespoon cornflour (cornstarch) or potato flour, mixed with 2 tablespoons water

DUCK STOCK
1 onion
2.5 cm (1 inch) ginger, bruised
2 slices dried mandarin peel
2 star anise

STUFFING
1½ cups (280 g) glutinous rice, soaked in plenty of water for at least 4 hours or overnight
¼ cup (60 ml) neutral oil
2 spring onions (scallions), finely chopped
2 garlic cloves, finely chopped
2 thin slices of ginger, finely chopped
2 slices dried mandarin peel
2 star anise
100 g (3½ oz) minced pork
3 links lap cheong (Chinese sausage), sliced into 3 cm (1¼ inch) coins (see page 37)
10 chestnuts (about 120 g/4¼ oz), peeled, boiled and skins peeled (see opposite; can be bought frozen)
1 tablespoon dried shrimp, soaked in ½ cup (125 ml) water for 10–15 minutes, drained
1 tablespoon oyster sauce
1 teaspoon light soy sauce
1 tablespoon Shaoxing wine
Salt and white pepper, to taste

The day before, soak the dried mushrooms in a bowl of hot water for 20 minutes. Drain and squeeze out excess water (reserve the water), discard the stems, then slice the caps. Refrigerate the caps overnight.

Bone the duck from the back by following the method on page 181, taking great care not to pierce the skin; failing that, you can cut through the backbone with scissors and remove the frame, keeping the legs intact. Reserve the bones. Season and add a splash of Shaoxing in the cavity. Cover and refrigerate overnight.

Also the day before, make the duck stock by placing all the ingredients in a stock pot with the reserved bones and the mushroom soaking liquid. Cover with water and bring to the boil, skimming the surface to remove impurities. Reduce to a simmer and simmer gently for 1 hour. Cool, then refrigerate overnight.

On the day of serving, for the stuffing, drain the rice, add 1 tablespoon oil and mix it through. Steam the rice on a piece of muslin set in a steamer over simmering water for 20 minutes or until translucent.

Heat 1 tablespoon oil in a wok over medium heat, add spring onion, garlic and ginger and stir-fry for 5 minutes or until the spring onions are soft. Add the mandarin peel and star anise, stir-fry for another minute, then add the pork mince, lap cheong, chestnuts, dried shrimp, oyster sauce, soy sauce, Shaoxing, soaked and chopped mushrooms and ½ cup (125 ml) duck stock. Stir to combine, then remove from the heat and stir in the rice. Season to taste with salt and white pepper, then leave to cool.

Lay the boned duck out on a clean board. If it's been tunnel-boned, stuff the duck with the stuffing (don't overfill it, or it can burst when cooking; it should just look natural), tie the neck end firmly with string to seal, and sew up the cavity tightly. If you've butterflied the duck, place the stuffing down the centre, fold the meat and skin around it to seal, then tie it up or preferably sew together with a larding needle.

Heat the oven to 180°C (350°F). Rub the thick soy and sugar all over the duck. Heat the oil over medium-high heat in a wok or frying pan until shimmering. Add the duck carefully, turning it to seal it quickly, for no more than 2 minutes. Remove to a roasting tin double-lined with baking paper. Add 1.25 litres (42 fl oz) duck stock along with the star anise from the stock, then toss in an extra star anise. Bake for 1.5 hours, basting three or four times and skimming away excess duck fat, until the duck is tender and has taken on a mahogany hue.

Lift the duck out very carefully with the help of the baking paper, to a platter. Gently remove the paper, remove any string, and keep warm (you can place it in the still-warm oven, for example, with the door closed and the oven off).

Pour the liquid in the baking tray into a saucepan and bring to a simmer over medium-high heat. Reduce until syrupy, adding a splash of soy, Shaoxing and a touch of sugar to taste, skimming the duck fat as you go. Add the cornflour slurry and stir to thicken the sauce.

Pour the sauce over the duck to serve, or serve it separately in a sauceboat.

✤ A simple salad with snow peas or stir-fried Chinese vegetables are perfect accompaniments.

KUNG PAO CHICKEN
GONG BAO JI DING

One of the most famous dishes from Sichuan, kung pao chicken is named after a Qing governor of Sichuan, Ding Baozhen, who is believed to have been very partial to this preparation. Hot and spicy, savoury and pungent, a version of this favourite is found in virtually any Chinese restaurant in Hong Kong. It's quick and easy to whip up, and its success lies in ensuring all ingredients are cut evenly.

SERVES 4–6

- 350 g (12 oz) skinless chicken thigh or breast, cut into 2 cm (¾ inch) cubes
- 2 tablespoons neutral oil
- 8–10 dried long red chillies, snipped into 1.5 cm (⅝ inch) pieces (shake out as many seeds as possible)
- 1 teaspoon Sichuan pepper
- 2 teaspoons minced ginger
- 2 garlic cloves, minced
- 3 spring onions (white part only), cut into 2 cm (¾ inch) lengths
- 1 tablespoon Shaoxing wine
- 100 g (3½ oz) roasted peanuts

MARINADE
- 2 teaspoons light soy sauce
- 1 teaspoon Shaoxing wine
- 1½ teaspoons cornflour (cornstarch)
- Salt, to taste

SAUCE
- 2 tablespoons chicken stock
- 1 teaspoon light soy sauce
- 1 teaspoon dark soy sauce
- 3 teaspoons Chinkiang vinegar
- 1 teaspoon sesame oil
- 3 teaspoons caster (superfine) sugar
- 1 teaspoon cornflour (cornstarch)

For the marinade, combine all the ingredients and 1 tablespoon water in a small bowl and mix well.

Place the chicken into a bowl with the marinade, toss to coat, and set aside for 15–20 minutes to marinate.

For the sauce, combine all the ingredients in a bowl, seasoning with salt and adjusting the quantities to taste – it should taste sweet-sour.

Heat 1 tablespoon oil in a wok over medium heat, add the chilli and Sichuan pepper, lifting the wok away from the heat in case it is too hot (chillies burn easily). Stir until the chillies are crisp and the oil is spicy and fragrant (about 1 minute).

Toss in the chicken quickly and stir-fry rapidly until the meat is just beginning to turn white. Dish out onto a plate.

Return the wok to the heat and add the remaining oil. Stir in the ginger, garlic and spring onions and stir-fry for 1–2 minutes until aromatic. Pour in the Shaoxing, toss a couple of times, then return the chicken and chilli mixture to the wok. Stir-fry for 30 seconds or until the meat is cooked through.

Mix the sauce, then stir it into the wok. As soon as it thickens, add the peanuts, toss to combine, then serve immediately.

✖ Prawns, calamari, pork, lamb and beef are all great substitutes for the chicken.

CURRY KAPITAN

SERVES 4–7

If you love hot, spicy food and if you haven't had curry kapitan before, you simply must make this. Bright, zesty and rich with the flavour of coconut, this curry is not only great to eat but it has also attained legendary status due to its name. While most know it as a Nyonya dish, no one knows why and where the name comes from.

Popular Peranakan legend suggests that the name came into being when a Chinese cook was asked by his Dutch master, 'What's its name?' to which he replied, 'Curry, kapitan'. Charming though this may be, I think it probably comes from the Portuguese term for a Chinese head man (the person who acts as the go-between for his own people and the rest of the community), which is kapitan.

As with all foods that are legendary, multiple versions of this fragrant curry exist. Some add lime or tamarind; others do not. I like squeezing in lime juice for the tangy twist.

- 1 teaspoon ground turmeric
- Pinch of salt, to taste
- 1 × 1.8 kg (4 lb) chicken, cut through the bone into pieces of around 7 cm (2¾ inches)
- 80 ml (2¾ oz) neutral oil
- 1 teaspoon caster (superfine) sugar
- 3 cups (750 ml) coconut milk
- 1 cup (250 ml) coconut cream
- Juice of 2 limes
- 2 makrut lime leaves, finely shredded
- Crisp-fried shallots, to serve
- 2 sliced long red chillies, to serve
- Steamed rice, sambal belacan (see page 261) and pickles, to serve

SPICE PASTE

- 5 dried red chillies
- 10 long red chillies, chopped
- 2.5 cm (1 inch) fresh turmeric or 1 teaspoon ground turmeric
- 2 lemongrass stalks (white part only)
- 6 candlenuts
- 6–7 shallots (eschalots; about 300 g/10½ oz)
- 4 garlic cloves, peeled
- 1 teaspoon belacan (shrimp paste)

Toss turmeric and a pinch of salt together, rub all over the chicken and refrigerate for 4 hours to marinate, or overnight.

For the spice paste, soak the dried chillies in a bowl of warm water to soften. Add to a food processor or blender with remaining ingredients and blend to a fine paste, adding a little water if necessary.

Heat the oil in a heavy-based saucepan or a wok over medium heat, add the spice paste and fry, stirring to make sure the paste doesn't catch, until fragrant (7–10 minutes).

Add the chicken and the sugar and fry, stirring occasionally, for another 5 minutes, allowing the flavours to really develop.

Add the coconut milk, season with salt, and bring gently to the boil, stirring every so often. Simmer, uncovered, until chicken is tender and the sauce is thick (35–40 minutes). Stir in the coconut cream and bring to the boil, then add the lime juice and makrut lime leaves.

Transfer the curry to a serving dish, top with fried shallots and sliced chillies and serve with rice, sambal belacan and pickles.

✖ This is the traditional method of making a proper curry. By this I mean coconut milk is added initially, then coconut cream is added later for richness.

VIETNAMESE HONEY-ROASTED QUAIL
CHIM CÚT RAN

Serves 6

This popular quail dish bears all the characteristics of a great Vietnamese dish – it's light, full flavoured and fresh. The fish sauce paired with spring onion oil is a perfect balance of yin and yang. This recipe may be deep-fried, as is often the case in Vietnamese restaurants, where the quail is partially boiled or steamed before frying, but I think it loses some of its flavour when it's fried, so this version is roasted. The marinating time is also important here, so plan to marinate it overnight if you can.

6 quails
2 garlic cloves
1 tablespoon honey
2 teaspoons caster (superfine) sugar
1 teaspoon Chinese five-spice powder
Pinch of salt, or to taste
½ teaspoon black pepper
2 tablespoons fish sauce
2 tablespoons Shaoxing wine
1 teaspoon dark soy sauce

SPRING ONION OIL
1 cup (250 ml) neutral oil
6–8 spring onions (scallions), green part only, thinly sliced

SPICED SALT
2 teaspoons salt
1 teaspoon black pepper, crushed
1 large lime, cut into wedges

For the spring onion oil, put the neutral oil and spring onion in a small saucepan over medium heat. Once the oil starts to bubble gently, remove from the heat immediately and leave to cool. Spring onion oil will keep refrigerated in a sealed jar or container for a week.

Rinse the quails and pat dry with paper towel, then place in a bowl with the remaining ingredients. Refrigerate for 2 hours, or preferably overnight, to marinate.

For the spiced salt, combine the salt and pepper and fry in a dry pan for a couple of minutes until fragrant. Cool, then grind in a spice grinder or mortar and pestle to a fine powder. Transfer to a small bowl and squeeze the lime juice in. Set aside until you're ready to serve.

To roast the quails, heat the oven to 200°C (400°F). Place the birds, breast-side up, on a baking tray and roast, turning after 10 minutes, for 15 minutes or until the skin is nicely golden. This will be slightly pink inside, but roast for up to another 10 minutes if you prefer it well done.

Serve at once with spiced salt and with spring onion oil to spoon over.

CHICKEN BUAH KELUAK
AYAM BUAH KELUAK

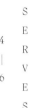

Native to Malaysia, Indonesia and Papua New Guinea, the pangium tree grows in mangrove swamps. It produces a poisonous nut called buah keluak (*Pangium edule*), made edible through a fermentation process using water, wood ash, banana leaves and earth over several days until the kernels turn from creamy white to dark brown or charcoal to yield a prized delicacy much loved by the Nyonya cooks of Singapore and Malacca. It tastes distinctive, almost smoky and quite velvety if the quality of the nuts is superior.

Chicken buah keluak is a classic. In fact, Peranakans from Singapore and Malacca wax lyrical about it because it bears all the characteristics of great cooking – balanced flavours with just that hint of spice and the intriguing aroma of the nut that's akin to manna from heaven.

Also called kepayang or pakem, buah keluak is sold dried without the shell in Indonesian and Malaysian grocers and online in Australia and elsewhere. Should you be put off after reading this, please don't be. Remember that eating raw or fresh morel mushrooms can make also you sick, and that they have to be cooked to remove their toxicity; buah keluak is just as safe if treated properly.

SERVES 4–6

Soak the buah keluak nuts for three days, changing the water daily. As the nuts tend to float, put a plate on top to keep them submerged.

On the fourth day, scrub the nuts of any sediment and rinse. Place in a saucepan filled with water, bring to the boil, and cook the nuts until soft, about 20–30 minutes, to facilitate easier handling. Once the nuts are cool enough to handle, crack the 'mouth' or 'lip' with a pestle or hammer and extract the seed/kernel with a teaspoon, discarding any hard ones. Mash the kernels to a paste and set aside. Reserve the shells.

Meanwhile, place the tamarind pulp in a bowl and cover with 1 cup (250 ml) warm water. Soak for 20 minutes, then, with your fingers, mash and squeeze the tamarind to extract as much juice as possible. Pour the juice through a sieve into a container and add 1 litre (4 cups) water. Set aside.

For the spice paste, add all the ingredients to a food processor and blend to a semi-smooth paste.

In a small bowl, add the pork or prawns, the salt, 1 teaspoon of sugar and three-quarters of the pounded buah keluak. Mix thoroughly to combine, then stuff this mixture into the reserved buah keluak shells. If there's any mixture left over, form it into tiny balls, about the size of cherries or marbles.

Heat the oil in a large saucepan, then fry the spice paste for 4–5 minutes together with the remaining buah keluak paste, the crushed lemongrass and the makrut lime leaves. When the oil separates, add the chicken drumsticks and continue to fry for 5 minutes, turning the chicken occasionally to coat it evenly.

Add the stuffed buah keluak shells, stir gently, then add the tamarind water and the remaining 2 teaspoons sugar, and season to taste with salt. Bring to the boil, then reduce to a simmer and cook for 30–45 minutes or until the chicken is tender and cooked through. Just before serving add any leftover buah keluak balls and simmer for 1–2 minutes until cooked through. Serve with hot steamed rice.

15–20 buah keluak nuts
100 g (3½ oz) tamarind pulp
150 g (5½ oz) minced pork or prawns, finely chopped
1 teaspoon salt, plus extra to taste
3 teaspoons caster (superfine) sugar
½ cup (125 ml) neutral oil
1 lemongrass stalk, bruised
2–3 makrut lime leaves, to taste
1.5 kg (3 lb 5 oz) chicken drumsticks
Steamed rice, to serve

SPICE PASTE
4 cm (1½ inch) piece fresh turmeric or 1 teaspoon ground turmeric
3 garlic cloves, peeled
1 onion (about 200 g/7 oz) or 15 shallots (eschalots)
2 lemongrass stalks (white part only), chopped
3 slices (20 g/¾ oz) galangal
8 long red chillies, chopped
8 candlenuts
1 tablespoon belacan (shrimp paste), roasted (see page 42)

STIR-FRIED CHICKEN WITH CASHEW NUTS

SERVES 4–6

A very quick dish to prepare, this classic is popular with all Chinese for the way tender chicken contrasts beautifully with sweet, crunchy cashew nuts. When cooked properly, it is stunning.

Place the chicken in a bowl with the egg white, salt and cornflour and mix well. Refrigerate for 20 minutes to marinate.

For the sauce, combine all the ingredients in a bowl and stir well.

Heat a wok or saucepan over high heat and add the neutral oil to a depth of 2.5 cm (1 inch). Once it's shimmering, add the chicken in batches and fry, stirring to prevent sticking, until it turns white. Remove with a slotted spoon, transfer to a colander set over a bowl, and continue until all chicken is cooked.

Remove excess oil from the wok and wipe it clean. Heat the wok over high heat until very hot, add 2 tablespoons neutral oil, then add the garlic. Stir-fry for 1 minute, then add the roasted cashew nuts, spring onions and capsicum. Return the chicken to the wok and add the sauce. Stir-fry for a couple of minutes or until the sauce thickens and the vegetables are just tender. Drizzle with sesame oil, transfer to a warm plate, garnish with coriander leaves and serve immediately with rice.

500 g (1 lb 2 oz) skinless chicken breast, cut into 2 cm (¾ inch) dice
1 egg white
½ teaspoon salt
2 teaspoons cornflour (cornstarch)
Neutral oil, for deep-frying
1 teaspoon chopped garlic
100 g (3½ oz) cashew nuts, roasted
2 spring onions (scallions), sliced
1 red capsicum (pepper), seeded, diced and blanched
1 teaspoon sesame oil
Coriander (cilantro) leaves, to serve
Steamed rice, to serve

SAUCE
2 teaspoons oyster sauce
1 tablespoon Shaoxing wine
1 teaspoon light soy sauce
100 ml (3½ fl oz) chicken stock
1 teaspoon caster (superfine) sugar
1 teaspoon potato flour

SLOW-COOKED SPATCHCOCK WITH JICAMA, BRUSSELS SPROUTS AND VADOUVAN

SERVES 4

Until a few years ago, I'd never heard of vadouvan, but it has crept up on me, becoming something I use more and more in my cooking. A spice blend originally from the former French colony of Pondicherry in Tamil Nadu, it is 'Frenchified' with slow-cooked onions and shallots. I was initially sceptical about it, but once I considered that most Southeast Asian and Indian curries start with a base of onions and garlic followed by spices, I started making it. The result is this chicken dish.

Vadouvan is easy to knock up but it needs time, so it's best to make a large batch and freeze it to use whenever it's required. The quantity in this recipe is generous enough to make sure you have some for later. It is wonderfully versatile, used in curries, purées, soups, dips and stir-fries, so you'll find plenty of homes for it in your kitchen.

---

4 spatchcocks (baby chickens), quartered, backbones and wing tips removed with kitchen shears
Salt and white pepper, to taste
2 tablespoons neutral oil
1 tablespoon butter
24 Brussels sprouts, halved, lightly blanched and refreshed in cold water
500 g (1 lb 2 oz) jicama or water chestnuts, cut into small cubes
2 cups (500 ml) chicken stock
⅔ cup (170 ml) coconut milk

VADOUVAN
1 kg (2 lb 4 oz) onions, coarsely chopped
500 g (1 lb 2 oz) shallots (eschalots), quartered
12 garlic cloves, chopped
1 teaspoon fenugreek
1 teaspoon ground black pepper
1 tablespoon ground cumin
1 teaspoon ground cardamom
1 teaspoon brown mustard seeds
1 teaspoon chilli powder
¾ teaspoon ground turmeric
½ teaspoon grated nutmeg
¼ teaspoon ground cloves
1 sprig fresh curry leaves, thinly sliced
½ cup (125 ml) neutral oil
1 tablespoon salt

For the vadouvan, heat the oven to 160°C (315°F). Pulse the onions in three batches in a food processor to a coarse paste (not to a mushy consistency). Add the shallots and garlic and repeat.

Grind the fenugreek finely with a spice grinder or a mortar and pestle, then combine it with the other spices.

Heat the oil in a wok over medium heat. Add the onion, shallots and garlic and cook, stirring frequently, until caramelised (25–30 minutes).

Add the spice mixture to the onion mixture with the salt and continue to cook, stirring, for another 5 minutes. Transfer to a large roasting tin lined with baking paper, spread it out evenly, then roast until there's almost no moisture left in the vadouvan, (30–40 minutes). Cool, then transfer to a sterilised container. Vadouvan will keep frozen in an airtight container for a month.

Pat the spatchocks dry with paper towel and season with salt and pepper. Heat the oil and melt the butter in a large heavy-based saucepan until foaming, then add the spatchocks in batches, skin-side down, and fry, turning occasionally, until golden. Transfer to a plate.

Pour off all but 1 tablespoon of oil from the pan, add the Brussels sprouts and stir until nicely caramelised (about 10 minutes). Season with salt to taste, and transfer to a plate.

Add the jicama to the pan along with a pinch of salt and cook, stirring, until cooked through but still with some crunch (about 2 minutes). Now add the chicken stock and bring to the boil, then stir in the coconut milk and ½ cup (around 80 g) vadouvan. Return the chicken pieces to the pan, skin-side up and gently simmer, partially covered with a lid, for 15 minutes or until cooked through.

Transfer the chicken to a platter and continue to simmer the sauce for 5 minutes or until it reaches a syrupy consistency. Add the Brussels sprouts to warm through, then spoon the mixture over the chicken to serve.

✤ If you are time poor, vadouvan is available in gourmet stores.

FRIED CHICKEN, NYONYA STYLE
INCHE KABIN

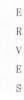

SERVES 4–6

Several moons ago, friends took me to the Penang Swimming Club and we ordered inche kabin, the local equivalent of KFC. I've had inche kabin before but this was magical. Perhaps it had something to do with the warm tropical sunset or the cool beer, but when it arrived on the platter decorated with fried bread fingers, it was the best fried chicken I've ever tasted. It was crisp, crunchy and succulent. And despite my friends' inability to offer any explanations of the name's origin, it didn't seem to matter that day. Perhaps it's a throwback to colonial times with bread fingers and Worcestershire sauce. Whatever it represents, this is definitely one of the most flavourful fried chicken recipes I have ever come across.

For the marinade, combine all the ingredients in a bowl and mix well.

Place the chicken Marylands in a dish, pour the marinade over, toss to coat, then cover and refrigerate for 4 hours, or preferably overnight, to marinate.

Once you're ready to cook, combine all the ingredients for the dipping sauce in a bowl.

Bring the chicken back to room temperature, then remove the chicken from the marinade, draining off the excess. Heat 5 cm (2 inches) oil in a wok over medium-high heat or place oil in a deep-fryer and heat to 165°C (330°F) on a thermometer. Fry the chicken in batches until golden brown and cooked through (about 15 minutes).

For a crisp skin, it is best to fry the chicken twice – fry on medium heat first, then remove the chicken pieces. Increase the heat to medium-high and fry the chicken again. A tablespoon or so of rice or tapioca flour dusted over the chicken just before frying gives that extra crunch. Remove with a slotted spoon and drain on paper towels.

Serve with croûtons or bread fingers and dipping sauce.

1.5 kg (3 lb 5 oz) chicken Marylands (thighs with the drumstick attached), cut through the bone into bite-sized pieces
Neutral oil, for deep-frying
Rice or tapioca flour, for dusting (optional)
Croûtons or fried bread fingers, to serve

MARINADE
1 tablespoon curry powder
1 tablespoon light soy sauce
2 tablespoons lime juice
100 ml (3½ oz) coconut cream
2 teaspoons caster (superfine) sugar
Salt, to taste

DIPPING SAUCE
100 ml (3½ oz) Worcestershire sauce
1 teaspoon ground mustard
1 long red chilli, seeds removed, thinly sliced
Juice of 1 lime

SEAFOOD

OYSTERS WITH MY DRESSING

SERVES 10–12

This is a dressing with very strong Thai overtones, the inspiration coming from the sweet, sour, salty and herbaceous flavours of Thai cooking. I have used this dressing with steamed mussels, Moreton Bay bugs and prawns, and it's also very good with steamed vegetables.

Don't go to Thailand expecting oysters served in this manner – it's not something you'll typically find. Though some imported oysters are served in this fashion, Thais traditionally prefer their oysters cooked.

You can use whatever oysters you prefer, but remember, the colder the climate, the better the eating – especially in summer when they tend to spawn, though that varies by location.

---

3 dozen freshly shucked oysters
Salmon roe (optional), to serve
Finger lime (optional), pearls squeezed out, to serve

DRESSING
200 g (7 oz) palm sugar (or jaggery)
¼ bunch coriander (cilantro), stems and leaves finely chopped, roots reserved
1 fat lemongrass stalk (white part only)
2 birdseye chillies, finely chopped
2 large makrut lime leaves, finely shredded
100 ml (3½ fl oz) best-quality fish sauce
160 ml (5¼ fl oz) lime juice (from about 4–5 limes)

For the dressing, place the palm sugar in a saucepan with the coriander roots and 1½ cups (375 ml) water, bring to a simmer, then reduce the heat to low and simmer very gently for 20 minutes until the liquid is reduced by a third. Cool, discard the roots, then transfer the liquid to a mixing bowl.

Chop or blend the lemongrass to a fine mince and add to the syrupy base along with the chilli and lime leaves. Add the chopped coriander stems and leaves to the dressing along with the fish sauce and lime juice and whisk to combine, adjusting to taste with more lime juice and fish sauce.

To serve, spoon some dressing over freshly shucked oysters. If you're using salmon roe and finger lime, spoon half a teaspoon of each on each oyster. Serve immediately.

✹ This dressing lasts for only 2 days as the chlorophyll deteriorates, making it less visually appealing.

THAI GREEN PAPAYA SALAD
SOM TAM

Green papaya salad is loved by just about every Southeast Asian country, but Thailand's version, som tam, from the north-east, is the most famous. Hot, salty and sour, it's traditionally made in a mortar and pestle and sold on just about every street corner in Thailand. Each province has its own version and you even find some recipes with salted crab or water-dwelling insects. Then there is pla ra or pickled fish, which is added to give the distinctive pungency much loved by northern Thais and Laotians. Seek out firm papayas for this dish and it'll be all the better.

Pound the garlic and chillies with a large mortar and pestle (or blitz in a food processor) to a fine paste.

Add the dried shrimp, continue to pound (or blitz) until coarsely crushed, then add the beans and tomatoes and pound (or blitz) until bruised and coarsely crushed.

Add the papaya, crush it lightly, then stir in the fish sauce, lime juice and palm sugar, adjusting to taste. Season to taste with salt and serve topped with prawns and peanuts.

✖ This salad is wonderfully versatile. Use any protein you like, such as roast pork or chicken.

3 garlic cloves, peeled
3–9 green or red birdseye chillies, according to taste
1 tablespoon dried shrimp
2 runner beans (or 5 green beans), cut into 3 cm (1¼ inch) lengths
1 firm tomato, coarsely chopped or 3 cherry tomatoes, halved
500 g (1 lb 2 oz) green papaya, peeled, seeds removed and shredded
2 tablespoons fish sauce
2 tablespoons lime juice
2 teaspoons palm sugar (or jaggery)
Salt, to taste
6 cooked prawns, peeled
1 tablespoon roasted peanuts, crushed

SHELLFISH WITH GARLIC, CORIANDER AND THAI BASIL

SERVES 4–6

Southeast Asians love eating seafood, and love mixing it with just about anything. This is one of those great versatile seafood dishes that regularly appear in many of the resort towns in Thailand and Malaysia. Simple to make and infused with an abundance of herbs, it's good enough to convert just about anyone into a seafood lover. You can change which shellfish you use depending on what's fresh near you.

500 g (1 lb 2 oz) mussels
250 g (9 oz) green prawns
250 g (9 oz) scallops or calamari
1 tablespoon neutral oil
1 cup (250 ml) chicken stock
1 tablespoon oyster sauce
1 tablespoon fish sauce
½ teaspoon palm sugar
½ cup (15 g) Thai basil leaves
Chopped coriander (cilantro), to garnish
Steamed rice or crusty bread, to serve

SPICE PASTE
½ teaspoon white peppercorns
2 birdseye or long red chillies, or to taste, chopped
3 garlic cloves, peeled
2 large coriander (cilantro) roots and stems, washed well and chopped

Scrub the mussels and peel the prawns. If using calamari, score it in a crisscross pattern. Set the seafood aside in the fridge until ready to cook.

To make the spice paste, use a mini food processor or a mortar and pestle to blend or pound the ingredients to a coarse paste.

Heat the oil in a wok over medium heat. Fry the spice paste for a couple of minutes or until fragrant. Stir in the stock, oyster sauce, fish sauce and palm sugar, then bring to the boil.

Add the mussels, cover and steam until they are just beginning to open. Add the prawns and cook for 30 seconds before adding the scallops or calamari.

Toss the Thai basil through the wok. Transfer the shellfish to serving plates. Top with the coriander and serve with steamed rice or crusty bread.

SINGAPORE CHILLI CRAB

SERVES 2

Eating crab is almost an obsession for many Singaporeans and Malaysians. Friends recently drove me across Singapore island in the middle of a tropical downpour to one of the colourful food centres to eat the sublime chilli crab. Over glasses of ice-cold beer, and with the cheeky persuasion from the waitstaff, we consumed six delicious crabs! The drive was definitely worth the effort, and the crab clearly lived up to its billing as one of the signature dishes of Singapore.

For those of you who find eating crab fiddly, do persevere. Besides, it's fun licking your fingers and sucking at every nook and cranny of this luxurious crustacean. Wear a bib or a tea towel so you can enjoy the experience of eating in casual mode.

If you don't have nerves of steel, ask your fishmonger to dispatch your crabs for you. However, the easiest and most humane method is to put them to sleep in the freezer for an hour. After that, flip the crab over, exposing its belly, find the tip of the triangle of the main belly, and stab it quickly with a sharp knife.

Clean the crabs and lever the shell from the bodies to expose the spongy 'dead man's fingers'. Discard these, then cut each body in half. Cut each half in two, keeping the legs attached. Bash the claws lightly with a cleaver or a mallet to allow the sauce to penetrate.

For the sauce, combine all the ingredients in a bowl and mix well.

Pound the ginger and chillies with a mortar and pestle or blend them in a food processor into a coarse paste.

Heat the oil in a wok over medium-high heat, swirl once or twice, then add the garlic and pounded ginger and chilli.

Stir-fry for 1 minute until fragrant, then add the crab and stir-fry for 2–3 minutes or until the shells turn slightly red.

Add the sauce, stirring well to coat evenly, then cover with a lid, reduce the heat to medium and simmer for 7–10 minutes until the crab is bright red and cooked through.

Remove the lid, stir in the beaten egg and cornflour slurry to thicken, then season to taste with salt and pepper. Serve immediately topped with spring onion curls.

✣ Prawns, lobsters and crayfish are great substitutes for crab in this recipe. Crusty bread is excellent to mop up the sauce.

1.4 kg (3 lb 2 oz) fresh live mud crabs
5 cm (2 inch) piece ginger
3 long red chillies, chopped
¼ cup (60 ml) neutral oil
4 garlic cloves, chopped finely
1 egg, lightly beaten
2 teaspoons cornflour (cornstarch) mixed with ¼ cup (60 ml) water
Salt and white pepper, to taste
2 spring onions (scallions), thinly sliced and soaked in cold water, to serve

SAUCE
1 cup (250 ml) light chicken stock or water
¼ cup (60 ml) chilli sauce
¼ cup (60 ml) tomato sauce (ketchup)
1 tablespoon light soy sauce
1 tablespoon caster (superfine) sugar
Salt and white pepper, to taste

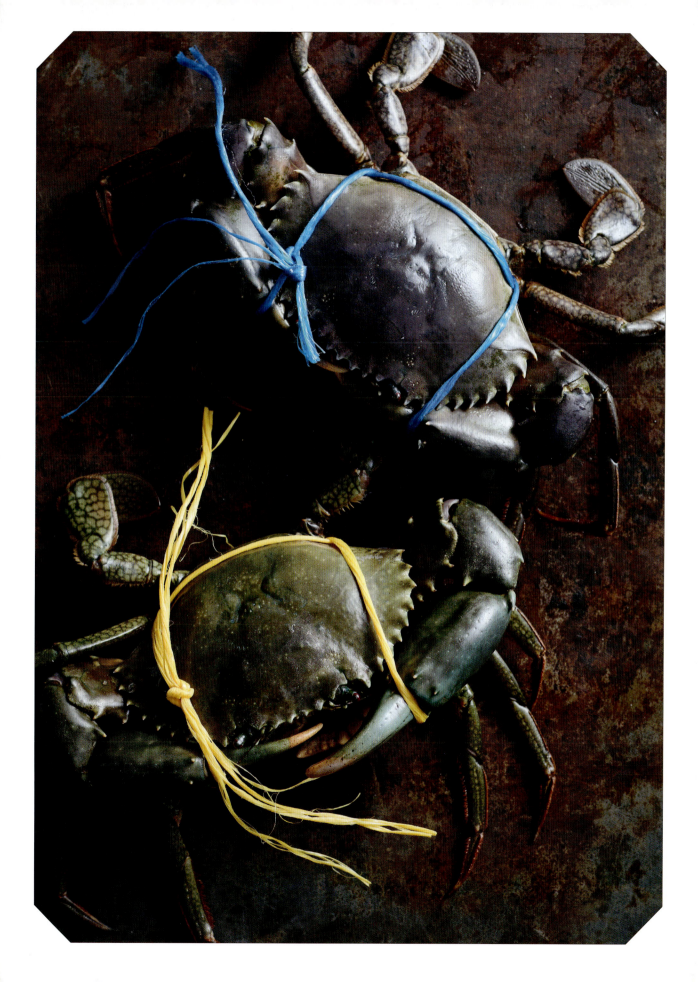

STIR-FRIED PIPIS WITH MALAYSIAN FLAVOURS
KAM HEONG LA LA

SERVES 2–4

This is a purely Malaysian dish because it is influenced by the country's three dominant cultures: Malay, Chinese and Indian. Popular cooking legend has it that it was created by a Cantonese chef in Kuala Lumpur for seafood and poultry dishes, because the name in Chinese is kam heong ('gold fragrance'), meaning that its flavours are as fragrant as heaven. It is made with curry leaves, dried shrimp, preserved soybeans, chillies and curry powder – and in this case it's served with pipis. On paper, the dish sounds strange but when you eat your first mouthful, you'll find it is incredibly delicious.

¼ cup (60 ml) neutral oil
2 garlic cloves, finely chopped
1 shallot (eschalot), finely chopped
2–4 long red chillies (to taste), thinly sliced
1 sprig curry leaves, picked
1 tablespoon dried shrimp, soaked briefly in hot water, chopped
1 kg (2 lb 4 oz) live pipis (or mussels or clams), purged
½ cup (125 ml) chicken stock
1 teaspoon preserved soybeans, crushed (or red miso)
1 tablespoon Malaysian curry powder (see page 137)
1 tablespoon oyster sauce
Dash of dark soy sauce
1 tablespoon Shaoxing wine
1 teaspoon caster (superfine) sugar
Sliced lemons or lime (optional), to serve

Heat the oil in a wok over medium-high heat until shimmering. Add the garlic and shallot and stir-fry for 30 seconds or until fragrant. Add the chilli, curry leaves and dried shrimp and stir-fry for another minute until the chilli softens.

Ramp up the heat to high, add the pipis, and give them a good shake before adding the remaining ingredients. Lower the heat a little, cover with a lid, and cook for another minute or two, then remove the lid and transfer any open pipis to a serving dish, continuing to remove the rest as soon as they pop open.

Pour the contents of the wok over the pipis and serve with lemon or lime.

✖ I have had great success serving this on a bed of noodles or pasta.

CALAMARI AND GREEN MANGO SALAD

SERVES 4

Similar to many Malaysian salads, this Thai-inspired dish is notable for its flexibility and use of the umami-packed shrimp paste belacan. That said, Malaysians and Thais take a rather cavalier approach, using whatever is available when making salads. In that spirit, I've used fresh prawns and mussels in this recipe, which isn't strictly traditional, but sure is enjoyable..

Wipe the calamari dry with paper towel, then cut it open along one edge to open it out. Score the flesh on the inside in a tight criss-cross pattern, then cut each hood into 5 cm (2 inch) pieces. Refrigerate until needed.

For the dressing, add the coriander roots to a mortar and pound to a coarse paste with a pestle. Add the chillies and lemongrass and continue to pound to a fine paste. Add the fish sauce, lime juice and palm sugar, adjusting quantities to suit your palate – it should be sour, hot, sweet and salty.

To cook the calamari, heat a barbecue or char-grill pan to high heat. Brush a thin layer of oil onto the grill. When hot, add the calamari and grill, turning once, until just cooked through (3–4 minutes).

Transfer to a large bowl, add the green mango, ginger, herbs and shallot, drizzle the dressing over everything. Toss well and serve with lime wedges.

✱ If you can't find fresh calamari, you can also use frozen.

500 g (1 lb 2 oz) fresh calamari hoods, cleaned
Neutral oil, for grilling
2 green mangoes (use the sour variety), shredded
40 g (1½ oz) ginger, sliced into fine strips
1 cup (20 g) firmly packed mint leaves
1 cup (30 g) firmly packed coriander (cilantro) sprigs
1 cup (50 g) firmly packed Thai basil leaves
2 shallots (eschalots), thinly sliced
Lime wedges, to serve

DRESSING
2 coriander (cilantro) roots, chopped
2 birdseye chillies, sliced
1–2 long red chillies (to taste), sliced
1 lemongrass stalk (white part only), finely chopped
2 tablespoons fish sauce
¼ cup (60 ml) lime or lemon juice
40 g (1½ oz) palm sugar (or jaggery), shaved with a knife

SPICY POMELO AND PRAWN SALAD
YAM SOM-O

SERVES 4–6

I love making this Thai street food whenever pomelo is in season. A tropical fruit resembling an oversized grapefruit, the pomelo is a member of the citrus family. There are two varieties: pink and pale yellow. During the hot summer months, Thais tend to snack on segments of pomelo with whatever sauce or prik is available. It must be ripened on the tree for the exquisite flavour to develop – check to see that the fruit feels heavy in your hand when you buy it, which means it's packed with juicy segments.

There are hundreds of versions of this popular salad; some are even presented in a hollowed-out pomelo intricately carved with floral designs. Regardless of presentation, I urge you to make this salad. I know it's not easy to find pomelo (if you can't, use grapefruit and add more palm sugar to cut the sourness) but when you do, it's like a world of sheer deliciousness exploding in your mouth. It's nothing short of ambrosia!

1 pomelo, peeled
2 tablespoons lime juice
1 tablespoon fish sauce
3–7 birdseye chillies, chopped
1 tablespoon palm sugar, or to taste
2 tablespoons nam prik pao (chilli jam)
150 g (5½ oz) cooked prawns, peeled and halved lengthways
½ cup (125 ml) coconut cream
2 tablespoons desiccated coconut, dry-roasted, plus extra to serve
1 tablespoon dried shrimp, finely chopped
5 makrut lime leaves, finely shredded
2 tablespoons crisp-fried shallots, to serve

Remove the membrane enclosing the pomelo segments, then break them into chunks, discarding seeds.

Place the lime juice, fish sauce, chilli, palm sugar and nam prik pao in a bowl and stir until the sugar dissolves.

Add the prawns, coconut cream, desiccated coconut, dried shrimp and lime leaves, stir to combine, then add the pomelo pieces, stir gently to avoid breaking up, and transfer to a serving plate. Serve sprinkled with fried shallots and extra dry-roasted coconut.

✖ I've sometimes substituted other shellfish, like mussels and calamari, for the prawns. Grilled chicken is also delicious with this salad, as is crisp, deep-fried pork.

WATERMELON WITH CRISP FISH

SERVES 40

This is what I call modern Southeast Asian food. The recipe came about one hot afternoon in Thailand when I was eating a delicious traditional dish called yam pla fuu, a crisp fish salad with green mango. In Malaysia, we tend to use dry-roasted coconut (kerisik) in many of our salads, including a lovely salad made with watermelon rind. The idea of combining these two cooking styles kept plaguing me and the following recipe was born.

While this recipe is modern cooking, its creation firmly entrenched in tropical Asia. Thai flavours, Malaysian innovation and Singaporean modernity are all represented in the dish. Many Asian chefs believe the joy of cooking has no boundaries but that it requires strong culinary grounding.

This dish speaks for itself – the contrast of flavours is quite phenomenal. Try it as a salad, but it also works perfectly as a finger food.

For the dressing, combine sugar, malt syrup, water, coriander root, garlic and chilli in a saucepan, bring to the boil, reduce the heat to medium and simmer until syrupy (about 8–10 minutes). Remove pan from heat, add rice vinegar and fish sauce and discard coriander roots. Cool, blend until smooth, then stir in the dried shrimp and coconut. Season to taste.

Heat oven to 180°C (350°F). Wash and pat dry the fish fillets, season all over with salt and place on a wire rack set over a roasting pan. Roast for 20–30 minutes until golden. Cool, then place in a food processor and pulse until the fish resembles fine breadcrumbs (take care not to overprocess the fish or it won't puff during frying).

Heat 5 cm (2 inches) oil in a wok over medium heat until shimmering. When the oil is hot, carefully drop a handful of fish into the oil (be careful; it can spit). It will immediately form a raft or nest. With a strainer or slotted spoon, pull the fish towards you. Once the oil stops bubbling, turn the fish over and fry until golden (about 2–3 minutes). Remove and drain on paper towel. Repeat with remaining fish.

If you're serving this as a salad, gently toss the watermelon with dressing to taste, scatter with Thai basil and fried shallots and top with fish to serve.

If you're serving this as finger food, place a dab of dressing on top of each piece of watermelon. Add a pinch of fried shallot, a tiny quantity of fish and top with a pinch of basil. Serve immediately on Chinese spoons.

300 g (10½ oz) skinless fillets of flathead or snapper (or any firm white fish)
Good pinch of salt, or to taste
Neutral oil, for deep-frying
2 kg (4 lb 8 oz) seedless watermelon, cut into 3 cm (1¼ inch) cubes
1 cup (30 g) Thai basil (or basil), shredded or torn
2 tablespoons crisp-fried shallots

DRESSING
½ cup (110 g) caster (superfine) sugar
2 tablespoons malt syrup
1 cup (250 ml) water
2 coriander (cilantro) roots
2 garlic cloves, peeled
3–4 long red chillies, chopped
1 tablespoon rice vinegar
2 tablespoons fish sauce, or to taste
2 tablespoons ginger, finely minced
1 tablespoon dried shrimp, dry-roasted and chopped
½ cup (35 g) freshly grated coconut (or desiccated), dry-roasted
Salt, to taste

SERVES 8

VIETNAMESE STUFFED SQUID OR CALAMARI

The difference between squid and calamari is slight: squid have smaller pointed flaps attached only to the narrow end of the body, looking like an arrow or bishop's hat, while calamari have long triangular flaps that run along each side of the body. When fresh, both vary in colour from pink to brown to greenish blue.

Whichever you choose, smaller squid or calamari are far better for several reasons. First, they taste sweeter and are easier to handle. Second, they present beautifully when sliced. But if you can't find them, big ones are still tasty.

This dish is excellent with homemade Asian pickles and salads.

10 squid or calamari, each weighing less than 125 g (4½ oz), cleaned, tentacles reserved
2 tablespoons neutral oil

NUOC CHAM

¼ cup (60 ml) fish sauce
2 tablespoons caster (superfine) sugar
1 tablespoon lime juice or rice vinegar
1 birdseye chilli, minced
1 garlic clove, minced
2 teaspoons finely chopped carrot

STUFFING

1 tablespoon neutral oil
3 shallots (eschalots), finely chopped
1 garlic clove, minced
1 birdseye chilli, minced
300 g (10½ oz) minced pork
Reserved squid or calamari tentacles (see above), finely chopped
¼ cup (25 g) dried glass noodles, soaked in cold water, drained and cut into 2 cm (¾ inch) pieces
¼ cup (25 g) shredded carrot
5 wood ear mushrooms, soaked in water, finely-chopped
1 small egg, beaten
1 tablespoon fish sauce
1 tablespoon light soy sauce
1 tablespoon coconut milk
1 teaspoon Chinese five spice powder

For the nuoc cham, place the fish sauce, sugar and ¼ cup (60 ml) water in a saucepan and bring to the boil. Stir to dissolve sugar, then remove from heat and cool before adding remaining ingredients. Nuoc cham will keep refrigerated for 2 weeks.

For the stuffing, heat the oil in a frying pan over medium heat, add the shallots and garlic and fry, stirring occasionally, until fragrant (2–3 minutes). Remove from heat and cool, then add to a bowl with the remaining ingredients and stir to combine. Quickly fry a morsel to check the seasoning, adjusting to taste.

Fill the squid or calamari hoods with the stuffing, leaving 3–4 cm (1¼–1½ inches) of space around the opening (the squid will shrink when it's fried). Secure with toothpicks.

Heat the oil in a frying pan or skillet over medium heat, and fry the squid until golden and cooked through, turning every couple of minutes and covering with a lid in between (10–15 minutes depending on size). Remove from the pan and slice into rings. Serve at once with nuoc cham.

✖ Glass noodles are also called mung bean or bean thread noodles. This dish is also lovely served with a green mango salad (page 217).

STEAMED SEAFOOD PUDDING
OTAK-OTAK

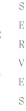

Called otak-otak in Malaysia, Singapore and Indonesia, hor mok in Thailand and amok in Cambodia, this dish is essentially a savoury seafood pudding, which is either grilled in coconut leaves or steamed in banana leaves. This steamed Nyonya version from Penang is far more delicate and truly delicious. If the words 'seafood' and 'pudding' together don't excite you, trust me – once you've eaten one, you'll be a convert. Since I don't have easy access to banana leaves, I make this pudding in dariole moulds. It's wonderful eating!

This recipe uses wild betel leaves (*Piper sarmentosum*), or daun kadok in Bahasa Malaysia, which are readily available in major cities that have a large Vietnamese population, particularly because they're used in making bo la lot, a popular grilled beef dish.

You'll need 10 dariole moulds.

SERVES 2–4

For the spice paste, blend all the ingredients in a food processor until smooth.

Blanch the betel leaves in a large saucepan of boiling water, refresh in a bowl of iced water, drain and pat dry.

Beat the eggs lightly in a bowl, then beat in the coconut milk, glutinous rice flour, sugar (adjusting to taste) and spice paste until well combined. Season with salt and pepper. Add the fish and makrut lime leaves and mix again to distribute evenly. Grease the dariole moulds lightly with oil and line them with blanched betel leaves (two per mould should be enough).

Ladle the mixture into the moulds, wrap them tightly with plastic wrap and steam in a steamer basket set over a wok of boiling water for 15 minutes, or bake in a bain-marie at 160°C (320°F) for 20 minutes, until just set with a slight wobble in the centre.

Meanwhile, for the sauce, combine all the ingredients, except the cornflour slurry, in a saucepan and cook, stirring occasionally, over low heat for 10 minutes until the flavours have developed. Taste, adjusting the seasoning with extra salt and sugar as needed, then add the cornflour slurry, stirring to thicken.

Unmould the otak-otak and serve with the coconut sauce.

20 betel leaves
4 eggs
300 ml (10½ fl oz) coconut milk
1 tablespoon glutinous rice flour
Caster (superfine) sugar, to taste
Salt and white pepper, to taste
600 g (1 lb 5 oz) white fish fillets (such as snapper or barramundi), cut into 1.5 cm (½ inch) pieces
7 makrut lime leaves, thinly sliced
Neutral oil, for greasing

SPICE PASTE
6 dried chillies, soaked in hot water to soften, or 1 tablespoon chilli powder
60 g (2¼ oz) shallots (eschalots)
1 lemongrass stalk (white part only), minced
2 garlic cloves, peeled
2 candlenuts
20 g (¾ oz) fresh turmeric or ½ teaspoon ground turmeric
1 slice galangal
20 g (¾ oz) belacan (shrimp paste), roasted (see page 42)

COCONUT SAUCE
2 cups (500 ml) coconut milk
1 cup (250 ml) fish stock
3 tablespoons julienned ginger
1 stalk lemongrass, bruised
1 teaspoon ground turmeric
Pinch of salt, to taste
Pinch of caster (superfine) sugar, to taste
2 teaspoons cornflour (cornstarch), mixed with 2 tablespoons water

GRILLED SCALLOPS WITH SWEETCORN SAUCE AND CURRY LEAVES

Scallops and sweetcorn are, to my mind, a perfect pairing. It's even more delicious if you add some Asian herbs, such as curry leaves and Thai basil. I don't remember where the original recipe comes from, but I have played with myriad combinations. If I want to lend complexity to the dish, I add a tiny spoon of shellfish oil to the scallops. Serve this with a rich white wine.

2 tablespoons ghee or olive oil
18 curry leaves or Thai basil leaves
18 large scallops, roe removed, muscle trimmed, drained on paper towel
Salt and white pepper, to taste
Shellfish oil (page 101), to serve

SWEETCORN SAUCE
¼ cup (60 g) butter or olive oil
1 small onion, finely chopped
1 garlic clove, finely chopped
1 tablespoon ginger, finely chopped
3 sweetcorn cobs, husks removed, kernels shaved off with a knife
200 ml (7 fl oz) chicken stock
200 ml (7 fl oz) single (pure) cream
Salt and white pepper, to taste

For the sweetcorn sauce, melt the butter in a saucepan over low heat, add the onion, garlic and ginger and cook, stirring occasionally, until translucent (about 5–6 minutes).

Add the corn kernels and give them a toss, then add the chicken stock and cream. Bring to the boil, then reduce the heat to low and simmer for 10 minutes or until the kernels are tender. Season to taste with salt and pepper, and allow to cool slightly.

Transfer to a blender and process until smooth. If the sauce feels a little coarse, pass it through a fine sieve. Transfer to a cleaned saucepan and keep warm.

Heat the ghee in a non-stick frying pan over medium-high heat, add the curry leaves (stand back; they'll pop in the heat), stir for about 10 seconds, then add the scallops and sear for 20–30 seconds on each side until golden and just opaque. Season to taste with salt and pepper.

To serve, place a dollop of sweetcorn sauce on six plates. Top with three scallops, fried curry leaves and a drizzle of shellfish oil. This dish can also be served on a platter.

BUTTER PRAWNS
NAI YOW HA

SERVES 6

This is a signature dish of Malaysia, but no one knows precisely when it was created. Most Malaysian food writers believe it originated in a Chinese restaurant in Johor state around 20 years ago. Since then, several versions have popped up all over the country. Combining Malay, Chinese, Indian and Western ingredients, and Chinese cooking techniques, this is a delicious example of a truly diverse Malaysian dish.

---

500 g (1 lb 2 oz) green prawns, shells on, antennae trimmed
Salt and white pepper, to taste
Neutral oil, for deep-frying, plus 2 tablespoons extra
2 egg yolks, lightly beaten
90 g (3¼ oz) butter
2 sprigs curry leaves
5–12 birdseye chillies, or to taste, roughly chopped
1 garlic clove, finely chopped
½ teaspoon light soy sauce
30 g (1 oz) desiccated coconut, dry-roasted until golden
2–3 teaspoons sugar, or to taste

Season prawns with salt and pepper, and set aside for 10–15 minutes to absorb the seasoning.

Half-fill a deep-fryer or a large saucepan with neutral oil and heat to 170°C (340°F); bubbles should form around a wooden chopstick when it's dipped in. In batches, deep-fry the prawns until just cooked (about 2 minutes). Remove and drain well on paper towels.

Heat 2 tablespoons of oil in a clean wok over medium heat. Add a pinch of salt to the beaten egg yolks and pour into the wok. Stir briskly with a fork or chopsticks to form fine strands. As soon as the yolks are cooked, remove from the wok and set aside.

Melt the butter in the wok over medium–high heat and fry the curry leaves for 10 seconds (be careful; they will spit), then add the chilli and garlic and fry for 1 minute or until fragrant.

Add the deep-fried prawns, soy sauce and roasted coconut and cook, stirring frequently, for 1 minute. Return the egg strands to the wok and add the sugar. Stir and toss for 30 seconds or until well mixed. Check the seasoning and serve hot.

✿ The original recipe calls for the prawns to be deep-fried with the shells on. However, they are equally delicious when stir-fried or shallow-fried and you can peel the prawns in this case.

SERVES 4 | 6

STEAMED PRAWNS WITH PICKLED LEEKS, GINGER AND SPRING ONIONS

The combination of ginger and spring onions is a Chinese classic. I have included pickled leeks to enhance this dish, which puts steamed prawns at the centre, although the combination also works well with fish. Prawns don't really require much embellishment – the inherent sweet flavour speaks for itself. Umeboshi, the pickled plums, are also delicious with this recipe.

- 500 g (1 lb 2 oz) green prawns, peeled and deveined, tails intact
- 2 tablespoons Shaoxing wine
- ¾ cup (185 ml) chicken stock
- 3 pickled leeks (see note), finely chopped
- 1 tablespoon finely chopped ginger
- 1 tablespoon light soy sauce
- ½ teaspoon sesame oil
- Pinch of caster (superfine) sugar
- Salt and white pepper, to taste
- 1 spring onion (scallion), finely chopped
- ¼ cup (60 ml) camellia tea oil or peanut oil
- Coriander (cilantro) sprigs, to serve

Butterfly the prawns by making a cut along the back to ensure even cooking. Place them side by side in a shallow bowl that will fit in your steamer, then pour in the Shaoxing and chicken stock and scatter with pickled leeks and ginger.

Place the bowl in a steamer basket and set it over a wok filled with boiling water. Cover and steam for about 5 minutes or until the prawns are just cooked. Carefully remove the bowl from the steamer and transfer prawns to a serving plate. Drizzle with the steaming juices, then top with soy, sesame oil, sugar, a pinch or two of salt and pepper and the spring onion.

Heat the oil in a dry wok over medium-high heat until smoking, then carefully pour it over the prawns. Serve topped with coriander.

✖ Chinese, Vietnamese and Thai pickled leeks are tiny. They are young shoots (5 cm/2 inches) and are pickled in a vinegar-sugar solution, with decorative sliced carrots at times. They are sold in Asian grocers.

OYSTER OMELETTE WITH CHILLI SAUCE

SERVES 4

Often called 'or luak' in hawker centres, this oyster omelette from the Hokkien and Teochew communities is one of the dishes I never skip when I'm back in Singapore. There are several versions of this local favourite – some are served soft and slightly runny while others are dry and well done – and it's often prepared with a generous addition of tapioca and rice starch batter for a sort of gooey texture. If you are in Penang, the same dish is called 'or chien'.

To make the chilli-vinegar sauce, place the ingredients in a blender and blitz until a smooth sauce forms. Chilli-vinegar sauce will keep refrigerated for 1 month.

Mix the beaten eggs with the fish sauce and set aside.

Combine the flours with ½ cup (125 ml) water in a small bowl and set aside.

Heat a wok or a non-stick frying pan over medium heat, add 1 tablespoon oil, add half the flour mixture, swirl it around on the base of the wok and allow it to just set. Pour the egg over the flour pancake and leave to set for about 10 seconds, then add the remaining flour batter followed by another tablespoon of oil.

Cook for 2–3 minutes until the omelette turns lightly golden, then move it to the side of the wok or pan. Reduce the heat to low-medium, add the remaining tablespoon of oil followed by the garlic, stir-fry until softened, then add the oysters and Shaoxing and stir quickly to warm through.

Mix the oysters into the omelette, transfer to a plate, top with coriander and serve with the chilli sauce.

✽ This omelette is not like a traditional French or Western-style omelette. It's more like scrambled eggs.

6 eggs, lightly beaten
1 tablespoon fish sauce, or to taste
2 tablespoons tapioca flour mixed with 1 tablespoon rice flour
¼ cup (60 ml) neutral oil
1 teaspoon finely chopped garlic
8 large fresh oysters
1 teaspoon Shaoxing wine (optional)
Salt and white pepper, to taste
Coriander sprigs, to serve

CHILLI-VINEGAR SAUCE
4 long red chillies, seeds removed if preferred
2 garlic cloves, peeled
100 ml (3½ fl oz) rice vinegar
Caster (superfine) sugar, to taste
Salt, to taste

HOT WOK, COLD OIL

After all these years of teaching and living in Australia, it still surprises me that so many people are mystified by woks. Then I realised that they haven't been properly taught how to use this most versatile of Chinese cooking vessels. For me, it starts by knowing its history. The wok has been around since the Han Dynasty (206 BCE to 220 CE) and for more than 2000 years, it has remarkably remained the same shape, which is a testament to its usefulness. It is only during the Ming Dynasty (1368–1644), however, that the wok came to enjoy widespread popularity.

Since that period, the wok has travelled from China to just about every corner of the world, the main reason being its versatility; it is one of the few pieces of cooking equipment that is great for not only stir-frying, but also steaming, deep-frying, blanching and smoking. Because of this multifunctional capability, the wok is the tool of choice for Chinese chefs and many home cooks.

Choosing a wok is easy, if you think about a few things first. First, woks come in different sizes, ranging from 28 to 50 centimetres (11 to 20 inches) in diameter. Second, they're made with different materials, from aluminium to cast iron to carbon steel. There are also stainless-steel and non-stick woks. Third, there's the shape. A traditional wok is bowl-shaped with curved sloping sides designed to fit directly over the hearth. Flat-bottomed woks, meanwhile, are a more recent invention, designed to fit a modern electric or induction stove.

There are also the handles to think about. Cantonese or southern Chinese woks are made with two loop handles mounted on opposite sides of the wok. Since they're made from metal, cooks use a thick towel to hold one of the handles to toss the food when cooking, an action that requires strong hands and wrists. Northern Chinese woks – aka pow woks – come with stick handles made from metal that are welded to the wok. Most of the handles are also mounted with wood for easier handling. Some of these woks also have a helper-handle on the opposite side.

> It's also important to consider your stove. Most domestic stove-tops are small, so pick a wok that will fit comfortably on it.

My wok, for example, is 36 centimetres (14 inches) in diameter, making it perfect for cooking dishes to feed up to four or five people, but my gas stove has a custom-made wok insert that can accommodate a round-bottomed wok. The fact it can churn out 18 megajoules of intense heat also means I can achieve the elusive wok hei much loved by discerning cooks. (For more on this phenomenon, see my notes on stir-frying on page 256.)

Consider also the wok's durability and weight. Properly treated, most woks can last a lifetime. It's essential, however, to note the density of the material used for making a wok and how it reacts to heat when you're cooking with it. Stainless-steel woks are expensive and heavy and take longer to heat. They also tend to stick. Aluminium woks are great when it comes to even heat distribution, but they cool down very quickly. Non-stick woks, though, are best avoided because the coating can break down and create toxic vapours when the temperature reaches 230°C (450°F).

In my opinion, the best wok you can buy is a carbon-steel one, which is typically the wok of choice for Chinese chefs. Not only is carbon steel durable, but it will withstand the high temperatures needed for quick stir-frying. Carbon-steel woks are also inexpensive. Of course, you may choose to buy a cast-iron wok, which has the benefit of being a beautiful vessel to braise or slow-cook in. The downside is that a cast-iron wok will tend to be heavier and more fragile than a carbon-steel wok. My carbon-steel wok, for example, weighs less than 950 grams (2 lb 1 ounce) and is 14 gauge, or about 2 millimetres (1/16 inch) thick.

The next consideration is how to season a new wok to create a durable non-stick surface – my wok, for example, has developed a patina from years of cooking with it. The traditional Chinese method is to use garlic chives and/or ginger and pork fat to season a wok. This has something to do with symbolism and superstition. American-Chinese author and cookery teacher Grace Young offers a detailed explanation of the reasoning and method in her outstanding book, *The Breath of a Wok*. My method is less romantic.

When you bring your carbon-steel wok back from the shop, the first thing to do is completely scrub off the protective oil coating with warm soapy water. Dry the wok thoroughly with paper towel, then place it over medium-high heat on a gas stove (if you don't have a gas stove, see below for alternatives). After 30 seconds, the wok will begin to smoke and change to a bluish colour. Turn and tilt the wok until the surface is blue and black all over. Remove from the heat, leave it to cool for 30 seconds, then dab half a teaspoon of high-smoke-point oil (such as grapeseed or rice bran oil) onto a piece of paper towel and rub the wok all over with the oil. Repeat this process three or four times until the non-stick patina is developed (this process is called polymerisation, which basically bonds the oil to the surface of the wok, creating a non-stick coating). After this process, the wok is seasoned and ready to use.

If you have an electric or induction stove, your flat-bottomed wok can be seasoned using a butane torch or in a 230°C oven. Or you can season it on a barbecue if you have one.

> One of the tests for whether you've succeeded in creating a non-stick patina is to fry an egg in a newly seasoned wok.

Heat the wok over high heat until a drop of water evaporates within 1 or 2 seconds. Add 2 tablespoons of grapeseed or rice bran oil. Once the oil is shimmering, crack an egg into the middle of the wok. With a spatula, baste the egg with the hot oil until cooked to your liking. If the egg does not stick to the wok, the wok has developed a patina.

As for how to maintain the non-stick surface, my best advice is to regularly use your wok. Just be aware that it's not great to cook anything acidic, like tomatoes or vinegar, during the first couple of uses – acid destroys the patina. Until the patina is built up through constant stir-frying, it's best to treat your new wok with tender loving care.

Some cooks believe it's not a good thing to use soap to clean a wok. I do and I don't. If I'm using my wok for deep-frying, I use a mild detergent to remove excess oil and it will not affect the patina. But generally, I wash my wok in hot water with a sponge immediately after cooking. Once cleaned, the wok is put back on the burner to dry off.

> Water is the enemy of a carbon-steel wok; you don't want it to rust. Once the surface has dried, rub a thin layer of oil onto the surface with paper towel to maintain the patina.

My preferred tools for wok cooking are the following: a metal wok spatula, a domed lid, a Chinese ladle and a wok ring. A wok spatula, made of stainless steel, is perfect for stir-frying because the curved contours fit perfectly within the sloping sides of the wok. A domed lid, meanwhile, that sits just below the rim of the wok, allows for maximum steam circulation and is also fantastic for heat control, especially for dishes that require slow cooking or braising. If you don't have a lid for your wok, I highly recommend buying one. As for the ladle, Chinese chefs use a ladle to stir-fry and to measure and combine sauce ingredients while stir-frying. They also use it to push the food away when stir-frying while they simultaneously jerk the wok to toss the food. This technique is achievable with practice and patience. The wok ring is to support a round-bottomed wok for gas stoves but it's not required for flat-bottomed woks.

People often ask me why I use a wok when a frying pan will do. My answers are that first, and rather simply, a wok has sloping sides so less oil is needed and the results are healthier. Second, a wok has the perfect shape to create the much-desired wok hei, that elusive fragrance that a frying pan just can't achieve. Because the heat source is concentrated at the base, it's easier to achieve a rich, charred flavour and maintain a sense of freshness – especially with vegetables – aided by the stirring and tossing action that ensures dishes are finished in mere minutes.

It's important to remember that a domestic range will never produce the intense heat of a professional range, but the wok will affect the flavour greatly. The flavour is a result of the combination of the patina – or the layers of polymerised oil – bonded to the surface of a carbon-steel wok and the heat. It sounds a bit far-fetched, but the next time you cook with your carbon-steel wok, notice the flavour. It is the qi or 'breath of the wok' at work.

If you want your stir-fry to taste like the ones in a Chinese restaurant, remember not to overcrowd a wok with too many ingredients. If a lot of ingredients are thrown into a wok, the temperature will drop, the contents will steam and the result will be something akin to a mish-mash of ingredients instead of a glorious integrated stir-fry. If the quantity of a dish is more than the wok can fit, it is best to cook the dish in batches to maintain the crisp wok flavour.

> I have seared steaks in my wok. I've cooked pasta in it. I have roasted nuts and seeds in it. I've also deep-fried pastries in it.

Thanks to its deep, sloped sides, I have made the perfect fried rice. I've steamed dumplings with it. The beauty of wok cooking is its limitless possibilities. Just remember one golden rule when you next stir-fry: hot wok, cold oil, and the world is your oyster.

SERVES 2–4

STEAMED MUSSELS WITH XO SAUCE

When I first wrote in *Gourmet Traveller* about cooking mussels with XO sauce, it must have struck a chord – it soon appeared on a few restaurant menus around town. XO sauce is the crème de la crème of sauces because it's so packed with umami.

To make this dish really sing, you need to make your own XO sauce using this recipe. It makes 1 kg (2 lb 4 oz) of sauce and will keep in the fridge for about a month. If you are pressed for time, by all means use a commercially made sauce.

XO SAUCE
50 g (1¾ oz) dried scallops
150 g (5½ oz) dried shrimp
2 cups (500 ml) neutral oil, plus extra to store
150 g (5½ oz) garlic, finely chopped
150 g (5½ oz) shallots (eschalots), finely chopped
100 g (3½ oz) jamón or prosciutto, finely shredded
50 g (1¾ oz) long red chillies, seeded and finely chopped
30 g (1 oz) dried long chillies, seeded, soaked and finely chopped
15 g (½ oz) dried birdseye chillies, finely chopped
10 g (¼ oz) belacan (shrimp paste)
1 tablespoon dried shrimp roe, crumbled (optional)
30 g (1 oz) sugar, or to taste
Salt, to taste

STEAMED MUSSELS
2 tablespoons neutral oil
1 baby carrot, finely diced
2 spring onions (scallions), thinly sliced
1 teaspoon grated ginger
2 makrut lime leaves
1 kg (2 lb 4 oz) mussels, scrubbed
3 tablespoons Shaoxing wine
⅓ cup (80 ml) XO sauce
1 long red chilli, chopped
Salt, to taste
Coriander (cilantro) sprigs, to garnish

Put the dried scallops and shrimp in separate bowls and add 1 cup (250 ml) hot water to each bowl. Soak until plump (preferably overnight).

Drain the scallops and shrimp, reserving the soaking water. Tear the scallops by hand into fine shreds and pat dry. Finely chop the shrimp.

Heat 1 cup (250 ml) of the oil in a wok or large saucepan over medium-high heat and deep-fry the scallops until very crisp (cover with a lid as they will spit). Drain the scallops in a fine metal sieve set over a heatproof container. Reserve both.

Wipe the wok dry and add the strained oil along with remaining oil. Heat over medium heat. Fry the garlic, shallots and dried shrimp, stirring constantly, for 5–10 minutes until golden. Add the jamón and fresh and dried chilli. Fry for a few seconds (watch carefully; chilli burns easily).

Stir in the belacan, fried scallops and reserved soaking water. Add the shrimp roe, if using, and season with sugar and salt. Cook over low heat, stirring regularly, until the sauce is fragrant and the water has completely evaporated (about 30 minutes).

Transfer the sauce to a large sterilised jar and cover the top with a layer of oil. Cool, then store in the fridge for up to a month, or freezer for up to 3 months.

Heat the oil in a wok over medium heat. Fry the carrot, spring onions, ginger and lime leaves for 1 minute.

Increase the heat and add the mussels, stirring well. Add ⅓ cup (80 ml) water and half the Shaoxing. Cover and steam for 1–2 minutes or until the mussels start opening.

Add the remaining Shaoxing along with the XO sauce, chilli and salt. Cover and steam for another 2 minutes or until the mussels open. Discard any mussels that don't open, and serve garnished with coriander.

PENANG NYONYA FISH 'CURRY' WITH SPICY TAMARIND SAUCE

GULAI IKAN

SERVES 4 | 6

From Penang, this Nyonya fish 'curry' is popular throughout Malaysia. Perfumed with the scent of tamarind, this dish is even more exciting if you have access to fresh torch ginger bud or flower. This tropical flower is now available fresh from Northern Queensland, and it's sold frozen in Asian grocers.

This is an extremely versatile dish, that works well with strong-flavoured fish, such as trevally and mackerel. I have also made this dish with prawns and Balmain bugs, known as slipper lobsters in Malaysia.

- 100 ml (3½ fl oz) neutral oil
- 70 g (2½ oz) tamarind pulp
- 2–3 teaspoons caster (superfine) sugar
- 1 ginger flower (torch ginger), finely chopped
- Salt, to taste
- 4–6 fish fillets (such as trevally), skin on, each weighing 120 g (4¼ oz)

SPICE PASTE

- 2 small onions or 5 large shallots (eschalots), chopped
- 10 dried chillies, or to taste, soaked in hot water until soft, drained
- 2 cm (¾ inch) piece galangal
- 2 stalks lemongrass (white part only), finely chopped
- 2 cm (¾ inch) piece turmeric or 1 teaspoon ground turmeric
- 3 long red chillies, chopped
- 20 g (¾ oz) belacan (shrimp paste)

For the spice paste, blend all the ingredients in a food processor to a fine paste. Set aside.

Place the tamarind pulp in a bowl and cover with 3 cups (750 ml) warm water. Soak for 20 minutes, then, with your fingers, mash and squeeze the tamarind to extract as much juice as possible. Strain the liquid into a container.

Heat the oil in a large saucepan over medium heat, add the spice paste and cook, stirring to prevent catching, until fragrant and the oil separates from the paste (6–8 minutes).

Add the sugar to the saucepan, stir-fry for another minute, then stir in the torch ginger and pour the strained tamarind liquid into the saucepan. Bring to the boil, then reduce the heat to medium-low and simmer for 10–15 minutes until the flavours are balanced with hot, sweet and sour notes.

Season to taste with salt, then add the fish. Simmer, stirring occasionally, for 5–10 minutes until the fish is just cooked through and flakes easily at a touch. Check the seasoning, adjusting to taste and serve.

✖ A gulai is a thin curry that originated from Indonesia. Some cooks also add a handful of okra into the hot sauce a minute or two before serving. Ginger flower (torch ginger) is sometimes sold fresh at florists. In Bahasa Malaysia, it is called bunga kantan.

SERVES 4

STIR-FRIED PRAWNS WITH DUCK-LIVER SAUSAGE

This recipe is inspired by the love of auspicious ingredients during the Lunar New Year. 'Waxed meats' like wind-dried duck, chicken and sausages grace the reunion dinner. Prawns are considered to be prosperous, and so are also a celebratory staple. This quick stir-fry brings the two together, with the funkiness of duck-liver sausage complementing the clean sweetness of the prawns. The result is rather gutsy, but once you've made it, I guarantee you'll make it again and again.

2 tablespoons neutral oil
2 duck-liver sausages (see note), scalded and diced finely
1 small onion, finely diced
1 tablespoon ginger, finely chopped
1 teaspoon garlic, finely chopped
1 long red chilli (optional), finely chopped
1 teaspoon Sichuan pepper (optional), crushed
500 g (1 lb 2 oz) green prawns, peeled and deveined
1 tablespoon Shaoxing wine
1 teaspoon light soy sauce
1 teaspoon dark soy sauce
Pinch of sugar
½ cup (125 ml) chicken stock
½ teaspoon sesame oil
1 teaspoon cornflour (cornstarch), mixed with 2 tablespoons water
Thinly sliced spring onions (scallions) or chives, to serve

Heat a wok over medium-high heat, add the oil and swirl it around once or twice. Add the duck-liver sausage and the onion, stir-fry for 20–30 seconds until the onion softens and the sausage turns crisp, then immediately add the ginger, garlic, chilli and Sichuan pepper and stir-fry for 10 seconds.

Add the prawns and continue to toss and fry until the prawns turn slightly opaque before splashing in Shaoxing, soy sauces, sugar and chicken stock. Bring to a rapid boil and cook until the sauce is slightly reduced and the prawns are cooked.

Add the sesame oil, followed by the cornflour slurry, stirring to thicken the sauce.

Served topped with spring onion.

✖ You can find duck-liver sausages, or yun cheong in Cantonese, in Chinese grocers.

TYPHOON SHELTER CRAB

SERVES 4–6

If you love garlic and punchy flavours, this classic Hong Kong dish ticks all the boxes. Named after the people who once lived on fishing boats in typhoon shelters and originally made the dish, it is garlic-laden and deliciously earthy and can be made with all types of seafood, but in particular crab.

This dish became so popular that it's now served in many Chinese restaurants. The crab in this recipe is cooked with shell on, so have bowls of water ready to clean fingers – and perhaps a bib.

If you don't have nerves of steel, ask your fishmonger to dispatch your crabs for you. However, the easiest and most humane method is to put them to sleep in the freezer for an hour. After that, flip the crab over, exposing its belly, find the tip of the triangle of the main belly, and stab it quickly with a sharp knife.

Break down the mud crab by first lifting the carapace from the body, then pull out the gills. Chop the body into quarters, then chop off the legs and pincers. Give the pincers a good bash with a hammer or heavy knife to allow the sauce to penetrate.

Heat the oil in a wok over low-medium heat until shimmering or it reaches 140°C (275°F). Add the garlic and, stirring continuously with chopsticks or a spatula to prevent clumping, fry for 3–4 minutes until just turning light golden. Carefully pour the garlic and oil into a fine (metal) sieve set over a heatproof bowl. Drain garlic on paper towel.

Return the oil to the wok and place it over medium-high heat. Once the oil is shimmering, add the crab pieces in batches (be careful; hot oil will spit) and deep-fry until the shells turn a glossy coral red (4–5 minutes a batch). Remove with a slotted spoon and drain on paper towel. Strain the oil into a heatproof bowl and reserve.

Wipe the wok clean and return to medium high-heat. Add 2 tablespoons reserved oil, heat until shimmering, then add the shallots and ginger and stir frequently until light golden and crisp (2–3 minutes).

Add the chilli and fermented black beans, stir-fry for 1 minute, then return the crab and half the garlic to the wok, and add the salt and sugar. Stir-fry for another minute, add the spring onion, toss a couple of times, then add the Shaoxing and check the seasoning, adjusting to taste.

Transfer to a bowl and top with remaining garlic to serve.

- 1.5 kg (3 lb 5 oz) live mud crabs
- 1 cup (250 ml) neutral oil
- 2 garlic bulbs (about 20 cloves or 120 g/4¼ oz), finely chopped
- 2 shallots (eschalots; about 60 g/2¼ oz), finely chopped
- 2 tablespoons finely chopped ginger
- 5–8 dried chillies (to taste), cut with scissors into 1 cm (½ inch) pieces
- 1 tablespoon fermented black beans (about 15 g/½ oz), chopped
- 1 teaspoon salt
- 1 teaspoon caster (superfine) sugar
- 1 spring onion (scallion), cut into 5 cm (2 inch) pieces
- 1 tablespoon Shaoxing wine (optional)

PAN-FRIED SNAPPER WITH VINEGAR SAMBAL

SERVES 2

This deceptively easy recipe comes from the Kristang community in Malacca. The secret is to really work on the spice paste until it takes on a caramel-like fragrance. Mackerel is traditionally used here, but snapper or any white fish is just as delicious – likewise, it works just as well if you prefer to grill it. It's a dish traditionally made with distilled vinegar, but I've used rice vinegar, which is milder than most vinegars; adjust accordingly if you're using something different, such as sugar-cane vinegar or coconut vinegar.

This homestyle dish featuring a tangy sambal is particularly delicious with a cucumber salad. Recipe adapted from *A Kristang Family Cookbook* by Melba Nunis.

For the spice paste, soak the dried chillies in hot water for 15–20 minutes to soften. Once softened, drain and transfer to a blender and add shallots and candlenuts. Blend to a fine paste, adding a couple of tablespoons of water if required.

For the marinade, combine the turmeric, chilli and salt in a bowl.

Add the snapper to the marinade, toss to coat and set aside for 15 minutes to marinate.

Heat ¼ cup (60 ml) oil in a wok or frying pan over medium-high heat. Once the oil is shimmering, add the fish and cook for 6 minutes, turning halfway, until cooked through (be careful; hot oil will spit). Transfer to a plate lined with paper towel to drain.

Wipe the wok clean and return to medium heat, then add remaining oil. Once it's shimmering, add the spice paste and fry, stirring continuously to prevent catching, for 5–6 minutes until fragrant and the oil separates. Add 1 cup (250 ml) water, vinegar, soy sauce and sugar, bring to the boil, then reduce to a simmer and cook until slightly thickened (3–5 minutes).

Return the fish to the wok to warm through and season to taste with salt. Serve topped with spring onion.

2–3 snapper cutlets (about 500 g/1 lb 2 oz total), or whole snapper or mackerel
⅔ cup (175 ml) neutral oil
⅓ cup (80 ml) rice vinegar (or distilled vinegar)
½ teaspoon dark soy sauce, preferably thick soy sauce
2 tablespoons caster (superfine) sugar, or to taste
Salt, to taste
Thinly sliced spring onion (scallion), to serve

SPICE PASTE
10 dried red chillies (about 30 g/1 oz), cut into pieces with scissors
10 shallots (eschalots) (about 200 g), chopped
7 candlenuts

MARINADE
1 teaspoon ground turmeric
½ teaspoon chilli powder
Salt, to taste

FISH HEAD CURRY
KARI KEPALA IKAN

SERVES 6–8

One of the most recognised dishes in Malaysia and Singapore, fish head curry is simple to prepare and terribly addictive. According to legend, this classic is thought to have been created by a South Indian cook in the 1950s in Singapore. Although many of us may be confronted by the idea of eating fish head, believe me, the tender fish cheeks are quite irresistible. Once you have overcome any initial hesitation, you will adore the flavours of curry leaves and lemongrass infused into the rich fish broth. If you can't get hold of a head (ask your fishmonger), fillets work perfectly, too.

Clean the fish head by giving it a thorough wash and stripping the gills and blood (if any). Season all over with the salt. Leave for 20 minutes, then rinse off the salt and pat dry with paper towel.

Meanwhile, for the spice paste, place all the ingredients in a food processor and blend until smooth.

Mix the tamarind pulp with 2 cups (500 ml) hot water. Mash the soaked tamarind with your fingers to extract as much pulp from the seeds as possible, then strain the mixture into a bowl. Set aside.

Heat the oil in a large wok or pan over medium-high heat, add the mustard seeds and swirl until they pop. Working quickly, add the curry leaves and fenugreek seeds. Stir for a few seconds, then add the spice paste along with the lemongrass and star anise. Reduce the heat to medium-low and cook, stirring frequently, until fragrant and the oil separates.

Add the fish curry powder, stir-fry for another 2 minutes, then add the coconut milk and strained tamarind juice and bring to the boil, stirring constantly.

Place the fish head in the sauce and lower heat to a gentle simmer. When the fish is almost cooked (about 6–8 minutes), add the okra and eggplant. Simmer for another 3–5 minutes, add sugar and salt, adjusting to taste, then just before serving stir in the tomato. Serve with rice.

✖ Use fresh curry leaves only – the dried variety doesn't have the distinctive fragrance that is essential to the dish. Malaysian fish curry powder is made with coriander, fennel, fenugreek and cumin seeds, black peppercorns, turmeric powder and roasted dried chillies. Alagappa's and Cap Burung Nuri (Parrot Brand) are among the best.

1 large fish head (preferably snapper; about 1.5 kg/3 lb 5 oz), cut in half
1 teaspoon salt
2 heaped tablespoons tamarind pulp
4 tablespoons neutral oil
¼ teaspoon mustard seeds
2 sprigs curry leaves
¼ teaspoon fenugreek seeds
1 lemongrass stalk (white part only), outer leaves removed, crushed
1 star anise
3 tablespoons Malaysian fish curry powder (see note)
2 cups (500 ml) thin coconut milk
5 small okra
1 small Japanese eggplant (aubergine), cut into wedges
Caster (superfine) sugar, to taste
Salt, to taste
1 tomato, cut into wedges

SPICE PASTE
5 dried long red chillies, soaked in hot water until soft, then drained
2 long red chillies, seeded and chopped
5 shallots (eschalots), sliced
3 garlic cloves
2 cm (¾ inch) piece fresh turmeric, sliced
2 cm (¾ inch) piece galangal, chopped
5 cm (2 inch) piece ginger, chopped
1 lemongrass stalk, thinly sliced

SERVES 10

FIVE-SPICE 'SMOKED' FISH WITH BROAD BEAN MASH AND SPICY WITLOF SALAD

Although this dish is from Sichuan province, it also appears in Shanghainese and northern Chinese restaurants. Despite its name, there is no smoking involved, though it was once made with smoked fish and was a traditional Chinese food. Apparently, the Chinese used to smoke fish but stopped, however the name stuck.

The fish must be marinated first, then deep-fried and finally cooked in a spiced sauce. Because full-flavoured fish is often used, I like to present it with a garnish of spring onion and pickled Chinese limes, which stand up to the flavour. The latter is sold in jars at Asian grocers.

As for the mashed broad beans, fresh is best, but you can now buy frozen double-peeled broad beans in Asian grocers. When infused with pickled mustard greens, these provide a lovely contrast. This is often served as a starter as part of a collection of salads, but I think it's perfect as a side too.

The best pickled mustard greens translate as 'red in snow' (poetically red, as in new life springing from the snow, rather than their literal colour) and are sold in foil packets. Finally, the Chinese love lightly pickled cabbage (wong bok) as a starter. In its place, use witlof for a modern touch.

1 kg (2 lb 4 oz) blue-eye, ling, trevally or salmon fillets, skin on, cut into 2 cm (¾ inch) pieces
Neutral oil, for deep-frying
2 spring onions (scallions), thinly sliced
1 preserved lime (or lemon), finely diced

MARINADE
40 g (1½ oz) ginger, chopped
1 spring onion (scallion), chopped
¼ cup (60 ml) light soy sauce
1 tablespoon Shaoxing wine
1 teaspoon salt, or to taste

SAUCE
2 tablespoons peanut oil
2 garlic cloves, finely chopped
2 teaspoons finely chopped ginger
2 spring onions (scallions), thinly sliced
2 star anise
2 pieces dried mandarin peel
2 pieces cassia bark, about 5 cm (2 inch) each
60–80 g (2¼–2¾ oz) rock sugar (to taste)
2 teaspoons dark soy sauce
2 tablespoons light soy sauce
½ teaspoon ground Sichuan pepper
1 teaspoon black peppercorns

For the marinade, pound the ginger with a mortar and pestle to extract the juice. Discard the pulp. Add the spring onion, pound together, then toss with the soy, Shaoxing and salt, adjusting to taste.

Place the fish and marinade in a bowl, toss to coat, and refrigerate for at least 2 hours to marinate.

Meanwhile, for the sauce, heat the oil in a wok over medium-high heat. Once shimmering, add the garlic, ginger and spring onion and stir-fry until fragrant (3–5 minutes). Add the remaining ingredients and 700 ml (24 fl oz) water, bring to the boil, then reduce the heat to low and simmer for 25–30 minutes until the liquid is reduced to about 400 ml (13½ fl oz). Strain, discarding the solids.

Once the fish is ready, pat it dry with paper towel (discard the remaining marinade) and heat the oil in a deep-fryer or large, deep saucepan, to 170–180°C (325–350°F; bubbles should form around a wooden chopstick when it's dipped in). Deep-fry the fish in batches, until crisp (5–6 minutes). Remove with a slotted spoon and drain well on a wire rack.

Bring the sauce back to the boil. Add the fried fish pieces and simmer gently, basting now and then, until the sauce has almost evaporated. Ladle onto a serving platter and scatter with lime and spring onion. Serve with the broad beans and witlof salad (see opposite).

BROAD BEAN MASH

¼ cup (60 ml) neutral oil
100 g (3½ oz) pickled mustard greens, rinsed well, drained and finely chopped
300 g (10½ oz) double-peeled broad beans (fresh or frozen)
1 cup (250 ml) chicken stock
1 teaspoon caster (superfine) sugar
Salt and white pepper, to taste
2 tablespoons thinly sliced spring onion (scallion)

Heat the oil in a wok over medium heat, add the pickled mustard greens and stir-fry for 1–2 minutes. Add the broad beans, stir-fry for 30 seconds, then add the chicken stock and sugar and season to taste with salt and pepper. Stir-fry over high heat until the stock is completely evaporated and absorbed. Transfer to a bowl, leave to cool, then mash coarsely and stir in the spring onion.

SPICY WITLOF SALAD

3 witlof (chicory)
Good pinch of salt, for pickling
3–5 Sichuan pickled chillies (from Asian grocers) or Thai pickled whole chillies, thinly sliced
2 tablespoons shredded ginger
1 tablespoon white wine vinegar, or to taste
1 tablespoon caster (superfine) sugar, or to taste

Pull off as many leaves as will come away easily from the witlof, then cut from the base to remove remaining leaves. Place the leaves in a bowl, sprinkle evenly with salt (enough to coat), tossing gently to coat well. Set aside for 30 minutes until the leaves are wilted.

Rinse off the salt, drain well, then slice the witlof into bite-sized pieces. Toss with the remaining ingredients and leave for 5–10 minutes to allow the flavours to meld before serving.

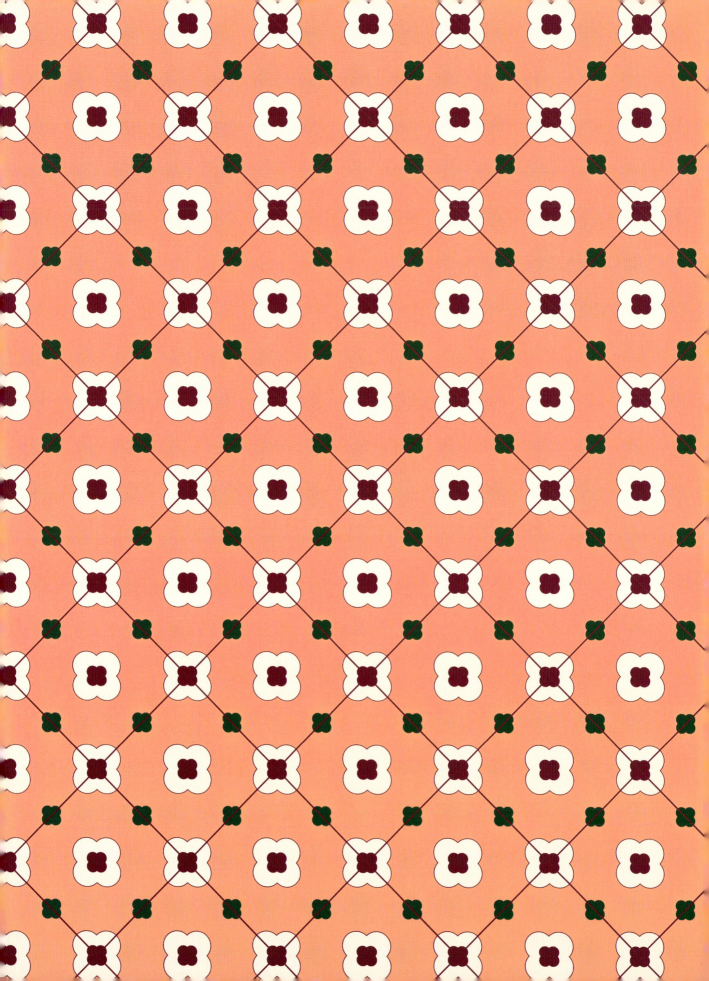

VEGETABLES

CHAR SIU CAULIFLOWER

SERVES 2–4

This recipe was born some time during lockdown. At that time I realised that if I'm to eat seasonally, there will be an abundance of the same vegetable. Hence the creation of char siu-flavoured cauliflower, which gave me one more exciting way to serve this brassica when I had a glut of it. Packed with the flavours of a great char siu, it's seriously delicious and a joy to eat. Presenting a whole cauliflower in its glorious roasted splendour is increasingly popular and also a visual treat.

1 tablespoon salt
1 cauliflower (about 500 g/1 lb 2 oz), leaves removed
Neutral oil, for drizzling
Thinly sliced spring onions (scallions), to serve
Steamed rice, to serve

MARINADE
2 garlic cloves, chopped
1 tablespoon light soy sauce
1½ teaspoons dark soy sauce
½ teaspoon white pepper
1 tablespoon hoisin sauce
2 cubes red fermented beancurd (see note), mashed
½ teaspoon Chinese five-spice powder
1 tablespoon honey or maltose, or to taste
1 tablespoon mei kuei lu chiew (rose dew cooking wine) or brandy
Few drops red food colouring (optional)

Heat the oven to 240°C (475°F). Fill a large pot two-thirds full with water and bring to the boil. Add a tablespoon of salt and submerge the cauliflower, leaving it to simmer for 10–12 minutes until just tender but not overcooked.

Meanwhile, blitz the marinade ingredients together with a stick blender until smooth.

Drain the cauliflower and pat dry. Transfer to a baking tray, smear the marinade all over it (if you like, you can reserve a little to pour over it at the end), then drizzle with oil.

Place the cauliflower in the oven and roast for 10 minutes, then reduce the heat to 180°C (375°F) and cook, brushing now and then with excess marinade, for another 20–30 minutes until beautifully caramelised and crisp.

Remove from the oven and cool for 5 minutes, then top with spring onion and serve with steamed rice.

✿ Red fermented beancurd is a funky ingredient sold in jars. It's called nam yue in Cantonese.

LEMONGRASS TOFU

SERVES 4–6

This tofu offering will convert the firmest of sceptics into a tofu lover. From Vietnam, this strikingly beautiful dish is all about textures and flavours: crisp tofu and bright tropical hits of lemongrass, ginger and a choice of herbs like wild betel leaves, coriander and Thai basil.

A departure from the ubiquitous fish sauce, which is often used in Vietnamese cooking, soy sauce not only adds flavour, but is fabulous for vegetarians. I make this dish whenever I crave clean, spicy flavours.

Combine lemongrass, soy sauce, chillies, turmeric and sugar in a bowl. Stir well, add tofu, toss gently to coat and leave to marinate for 30 minutes.

Heat half the oil in a non-stick frying pan or well-treated wok over medium-high heat. Add the onion, garlic and ginger and stir-fry until aromatic and softened but not burnt (about 1 minute). Transfer to a plate.

Add the remaining oil to the pan and reduce the heat to medium. Carefully add the tofu (it will spit) and fry, turning, until the cubes are golden all over (4–5 minutes).

Return the onion mixture to the pan and cook, stirring occasionally, for another 2–3 minutes, adding a little water or stock if it's cooking too quickly. Check seasoning, adjusting to taste, then add the nuts and betel leaves, tossing them through just before dishing. Serve with steamed rice.

2 lemongrass stalks (white part only), finely chopped
2 tablespoons light soy sauce
2 birdseye chillies, minced
½ teaspoon ground turmeric
1 teaspoon caster (superfine) sugar, or to taste
400 g (14 oz) firm tofu, drained, patted dry and cut into 3 cm (1¼ inch) cubes
⅓ cup (80 ml) neutral oil
1 small onion, thinly sliced
2 garlic cloves, minced
2 thin slices of ginger, finely chopped into strips
Dash of water or chicken stock (optional)
Salt and white pepper, to taste
⅓ cup (50 g) roasted peanuts or pinenuts, chopped
10–15 betel leaves, shredded, or ¾ cup (10 g) Thai basil or coriander (cilantro)
Steamed rice, to serve

SERVES 4

SPICY SICHUAN MUNG BEAN NOODLES

This is a wonderful refreshing homemade noodle salad, especially popular during the hot summer months. Since the dish is from Sichuan, a province in western China famous for its hot, fragrant dishes, it is highly aromatic and very spicy. You can, however, always reduce the quantity of chilli to suit your palate.

Homemade mung bean noodles require practice, but once you've mastered the technique, they're so easy to make. In Australia, mung bean flour typically comes from Thailand, so you'll find it most commonly sold in packets in Thai grocers. For making these noodles, you'll need a large plastic tray around 28 x 36 cm (11 x 14 inches) – this helps to prevent the dough from sticking. If you don't have the time to make the noodles, you can use wheat or rice noodles instead.

60 g (2¼ oz) mung bean flour
150 ml (5 fl oz) cold water
Roasted peanuts (optional) and thinly sliced spring onion, to serve

SICHUAN CHILLI SAUCE
1 tablespoon light soy sauce
1 tablespoon Chinkiang vinegar
Pinch of caster (superfine) sugar, to taste
Salt, to taste
⅓ cup (80 ml) light neutral oil
2 teaspoons sesame oil
30 g (1 oz) ginger, minced
2 spring onions (scallions), finely chopped
1 tablespoon roasted sesame seeds
1–2 teaspoons chilli powder, to taste
1 teaspoon roasted Sichuan pepper, ground

To make the noodles, thoroughly whisk the mung bean flour into the cold water. Set aside and bring 2 cups (500 ml) water to the boil in a saucepan. As soon as it boils, whisk the mung bean flour mixture again and, in a steady stream, pour it into the hot water. Whisk immediately and vigorously until it becomes a translucent, starchy mass.

Tip this dough immediately into a large ungreased plastic tray. Working quickly, spread the mixture all over the tray by tipping it in all directions until it's evenly spread. Leave to cool at room temperature, then refrigerate until firm (about 15 minutes).

Meanwhile, for the sauce, combine the soy sauce and vinegar in a bowl, add the sugar and salt and whisk to dissolve. Add remaining ingredients and stir to combine well.

To serve, roll the sheet of dough up lengthways to form a sausage. Carefully lift the sausage from the tray and onto a chopping board. Cut into thin noodles, serve with sauce and top with crushed peanuts and spring onion.

GRILLED EGGPLANT SALAD WITH CHILLI JAM
YAM MAKUA POW

SERVES 6–8

In Thailand, eggplant is often grilled over an open fire, which gives the dish a smoky character. Combined with the signature punch and sweetness of nahm prik pao, this dish is sprightly and addictive.

Chilli jam, or nam prik pao as it's known in Thailand where it's often served as a table condiment, is extremely versatile, just like the sambals of Malaysia. I have used it in stir-fries and even in soups.

2–3 eggplants (aubergines), preferably Asian
1 tablespoon dried shrimp, pounded to a coarse powder
1 tablespoon fish sauce
¼ cup (60 ml) lime juice (from about 2 limes)
1 teaspoon caster (superfine) sugar
1 spring onion (scallion), finely chopped
Coriander (cilantro) leaves, to serve

CHILLI JAM (NAHM PRIK PAO)
2 garlic bulbs
120 g (4¼ oz) shallots (eschalots)
10–15 dried long red chillies
1 tablespoon dried shrimp
1 cup (250 ml) neutral oil
1 teaspoon salt
2 tablespoons palm sugar (or jaggery)

Prick the eggplants all over with a fork and sit them directly on the naked flame of your stove burner set to medium-low (or place them on the grill of a barbecue over medium-low heat). Cook, turning constantly, for at least 10 minutes until the whole eggplant is blackened and blistered. Transfer to a bowl and cover with plastic wrap. Leave to cool, then peel off the skin to reveal the flesh. Slice the eggplant into 5 cm (2 inch) pieces.

Heat the oven to 200°C (400°F). Break the unpeeled garlic bulbs apart just a little and wrap in foil. Wrap the shallots separately in foil, then roast both on the top shelf of the oven for 30 minutes or until soft to the touch. Remove, cool and then peel.

Roast or pan-fry the chillies in a frying pan over low heat for 2–3 minutes or until light brown. Discard the stems, and remove the seeds if you prefer a milder flavour, then blend finely in a food processor. Blend in the dried shrimp, then add the peeled garlic and shallots and blend until smooth.

Combine the remaining ingredients, except the coriander, in a bowl with 3 tablespoons of nahm prik pao. Add the eggplant and stir just enough to coat. Transfer to a serving plate and top with coriander to serve.

Heat the oil in a wide saucepan or wok over medium heat and add the chilli mixture. Reduce the heat to low and cook, stirring frequently, for 5–6 minutes until the mixture is slightly oily and sticky. Add the salt and stir to mix, then add the sugar and mix until dissolved to make a thick, slightly oily sauce. Remove from the heat, cool and store in an airtight container in the fridge for up to 2 weeks.

STIR-FRIED CHINESE SPINACH OR AMARANTH

SERVES 2–4

Sold as entire plants, the amaranth family is a large group of plants, originating in the American, African and Asian tropics but now spread all over the tropics. In Asia, amaranth has been cultivated for centuries for its leaves, while in Latin America it's harvested for its seeds.

Exceptionally nutritious, it is considered by experts to be as rich in protein as most podded beans. As it has a tendency to wilt like English spinach, it is known as Chinese spinach (though it is not a spinach) in many cookbooks. There are mainly two varieties sold here in Australia: one with green leaves and the other splotched and veined with red.

For Western cooking, it can be sautéed with bacon or baked with cheese or seafood. In Chinese cooking, it is often made into a soup or quickly stir-fried with white fermented beancurd (fu yu), though adding some meat and seafood is equally as delicious. It is also great with coconut, lentils and flowering chives.

This preparation strips it back to the essentials, keeping the focus on the leaves in a quick stir-fry to accompany dishes like braised pork belly with soy sauce (page 151) and pan-fried snapper with vinegar sambal (page 239).

Pick off the tender tips and leaves of the amaranth and discard the central stems and roots. Rinse, then drain.

Heat the oil in a wok over low heat, add the garlic and fry, stirring, until it turns pale golden. Add the amaranth, increase the heat to medium-high and stir-fry until the leaves begin to wilt.

Add a splash of water (or stock), followed by the oyster sauce and sugar. Stir for another minute, then dish out and serve with steamed rice.

500–700 g (1 lb 2 oz–1 lb 9 oz) amaranth
2 tablespoons neutral oil
1 large garlic clove, finely chopped
Splash of water or chicken stock
2 tablespoons oyster sauce
Pinch of caster (superfine) sugar
Steamed rice, to serve

MASTERING STIR-FRY

Much has been written about stir-frying, a cooking technique that originated in China and is now used globally. We all know it involves cooking chosen ingredients rapidly with a small amount of oil in a heated wok to then be served immediately. But what about wok hei, the Cantonese term that refers to the energy or 'breath' of the wok that so many chefs and writers talk about? What happens when there is none of the elusive fragrance emanating from a perfectly executed stir-fry? What happens when the ingredients in a wok are not tossed dramatically in the air like one sees in a Chinese restaurant? Well, here are some tips and explanations.

To begin with, the term stir-fry apparently was only coined last century. It is used to explain the action of cooking either proteins, like meat and seafood, or vegetables briskly while moving the food around in a hot wok so that they're done in minutes. Called chau in Chinese, this method of cooking is immensely popular in China because it is time- and fuel-efficient. Stir-frying also results in tender-crisp vegetables that retain more nutrients than if they were boiled.

Before you begin to stir-fry, it is essential to prepare all the ingredients ahead of time. All the ingredients that go into the wok must be cut uniformly so that they cook evenly. Meats should be cut across the grain, and vegetables should be washed and properly drained to avoid adding moisture to the dish.

If meat or seafood needs to be velveted – a marinating technique involving an egg white, 1 tablespoon of cornflour or tapioca flour and a dribble of water or rice wine to form a slurry – it should be done at least 10 minutes before cooking.

When you're ready to stir-fry, there are two things to remember. One: have all your sauces and flavouring ingredients close by and measured out, because as soon as the process of stir-frying begins, there's no turning back. And two: select an oil with a high smoke point – the Chinese prefer peanut oil, although just about any neutral oil with a high smoke point will be fine.

> To ensure a great result, always use the 'hot wok, cold oil' technique.

Depending on your heat source, a wok may take a few seconds to a couple of minutes to reach the high heat required for stir-frying (a good test is to splash a drop or two of water into the wok; if it evaporates in seconds, the wok is ready). Add a little oil and swirl it around to cover the surface. This essential step seals the surface to prevent ingredients from sticking. As soon as the oil shimmers, add your aromatics, like ginger, chillies and spring onions. I tend to add garlic a couple of seconds later as it tends to burn a little more easily. Stir-fry the aromatics quickly, then add the main ingredient. If you're adding meat, separate the pieces and stir-fry or toss briskly in the air until lightly browned but not cooked through. The cooking time depends on how finely the meat is cut and the heat source, but it should be no more than a minute. If the meat is searing too quickly, move the wok to the side or turn the heat down or even off as Chinese restaurant chefs do in their kitchens.

Understanding heat and controlling it is part of the journey of learning about stir-frying.

Check out a professional Chinese or Asian kitchen and you'll see a lever about knee height. Wok chefs use this to control the heat of the gas with their knee while they are tossing and frying the food in the wok.

To finish your stir-fry, once the main ingredient is partially cooked through, add any other ingredients in your recipe and continue to toss and fry. Just before the final flourish, add a splash of soy sauce, or whatever sauce you're using, to the side of the wok and toss again. Your stir-fry is ready.

In some cases, especially in restaurant cooking, velveted ingredients are blanched briefly in hot oil or simmering water with a dollop of oil to create that luscious mouthfeel much loved by the Chinese. This additional step, called guo you, results in silky-smooth morsels of meat or seafood. These bite-sized pieces are added to a stir-fry to finish off a dish. This blanching method is sometimes also used to hasten the cooking time of vegetables like Chinese broccoli, meaning that when it's added to a stir-fry, it will cook in roughly the same amount of time as the other ingredients.

Wok hei tends to be used as a yardstick to determine if a cook is proficient with stir-frying. To achieve this elusive fragrance, professional chefs cook on stoves with 20 times the power of a domestic range. Unless a dedicated wok burner is available, wok hei is the bane of so many home cooks. My mother, who was an amazing cook, could never match the wok fragrance of the professional chefs in our restaurant because she was cooking on a domestic stove.

My thoughts regarding this issue are these. So long as the stir-fry is full of nutritional goodness and delicious fresh flavours, it doesn't matter. In her ground-breaking book, *The Breath of A Wok*, Grace Young writes that the legendary food authority Florence Lin had said that only the Cantonese stressed the importance of wok hei.

Throughout Southeast Asia, the wok is the favourite tool for stir-fries in thousands of domestic kitchens. Practically all the stir-fries I've enjoyed deliver none of the much-talked-about wok hei but they are fresh, punchy, delicious and deeply satisfying.

Why? The cooks there don't overcrowd their woks with too many ingredients, they cut their ingredients uniformly, they use the right oils and they are highly organised when they stir-fry.

These valuable assets are what stir-frying is all about.

STIR-FRIED MIXED VEGETABLES

SERVES 6

A lovely, simple and quick stir-fry with different textures, including soft leafy greens, such as wombok and bok choy, silky shiitake mushrooms and crunchy asparagus and carrot. Vegetarian oyster sauce is a great option in this dish, too. You can use any vegetables you like, including zucchini (courgette), capsicum (pepper), green tomatoes and any leafy green of your choice such as silverbeet (swiss chard) or spinach. I even use cabbage and lettuce from the garden!

Pour a litre (4 cups) water into a wok and bring to the boil. Quickly blanch the carrots for 30 seconds, refresh in iced water, then drain. Tip the water out of the wok and return to high heat.

Once the wok is smoking, add the neutral oil, swirl once or twice, then add the shallot and ginger and stir-fry for 15 seconds before adding the garlic and tossing for another 15 seconds or so.

Add the asparagus, shiitake mushroom and blanched carrot, stir-fry for 30 seconds, then add the water or stock and simmer for 1–2 minutes until reduced.

Add the wombok and bok choy followed by the soy sauce, oyster sauce, sugar and Shaoxing and stir-fry for another 2–3 minutes until the leafy vegetables are wilted. Sprinkle with salt and pepper to taste, add sesame oil and give it all brief stir before serving.

- 200 g (7 oz) carrots, thinly sliced on the diagonal
- 2 tablespoons neutral oil
- 1 large shallot (eschalot), finely sliced
- 2 teaspoons finely chopped ginger
- 1 large garlic clove, finely chopped
- 200 g (7 oz) asparagus or bamboo shoots, sliced diagonally at 4 cm (1½ inch) intervals
- 150 g (5½ oz) fresh shiitake mushrooms, sliced
- 2–3 tablespoons water or chicken stock
- 250 g (9 oz) wombok (Chinese cabbage), shredded
- 200 g (7 oz) bok choy, shredded
- 1 teaspoon light soy sauce
- 1 tablespoon oyster sauce (see above)
- 1 teaspoon caster (superfine) sugar
- 1 tablespoon Shaoxing wine
- Salt and white pepper, to taste
- 1 teaspoon sesame oil

SERVES 2–4

STIR-FRIED BEAN SHOOTS WITH SALTED FISH

Rich in nutrients and low in calories, bean shoots are surprisingly unpopular in Western countries. Often eaten raw in the West but mostly cooked in Asia, they pop up in Indian curries, Chinese stir-fries, lightly blanched in Japanese dishes and in the form of banchan in Korean cooking.

I think bean shoots get a bad rap in the West because most of them are sold with the unsightly tail on; most Asian cooks nip the tail off before cooking. While most of us find this chore tedious, if you share the work with someone, it'll be done in next to no time at all.

This dish was all the rage in Chinese restaurants some years ago. Since then, everyone has created their version of this simple stir-fry. For the dish to really shine, you need to stir-fry quickly and source salted fish made from snapper or threadfin (available at Asian grocers), although I've used baccalà before and it's worked beautifully.

¼ cup (60 ml) neutral oil
30 g (1 oz) salted fish (see above), cut into 1 cm (½ inch) pieces
2 garlic cloves, minced
1 long red chilli, finely chopped
300 g (10½ oz) bean shoots (see note), tails trimmed
2 spring onions (scallions), cut into 5 cm (2 inch) lengths
Splash of water or chicken stock (optional)
½ teaspoon caster (superfine) sugar
Salt and white pepper, to taste

Heat the oil in a wok or saucepan over medium heat, add the salted fish and fry, stirring occasionally, until crisp (2–3 minutes). Remove with a slotted spoon and drain on paper towels.

In the same oil, fry the garlic until golden, then add the chilli, bean shoots and spring onions and stir-fry quickly over high heat for a minute, sprinkling in some water or stock if necessary. Add the sugar and season to taste with salt and pepper.

Return the salted fish to the wok, stir-fry another minute until well combined, transfer to a plate and serve hot.

✽ If you have a large wok and are used to cooking with it, use 500 g (1 lb 2 oz) of bean shoots.

WOOD-EAR MUSHROOMS AND SHREDDED CHICKEN, NYONYA STYLE
KERABU BOK NEE

SERVES 2–4

This salad embraces elements of both Chinese and Malay cooking styles – Chinese because wood-ear mushrooms are usually associated with Chinese cooking, and Malay because salads are commonly served at mealtimes. It's a favourite with the Peranakans from Penang.

Wood-ear mushrooms, commonly called bok nee in Hokkien or mock yee in Cantonese, are usually sold dried in most Asian grocers. It is closely related to the more common cloud-ear fungus. Both these fungi are black and will swell to about three times their dried size once soaked.

Wood-ears are eaten for their crunchy texture but when simmered for a long time, they become slightly gelatinous. This recipe comes courtesy of my friend Annie Lee in Penang.

Soak the wood-ear mushrooms in 2 cups (500 ml) boiling water for 15 minutes. When cool enough to handle, drain and slice into very fine matchsticks.

Put the chicken breast, along with the salt, in a small saucepan, cover with water and bring to a simmer over medium heat. Simmer for 3–5 minutes, then turn off the heat, cover with a lid and leave to steep for 20 minutes until cooked through. Remove, cool and shred finely with your hands.

Meanwhile, for the sambal belacan, grind the chillies, belacan, sugar and salt to a fine paste with a mortar and pestle.

Place the sambal belacan in a large bowl, add the wood-ear mushrooms, chicken, shallots, ginger flower and coconut, toss well, then add the cumquat juice and sugar. Give the salad a good toss, taste, adding some salt if it needs it, then serve.

✖ I've used desiccated coconut for this recipe, but kerisik (which is the Malay word for fresh shredded and roasted coconut) would be the traditional ingredient if you can find it. Ginger flower (torch ginger) is sometimes sold fresh at florists, and is sold frozen in select Asian grocers. In Bahasa Malaysia, it is called bunga kantan.

30 g (1 oz) dried wood-ear mushrooms
300 g (10½ oz) chicken breast
1 teaspoon salt, plus extra to taste
150 g (5½ oz) shallots (eschalots), thinly sliced
25 g (⅞ oz) finely chopped ginger flower (torch ginger)
30 g (1 oz) desiccated coconut, dry-fried in a pan until golden brown
¼ cup (60 ml) cumquat juice or lime juice
1 tablespoon caster (superfine) sugar, or to taste
Salt, to taste

SAMBAL BELACAN
6–7 long red chillies, seeds removed and chopped
20 g (¾ oz) belacan (shrimp paste), roasted (see page 42)
Pinch of caster (superfine) sugar
Pinch of salt, or to taste

SERVES 2

EDIBLE CHRYSANTHEMUM LEAF AND TOFU SALAD

Not to be confused with the ornamental chrysanthemum, this edible variety's proper name is garland chrysanthemum. Originally from the Mediterranean, it is cultivated as a vegetable in northern and Southeast Asia. Generally, there are two varieties – serrated and broad-leaved – sold in Chinatown and Asian grocers. Just keep in mind that it pays to check that the chrysanthemum has tender stems, which are far more appealing to eat.

Its flavour is distinctly tangy and pleasant, and its texture succulent. The leaves are often used in hot pots and stir-fries, but work brilliantly in salads such as this one, where silken tofu brings a luscious texture.

- 1 bunch of (about 500 g/1 lb 2 oz) garland chrysanthemum leaves
- 150 g (5½ oz) silken tofu, lightly mashed
- 2 teaspoons roasted sesame seeds, coarsely ground with a mortar and pestle
- 1 tablespoon neutral oil
- 2 teaspoons light soy sauce
- 1 crushed garlic clove (optional)
- 1 teaspoon rice vinegar
- 1 teaspoon spring onion (scallion), thinly sliced
- 1 teaspoon brown sugar, or to taste
- 1 teaspoon black peppercorns, ground

Pick the chrysanthemum leaves, discarding any stems that are tough and woody. Cut tender stems into 2 cm (¾ inch) pieces.

Bring a pot of water to the boil, blanch stems first for 30 seconds, then add the leaves to cook both together until wilted. Tip into a colander and refresh under cold running water. Drain well and squeeze dry.

Place in a salad bowl, add the mashed tofu along with the rest of the ingredients, toss well with a pair of chopsticks and serve.

✻ You can vary this delicious salad by adding a couple of drops of sesame oil and some roasted pinenuts.

GAI LAN WITH LOTUS ROOT OR BEEF

SERVES 2–4

Belonging to the same family as cauliflower and kale, gai lan or Chinese broccoli is much loved by everyone who comes to my cooking classes. It is extremely nutritious and a breeze to cook – look out for those with thick stems and glossy dark-green leaves. Teamed with lotus root or beef, gai lan not only provides textural interest but also visual contrast to these other ingredients.

Fresh lotus root is still not that well known in the West. But frozen lotus root is readily available in Asian grocers.

Bring a litre (4 cups) water to the boil in a wok. Add a pinch of salt and 1 tablespoon of oil, then the gai lan and lotus root, if using. Blanch for a minute, then tip into a colander and refresh under cold running water. Drain well.

Wipe the wok dry with paper towel, return to high heat and add the remaining oil. Add the ginger and garlic and stir-fry for a few seconds until fragrant.

If you're using lotus root, add the gai lan and lotus root, stir-fry for 45 seconds, then add the Shaoxing, sugar, oyster sauce, soy sauce and stock.

Bring to the boil, stir in the cornflour slurry to thicken, season with salt and pepper and serve immediately.

Alternatively, if you're using beef, add it to the ginger and garlic and stir-fry until the meat is just cooked (around 1 minute). Then add the gai lan and continue to stir-fry for a minute. Add Shaoxing, sugar, oyster sauce, soy sauce and stock. Bring to the boil for 30 seconds, then stir in the cornflour slurry. Stir to thicken, adjust the seasoning with salt and pepper and serve immediately.

✖ To slice beef finely, you can partially freeze the fillet or rump until firm, which makes it easier to slice.

Salt and white pepper, to taste
2 tablespoons neutral oil
300 g (10½ oz) gai lan (Chinese broccoli), trimmed
100 g (3½ oz) paper-thin slices of lotus root or beef (see note)
4 slices ginger, cut into fine strips
1 garlic clove, minced
1 tablespoon Shaoxing wine
½ teaspoon caster (superfine) sugar
1 tablespoon oyster sauce
1 teaspoon light soy sauce
100 ml (3½ fl oz) chicken stock or water
1 teaspoon cornflour (cornstarch) dissolved in 1 tablespoon water

GRILLED ASPARAGUS WITH WALNUT PESTO

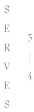

This recipe is based on a dish I ate at Contra in New York a few years ago. It also has roots in the condiments used in China and Japan and the sambals eaten in Malaysia and Singapore.

Asparagus is still relatively new in Asia as it's a vegetable from the West. The walnut pesto is pretty flexible. For instance, if you don't have miso, you can also use fermented tofu.

700 g (1 lb 9 oz) asparagus, trimmed
¼ cup (60 ml) neutral oil
Lemon wedges, to serve

WALNUT PESTO
100 ml (3½ fl oz) neutral oil
1¼ cups (150 g) walnuts
3 garlic cloves, finely chopped
50 g (1¾ oz) white (shiro) miso or fermented tofu
1 teaspoon fish sauce
1 tablespoon rice vinegar
Pinch of chilli powder, or to taste
Salt, to taste

First, make the walnut pesto. Heat the oil in a saucepan over medium heat. Add half the walnuts and fry until lightly toasted. Remove with a slotted spoon to a heatproof bowl. Repeat with remaining walnuts.

While the oil is still hot, fry the garlic until golden. Tip the garlic and oil into the bowl with the walnuts. Remove a small handful of walnuts to serve, then blend the rest in a food processor with the remaining pesto ingredients until smooth. Taste, and adjust seasoning with salt if it needs it.

To serve, heat a barbecue or char-grill pan to high. Toss the asparagus in the oil and grill, turning occasionally, until nicely charred but still crisp (about 3 minutes).

Transfer to a plate and dress with the pesto and reserved walnuts. Serve with lemon wedges.

✤ Some brands of miso and fermented beancurd can be salty; so don't add any salt until you have tasted the pesto.

PINEAPPLE CURRY
PAJERI NENAS

SERVES 6

This is definitely one of the Malay dishes adopted by the Nyonyas as their own. In Penang, it's called pajelis ong lai, while in Malacca it's known as pajeri nenas. This dryish pineapple pajeri is derived from a Telugu or Tamil word meaning pickle. It's hot and spicy, but you can tone down the spices to your liking. It is fabulous with grilled seafood.

For the spice paste, put all the ingredients in a food processor or spice grinder and blend to a smooth paste.

Heat the oil in a wok or large saucepan over medium heat, add the star anise and cinnamon and fry, stirring occasionally, for 2 minutes or until aromatic. Add the spice paste and fry, stirring, for another minute.

Add the pineapple and stir-fry for a minute before adding the coconut milk, ¾ cup (185 ml) water, sugar and salt, adjusting to taste. Simmer for 5–8 minutes, stirring occasionally, until the sauce is syrupy. Check the seasoning once again, then transfer to a plate, top with red chillies and serve with steamed rice.

½ cup (125 ml) neutral oil
2 star anise
5 cm (2 inch) piece cinnamon
1 half-ripe pineapple (about 700 g), peeled, quartered, core removed, then cut into chunks
200 ml (7 oz) coconut milk
2 tablespoons brown sugar or palm sugar (or jaggery)
Salt, to taste
1 long red chilli, thinly sliced, to serve
Steamed rice, to serve

SPICE PASTE
5 shallots (eschalots; about 200 g/7 oz), thinly sliced
3 garlic cloves, finely chopped
5 dried long red chillies, soaked in hot water to soften, drained, chopped
2 long red chillies, chopped
1 cm (½ inch) piece turmeric (about 10 g/¼ oz) or ½ teaspoon ground turmeric
2 tablespoons dry-roasted coriander seeds

MY DHAL

I grew up eating this soupy lentil curry. In Malaysia, it's frequently served with roti canai, the flatbread from India that's popular throughout Southeast Asia. This recipe uses yellow split peas (mung dhal) but you can use whatever lentils you like — you'll just need to adjust the cooking time so the lentils are tender. The dhal is mild in spiciness (amp up the heat if you like), but rich in flavour. It's great with rice and kids love it.

3 tablespoons neutral oil
1 sprig curry leaves, picked
1 cinnamon stick
2 green chillies
1 cup (220 g) yellow split peas
2 cups (500 ml) coconut milk
1 teaspoon sugar, or to taste
Salt, to taste
Chilli powder, to taste
Steamed rice, to serve
Roti canai, to serve (see page 106)

CURRY PASTE
2 garlic cloves, chopped
1 tablespoon chopped ginger
1 onion, chopped
2 tablespoons Malaysian curry powder

Coarsely blend the curry paste ingredients in a food processor – do not overblend into a mush.

Heat the oil in a saucepan over medium heat. Add the curry leaves, cinnamon stick and green chillies and fry for 5 minutes. Reserve a few fried curry leaves for garnish, then add the curry paste and gently cook for another 3–5 minutes until fragrant.

Add the split peas, 1 cup (250 ml) water and coconut milk. Bring to the boil, then reduce the heat and simmer for 30–45 minutes until the split peas are soft and tender.

Add the sugar, salt and a pinch of chilli powder to taste. Serve with steamed rice and roti.

✱ If the liquid is evaporating too quickly, add another 1 cup (250 ml) water.

RAJASTHANI WATERMELON CURRY

Many years ago, I came across the idea of this delightful curry in Camellia Panjabi's book, 50 Great Curries of India. It is usually eaten during the long, hot summers in Rajasthan when not many vegetables are available. A semi-dry curry, it's delicious with rice or chapati, naan or roti (page 106). You could even combine it with my biryani (page 54).

Note, however, that the quality of this curry is dependent on the age and type of watermelon – some watermelons give out plenty of juice while others are powdery. Select heavy seedless watermelons, and try to cook the dish in a wide pan, which will help keep the fruit from breaking apart.

SERVES 6–8

Blend 1 cup (175 g) watermelon in a food processor or blender to make juice, then strain and discard the pulp. To the juice, add the chilli, turmeric, coriander and garlic, and stir to combine.

Heat the oil in a large saucepan over medium-high heat. Stir in the cumin and mustard seeds, and as soon as they change colour and start to pop, about 5–10 seconds, add the watermelon juice.

Reduce the heat to medium and simmer until the liquid is reduced by half. Season to taste with salt and sugar, add the chopped watermelon and toss gently until the pieces are coated with the spice mixture, then cook, stirring gently, over low heat for 2–3 minutes until just soft.

Stir in the lime juice, then ladle the watermelon pieces into a heatproof serving bowl. Place in a warm oven to keep warm, then keep reducing the sauce in the saucepan until it is syrupy (1–2 minutes).

Spoon the sauce over the watermelon and serve with roti and steamed rice.

✖ The flavour should be hot, sweet and sour. Add a pinch of paprika to achieve a better colour to the sauce if it looks insipid. Brown mustard seeds come from the vast brassica family. Yellow or white mustard seeds and black mustard seeds are native to Europe and brown mustard seeds are native to Asia, hence this variety is often seen in Asian cookbooks.

2 kg (4 lb 8 oz) seedless watermelon, rind removed, flesh cut into 5 cm (2 inch) cubes
1½ teaspoons chilli powder
½ teaspoon ground turmeric
1 teaspoon ground coriander
1 teaspoon minced garlic
¼ cup (60 ml) neutral oil
½ teaspoon cumin seeds
½ teaspoon brown mustard seeds
Pinch of salt, or to taste
Pinch of caster (superfine) sugar, or to taste
Juice of 1 lime, or to taste
Roti canai, to serve (page 106)
Steamed rice, to serve

SRI LANKAN SPICY CASHEW CURRY

SERVES 4–6

Creamy and rich with coconut milk, this Sri Lankan dish – fabulous for vegetarians – is much loved not only in Sri Lanka but also in Malaysia where the burghers, Jaffna Tamils and Sri Lankans have settled since the 1900s. The recipe uses raw or unroasted cashews but if roasted is all you have, you can soak the nuts in warm water to soften before cooking.

3¼ cups (500 g) raw cashews
100 ml (3½ fl oz) neutral oil
1 teaspoon brown mustard seeds
1 teaspoon cumin seeds
3 × 5 cm (2 inch) pieces pandan leaves
2 sprigs curry leaves
2 onions, thinly sliced
1 cinnamon stick
1 cup (250 ml) thin coconut milk
Salt, to taste
1 tablespoon lime or lemon juice
2 tomatoes, chopped
3 tablespoons chopped coriander
Rice, papadams and pol sambal (recipe opposite), to serve

SPICE PASTE
1 teaspoon ground turmeric
1 teaspoon ground cumin
2 teaspoons ground coriander
1 teaspoon chilli powder

Cover cashew nuts in warm water and leave to soak for 2 hours to soften, then drain.

For the spice paste, combine all the ingredients in a bowl, add ½ cup (125 ml) water and stir to a paste.

Heat the oil in a saucepan over medium-high heat. Add the mustard seeds, cumin, pandan and curry leaves and fry until aromatic – this takes only a few seconds, so make sure the seeds don't burn. Add the onion and cinnamon and sauté until the onion is golden (3–4 minutes).

Add the spice paste and cook, stirring, for another minute, then add the cashews and coconut milk and season to taste with salt. Bring to a simmer and cook until the nuts are just tender, topping up with water if the liquid is reducing too quickly (6–8 minutes). Stir in lime juice, tomato and coriander.

Serve with rice, papadams and pol sambol.

POL SAMBOL

MAKES 500 G (1 LB 2 OZ)

I love this sambol. I think the first time I ate it was at the home of my Sri Lankan art teacher, Mr Piyadasa, with nothing more than steamed rice, but every mouthful was a taste sensation. The next time I ate it was with string hoppers, and it was just as memorable. When I ate it in a restaurant in Melbourne, it was so delicious that it took me back to my school days in Malaysia when I had Sri Lankan schoolmates.

I used frozen fresh grated coconut, which is readily available in many Indian and Sri Lankan grocers. Sweet, hot and sour, this sambol is fantastic with roti, hoppers and curries.

For the tempering ingredients, heat the oil in a small saucepan over medium heat until shimmering. Add the curry leaves and mustard seeds. As soon as they start to sizzle, transfer to a bowl.

Add the coconut, chilli, onion and paprika to the bowl and mix well by hand. Squeeze and rub until well blended.

Season to taste with lime juice and salt. Serve immediately.

✤ This is a condiment that varies from family to family – some cooks add ground Maldive fish and green chillies to the sambol.

500 g (1 lb 2 oz) fresh or frozen grated coconut
1 dried chilli, finely chopped
1 small onion, finely chopped
1 teaspoon sweet paprika
¼ cup (60 ml) lime juice
Salt, to taste

TEMPERING INGREDIENTS
1 tablespoon neutral oil
1 sprig curry leaves, stripped
1 teaspoon brown mustard seeds

MAKES 250 G (9 OZ)

SEITAN

TL

If you've ever been to a Buddhist temple and enjoyed a vegetarian banquet, chances are you have eaten seitan, the name it's commonly known as in the West and the Japanese word for pure wheat gluten. In Mandarin it's called mian jin.

Food writers believe it was invented some time around the 6th century when Buddhism came to China. As strict vegetarians, Buddhist monks probably discovered that by 'washing' flour dough in water, starch granules were removed and what was left behind was a wobbly, stretchy mass of wheat gluten.

As an ingredient, wheat gluten is bland but it's fantastic when it is cooked in various stocks, like mushroom stock for instance. When I was part-owner of Shakahari restaurant in Melbourne, the seitan was cooked in a stock of ginger, garlic and soy sauce. If you add yeast to seitan, it becomes kaofu, the seitan puffs you find in Buddhist temples and Asian grocers.

3⅓ cups (500 g) high-gluten flour or bread flour
¼ teaspoon salt
1¼–1½ cups (310–375 ml) warm water

Place the flour in a large bowl and add the salt. Stirring the flour with a pair of chopsticks, gradually add the warm water until the flour turns into a shaggy mess (you may not need all the water). Tip the dough onto a clean bench and knead for 5–10 minutes until soft and pliable. Place it in a large bowl to rest for 10 minutes.

Knead the dough again for 5–10 minutes. By now it should be soft, and if you press the dough with your finger, it should spring back. Cover with water and leave it for 2 hours. I leave mine overnight.

The next day, place the bowl in the sink. This is when you start the 'washing' process. You need three washes at least, changing the water after each wash. First, fill the bowl with the dough to the brim with lukewarm water. It should be at least filled with a litre of water; otherwise transfer the dough to a larger bowl. Stick your hands into the dough and pick up a large piece and start massaging or kneading it gently in the water. You will start to see the starch separating from the gluten. By now the water will look milky or cloudy.

Keep kneading until all the starch is extracted and the dough is beginning to stretch. Tip the dough and water into a sieve over a large clean bowl. Return the dough and any trapped bits to your original bowl and repeat this process, keeping the 'washing' water from the first and second washes to make the noodles (see note opposite).

Otherwise, to cook it, slice the seitan into 2–3 strips, cover with master stock, or chicken stock infused with flavours of your choice (I like a dash of smoked paprika) and simmer for 25–30 minutes until firm. It's now ready to eat as is or use in a stir-fry, or in simmered or grilled dishes.

✖ This dough can also be made into gluten puffs, or kaofu, by rolling it into balls weighing no more than 10 g (⅜ oz) and deep-frying them in oil at 150°C (300°F) for 5–6 minutes, then draining well. Gluten puffs are great with braised mushrooms.

STIR-FRIED SEITAN WITH MUSHROOMS AND CAPSICUM

SERVES 2 | 4

Seitan is wonderfully versatile once it is cooked. Here is a simple, quick stir-fry with mushrooms and capsicum. You will find the seitan a bit chewy like calamari.

2 tablespoons neutral oil
250 g (9 oz) cooked seitan (see opposite), cut into bite-sized pieces
2 garlic cloves, chopped
1 spring onion (scallion), white part finely chopped, green tops reserved and thinly sliced to serve
1 teaspoon Sichuan pepper
1 red capsicum (pepper), cut into 2 cm (¾ inch) cubes
300 g (10½ oz) mixed mushrooms, chopped
Dash of sesame oil
Salt and white pepper, to taste
Steamed rice, to serve

SAUCE

½ cup (125 ml) chicken or vegetable stock
1 tablespoon oyster sauce
1 tablespoon Shaoxing wine
2 teaspoons light soy sauce
1 teaspoon dark soy sauce
1 teaspoon caster (superfine) sugar, or to taste
1 teaspoon cornflour (cornstarch) mixed with 2 tablespoons water

For the sauce, place all the ingredients in a bowl and stir well to combine.

Heat a wok over medium-high heat and add the oil. Once the oil is shimmering, add the seitan and stir-fry until golden (2–3 minutes). Add the garlic, spring onion and peppercorns, stir-fry for 30 seconds, then add the capsicum and mushrooms. Continue to stir-fry for 1–2 minutes until softened, then add the sauce, cover with a lid and leave to simmer for another minute until thickened. Add a dash of sesame oil, adjust seasoning to taste with salt and pepper and serve with rice.

✖ Make liang pi – a silky noodle from Shaanxi province that's great on summer days with chilli oil and vinegar – with the 'washing' water from the seitan (opposite). Collect the liquid from the first and second washes, and leave it to settle completely overnight. The next day, tip off the water to expose the collected flour mixture, weigh out 250 g (9 oz) and mix it with 150 ml (5 fl oz) fresh water and a pinch of salt. Brush a container with oil, pour in a ladle of flour mixture and steam for 2 minutes. Lift out when cool enough to handle, brush the top with oil and transfer to an oiled plate. Continue until all mixture is used up. Cut into ribbons and toss with chilli oil and vinegar.

MAKES 20

STEAMED RICE CAKE
CHWEE KUIH

Every time I serve chwee kuih, meaning 'water cake', those in the know are ecstatic. For those who've never eaten it before, there's an initial look of surprise, but once they bite into these pillowy soft treats, they are converted. One of the most popular street foods in Malaysia and Singapore, it migrated with the Chiu Chow people from southern China.

Super easy to make, this scrumptious snack has two parts: the rice cake and the topping. The rice cake is made with rice and tapioca flour (though some recipes use cornflour and wheat starch), while the topping is made with umami-packed preserved daikon known as chai poh (erroneously called preserved turnip). Chilli sauce is served alongside for that extra kick.

While it's not the purist's way, just about any topping will go with this. In fact, a strikingly similar rice cake called banh beo in Vietnam is served with dried shrimp, spring onion oil and fish sauce. You'll need some Chinese dipping sauce plates, around 7 cm (2¾ inches) in diameter.

---

150 g (5½ oz) rice flour
25 g (1 oz) tapioca flour
2 teaspoons neutral oil, plus extra for greasing
¼ teaspoon salt, or to taste
300 ml (10½ fl oz) water, at room temperature
400 ml (14 fl oz) boiling water

TOPPING
200 g (7 oz) chai poh (preserved daikon; see note)
2 tablespoons neutral oil or lard
2 shallots (eschalots), minced
2 garlic cloves, chopped
1 teaspoon fish sauce
½ teaspoon caster (superfine) sugar
½ teaspoon thick dark soy sauce (kecap asin; see page 37)
½ teaspoon white pepper

First, make the topping. Rinse the chai poh if it's too salty, then drain well. Add the oil or lard to a wok over medium heat, add the shallots and fry, stirring occasionally, until it's beginning to turn a pale shade of gold, then add the garlic followed by the chai poh. Stir-fry until fragrant, then add fish sauce, sugar, dark soy and pepper. Stir well and set aside.

Next, make the rice cake batter. In a large bowl, combine the rice flour, tapioca flour, oil, salt and the room temperature water. Mix well, then gradually add the boiling water, mixing as you go (do not pour it in all at once because it will turn into a lumpy dough). What you want is a slightly thickened mixture, the consistency of runny honey. Pour into a jug.

Brush some Chinese dipping sauce plates (about 40 ml/1½ fl oz) capacity) lightly with oil and place them in a steamer set in a wok of simmering water to warm up. Stir the batter, pour into the plates and steam for 15–20 minutes over medium-high heat, topping up water as necessary, until set. Repeat as needed until you've used all the batter.

Remove and leave to cool for 5 minutes before unmoulding with a palette knife or spatula. Serve topped with the chai poh topping.

✤ Preserved daikon, or chai poh, is sold in Asian supermarkets, but is often erroneously called preserved turnip. Some brands are salted and others are sweetened. Depending on the brand, sometimes it is best to rinse it to get rid of excess salt.

If you can't be bothered to make the rice cakes, the topping is great with bread or noodles.

SPICY FRIED TEMPEH
SAMBAL TEMPE

From Indonesia, tempeh is a fermented plant-based food traditionally made with soybeans. Its pleasant nutty flavour is used in several Indonesian regional dishes but it is in Java that tempeh is the most popular. This is a spicy dish that is very popular with several Southeast Asian communities.

To make fried tempeh, add oil to a depth of 5 cm (2 inches) in a wok over medium-high heat. When the oil reaches 180°C (350°F; bubbles should form around a wooden chopstick when it's dipped in), fry the tempeh in batches for 3–4 minutes until golden. Transfer to paper towel with a slotted spoon.

Pour the frying oil into a heatproof dish. Return 2 tablespoons of it to the wok and stir-fry the shallots, garlic, chillies, galangal and belacan over medium heat for 2–3 minutes until fragrant. Add the palm sugar and stir over low-medium heat until dissolved.

Place the tamarind pulp in a bowl and cover with 200 ml (7 fl oz) warm water. Soak for 20 minutes, then, with your fingers, mash and squeeze the tamarind to extract as much juice as possible.

Strain the tamarind water into a bowl, discarding the solids, then pour the tamarind juice into the wok and add the deep-fried tempeh. Cook, stirring frequently, until the sauce is reduced and caramelised (4–5 minutes). Season with salt and serve with sliced birdseye chillies.

Neutral oil, for frying
400 g (14 oz) tempeh, cut into 1 cm strips
3 shallots (eschalots; about 130 g/4¾ oz), thinly sliced
2 garlic cloves, thinly sliced
2 long red chillies, thinly sliced
2 cm (¾ inch) piece galangal, thinly sliced
½ teaspoon belacan (shrimp paste), roasted (see page 42)
2 tablespoons dark palm sugar (gula jawa)
50 g (1¾ oz) tamarind pulp
Salt, to taste
3–5 birdseye chillies, sliced, to serve

ROAST POTATOES WITH FERMENTED BEAN SAUCE

SERVES 2–4

In my cooking classes, students often ask what to do with the array of Asian condiments they have in their pantry. My response is simple: just like in Western cooking how we use so many condiments to make a variety of dishes, such as mayonnaise and balsamic vinegar, Asian condiments can be used similarly.

I use miso not only in Japanese dishes but also in ice-creams and desserts; gochujang is fabulous in pasta; and doubanjiang is great in meat pies. What's undeniable, though, is that all three of these are brilliant with potatoes. Serve this with my mother's roast chicken (page 189) and it's a feast.

500 g (1 lb 2 oz) new potatoes, cut into chunks
2–3 tablespoons white (shiro) miso paste or gochujang (red chilli paste) or doubanjiang (chilli bean paste), plus extra to serve
2–3 tablespoons butter or olive oil
Salt and white pepper, to taste
1 tablespoon thinly sliced chives
2 tablespoons dill or fennel fronds

Preheat the oven to 200°C (400°F). Place the potatoes in a roasting tray and toss with your choice of miso or gochujang or doubanjiang along with the butter or olive oil and sprinkle with salt and pepper to taste.

Roast for 40–50 minutes, shaking the pan a couple of times to dislodge any stuck ones, until potatoes are crisp and tender.

Sprinkle with chives and dill and add a dollop of additional sauce (either the miso, gochujang or doubanjiang) if you feel they need it. Toss well and serve.

✤ Sweet potatoes are also a delicious alternative for this recipe.

TARO GNOCCHI TWO WAYS

SERVES 6

This recipe is based on a kind of Hokkien 'gnocchi' called suan pan zi, meaning abacus seeds. It is traditionally made with taro, which means it tends to be rather heavy. I've added potatoes to lighten the dish. Fresh taro is sometimes hard to find, so I've used frozen taro instead. This being the case, you have to ensure there's not too much moisture in the frozen taro or it will affect the recipe.

Taro is a root vegetable that's much loved in Asia, Polynesia and Latin America. Its distinctive flavour and starchy character has given rise to many dishes, including desserts, most notably taro ice-cream and sweet taro soup. Although there are some 200 varieties, the ones we know most here in Australia are the large, narrow-topped ones with brownish skin. The flesh is pinkish purple, white and beige.

Both the tuber and the leaves contain calcium oxalate crystals so they must be thoroughly cooked before use. Like the potato, it is often teamed with oily foods as it can absorb the fats readily. This recipe is adapted from one by Patricia Yeo, a Singaporean chef in New York. I've offered it two ways; first simply in brown butter, and then with mushrooms and dried shrimp.

---

500 g (1 lb 2 oz) taro, scrubbed
500 g (1 lb 2 oz) floury potatoes (Coliban, Desiree, Dutch Cream)
½ teaspoon Chinese five-spice powder
Freshly grated nutmeg, to taste
Salt, to taste
3 egg yolks
½ cup (75 g) plain (all-purpose) flour
150 g (5½ oz) unsalted butter
Chopped coriander (cilantro) or parsley, to serve

Preheat the oven to 180°C (350°F). Bake the taro (if your taro is large, you may need to halve it and wrap it in foil) for 45 minutes to 1 hour until the taro is soft. If it's still not soft, bake for another 15 minutes.

Halfway through baking, cover the potatoes with water in a large saucepan, bring to the boil and cook until tender (10–15 minutes; avoid testing them with a fork or a knife too much, or they may become waterlogged).

Remove the taro from the oven, and drain the potatoes. Once both are cool enough to handle, peel both and put them through a mouli or a potato ricer directly onto a clean bench.

Mix in the Chinese five-spice, nutmeg and salt, adjusting to taste, then working quickly, work in the egg yolks. Sprinkle some of the flour over the surface and knead lightly into the mixture. Continue adding flour and kneading until a dough forms (you may not need all the flour).

Meanwhile, bring a pot of boiling salted water to the boil. Roll out the taro dough into a thin sausage (no thicker than a thumb) and cut it into 2.5 cm (1 inch) pieces. Cook a few in boiling water to test; if they disintegrate, knead more flour into the dough.

Boil the gnocchi until they rise to the surface (2–3 minutes). Scoop them out with a slotted spoon and transfer to a warm buttered dish.

Just before serving, melt half the butter in a frying pan over high heat. Add half the gnocchi and cook, shaking the pan occasionally, until heated through and browned (about 2 minutes). Transfer to a serving platter and keep warm. Wipe out the pan with paper towel and repeat with the remaining butter and gnocchi. Serve immediately with chopped herbs. Alternatively, serve the gnocchi with stir-fried mushrooms and dried shrimp (see opposite).

MUSHROOMS AND DRIED SHRIMP

1 tablespoon dried shrimp
4 dried shiitake mushrooms
2 tablespoons neutral oil
2 garlic cloves, finely chopped
1 tablespoon julienned ginger
500 g (1 lb 2 oz) king mushrooms, sliced into thin strips
1 tablespoon light soy sauce
1 teaspoon doubanjiang (chilli bean paste), or to taste
Chopped coriander (cilantro), to serve

Soak the dried shrimp in ½ cup (125 ml) hot water for 20 minutes. Drain, reserving soaking liquid, then chop coarsely.

Meanwhile, soak the mushrooms in 1 cup (250 ml) hot water for 20 minutes. Drain, reserving soaking liquid, then squeeze out excess liquid, discard stems and slice caps into thin strips.

Heat the oil in a wok over high heat, add the oil, then, once it's shimmering, add the garlic and ginger, toss briefly, then add the shrimp and mushrooms and stir-fry until fragrant (about 2 minutes). Add the reserved shrimp and mushroom soaking liquids, then add the soy sauce and doubanjiang. Bring to the boil and simmer until syrupy.

Pour this sauce over the freshly boiled taro gnocchi and serve topped with chopped coriander.

SILKEN TOFU WITH ROASTED CAPSICUM AND FERMENTED CHILLI

Serves 2

Silken tofu is very popular with the Chinese and every family has its own take on this very homestyle dish. Served cold, it graces the table sometimes with nothing more than chopped garlic and spring onions with a splash of soy and sesame oil, and other times with fried ginger, garlic and chillies.

Here, some oyster sauce and soy sauce are added along with stock, before the whole thing is poured over the soft tofu. Super fast and easy to make, this is a dish that's especially enjoyable on a warm day. If you don't want to make the fermented chilli, you can use sambal oelek.

- 1 red capsicum (pepper), halved, seeds and membrane removed
- 1 tablespoon neutral oil
- 1 tablespoon finely chopped ginger
- 2 garlic cloves, finely chopped
- 1 tablespoon oyster sauce
- 1 tablespoon light soy sauce
- 2 tablespoons chicken stock or water
- Pinch of caster (superfine) sugar
- 300 g (10½ oz) silken tofu
- 2 tablespoons thinly sliced spring onions (scallions)

FERMENTED CHILLI
- 500 g (1 lb 2 oz) cayenne chillies, chopped
- 40 g (1½ oz) salt
- 3 tablespoons baijiu (or other distilled liquor)
- 1 bulb garlic, peeled (optional)

For the fermented chilli, place the chopped chillies, salt, baijiu and garlic (if using) in a food processor and blend into a coarse paste. Transfer to a sterilised jar and cover loosely with a muslin or clean cloth. Leave the jar in the sun for 1–2 days. Then seal with a lid and refrigerate for a week before using. Kept in the fridge, it will last for 4 weeks.

Preheat the oven to 230°C (450°F). Roast the halved red capsicum skin-side up on a lined baking tray for 25–30 minutes, or until blistered and blackened. Transfer to a bowl and cover with a plate to trap the steam. After 20 minutes, or when cool enough to handle, peel off the skin and chop into 1 cm (½ inch) cubes.

Heat the oil in a wok over medium heat until shimmering. Add the ginger and stir-fry for 1–2 minutes until light golden, then add the garlic and stir-fry until just turning pale golden, then toss in 1 tablespoon of the fermented chilli.

Add the oyster sauce, soy sauce, stock and sugar. Bring to the boil, stirring well, then turn off the heat.

Turn out the tofu onto a serving plate, pour the sauce over the top and serve with the capsicum and a scattering of spring onion.

SPICY PICKLED CHINESE CABBAGE

MAKES 1 LITRE (33 FL OZ)

Pickled Chinese cabbage (pictured on page 285) is a simple appetiser that usually graces the better Chinese restaurants. Its sweet–sour flavour and crisp texture make it a classic. A staple in my family, it's not only extremely easy to make but it complements so many dishes; I love it with roast meats and fried seafood.

Although there are two varieties of Chinese cabbage commonly available, in my family the barrel-shaped, loose-headed variety called wombok or napa cabbage (also called siu choy in Cantonese) is preferred for making this pickle. The longer cylindrical variety is often used in stir-frying.

For the pickling solution, combine all the ingredients and ½ cup (125 ml) water in a saucepan and bring to the boil, stirring to dissolve the sugar. Remove from heat and leave to cool.

Separate the cabbage leaves from the base, then wash the leaves and pat dry. Place leaves in a stack, halve the leaves lengthways, then cut crossways into strips. Place in a large bowl add the salt, mixing well to distribute it evenly. Set aside for 30 minutes to draw out the juices.

Drain off the juices from the cabbage, then rinse under running water to remove excess salt. Transfer to a sterilised jar and pour the cooled pickling solution over to cover.

Refrigerate overnight before serving. Pickled cabbage will keep, refrigerated for up to 2 months, topping up with vinegar to ensure it's covered.

✤ When making this pickle, many Chinese families use vast quantities of cabbages to ensure they have this appetiser to last them for several days. You may add extra chilli if preferred.

500 g (1 lb 2 oz) wombok (Chinese cabbage)
1 tablespoon salt

PICKLING SOLUTION
1–2 large red chillies, or to taste, seeds discarded and sliced, or ½ teaspoon dried chilli flakes
⅔ cup (150 g) caster (superfine) sugar
1½ cups (375 ml) rice vinegar

MAKES 1 LITRE (33 FL OZ)

PICKLED YOUNG GINGER

Spicy, briny and sweet, pickled ginger (pictured on page 285) is offered in many restaurants from Japan to Southeast Asia. It's frequently teamed with sushi or century eggs, but it's also enjoyed on its own for its refreshing flavour.

Not only is homemade pickled ginger simple to prepare, the result is far superior to the stuff you buy in shops. You can make this with mature ginger at a pinch, but young ginger with tender flesh and fine, papery skin is best for pickling. Look for rhizomes with creamy white flesh, thin skin and pinkish knobs as opposed to mature ginger, which is darker and more fibrous.

500 g (1 lb 2 oz) fresh young ginger, thinly sliced with a mandoline
2 tablespoons salt
1 cup (250 ml) rice vinegar
250 g (9 oz) caster (superfine) sugar
1 extra teaspoon salt (optional)

Mix the ginger and salt in a bowl, tossing well, and leave for 20 minutes to draw out excess moisture. Transfer the ginger to a colander and rinse under cold running water. Pat dry with paper towel and set aside in a heatproof bowl.

Combine the rice vinegar, sugar, salt, if using, and ½ cup (125 ml) water in a saucepan. Bring to the boil, reduce to a simmer and stir until sugar has dissolved.

Pour the vinegar-sugar solution over the ginger, ensuring the ginger is completely covered (it will turn light pink within 5 minutes). Cover the bowl, cool to room temperature and transfer to a sterilised jar. Seal and refrigerate for a week to pickle.

Pickled young ginger can be kept in the refrigerator for a month, topping up with vinegar to ensure it's covered.

PICKLED GREEN CHILLIES

MAKES 750 ML (25 FL OZ)

This fast and easy pickle (pictured on page 285) is a constant in my refrigerator, and in Southeast Asia, this pickle graces the tables of many eateries. It perks up just about anything, especially noodles and pasta.

Except for birdseye chillies or habanero, which are too hot for some, you can use whatever chillies you find for the recipe. I've used green cayenne chillies – or long green chillies. The purpose of this pickled condiment is to complement a dish, not to overpower it, so use it sparingly.

Place the chillies in a heatproof bowl. Pour boiling water over to cover, leave for 20 seconds, then drain in a sieve, retaining the seeds if you prefer a hotter flavour. Set aside.

Combine the rice vinegar, salt and sugar in a small saucepan. Bring to the boil, reduce to a simmer and stir until sugar has dissolved.

Place chillies in a sterilised jar. Pour in the hot vinegar mixture, making sure the chillies are submerged; if not, you'll need to make a little more solution. Allow to cool, then seal and transfer to the fridge to chill. Pickled chillies are ready to eat when they turn a khaki green, which should happen overnight. This keeps indefinitely, refrigerated, topping up with vinegar to ensure the chillies are covered.

250 g (9 oz) long green chillies, stems removed, sliced 1 cm (½ inch) thick
1½ cups (375 ml) rice vinegar
1 teaspoon salt
½ teaspoon caster (superfine) sugar

PENANG NYONYA PICKLES
ACAR AWAK

MAKES 4 LITRES (134 FL OZ)

Pickles are often considered by Nyonyas as the hallmark of a good cook, and acar awak is still made with love in Peranakan homes. Wonderfully aromatic and complex, this pickle is nutty, spicy, hot, sweet and sour and terribly moreish. It's also a visual treat, because the vegetables are cut to resemble a pool of dainty jewels. This pickle complements and enhances several dishes in the book, in particular curry kapitan and Nyonya braised pork.

---

1 kg (2 lb 4 oz) cucumber, seeded and sliced into 5 cm (2 inch) batons
1 tablespoon salt, plus extra to taste
80 g (2¾ oz) snake beans, cut into 5 cm (2 inch) lengths
80 g (2¾ oz) green beans, cut into 5 cm (2 inch) lengths
80 g (2¾ oz) cabbage, cut into 2.5 cm (1 inch) wide strips
250 g (9 oz) carrots, peeled and cut into 5 cm (2 inch) batons
250 g (9 oz) cauliflower, cut into florets
4 long red chillies (whole, or split in half lengthways)
4 long green chillies (whole, or split in half lengthways)
¾ cup (185 ml) neutral oil
50 g (1¾ oz) garlic, minced or sliced
¾ cup (185 ml) rice vinegar, plus extra for topping up
100 g (3½ oz) caster (superfine) sugar, or to taste
2 tablespoons salt, or to taste
100 g (3½ oz) roasted peanuts, crushed
80 g (2¾ oz) sesame seeds, dry-roasted and crushed

SPICE PASTE
15–20 dried red chillies (see note)
1½ tablespoons fresh minced turmeric or 1 tablespoon turmeric powder

BLANCHING VINEGAR
700 ml (24 fl oz) rice vinegar
2 tablespoons caster (superfine) sugar
1 teaspoon ground turmeric

For the spice paste, soak the dried chillies in hot water until soft (15–20 minutes). Blend with the turmeric to a paste.

Toss cucumber with salt in a bowl and leave for 15 minutes to draw out excess moisture. Drain and set aside.

For the blanching vinegar, pour the vinegar into a large saucepan, add sugar, turmeric and 350 ml (12 fl oz) water and bring to the boil. Except for the garlic, blanch the vegetables separately in the solution for 30 seconds to 1 minute. Drain each batch in a colander, then squeeze the vegetables in a muslin bag to remove excess liquid.

Heat the oil in a wok or frying pan over medium heat and stir-fry the garlic until just golden (keep your eyes on it – it can burn quickly). Remove at once and strain in a sieve over a container, reserving the oil.

Return the oil to the wok and fry the spice paste, stirring frequently, over medium heat until nicely fragrant. Add the vinegar, sugar and salt, bring to the boil, then remove from heat and leave to cool.

Once cooled, combine the spice-paste mixture with the vegetables, peanuts and sesame seeds in a large bowl. Mix well, then transfer to sterilised jars. Top up with vinegar to ensure it's covered, then leave overnight for the flavours to mature. Acar awak will keep refrigerated for 4 weeks.

✤ When using long dried chillies, they are about 8 cm (3¼ inches) in their dried form. I use dried chillies from Malaysia, Thailand and Kashmir.

Clockwise from top: Spicy pickled Chinese cabbage (page 281); Pickled green chillies (page 283); Pickled young ginger (page 282); Penang Nyonya pickles (page 284)

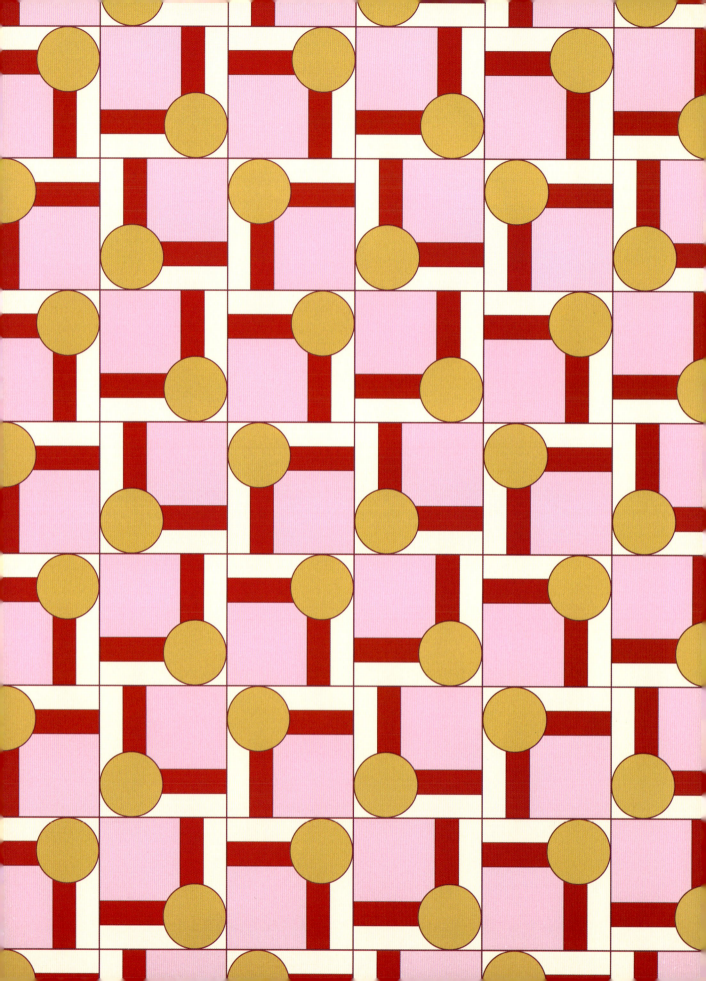

SWEETS

PANDAN PANNA COTTA WITH RED RUBIES

This recipe combines Western ingredients and method with Eastern flavourings in the form of panna cotta combined with a Thai dessert, tab tim krob. These are tiny diced water chestnuts coloured red and served with sweetened coconut milk, hence the name red rubies. I don't have a sweet tooth, so I tend to add a little less sugar than is traditional.

You'll need 8 x 120 ml (4 fl oz) dariole moulds.

Serves 8

1 litre (4 cups) single (pure) cream
1 vanilla bean, split
4 pandan leaves, knotted
1–1⅓ cups (150–200 g) shaved palm sugar (or jaggery)
2 gelatine leaves (titanium-grade)

RED RUBIES
1 cup (175 g) finely diced water chestnuts
Few drops red food colouring
½ cup (60 g) cornflour (cornstarch) or tapioca flour
100 g (3½ oz) caster (superfine) sugar
1 pandan leaf
200 ml (7 fl oz) coconut milk

For the red rubies, sprinkle the water chestnuts with red food colouring and stir until bright red, adding more food colouring if needed.

Put the cornflour in a plastic bag, add the water chestnuts and shake well so the pieces are well coated. Tumble into a sieve and shake to remove excess flour.

Bring 1.5 litres (6 cups) water to the boil in a large saucepan. Add the water chestnuts and boil for 3–5 minutes until softened. Drain, then plunge into cold water to refresh. Drain again and set aside until ready to serve.

Place the sugar, pandan leaf and 200 ml (7 fl oz) water in a saucepan and bring to the boil, stirring to dissolve sugar. Cool, then stir in the coconut milk and refrigerate to chill.

To make the panna cotta, put the cream, vanilla bean, pandan leaves and palm sugar in a saucepan. Over low heat, bring slowly to a simmer, stirring occasionally. Remove from heat and cover with a lid and set aside for 20 minutes to allow the flavour of the pandan to infuse the cream.

Place the gelatine leaves in a little cold water until soft, then wring out the excess water. Remove the pandan and vanilla bean from the sweet cream, then stir in the softened gelatine leaves until dissolved.

Pass the cream through a fine sieve and pour into the dariole moulds. Chill for at least 8 hours until set.

Unmould the panna cottas onto plates (run a knife around the edge of the moulds if they're not releasing). Finish off the red rubies by mixing the water chestnuts with the coconut cream, and put a tablespoon of these around each panna cotta to serve.

WATERMELON GRANITA WITH COCONUT JELLY AND BERRY COMPOTE

SERVES 8–10

A lovely dessert that's refreshing on warm nights, and especially good after a curry dinner. I don't remember exactly where I got the idea of combining these elements – probably from the days when I used to munch on coconut jelly back in Malaysia – but the coconut jelly gives the granita a wonderful textural dimension. That said, if I'm pressed for time, I replace it with silken tofu steeped in heavy sugar syrup – worth a go! Sometimes, I'll even mix a pinch of hot chilli powder into the berries to give the dessert a distinctive twist.

Agar agar, the setting agent here, is sold in two forms: powdered or in strands. I find the former is best, but sometimes it's not so readily available. If you can find it, grab a packet or two.

Blitz the watermelon in a food processor until smooth, then strain through a fine sieve into a bowl.

In a saucepan, combine the sugar with 150 ml (5 fl oz) water and heat gently, stirring until sugar is dissolved. Cool, then combine with the puréed watermelon, vodka and lemon juice. Pour into a shallow container and freeze for 3–4 hours, stirring with a fork every 30–40 minutes to form small flakes.

For the coconut jelly, soak the agar agar strands in cold water for at least 2 hours to soften, then drain. (If you're using powdered agar agar, soak it in 450 ml (16 fl oz) water, then add this to the saucepan in the next step.)

Add the agar agar, coconut milk, sugar and 450 ml (16 fl oz) water to a saucepan and bring to the boil, stirring constantly. Reduce the heat to medium, and simmer for 10 minutes or until agar agar is dissolved. Strain through a fine sieve, then add a dash of rose essence, pour into flat trays (like large baking trays) and refrigerate for 2 hours to set. Cut it into cubes.

Meanwhile, for the berry compote, combine the sugar and ½ cup (125 ml) water in a saucepan. Place over medium heat, stir until the sugar dissolves, then bring to the boil. Place the berries in a heatproof bowl, then pour the boiling syrup over the berries and leave to cool. Stir in the rose essence, then chill.

To serve, spoon the berry compote and then coconut jelly into cocktail glasses and top with watermelon granita.

1 kg (2 lb 4 oz) watermelon, peeled and chopped
⅓ cup (80 g) caster (superfine) sugar
¼ cup (60 ml) vodka
2 tablespoons lemon juice

COCONUT JELLY
6 g (⅛ oz) agar agar
400 ml (14 fl oz) coconut milk
150 g (5½ oz) caster (superfine) sugar, or to taste
Dash of rose essence

BERRY COMPOTE
125 g (4½ oz) caster (superfine) sugar
4 cups (500 g) fresh or frozen raspberries
3⅓ cups (500 g) strawberries
Dash of rose essence

MATCHA ICE-CREAM WITH SAGO AND DRIED PERSIMMON

SERVES 6

In many parts of Asia you will find matcha fanatics enjoying deep-green matcha-flavoured ice-cream with sponge cakes, chocolate sauce, chestnut cream and plenty more. Me? I prefer it with fruit, such as diced mango, lychee or, in this case, chewy dried persimmon that I make in the autumn. Coconut sago adds a creamy element that's undeniably delicious. Try to find high-quality matcha at Japanese grocers.

Combine the milk and cream in a saucepan and add the vanilla seeds. Bring just to the boil, then remove from the heat, cover and set aside to infuse for at least 15 minutes.

Meanwhile, whisk the egg yolks, sugar, cornflour, matcha powder and a pinch of salt in a large heatproof bowl until smooth.

Strain the milk mixture into the eggs, stir well, then return to saucepan over medium heat and cook, stirring with a wooden spoon until the mixture coats the back of the spoon (or until it reaches 76°C/170°F). Cool, then refrigerate until set. Once cooled, churn in an ice-cream machine according to manufacturer's instructions. Transfer to a container and freeze until ready to serve.

For the sago, bring 1 litre (4 cups) water to a rolling boil in a saucepan. Slowly dribble the sago into the water, boil for 7 minutes, then turn off the heat and cover with a lid. Remove from the heat and stand, covered, for 20 minutes to allow the sago to turn completely transparent. Strain in a fine sieve and wash off excess starch under cold water. Cool, then refrigerate.

Meanwhile, make a sugar syrup by combining sugar and ½ cup (125 ml) water in a small saucepan, bringing it to the boil and swirling until dissolved. Cool, then refrigerate.

Stir the sago, sugar syrup and coconut milk together, divide among bowls and serve topped with scoops of matcha ice-cream and hoshigaki.

❉ If you have a glut of persimmons, you can turn them into hoshigaki (dried persimmons) – all you need is time, sunshine and plenty of air circulation. After hanging or placing them on a drying rack (make sure they are not touching each other) for some two months, they are ready to eat. In this dessert recipe, I've used 4–5 diced hoshigaki.

450 ml (16 fl oz) milk
1 cup (250 ml) single (pure) cream
1 vanilla bean, split, seeds scraped
6 egg yolks
120 g (4½ oz) caster (superfine) sugar
2 teaspoons cornflour (cornstarch)
20 g (¾ oz) matcha powder
Pinch of salt
Diced hoshigaki (dried persimmons; see note), to serve

SAGO
¼ cup (50 g) sago
½ cup (110 g) sugar
400 ml (14 fl oz) coconut milk

KULFI ICE-CREAM

SERVES 10

If you haven't had kulfi before, you're in for a treat. An egg-free and churn-free ice-cream popular in India, all that is required is to reduce milk down before enriching it with a heavily reduced caramelised cream (think dulce de leche) called khoya or mawa. Perfume it with your choice of saffron, cardamom or rosewater with some sugar and you have kulfi.

As simple as it is, it takes time to make proper khoya (though you can buy it from good Indian grocers). Here, I've shortened the process considerably by using milk powder, milk, cream and butter, and it's made in a matter of minutes.

You'll need 10 kulfi or popsicle moulds (see note) and 10 popsicle sticks.

2 litres (8 cups) milk
½ teaspoon ground cardamom
½ teaspoon saffron threads
⅓ cup (80 g) caster (superfine) sugar
1 tablespoon corn syrup or liquid glucose
¼ cup (30 g) pistachios (optional), crushed

KHOYA
1 cup (250 ml) single (pure) cream
½ cup (125 ml) full-cream milk
1 cup (110 g) milk powder
2 teaspoons unsalted butter

Bring the milk to the boil in a heavy-based, non-stick saucepan. As soon as the milk begins to rise, reduce the heat to very low and simmer gently for about 1 hour, stirring now and then to prevent scorching, until the milk is reduced by half its volume. Add the cardamom, saffron, sugar and corn syrup and stir well to dissolve.

Meanwhile, for the khoya, add all the ingredients to a separate saucepan over low-medium heat and stir until combined. Cook, stirring with a spatula, until it has the consistency of thick porridge or clotted cream (about 10 minutes).

Add the khoya to the reduced milk, followed by the pistachios and stir until combined. Leave to cool, then pour into kulfi or popsicle moulds and insert sticks. Freeze until set – about 8 hours, depending on your fridge.

✤ The final mixture should be 1.3–1.35 litres (44–48 fl oz). Kulfi moulds are available online or sold in some Indian grocers; alternatively, freeze kulfi ice-cream in a freezer-safe container. Some Indian restaurants and families serve kulfi with silver leaf called 'vark', though nowadays, it's served with just about anything, ranging from fruit to chocolate.

FLUFFY PANCAKES WITH ROASTED PEANUTS AND SESAME SEEDS
BAN CHANG KUIH

SERVES 8

Also called apom balek, this street food – a delicious fluffy pancake with crisp edges that's filled with crushed roasted peanuts and sesame seeds – is pure nostalgia for anyone from Malaysia, Singapore or Indonesia. It is always formed into a half-moon, and while the traditional filling is peanuts and sesame seeds, now creamed corn, chocolate and condensed milk are also popular.

Its origin is probably southern Indian or Sri Lankan – a similar sweet called an appam is sold by Indian vendors in Penang. In fact, the only difference is that Indian pancake-makers use fermented palm toddy as the starter, while most other vendors prefer baking powder or yeast.

Origins aside, once you've eaten one, with its crumpet-like texture, I can vouch that you'll be craving another for a long time.

For the batter, sift the flour, sugar, baking powder and salt into a bowl. Make a well in the centre and drop in the egg, oil and 2 cups (500 ml) water. Mix into a smooth batter, then cover and set aside for 2 hours to rest.

Meanwhile, for the filling, crush the peanuts to a coarse powder with a mortar and pestle. In a separate bowl, combine the roasted sesame seeds and the sugar.

To cook the pancakes, heat a 15 cm (6 inch) non-stick frying pan over low heat. Stir the batter well, then spoon ½ cup (125 ml) of batter into the pan and spread it evenly. Cover with a lid, reduce the heat to low and cook for 2 minutes or until bubbles appear.

Sprinkle the peanuts and the sesame seed-sugar mixture evenly over the surface. Dab with butter, then flip half the pancake over itself to form a half moon. Re-cover the pan and cook for another minute or until the pancake is crisp on the outside and soft in the centre.

Remove from the pan, keep warm under a tea towel, and repeat until you've used all the batter. Serve hot, covered with a dusting of icing sugar.

✖ Ban chang kuih is the Penang Hokkien term for this pancake. It is traditionally made in a heavy cast-iron pan set over a coal fire.

1⅔ cups (250 g) plain (all-purpose) flour
2 teaspoons caster (superfine) sugar
3 teaspoons baking powder
½ teaspoon salt
1 large egg, beaten
1 tablespoon neutral oil

FILLING
80 g (2¾ oz) peanuts, roasted
⅓ cup (50 g) roasted sesame seeds
2 tablespoons caster (superfine) sugar, or to taste
50 g (1¾ oz) unsalted butter, softened
Pure icing (confectioners') sugar, for dusting

PANDAN CRÊPES WITH COCONUT FILLING
KUIH DADAR

Light and delicious, this crêpe with coconut filling, called kuih dadar, is popular throughout Malaysia, Singapore and Indonesia. The secret lies in the batter, which is redolent of pandan juice, thus making the crêpe rather special in both looks and its luscious tropical flavour.

It is best not to overcook the crêpes as the batter is one that turns firm easily. As for the filling, freshly grated coconut makes a vast difference to the result, although I've used desiccated coconut when fresh coconuts are not available.

This Nyonya version is served with coconut sauce. Should you come across a pancake called kuih tayap, it is more or less the same thing without the coconut.

To make the batter, place the pandan and spinach leaf in a blender with 1 cup (250 ml) water and blend on high for a minute. Pour through a fine sieve into a bowl, squeezing the solids to extract as much green juice as possible. Discard the solids.

Sift the flour into a bowl and whisk in the egg, milk, butter, a pinch of salt and the strained pandan juice. Stir the batter until smooth, adding a little extra milk if it's too thick; the batter should have a thin consistency. Strain through a sieve and set aside to rest for 30 minutes.

For the filling, combine the pandan leaves and palm sugar with 1½ cups (375 ml) water in a saucepan over medium heat. Simmer until sugar is melted, then add the coconut and a pinch of salt. Stir well, then discard pandan leaves and set aside to cool.

For the sauce, combine all the ingredients with ½ cup (125 ml) water and a pinch of salt in a saucepan. Gradually bring to the boil, stirring frequently. Cool before use.

Heat a 15–20 cm (6–8 inch) crêpe or non-stick frying pan over medium heat. Wipe with a little oil or butter, then ladle in ½ cup (125 ml) batter, swirling quickly to the edges. Cook gently for 1 minute, then flip and cook the other side until set. Remove to a plate, and repeat with remaining batter, stacking the crêpes as you go.

To serve, put 2–3 tablespoons of filling in each crêpe, tuck the edges in and roll into a small cigar-shape. Serve with a spoonful of coconut sauce.

✤ The spinach is purely for colour; you can also use green food colouring.

10 frozen pandan leaves or 2 fresh, thinly sliced
1 large spinach leaf, chopped (see note)
1 cup (150 g) plain (all-purpose) flour
1 egg
⅓ cup (80 ml) milk, plus extra as needed
2 teaspoons butter, melted
Pinch of salt
Neutral oil or butter, for frying

COCONUT FILLING
3 pandan leaves, knotted
1 cup (150 g) coarsely grated palm sugar (or jaggery)
2 cups (180 g) desiccated coconut or freshly grated coconut
Pinch of salt

COCONUT SAUCE
½ cup (125 ml) coconut milk
2 pandan leaves, knotted
1–2 teaspoons caster (superfine) sugar
1 teaspoon cornflour (cornstarch)

GLUTINOUS RICE WITH COCONUT CUSTARD
PULUT SERIKAYA

Glutinous rice is used in sweets and savoury dishes across Southeast Asia. The following sweet dish, consisting of a layer of steamed glutinous rice topped with a layer of coconut-milk custard, is very popular with Straits Chinese families. Served in dainty wedges, pulut serikaya (also called kuih sarlat in parts of Malaysia and Singapore, and gading galoh in Malacca) is traditionally eaten during breakfast and mid-morning coffee breaks, although I like to serve it as a small dessert, more like a palate cleanser after meals.

MAKES 40

2½ cups (500 g) glutinous rice, soaked for 6 hours or overnight
2 pandan leaves
350 ml (12 fl oz) coconut milk
350 ml (12 fl oz) coconut cream
1½ teaspoons salt

CUSTARD
6 pandan leaves, chopped
450 g (1 lb) coconut milk
250 g (9 oz) caster (superfine) sugar
5 eggs
60 g (2¼ oz) plain (all-purpose) flour
½ teaspoon vanilla extract
Few drops green food colouring

Thoroughly rinse and drain the soaked glutinous rice in a sieve. Spread into a 28 cm (11 inch) cake tin and mix in the pandan leaves. Steam over a wok of boiling water for 20 minutes, then discard the leaves, and mix in the coconut milk, coconut cream, salt, and steam for another 15 minutes. Remove from the steamer to cool. Stir again, then pat the rice with a spatula to compress it.

For the custard, place the pandan leaves in a blender with 100 ml (3½ fl oz) water and blend for a minute. Pour through a fine sieve into a bowl, squeezing the solids to extract as much green juice as possible. Discard the solids.

Combine the pandan water with the remaining ingredients, whisk until combined, then pour onto the rice. Return rice to the wok and steam over gently simmering water for 20 minutes until custard is set – a wooden skewer inserted should come out clean. If it's not quite set, steam for another 10 minutes.

Remove the pulut serikaya from the steamer and allow to cool completely before cutting. Serve at room temperature. Pulut serikaya is best eaten on the day it's made; it'll harden up too much in the refrigerator.

�֍ You may need 50 ml (1¾ fl oz) more coconut milk as glutinous rice sometimes absorbs more and sometimes less water.

SERVES 8

RHUBARB, CARDAMOM AND ROSEWATER SORBET, BOOZY WATERMELON AND SAGO

A stunning late-summer dessert that's not only delicious but pretty simple to make if you happen to have an ice-cream churner. If you don't, you can always turn the sorbet into a granita by following the method on page 291.

The following recipe may not sound terribly Asian — I have yet to come across an Asian recipe using rhubarb, and I have two (there's another on page 313) — but I do know that it features in traditional Chinese medicine, which I feel is just enough of a link to justify me including it here.

The beauty of this dessert, apart from the refreshing flavours, is that it can all be made ahead, which if you're hosting gives you plenty of time to enjoy the moment. Traditionally, sago is a starch made from the pith of palm stems, but these days it's often made from tapioca. Buy it in Asian grocers.

RHUBARB SORBET
500 g (1 lb 2 oz) rhubarb, cut into 2 cm (¾ inch) pieces
¾–1 cup (165–220 g) caster (superfine) sugar, to taste
½ teaspoon ground cardamom
Pinch of salt
2 tablespoons glucose or corn syrup
1 teaspoon rosewater, or to taste

SAGO
¼ cup (50 g) sago
½ cup (110 g) caster (superfine) sugar
400 ml (14 fl oz) coconut milk

BOOZY WATERMELON
600 g (1 lb 5 oz) watermelon, cut into small cubes
1 tablespoon caster (superfine) sugar
½ cup (125 ml gin)

For the rhubarb sorbet, place the rhubarb in a saucepan with sugar, cardamom, a pinch of salt and 600 ml (21 fl oz) water. Bring to the boil, reduce to a simmer, then cook until the rhubarb is falling apart (about 10 minutes). Turn off the heat and cover to infuse for 20 minutes.

Transfer to a blender, blitz to a purée, then pass through a fine sieve. Stir in the glucose and rosewater, and refrigerate until cool. Once cooled, churn in an ice-cream machine according to manufacturer's instructions. Transfer to a container and freeze until ready to serve.

For the sago, bring a litre (4 cups) water to a rolling boil in a saucepan. Slowly dribble the sago into the water, boil for 7 minutes, then turn off the heat and cover with a lid. Remove from the heat and stand, covered, for 20 minutes to allow the sago to turn completely transparent. Strain in a fine sieve and wash off excess starch under cold running water. Refrigerate until needed.

Meanwhile, make a sugar syrup by combining the sugar and ½ cup (125 ml) water in a small saucepan, bring it to the boil and swirl until dissolved. Cool, then refrigerate until needed.

For the boozy watermelon, an hour before serving, mix the watermelon with the sugar and gin and chill for an hour.

To serve, stir the sago, sugar syrup and coconut milk together in a bowl, then place 2–3 tablespoons of it in each cocktail glass. Top with a scoop of rhubarb sorbet and cubes of boozy watermelon to serve.

BLACK RICE PUDDING WITH ROASTED-COCONUT ICE-CREAM
BUBUR PULUT HITAM

SERVES 4–6

If you adore rice pudding, you will love this dessert. Enjoyed more often as a snack than a dish, it is nevertheless very popular in Southeast Asian restaurants everywhere. It is extremely easy to make but it requires two non-negotiable ingredients to make it shine: black sticky or glutinous rice and dark palm sugar. Traditionally, it is served with a drizzle of coconut cream but I've upped the ante by serving it with roasted-coconut ice-cream. Start a day ahead to soak the black sticky rice.

250 g (9 oz) black sticky rice (see note)
3 pandan leaves
¾ cup (130 g) finely chopped dark palm sugar (gula jawa)
20 g (¾ oz) caster (superfine) sugar
½ teaspoon salt
400 ml (14 fl oz) coconut milk
Coconut cream and freshly grated coconut (optional), to serve

ROASTED-COCONUT ICE-CREAM
300 ml (10½ fl oz) single (pure) cream
300 ml (10½ fl oz) full-cream milk
50 g (1¾ oz) toasted desiccated coconut
100 g (3½ oz) dark palm sugar (gula jawa) or palm sugar (or jaggery)
6 egg yolks
1 tablespoon dark rum (optional)

For the roasted-coconut ice-cream, combine the cream, milk, coconut and palm sugar in a saucepan and bring to a simmer over low heat. Simmer, stirring, for a minute, then remove from the heat, cover with a lid and leave to infuse for 10 minutes.

Beat the egg yolks in a heatproof bowl until smooth. Whisk the hot cream mixture into the egg yolks, then place the bowl over a saucepan of simmering water (don't let the base of the bowl touch the water) and cook, stirring, until the mixture coats the back of a spoon (12–15 minutes).

Strain the custard through a fine sieve, discarding the coconut solids, then stir in the rum. Cool, refrigerate until chilled, then churn in an ice-cream machine according to manufacturer's instructions. Transfer to a container and freeze until ready to serve.

To make the sticky rice, wash the rice thoroughly, strain, then cover with water and leave overnight to soak.

The next day, drain the rice, then place in a saucepan with 2 pandan leaves and 1.5 litres (6 cups) water. Bring to the boil, then reduce to a simmer and cook, stirring now and then to prevent the rice from sticking, until the grains are soft, plump and partially split (30–40 minutes). If the pudding becomes too thick while simmering, add more hot water.

Meanwhile, combine the palm sugar and caster sugar in a separate saucepan with the remaining pandan leaf and 1 cup (250 ml) water. Bring to a simmer and cook, stirring occasionally, until the sugar dissolves and the water is reduced by half.

Strain through a fine sieve, then add to the rice, stirring to combine. Remove the pandan leaves, then add the salt to the rice, along with the coconut milk.

Spoon the rice pudding into bowls, top with a dollop of roasted-coconut ice-cream and serve topped with a drizzle of coconut cream and a sprinkle of grated coconut.

✖ Black sticky rice is available from Asian grocers.

INDIAN RICE PUDDING

PAYASAM

SERVES 6–8

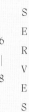

A payasam is a sweet, rich rice pudding, usually quite thick, that's served on special occasions in India, such as weddings. It is usually very calorific, packed with ghee and all sorts of nuts and dried fruits fried in ghee. Despite this version featuring rice, it can be made with many other ingredients, including mung beans and sago.

In South India, payasam is made with both cow's milk and coconut milk, and if you see the words seviyan payasam, it means a milk pudding made with extra-fine wheat noodles. In Singapore and Malaysia, meanwhile, you'll find this dessert served in the home or perhaps in some upmarket North Indian restaurants.

I prefer my version, which is less thick – more like the consistency of light cream. I guess this has something to do with my years of living in Australia.

Pour the milk into a large saucepan and bring to just below boiling. Reduce the heat to low, then add the rice, cardamom, lemon zest and half the raisins. Cook the rice, stirring frequently, for about 1 hour or until it's really soft, thick and creamy. Take care the rice does not stick – if you have one, use a heat mat.

When the rice is done, remove the lemon zest, stir in the sugar until dissolved, then add the coconut cream and remove from heat. Cover and set aside. At this stage, you may wish to add extra sugar to suit your taste.

Melt the ghee in a small frying pan over medium heat. Add the cashews and fry, stirring occasionally, until lightly brown. Toss in the remaining raisins, then spoon half the nut mixture through the rice, reserving the rest to serve.

Serve rice pudding hot or cold with a sprinkling of cardamom and the reserved nut mixture.

✖ Some cooks add a few saffron strands or rosewater for extra flavour while others like to sprinkle some fresh rose petals over the pudding.

1.5 litres (6 cups) milk
100 g (3½ oz) medium-grain rice (such as arborio or sushi rice), rinsed and drained
¼ teaspoon cardamom seeds, finely ground, plus extra to serve
1 strip lemon zest
⅓ cup (60 g) raisins or sultanas
2–3 tablespoons caster (superfine) sugar
½ cup (125 ml) coconut cream
50 g (1¾ oz) ghee or unsalted butter
⅔ cup (100 g) cashews

SERVES 6

SRI LANKAN COCONUT CUSTARD WITH PEAR AND PERSIMMON
WATALAPPAN

Also called vattalappam, this rich custard made with Sri Lankan palm sugar – known as jaggery – is very popular with the Singhalese community in Malaysia. I suspect this dessert is originally of Portuguese origin because of the large number of egg yolks used. I've suggested using nashi pear and crunchy persimmon in the accompanying fruit salad, but feel free to follow your gut and the season – any crunchy pear with strawberries can also work well, or any fruit of your choice.

Jaggery is ideal for this recipe, if you can find it at an Asian grocer. Kithul treacle or honey is palm sugar sold in bottles. You'll need 6 x 125 ml (½ cup) dariole moulds.

---

120 g (4¼ oz) palm sugar (or jaggery), chopped or shaved
2 cups (500 ml) thin coconut milk
100 ml (3½ fl oz) milk
2 eggs, plus 6 egg yolks
½ teaspoon ground cardamom
¼ teaspoon ground cloves
¼ teaspoon ground nutmeg
½ teaspoon ground cinnamon
2 teaspoons rosewater, or to taste
Coconut wafers and extra melted jaggery or kithul (see above), to serve

FRUIT SALAD
1 large nashi pear, peeled and diced
1 large Fuji or fuyu persimmon, peeled and diced
Strained juice of 3 passionfruit
½ teaspoon caster (superfine) sugar

Preheat the oven to 150°C (300°F). Bring the palm sugar, coconut milk and milk to a simmer point in a saucepan over medium heat, stirring gently to melt the palm sugar.

Meanwhile, whisk the eggs and egg yolks in a heatproof bowl.

Slowly pour the hot milk into the eggs, whisking continuously, then strain through a fine sieve. Add the spices and rosewater, stir well, then pour into oiled dariole moulds, removing any surface bubbles with a spoon.

Place the moulds on a tea towel in a deep baking tray, place in the oven, then pour in enough boiling water to come halfway up the sides. Bake for 30–40 minutes until just set, checking after 20 minutes and turning the tray around if necessary.

Carefully remove the tray from the oven and leave the custards to cool in the bath. Once cooled, remove from the water and chill in the refrigerator, covered with plastic wrap, for at least 4–5 hours or ideally overnight.

For the fruit salad, combine all the ingredients in a bowl and toss well.

To serve, carefully unmould the custards onto plates, running a small, sharp knife around the edge if it's proving difficult. Serve with fruit salad, coconut wafers and a drizzle of the melted jaggery.

✄ This recipe can stretch to 8 if the moulds aren't filled to the brim.

CHINESE ALMOND BISCUITS
HANG YEN PAENG

Almond biscuits are especially popular during Chinese New Year because they resemble coins, which means they bring good fortune. Beautifully crumbly and fragrant, they're a cinch to make, whether you use butter as I have, or go for lard, which is equally delicious.

Preheat oven to 180°C (350°F). Spread the blanched almonds on a tray and bake for 8–10 minutes until golden. Remove from oven and leave to cool.

Sift the flour, baking powder and bicarbonate of soda into a bowl. Set aside.

In a separate bowl, beat the caster sugar, butter and salt with an electric beater until pale and creamy. Add the egg, almond extract and vanilla extract and beat until combined.

With a spatula, gradually mix the sifted flour into the egg mixture, followed by the almond meal, stirring until combined.

Take a teaspoonful of dough, form it into a ball and place it on a baking tray lined with baking paper. Repeat with remaining dough, then lightly flatten the balls with a fork. Brush with the egg wash and gently press a roasted almond into the centre of each.

Bake for 10–12 minutes or until light golden, then transfer to a wire rack to cool. Almond biscuits will keep in an airtight container for 2 weeks.

- 40 blanched almonds
- 1⅓ cups (200 g) plain (all-purpose) flour
- ½ teaspoon baking powder
- ½ teaspoon bicarbonate of soda (baking soda)
- 130 g (4½ oz) caster (superfine) sugar
- ½ cup (125 g) unsalted butter, softened
- Pinch of salt
- 1 egg, beaten
- ½ teaspoon almond extract
- ½ teaspoon vanilla extract
- ¾ cup (80 g) almond meal
- 1 egg yolk, beaten with 1 tablespoon milk, for brushing

MAKRUT LIME LEAF CRÈME BRÛLÉE

SERVES 6–7

The secret of this crème brûlée, beautifully fragrant with makrut lime, is not to cook the custard in the oven as in most recipes, but to cook it like making a stirred custard. The result is creamier and smoother, as long as you make sure that the protein in the yolks sets the custard so it'll firm up in the fridge before you top and torch it to give that signature brûlée finish.

The crème brûlée mixture can be made a day ahead to allow the flavours to infuse that little bit more. This dessert is lovely with any biscuit like my Chinese almond biscuits on page 305. You'll need 6–7 x 100–110 ml (3½–3¾ fl oz) ramekins.

Grind the makrut lime leaves to a fine powder in a spice grinder or with a mortar and pestle. Place in a saucepan with the lime zest and the cream and heat to just below boiling point.

Meanwhile, beat the egg yolks and the sugar in a heatproof bowl until combined.

Just before the cream reaches boiling point, pour it into the egg mixture in a steady stream, beating well with a whisk. Return the mixture to the saucepan and cook the custard, stirring, over low heat until it thickens and coats the back of a spoon (12–15 minutes).

Remove from the heat, add the lime juice and stir well.

Strain through a fine sieve, then ladle into ramekins. Refrigerate, uncovered, until set – about 8 hours or preferably overnight.

Sift the sugar evenly over the crèmes, then either place them under a grill set to high until caramelised (about 2–3 minutes), or caramelise the tops lightly and evenly with a blowtorch. Serve immediately.

5 makrut lime leaves
Finely grated zest of 1 makrut lime (optional, or use lime zest)
600 ml (21 fl oz) single (pure) cream
7 egg yolks
⅓ cup (75 g) caster (superfine) sugar, or to taste
Juice of 2 limes
¼ cup (60 g) rapadura sugar or dark brown sugar

ONDE ONDE

SERVES 6–7

Onde onde are tiny balls typically made with glutinous rice flour and sweet potato, with a palm sugar filling, served coated with freshly grated coconut and often eaten at breakfast. They are absolutely delicious, and like most sweet things in Southeast Asia, they are usually coloured green. Enjoy them on their own or serve them with the roasted-coconut ice-cream on page 302.

½ coconut, flesh freshly grated (about 200 g/7 oz; see note)
Pinch of salt
Roasted-coconut ice-cream (page 302; optional), to serve

ONDE ONDE
100 g (3½ oz) yellow sweet potato
5–6 fresh or frozen pandan leaves, chopped
2 large spinach leaves, chopped (see note)
250 g (9 oz) glutinous rice flour, plus extra for dusting

ONDE ONDE FILLING
150 g (5½ oz) palm sugar (or jaggery), grated or chopped into small pieces
1 tablespoon caster (superfine) sugar

For the onde onde, steam the sweet potato in a steamer set over boiling water until tender (10–15 minutes; a knife should be able to slide in easily), being careful that it doesn't turn to mush.

Meanwhile, place the pandan leaves and spinach in a blender with 100 ml (3½ fl oz) water and blend for a minute. Pour into a fine sieve over a bowl, squeezing the leaves to extract as much green juice as possible. Discard the solids.

When the sweet potato is cool enough to handle, peel and mash it (discarding any fibres) in a bowl with the glutinous rice flour to form a dough. Add the pandan extract, a little at a time, mixing with a spatula to form a green-coloured dough. If needed, add 150 ml (5 fl oz) warm water to the dough, a little at a time, until the dough is stiff but pliable. Turn dough out onto a bench dusted with rice flour and knead by hand until it's no longer sticking to your fingers. Rest for 5 minutes.

Meanwhile, for the onde onde filling, mix the palm sugar and caster sugar in a bowl until well combined.

Bring a large saucepan of water to a rolling boil. Form the dough into a long sausage, about 3 cm (1¼ inches) in diameter. Cut into pieces about the size of a small marble, then flatten each piece with your hand and put ½ teaspoon of filling in the centre. Draw each piece of dough together to form a small ball around the filling.

Add the balls to the boiling water a few at a time and cook until they float to the surface (3–5 minutes). Remove with a slotted spoon and drain well.

Working quickly, toss the onde onde into a bowl, add the grated coconut and a pinch of salt, and toss to coat. Serve as is, or with ice-cream if you like.

✱ If you can't find fresh coconuts, you can buy frozen grated fresh coconut in Asian grocers.

Mixing in spinach leaves with the pandan leaves when you blend them is great for the colour.

SNOW SKIN MOONCAKE WITH CUSTARD FILLING

MAKES 20

T L

I learnt this fabulous mooncake recipe from the Chinese chefs at Xin Cuisine in Kuala Lumpur. At that time, it was a chore to make snow skin mooncakes unless it was made with a combination of rice and glutinous rice flours and wheat starch. This flour combination is steamed until cooked before it can be used. Now, it's much easier because cooked glutinous rice flour is readily available.

Why this mooncake is called snow skin is because the pastry surrounding the filling is made with white glutinous rice flour, however different colours made with chocolate, matcha and butterfly pea flower are also popular. The texture of snow skin mooncakes is like mochi and it is never baked. This style of mooncake became popular partly due to consumer demand. Traditional baked mooncakes are deemed oily.

The following recipe is made with a custard filling, but nut fillings and fruit fillings are also popular. You'll need a 50 g (1¾ oz) mooncake mould.

SNOW SKIN

- 120 g (4¼ oz) pure icing (confectioners') sugar
- 160 g (5½ oz) cooked glutinous rice flour, plus extra for dusting (see note)
- 2 tablespoons neutral oil

CUSTARD FILLING

- 3 eggs
- 60 g (2¼ oz) caster (superfine) sugar, or to taste
- 70 g (2½ oz) milk powder
- ⅓ cup (40 g) cornflour (cornstarch)
- ⅔ cup (170 ml) full-cream milk
- 1 teaspoon vanilla extract
- 60 g (2¼ oz) butter

For the custard filling, whisk all the ingredients, except the butter, together in asaucepan and cook, stirring, over low-medium heat until thickened, about 5 minutes. Add the butter and stir well to combine. Transfer to a container to cool, cover the surface directly with plastic wrap and refrigerate until needed. When ready to make mooncakes, form into 25 g (1 oz) balls.

For the snow skin, sift the icing sugar into a bowl, add the cooked glutinous rice flour and mix well. Add 230 ml (7¾ fl oz) water and mix until it is a shaggy mass, then add the oil and mix until it forms into a ball. Knead on a clean surface for 2–3 minutes, then wrap in plastic wrap and leave for 2 hours to rest. When ready to make mooncakes, divide dough into 25 g (1 oz) balls.

Flatten each ball of dough into a 10 cm (4 inch) disc, large enough to wrap the custard. Place a ball of custard in the centre of a disc of dough and form into a ball.

Dust generously with cooked glutinous rice flour and carefully put it into your mooncake mould set on a work surface. Gently press the spring bar on the mould. When you feel some resistance, release the spring bar and the mooncake is formed. Repeat with remaining dough and custard.

If you're not eating these immediately, best to dust with extra glutinous rice flour and refrigerate in a container.

✖ You can buy cooked glutinous rice flour at Asian supermarkets.

To achieve the pink effect on the tops of the mooncakes, reserve 25 g (¾ oz) of the dough, and mix with 2 drops of red food colouring. Roll into a long thin pencil, and cut into tiny pieces which you can then press into the tops of the individual balls of white dough.

MAKES 40

PINEAPPLE TARTS

Pineapple tarts are a favourite with the Peranakans, the early Chinese settlers who married into the local community in Malaysia and Indonesia. I suspect it's a preparation borrowed from the Dutch, since pastry-making in the Western sense didn't really come into the Nyonya repertoire until the 18th century, when Dutch rule was firmly established in Indonesia and Melaka. It's also possible, however, that it was adapted from the British – the Malay name 'tart nenas' suggests it has Anglo leanings, given tart is an English word.

In Hokkien and Cantonese, the word for pineapple (ong lai or wong lai respectively) means yellow – and since gold is yellow, it is auspicious, hence why it's enjoyed during Chinese New Year in Singapore and Malaysia. These tarts are dainty and traditionally a lot of work goes into creating the most intricate patterns.

---

2 pineapples, peeled
1 cup (220 g) caster (superfine) sugar for every 1½ cups (390 g) pineapple
1 cinnamon stick
5 cloves
½ star anise
350–400 g (12–14 oz) your favourite shortcrust pastry (see note)

Coarsely grate the pineapple, discarding the core, and place the pulp in a fine sieve set over a bowl and leave it to strain for 30 minutes. (If you are pressed for time, squeeze out the juice lightly with muslin or a clean tea towel). Reserve the solids and drink the juice.

Measure the pineapple solids into a saucepan with a cup measure, and for every 1½ cups (390 g) of pineapple, add 1 cup (220 g) of sugar. Add cinnamon, cloves and star anise and place over medium heat. Bring to a simmer, then reduce the heat to low and cook, stirring frequently to prevent burning, for 1–1.5 hours until pineapple jam is very thick and golden, almost solid.

Pour into sterilised jars, seal and cool. It will keep refrigerated for a month.

To make the pineapple tarts, heat the oven to 180°C (350°F) and roll out your favourite shortcrust pastry on a lightly dusted surface to 5 mm (¼ inch) thick.

Cut it into rings with a 5 cm (2 inch) ring cutter and plop the pastry discs into greased miniature tart tins (or straight onto baking paper). Fill these with cold pineapple jam and bake until golden (about 20 minutes).

Cool on a wire rack before serving. Store extras in an airtight container for up to 2 weeks.

✖ If you aren't in the habit of making shortcrust pastry, look for a good-quality one such as Carême in your supermarket.

If your jam is runny, it will spread in the oven. Ensure it's thickened enough to sit on the tart, particularly if you're not using tart tins.

RHUBARB CRUMBLE WITH RHUBARB SORBET

SERVES 8

Along with citrus fruits, apples and pears, rhubarb is a great winter staple. If you grow your own like I do, it tends to be a most forgiving plant – I neglected mine when I first moved to Trentham, and it thrived anyway. I now have three rhubarb plants, and harvest the stalks for all sorts of sweet things and occasionally for savoury.

A crumble may not sound particularly Asian, but this one has hints of warmth and heat that transport it a little from the British village crumble feel. When I don't have enough rhubarb, I like to add a couple of apples or pears to bulk it out and add another dimension.

Toss the rhubarb with the sugar and your choice of spices in a baking dish and roast in an oven at 160°C (320°F) until soft (about 10 minutes). Set aside to cool.

For the rhubarb sorbet, place the rhubarb in a saucepan with sugar, orange zest, chilli powder, a pinch of salt and 600 ml (21 fl oz) water. Bring to the boil, reduce to a simmer, then cook until the rhubarb is falling apart (about 10 minutes). Turn off the heat and cover to infuse for 20 minutes.

Transfer to a blender, blitz to a purée, then pass through a fine sieve. Stir in the glucose, and refrigerate until cool. Once cooled, churn in an ice-cream machine according to manufacturer's instructions until frozen. Transfer to a container and freeze until ready to serve.

For the crumble, mix the sugar, baking powder and cinnamon in a small bowl to combine. In a separate bowl, rub the butter and flour together with your hands to form pea-sized pieces. Add to the sugar-cinnamon mixture and stir to combine.

Preheat oven to 180°C (350°F). Spoon the cooked rhubarb into 8 ceramic ramekins (avoid aluminium ones as they react with the rhubarb) and top with the crumble topping, packing it down gently. Bake for 8–10 minutes until the topping is golden and the rhubarb is bubbling at the edges.

Serve with the rhubarb sorbet and whipped cream.

---

1 kg (2 lb 4 oz) rhubarb, cut into 3 cm (1¼ inch) pieces
160–200 g (5¾–7 oz) raw sugar
1–2 star anise (optional)
5 cm (2 inch) cinnamon stick (optional)
1 tablespoon ground coriander (optional)
Whipped cream, to serve

RHUBARB SORBET
500 g (1 lb 2 oz) rhubarb, cut into 5 cm (2 inch) pieces
¾–1 cup (165–220 g) caster (superfine) sugar, to taste
2 teaspoons grated orange zest
½ teaspoon chilli powder
Pinch of salt, or to taste
2 tablespoons liquid glucose or corn syrup

CRUMBLE
½ cup (90–100 g) brown sugar, or to taste
1 teaspoon baking powder
½ teaspoon ground cinnamon (or cardamom)
⅓ cup (90 g) butter, cubed
1 cup (150 g) plain (all-purpose) flour

CHEESECAKE WITH RED FERMENTED TOFU

SERVES 8–10

This baked cheesecake was born from me thinking about the jars – yes, jars plural – of fermented doufu or tofu called nanru (in Mandarin) or nam yue (in Cantonese) I have tucked away in the fridge. The result is a cheesecake that's very much a dessert but is almost more savoury than sweet, with the spotlight on the flavour of the fermented tofu. If you have a sweet tooth, by all means, add 50 g (1¾ oz) more sugar.

I like to bake this at a low temperature because cheesecakes are prone to cracking, and it's always a good idea to line your tin thoroughly with foil, just in case the batter seeps. Finally, take care when you're beating the batter – overbeat it and it'll deflate during baking.

Brush a 22 cm (8½ inch) springform cake tin with a little of the melted butter, making sure the base is inverted, which makes it easier to slide out the cheesecake. Tear off an 80 cm (31½ inch) sheet of foil and fold it in half so it measures 40 cm (16 inches) in length. Wrap it around the outside of the cake tin, paying attention to sealing around the gaps and folding back the excess so there's plenty of room to pour the batter in.

Pulse the biscuits in a food processor until crumbled, then add the remaining butter and process until it feels sandy. Tip the mixture into the cake tin and use a smooth-sided glass to press it in around the edges until firm, then pop it into the fridge to chill until firm.

Preheat the oven to 150°C (300°F). Blend the cream cheese, sugar and beancurd cubes in a food processor until smooth. Add the cornflour, then add the eggs one at a time, beating until smooth between each addition.

Add the sour cream, cream and a pinch of salt, beat until smooth, then pour the batter into the tin and bake for 50 minutes or until the cake is just firm, with a slight wobble in the centre. Turn off the oven, leave the cake to cool in the oven for 1 hour, then remove from oven and cool completely on a wire rack.

Refrigerate overnight and serve with strawberry compote.

✖ Sometimes I use a water bath to bake the cheesecake to allow the eggs to cook more slowly, resulting in an even creamier texture. It'll take slightly longer to cook, around 1 hour.

- 100 g (3½ oz) unsalted butter, melted
- 300 g (10½ oz) Chinese almond biscuits (page 305) or digestive biscuits
- 2¼ cups (500 g) Philadelphia cream cheese, at room temperature
- 100 g (3½ oz) caster (superfine) sugar
- 10 cubes red fermented beancurd (see page 248)
- 1 tablespoon cornflour (cornstarch)
- 3 eggs, beaten
- 1 cup (245 g) sour cream, at room temperature
- 1 cup (250 ml) pure cream
- Pinch of salt
- Strawberry compote, to serve

PANDAN CHIFFON CAKE

SERVES 8

Such is the glamour of chiffon cake that it's hard to believe a century ago it didn't exist. Created by American Harry Baker in the 1920s, it quickly swept the US like a gossamer cloud. But even as its popularity declined, the cake – which has more air than sugar yet is beautifully rich – caught on in Asia.

I remember eating my first pandan chiffon cake, baked by a friend, in Kuala Lumpur. Laced with coconut milk and scented with pandan, it was a revelation. My next encounter with it was one I bought in Melbourne that was lurid green and tasted like cardboard. It was awful.

Finally, my dear friend Chui Lee Luk, the former owner-chef of Claude's restaurant in Sydney (and baker of my recent wedding cake!), gave me this stunning recipe. She graciously agreed to let me share it with the world. For this cake to really sing, use fresh pandan leaves. You'll need a 25 cm (10 inch) chiffon cake tin.

- 18 fresh pandan leaves, finely shredded
- ¾ cup (185 ml) coconut milk, plus 2 tablespoons extra
- 6 egg yolks (about 120 g), plus 10 egg whites (about 300 g/10½ oz)
- 250 g (9 oz) caster (superfine) sugar
- ½ cup (125 ml) neutral oil
- 180 g (6½ oz) plain (all-purpose) flour
- 2 teaspoons baking powder
- ½ teaspoon salt
- 1 teaspoon cream of tartar
- Whipped cream, to serve (optional)
- Coconut shavings and pure icing (confectioners') sugar, to serve (optional)

Heat oven to 160°C (315°F). Place the shredded pandan leaves in a blender with the ¾ cup (185 ml) coconut milk, blend until smooth, then strain through a fine sieve into a large bowl, discarding solids. Some coconut milk will be lost in the process; you should end up with ¾ cup (185 ml) total.

Add the egg yolks, 200 g (7 oz) of the sugar and the oil to the coconut milk and whisk with electric beaters or in a stand mixer fitted with the whisk attachment for 1 minute or until smooth.

Sift the flour, baking powder and salt together into a separate bowl. Make a well in the centre, then pour in the coconut milk mixture and beat until smooth.

Clean and thoroughly dry the beaters (or transfer the batter to another bowl and clean and dry the stand mixer), then beat the egg whites until frothy. Add the cream of tartar and continue beating for 10 minutes or until soft peaks form. Beat in the remaining sugar until dissolved and stiff peaks form.

With a balloon whisk, fold a third of the egg whites into the batter to loosen, then fold in the remaining egg whites until just combined.

Pour into a chiffon cake tin and run a skewer or knife through the middle of the cake batter to get rid of any air bubbles.

Bake for 50–55 minutes until a skewer inserted in the middle comes out clean and the cake springs back when pressed in the centre.

Remove from the oven and invert the tin, placing the upside-down tin onto the neck of a glass bottle. Leave inverted to cool completely, about an hour or so.

Once it's cooled, run a bread knife or long metal spatula around the side of the tin, pressing against the sides to keep the exterior of the cake attractive. Remove the centre of the pan, lifting the cake with it, then with a thin, sharp knife, loosen the core of the cake from the tin, then do the same with the base. Invert onto a cake platter and serve, either unadorned, or with whipped cream and showered with coconut shavings and a dusting of icing sugar.

✣ Always fold flour gently but thoroughly and use the correct tin size. When the cake is unmoulded, wrap cake well to avoid drying. Make sure there's no egg yolk in your egg white otherwise it will not whip.

ACKNOWLEDGMENTS

What a whirlwind few years. It all started in late 2021 when Kerrie O'Brien and Jane Willson visited me at my cooking school in Trentham. Kerrie is a journalist who has been a friend for at least a decade, and Jane I had met on a few occasions around town; she has a reputation of being one of the best publishers/editors around. My memory of that day is patchy; I was too focused on conducting my cooking class. Perhaps the idea of writing a second cookbook started germinating then, I don't know.

Soon after, Jane arrived on my doorstep with another powerhouse woman, Jane Morrow. The conversation with the pair, both razor-sharp and marvellous publishers at Murdoch Books, was invigorating and exciting, and a contract was sealed. Then in March 2023, I met my extraordinary editorial manager, Justin Wolfers, on a fancy pontoon on the Yarra River. Before I knew it, an ace team was assembled for this turbocharged adventure.

First cab off the rank was design manager Kristy Allen. Kristy's vision was beautiful and expressive. She and designer George Saad have delivered a package that has me spellbound. And leading the equally important next part of the process is dogged campaign manager Sarah Hatton, whose self-appointed title for the publicity of my book is Campaign Dumpling Manager. Good, eh?

All this is to express my deep gratitude and appreciation for the team at Murdoch Books standing by me. Special thanks to Jane Willson and Justin Wolfers for your wisdom, patience, encouragement and support for this mammoth book. Your unwavering belief in me kept me going when I felt all the air was sucked out of me. Special thanks also to David Matthews, my editor and friend. I felt you cooked with me through the recipes. And to another mate, Toni Mason, for the final read. Thank you.

To Mark Roper, the quiet, talented photographer, thank you for the fantastic images. And to Lee Blaylock, whose eye for detail as a food stylist is second to none. You two are legends.

I also want to thank a handful of selfless chefs (and friends) for their unstinting support. When I mentioned I needed help, the chefs of Surly Goat (one of the best regional restaurants in Victoria) jumped in without second thoughts. That's chefs' camaraderie. Thank you, David Willcocks, Rob Kabboord and Michael de Jong. Your skill, professionalism and big-heartedness are much appreciated. Equal thanks also to another talented chef, Jenna Abbruzzese.

I owe my thanks to Jo Corrigan, Matt Donnelly, Matt Jeffrey and Joel Milligan for friendship and roses. Also, thanks to Brad Swartz for his friendship and for designing my website.

Thank you to the generous team at Gaggenau, without whose help the cooking school would not be what it is today. To Mario, Helen and Madeleine Marson of Vinea Marson, thank you for your delicious wines and generosity. My deep gratitude to all the lovely participants who've made the trek to Trentham to cook and learn with me.

To my family, the Tan clan and the Lim clan, thank you for being there. And finally, to Terry, for sharing my dreams and life's adventures. Terima kasih.

FURTHER READING

Alexander, Stephanie, *The Cook's Companion* (Penguin-Lantern, 2004)

Alvarez, Danielle, *Recipes for a Lifetime of Beautiful Cooking* (Murdoch Books, 2023)

Brennan, Jennifer, *Curries and Bugles – A Cookbook of the British Raj* (Viking, 1990)

Bush, Austin, *The Food of Northern Thailand* Clarkson Potter, 2018)

Chang, K.C., *Food in Chinese Culture: Anthropological and Historical Perspectives* (Yale University Press, 1997)

Carey, O Tama, *Lankan Food: Serendipity and Spice* (Hardie Grant Books, 2022)

Chin, H.F., *Malaysian Vegetables in Colour – A Complete Guide* (Tropical Press Book, 1999)

Davidson, Allan, *The Oxford Companion to Food* (Oxford University Press, 1999)

Dunlop, Fuchsia, *Every Grain of Rice: Simple Chinese Home Cooking* (Bloomsbury, 2012)

Dunlop, Fuchsia, *Land of Fish and Rice: Recipes from The Culinary Heart of China* (Bloomsbury, 2016)

Ford, Eleanor, *The Nutmeg Trail: A Culinary Journey Along the Ancient Spice Routes* (Murdoch Books, 2022)

Hemphill, Ian, Spice Notes: *A Cook's Compendium of Herbs and Spices* (Macmillan, 2000)

Holttum, R.E. *Plant Life in Malaya* (Longman, 1954)

Jaffrey, Madhur, *A Taste of India* (Pavilion, 1985)

Long, Sorey & Linden, Kanika, *Authentic Cambodian Recipes* (Marshall Cavendish, 2010)

Nguyen, Andrea, *Into the Vietnamese Kitchen* (Ten Speed Press, 2006)

Ong, Jin Teong, *Nonya Heritage Kitchen* (Landmark Books, 2016)

Oseland, James, *Cradle of Flavor: home cooking from the spice islands of Indonesia, Malaysia and Singapore* (W.W. Norton, 2006)

Panjabi, Camellia, *50 Great Curries of India* (Kyle Books, 2004)

Sanmugam, Devagi, *Banana Leaf Temptations* (VJ Times, 1997)

Sharma, Nik, *Season* (Chronicle Books, 2018)

So, Yan-kit, *Classic Food of China* (Macmillan, 1992)

Solomon, Charmaine, *Charmaine Solomon's Encyclopedia of Asian Food* (Willian Heinemann, 1996)

Stobart, Tom, *Herbs, Spices and Flavorings* (The Overlook Press, 2000)

Tan, Christopher, *The Way of Kueh* (Epigram, 2019)

Tan, Tony, *Hong Kong Food City* (Murdoch Books, 2017)

Thompson, David, *Thai Food* (Viking 2002)

Tsuji, Shizuo, *Japanese Cooking – A Simple Art* (Kodansha International, 1980)

Young, Grace, *Stir-Frying to the Sky's Edge* (Simon & Schuster, 2010)

INDEX

A
Acar awak 284
Alice's ultimate meat patties 120
almonds
  Cheesecake with red fermented tofu 315
  Chinese almond biscuits 305
amaranth 24
  Stir fried Chinese spinach or amaranth 255
anchovies
  green herb sauce 128
  Jewelled-rice congee with sweetcorn and whitebait fritters 49
  Nasi lemak 52
  sambal ikan bilis 52
  stock 59
asam keping
  Grilled chicken with savoury coconut sauce 176–7
  Traders' rice 53
Asam laksa 38
asparagus
  Grilled asparagus with walnut pesto 264
  Stir-fried mixed vegetables 259
aubergines *see* eggplants

B
Balinese dry-spiced shredded beef 124
Balinese roast duck 191
Balinese roast pork 157
Balinese-style roast spatchcock with glutinous rice 182
bamboo shoots 14
  Braised lamb with beancurd sticks and tangerine peel 152
  Chicken and prawn windmill dumplings 71
  Deep-fried glutinous rice dumplings 72
  Duck breast with sweet osmanthus sauce and baby bamboo shoots 173
  Har gow 84
  Stir-fried mixed vegetables 259
  Thai duck curry dumplings 77
  Top hats 109
banh cuon batter 74
bao
  bao dough 92
  gai bao dough 73
  Steamed chicken bao 73
  Steamed pork buns with fermented black beans and chilli 92
Barbecued pork 93
bean pastes 21
  Beef fillet with Sichuan sauce 141
  Glass noodles with minced pork shiitake and garlic chives 50
  mushrooms and dried shrimp gnocchi 279
  Roast potatoes with fermented bean sauce 276
  Sichuan sauce 141
  Sichuan twice-cooked pork 153
  Stir-fried chicken with ginger and wood-ear mushrooms 164
  Taro gnocchi two ways 278–9
  see also miso
bean shoots, Stir fried, with salted fish 260
bean sprouts, pickled 145
beancurd 14
  Braised lamb with beancurd sticks and tangerine peel 152
  Char siu cauliflower 248
  Cheesecake with red fermented tofu 315
  Crisp beancurd skin dumplings 87
  Laksa lemak 42
  Zucchini dumplings 99
  see also tofu
beans 16, 30
  black bean sauce 181
  broad bean mash 243
  Chicken with black bean sauce 181
  Chinese Bolognese 61
  Duck breast with sweet osmanthus sauce and baby bamboo shoots 173
  Eggplant with minced pork 126
  Five-spice 'smoked' fish with broad bean mash and spicy witlof salad 242–3
  Fragrant duck, Shanxi style 190
  Grilled chicken with savoury coconut sauce 176–7
  kerabu rice salad 177
  mung bean noodles 62
  Penang Nyonya braised pork 142
  Penang Nyonya pickles 284
  Sichuan twice-cooked pork 153
  Spicy Sichuan mung bean noodles 252
  Steamed pork buns with fermented black beans and chilli 92
  Steamed pork spare-ribs 97
  Stir fried pipis with Malaysian flavours 214
  Tamarind pork 158
  Thai green papaya salad 209
  Typhoon shelter crab 237
  see also beancurd, bean pastes, miso, tofu
beef
  Alice's ultimate meat patties 120
  Balinese dry-spiced shredded beef 124
  Beef cooked in sweet soy sauce 148
  Beef fillet with Sichuan sauce 141
  Beef rendang 119
  Beef salad with roasted beetroot, preserved lemon and herb dressing 128
  Beef with mandarin peel 146
  Gai lan with lotus root or beef 263
  Macanese beef 'curry' with daikon 138
  Massaman curry of beef 139
  My family's beef brisket 123
  Nasi lemak 52
  Roti john 104
  Thai grilled beef salad 125
  Vietnamese shaking beef 145
beetroots
  Beef salad with roasted beetroot, preserved lemon and herb dressing 128
  beetroot salad 128
belacan 16 137
  Asam laksa 38
  Balinese roast duck 191
  Braised pork belly with soy sauce 151
  Chicken buah keluak 199
  Curry kapitan 197
  Hae mee 59
  Laksa lemak 42
  Nasi lemak 52
  Nyonya pork satay 132–3
  Penang Nyonya fish 'curry' with spicy tamarind sauce 235
  sambal belacan 261
  sambal ikan bilis 52
  satay spice paste 133
  Spicy fried tempeh 275
  Steamed mussels with XO sauce 232
  Steamed seafood pudding 221

321

stock 59
Tamarind pork 158
Traders' rice 53
Wood ear fungus and shredded chicken, Nyonya style 261
XO sauce 232

berries
berry compote 291
Cheesecake with red fermented tofu 315
Drunken chicken with shaved ice 168
Watermelon granita with coconut jelly and berry compote 291

biryani, Rose-scented chicken 54–5
biscuits, Chinese almond 305
black bean sauce 181
Black rice pudding with roasted-coconut ice-cream 302
blanching vinegar 284

bok choy 24
Stir-fried mixed vegetables 259

boozy watermelon 300
Braised chicken with lemongrass 187
Braised lamb with beancurd sticks and tangerine peel 152
Braised pork belly with soy sauce 151

bread
Roti canai 106–7
Roti jala 108
Spring onion pancakes 103

brisket, My family's beef 123
broad bean mash 243
brussels sprouts: Slow-cooked spatchcock with jicama, brussels sprouts and vadouvan 202
buah keluak: Chicken buah keluak 199
Butter prawns 225

C

cabbage
Grilled chicken with savoury coconut sauce 176–7
kerabu rice salad 177
Penang Nyonya pickles 284
Pork and Chinese cabbage dumplings 80–1
see also wombok

cakes
Cheesecake with red fermented tofu 315
Pandan chiffon cake 316
Snow skin moon cake with custard filling 311
Steamed rice cake 274

calamari
Calamari and green mango salad 217
Shellfish with garlic, coriander and Thai basil 210
Vietnamese stuffed squid or calamari 220

candlenuts 16
Balinese roast duck 191
Balinese-style roast spatchcock with glutinous rice 182
Chicken buah keluak 199
Curry kapitan 197

Grilled chicken with savoury coconut sauce 176–7
Laksa lemak 42
Pan-fried snapper with vinegar sambal 239
Steamed seafood pudding 221
Tamarind pork 158
Cantonese fried rice 44

capsicums
black bean sauce 181
Chicken with black bean sauce 181
Sichuan twice-cooked pork 153
Silken tofu with roasted capsicum and fermented chilli 280
Stir-fried chicken with cashew nuts 201
Stir-fried seitan with mushrooms and capsicum 273
Xinjiang lamb skewers 131

caramel 113

carrots
Beef cooked in sweet soy sauce 148
Chicken and prawn windmill dumplings 71
nuoc cham 220
Pearl balls 68
Penang Nyonya pickles 284
Prosperity toss 41
shellfish oil 101
Steamed mussels with XO sauce 232
Stir-fried mixed vegetables 259
Stir-fried vegetarian hokkien noodles 63
Top hats 109
Vietnamese stuffed squid or calamari 220

cashews 16
Indian rice pudding 303
Rose-scented chicken biryani 54–5
Sri Lankan spicy cashew curry 270
Stir-fried chicken with cashew nuts 201

cauliflower
Char siu cauliflower 248
Penang Nyonya pickles 284

celery
My family's beef brisket 123
shellfish oil 101
Soba noodles with seafood 58

Char kway teow 37
Char siu 93
Char siu cauliflower 248
Char siu sou 94
Chawanmushi with shellfish oil and crab meat 100–1
Cheesecake with red fermented tofu 315

chestnuts
Slow-cooked duck with fragrant stuffing – the duck that won 1000 hearts 192–3
see also water chestnuts

chicken
Alice's ultimate meat patties 120
Balinese-style roast spatchcock with glutinous rice 182
Braised chicken with lemongrass 187
Chicken and prawn windmill dumplings 71
Chicken buah keluak 199
Chicken with black bean sauce 181
Curry kapitan 197

Chinese almond biscuits 305
Chinese Bolognese 61
Chinese broccoli see gai lan
Chinese olive fried rice 45
Chiu chow dumplings 78
chocolate: Sesame doughnut with custard and chocolate 114

chrysanthemum 24
Edible chrysanthemum leaf and tofu salad 262

clams: Stir fried pipis with Malaysian flavours 214

coconut 18
Balinese-style roast spatchcock with glutinous rice 182
Beef rendang 119
Black rice pudding with roasted-coconut ice-cream 302
Butter prawns 225
Coconut jam 113
coconut jelly 291
coconut sauce 221, 297
Curry kapitan 197
curry sauce 77
custard 298
Fish head curry 241
Fried chicken, Nyonya style 203
Glutinous rice with coconut custard 298
Grilled chicken with savoury coconut sauce 176–7
Indian rice pudding 303
kerabu rice salad 177
Laksa lemak 42
Massaman curry of beef 139
Matcha ice-cream with sago and dried persimmon 293
My dhal 266
Nasi lemak 52
Nyonya pork satay 132–3
Onde onde 308
Pandan chiffon cake 316
Pandan crêpes with coconut filling 297
Pandan panna cotta with red rubies 288
Peanut crackers 112
Pineapple curry 265
pineapple satay sauce 133
Pol sambol 271
red rubies 288
Rhubarb, cardamom and rosewater sorbet, boozy watermelon and sago 300
roasted-coconut ice-cream 302
Roti jala 108
sago 293, 300
Slow-cooked duck with cumin and black pepper 183
Slow-cooked spatchcock with jicama, brussels sprouts and vadouvan 202
Spicy pomelo and prawn salad 218
Sri Lankan coconut custard with pear and persimmon 304
Sri Lankan spicy cashew curry 27
Steamed seafood pudding 221
Thai duck curry dumplings 77
Thai red duck curry with lychee 175
Traders' rice 53

Vietnamese stuffed squid or calamari 220
Watermelon granita with coconut jelly and berry compote 291
Watermelon with crisp fish 219
Wood-ear mushrooms and shredded chicken, Nyonya style 261
compote, berry 291
congee: Jewelled-rice congee with sweetcorn and whitebait fritters 49
corn
Grilled scallops with sweetcorn sauce and curry leaves 222
Jewelled-rice congee with sweetcorn and whitebait fritters 49
sweetcorn sauce 222
crabs
Chawanmushi with shellfish oil and crab meat 100–1
Singapore chilli crab 211
Top hats 109
Typhoon shelter crab 237
Crackers, Peanut 112
creme brulee, Makrut lime leaf 307
crêpes, Pandan, with coconut filling 297
Crisp beancurd skin dumplings 87
crumble, Rhubarb, with rhubarb sorbet 313
cucumbers
Asam laksa 38
Chinese Bolognese 61
Grilled chicken with savoury coconut sauce 176–7
kerabu rice salad 177
Nasi lemak 52
Nyonya pork satay 132–3
Penang Nyonya pickles 284
Thai grilled beef salad 125
cumquats
Beef salad with roasted beetroot, preserved lemon and herb dressing 128
beetroot salad 128
Wood-ear mushrooms and shredded chicken, Nyonya style 261
curries
Beef rendang 119
Curry kapitan 197
curry paste 266
curry sauce 77
Fish head curry 241
Macanese beef 'curry' with daikon 138
Massaman curry of beef 139
My dhal 266
Penang Nyonya fish 'curry' with spicy tamarind sauce 235
Pineapple curry 265
Rajasthani watermelon curry 269
red curry paste 175
Roti john 104
Sri Lankan spicy cashew curry 270
Thai red duck curry with lychee 175
Curry kapitan 197
curry oil 66
custards 100, 115, 298

Sri Lankan coconut custard with pear and persimmon 304

D
daikon 28
Char kway teow 37
Chiu chow dumplings 78
Deep-fried glutinous rice dumplings 72
Macanese beef 'curry' with daikon 138
Prosperity toss 41
Roast stuffed spatchcock with daikon 186
Steamed rice cake 274
dashi 100
Deep-fried glutinous rice dumplings 72
dip, Sichuan pepper-salt 190
dipping sauces 203
Sichuan-style dipping sauce 68
soy dipping sauce 81
soy-vinegar dipping sauce 96, 99
vinegar-ginger dipping sauce 96, 99
xiao long bao dipping sauce 89
doubanjiang see bean pastes
doughnut, Sesame, with custard and chocolate 114
dressings 41, 58, 62, 206, 217, 219
chilli jam 254
Drunken chicken with shaved ice 168
duck 170–1
Balinese roast duck 191
Duck breast with sweet osmanthus sauce and baby bamboo shoots 173
duck stock 193
Fragrant duck, Shanxi style 190
Slow-cooked duck with cumin and black pepper 183
Slow-cooked duck with fragrant stuffing – the duck that won 1000 hearts 192–3
Stir-fried prawns with duck-liver sausage 236
Teochew duck 174
Thai duck curry dumplings 77
Thai red duck curry with lychee 175
dumplings 21
Chicken and prawn windmill dumplings 71
Chiu chow dumplings 78
Crisp beancurd skin dumplings 87
Deep-fried glutinous rice dumplings 72
Har gow 84
Lamb dumplings, Xi'an style 69
Mushroom dumplings with curry oil 66
Pearl balls 68
Pork and Chinese cabbage dumplings 80–1
Potsticker dumplings 96
squid-ink dumpling dough 90
Squid-ink potstickers 90
Thai duck curry dumplings 77
wheat starch dough 84
Xiao long bao 88–9
Zucchini dumplings 99

E
Edible chrysanthemum leaf and tofu salad 262

eggplant 24
Eggplant with minced pork 126
Fish head curry 241
Grilled eggplant salad with chilli jam 254
Thai red duck curry with lychee 175
eggs
Alice's ultimate meat patties 120
Black rice pudding with roasted-coconut ice-cream 302
Butter prawns 225
Cantonese fried rice 44
Char kway teow 37
Chawanmushi with shellfish oil and crab meat 100–1
Chinese olive fried rice 45
Coconut jam 113
custard 100, 115, 298
Egg tart 115
Fried rice with chicken, salted fish and bean shoots 43
Fried rice with pineapple 46
Glutinous rice with coconut custard 298
Hae mee 59
Jewelled-rice congee with sweetcorn and whitebait fritters 49
Makrut lime leaf creme brulee 307
Matcha ice-cream with sago and dried persimmon 293
Nasi lemak 52
noodles 61
Oyster omelette with chilli sauce 227
Pandan chiffon cake 316
roasted-coconut ice-cream 302
Roti jala 108
Roti john 104
Scrambled eggs with curry leaves and green chillies 110
Sesame doughnut with custard and chocolate 114
Slow-cooked duck with cumin and black pepper 183
Snow skin moon cake with custard filling 311
squid-ink noodles 39
Sri Lankan coconut custard with pear and persimmon 304
Steamed seafood pudding 221
Taro gnocchi two ways 278–9
Teochew duck 174
whitebait fritters 49

F
fennel: shellfish oil 101
fish
Asam laksa 38
Chawanmushi with shellfish oil and crab meat 100–1
dashi 100
Fish head curry 241
Five-spice 'smoked' fish with broad bean mash and spicy witlof salad 242–3
Fried rice with chicken, salted fish and bean shoots 43
Glass noodles with pan-fried fish, and saffron broth 48

Pan-fried snapper with vinegar sambal 239
Penang Nyonya fish 'curry' with spicy tamarind sauce 235
Soba noodles with seafood 58
Steamed seafood pudding 221
Stir fried bean shoots with salted fish 260
Traders' rice 53
Watermelon with crisp fish 219
whitebait fritters 49
see also anchovies, salmon
Five-spice 'smoked' fish with broad bean mash and spicy witlof salad 242–3
Fluffy pancakes with roasted peanuts and sesame seeds 295
Fragrant duck, Shanxi style 190
Fried chicken, Nyonya style 203
fried rice, Cantonese 44
fried rice, Chinese olive 45
Fried rice with chicken, salted fish and bean shoots 43
Fried rice with pineapple 46
fritters, whitebait 49
fruit salad 304

G
gai bao dough 73
gai lan 24
Gai lan with lotus root or beef 263
ginger, Pickled young 282
Glass noodles with pan-fried fish, and saffron broth 48
glaze, mustard 189
glossary 14–31
Glutinous rice with coconut custard 298
granita, Watermelon, with coconut jelly and berry compote 291
green herb sauce 128
Grilled asparagus with walnut pesto 264
Grilled chicken with savoury coconut sauce 176–7
Grilled eggplant salad with chilli jam 254
Grilled scallops with sweetcorn sauce and curry leaves 222

H
Hae mee 59

I
ice-cream
Kulfi ice-cream 294
Matcha ice-cream with sago and dried persimmon 293
roasted-coconut ice-cream 302
Inche kabin 203
Indian rice pudding 303
ingredients 14–31
Isaan-style grilled chicken wings 167
Itik golek 183

J
jam
chilli jam 254
Coconut jam 113

jelly, coconut 291
Jewelled-rice congee with sweetcorn and whitebait fritters 49
jiaozi pio 80
jicama
Rice rolls with pork and wood-ear mushrooms 74–5
Slow-cooked spatchcock with jicama, brussels sprouts and vadouvan 202
Top hats 109

K
Kaya 113
kerabu rice salad 177
khoya 294
Kulfi ice-cream 294
Kung pao chicken 194

L
laksa
Asam laksa 38
Laksa lemak 42
lamb
Braised lamb with beancurd sticks and tangerine peel 152
Lamb dumplings, Xi'an style 69
Roast lamb with saffron and tandoori spices 155
Roti john 104
Stir-fried lamb with spring onions and steamed buns 147
Xinjiang lamb skewers 131
lap cheong 17
Cantonese fried rice 44
Char kway teow 37
Fried rice with pineapple 46
Slow-cooked duck with fragrant stuffing – the duck that won 1000 hearts 192–3
Stir-fried squid ink noodles with prawns, lap cheong and tomato 39
leeks
Prosperity toss 41
shellfish oil 101
Sichuan twice-cooked pork 153
Stir-fried lamb with spring onions and steamed buns 147
Steamed prawns with pickled leeks, ginger and spring onions 226
Lemongrass tofu 251
lentils: My dhal 266
lotus root 28
Gai lan with lotus root or beef 263
lychees: Thai red duck curry with lychee 175

M
Macanese beef 'curry' with daikon 138
Makrut lime leaf creme brulee 307
mangoes: Calamari and green mango salad 217
mantou 147
marinades 93, 129, 133, 138, 145, 146, 147, 152, 155, 167, 168, 177, 181, 190, 194, 203, 239, 242, 248,
lamb and marinade 131

wine marinade 173
mash, broad bean 243
Massaman curry of beef 139
Matcha ice-cream with sago and dried persimmon 293
miso
Grilled asparagus with walnut pesto 264
Roast potatoes with fermented bean sauce 276
Stir-fried chicken with ginger and wood-ear mushrooms 164
Stir fried pipis with Malaysian flavours 214
walnut pesto 264
moon cake, Snow skin, with custard filling 311
Glass noodles with minced pork shiitake and garlic chives 50
mung bean noodles 62
mushrooms 25
Chicken and prawn windmill dumplings 71
Chiu chow dumplings 78
Deep-fried glutinous rice dumplings 72
Glass noodles with minced pork shiitake and garlic chives 50
Mushroom dumplings with curry oil 66
mushrooms and dried shrimp gnocchi 279
Pearl balls 68
Rice rolls with pork and wood-ear mushrooms 74–5
Roast stuffed spatchcock with daikon 186
Slow-cooked duck with fragrant stuffing – the duck that won 1000 hearts 192–3
Steamed chicken bao 73
Stir-fried chicken with ginger and wood-ear mushrooms 164
Stir-fried mixed vegetables 259
Stir-fried seitan with mushrooms and capsicum 273
Stir-fried vegetarian hokkien noodles 63
Taro gnocchi two ways 278–9
Vietnamese stuffed squid or calamari 220
Wood-ear mushrooms and shredded chicken, Nyonya style 261
Zucchini dumplings 99
mussels
Shellfish with garlic, coriander and Thai basil 210
Soba noodles with seafood 58
Steamed mussels with XO sauce 232
Stir fried pipis with Malaysian flavours 214
mustard greens
broad bean mash 243
Chinese olive fried rice 45
Five-spice 'smoked' fish with broad bean mash and spicy witlof salad 242–3
My family's beef brisket 123
Stir-fried vegetarian hokkien noodles 63
mustard glaze 189
My dhal 266
My family's beef brisket 123
My mother's roast chicken 189

N
nahm prik pow 254

Nasi lemak 52
nectarines: Plum sauce 26
noodles 25, 34–5, 61
    Asam laksa 38
    Char kway teow 37
    Chinese Bolognese 61
    Glass noodles with pan-fried fish, and saffron broth 48
    Hae mee 59
    Laksa lemak 42
    Glass noodles with minced pork shiitake and garlic chives 50
    mung bean noodles 62
    noodles 61
    Prosperity toss 41
    Soba noodles with seafood 58
    Spicy mung bean noodle salad 62
    Spicy Sichuan mung bean noodles 252
    squid-ink noodles 39
    Stir-fried squid ink noodles with prawns, lap cheong and tomato 39
    Stir-fried vegetarian hokkien noodles 63
    Vietnamese stuffed squid or calamari 220
nuoc cham 75, 220
nuts *see* almonds, buah keluak, candlenuts, cashews, chestnuts, peanuts, pistachios walnuts, water chestnuts
Nyonya pork satay 132–3

O

oil dough 94
oils 82–3
    curry oil 66
    shellfish oil 101
    spring onion oil 198
okra: Fish head curry 241
olives: Chinese olive fried rice 45
omelette, Oyster, with chilli sauce 227
Onde onde 308
oysters
    Oyster omelette with chilli sauce 227
    Oysters with my dressing 206

P

Pan-fried snapper with vinegar sambal 239
pancakes
    Fluffy pancakes with roasted peanuts and sesame seeds 295
    Pandan crêpes with coconut filling 297
    Spring onion pancakes 103
Pandan chiffon cake 316
Pandan crêpes with coconut filling 297
Pandan panna cotta with red rubies 288
panna cotta, Pandan, with red rubies 288
papaya: Thai green papaya salad 209
passionfruit
    fruit salad 304
    Sri Lankan coconut custard with pear and persimmon 304
pastries, Flaky barbecue pork 94
pastry
    egg tart pastry 115
    pastry shells 109
    yeast pastry 86
patties, Alice's ultimate meat 120

peanuts
    Chiu chow dumplings 78
    Fluffy pancakes with roasted peanuts and sesame seeds 295
    Kung pao chicken 194
    Lemongrass tofu 251
    Massaman curry of beef 139
    Nasi lemak 52
    Nyonya pork satay 132–3
    Peanut crackers 112
    Penang Nyonya pickles 284
    pineapple satay sauce 133
    Prosperity toss 41
    Spicy mung bean noodle salad 62
    Spicy Sichuan mung bean noodles 252
    Thai green papaya salad 209
pears
    fruit salad 304
    Sri Lankan coconut custard with pear and persimmon 304
    Pearl balls 68
Penang Nyonya braised pork 142
Penang Nyonya fish 'curry' with spicy tamarind sauce 235
Penang Nyonya pickles 284
peppers *see* capsicums
persimmons
    fruit salad 304
    Matcha ice-cream with sago and dried persimmon 293
    Sri Lankan coconut custard with pear and persimmon 304
pesto, walnut 264
pickles
    Penang Nyonya pickles 284
    pickled bean sprouts 145
    Pickled green chillies 283
    Pickled young ginger 282
    pickling solution 281
    Spicy pickled Chinese cabbage 281
pineapple
    Asam laksa 38
    Fried rice with pineapple 46
    Nyonya pork satay 132–3
    Pineapple curry 265
    pineapple satay sauce 133
    Pineapple tarts 312
    Thai red duck curry with lychee 175
pipis: Stir fried pipis with Malaysian flavours 214
pistachios: Kulfi ice-cream 294
plums
    Duck breast with sweet osmanthus sauce and baby bamboo shoots 173
    Plum sauce 26
Pol sambol 271
pork
    Alice's ultimate meat patties 120
    Balinese roast pork 157
    Braised pork belly with soy sauce 151
    Char siu 93
    Char siu sou 94
    Chicken buah keluak 199
    Chinese Bolognese 61
    Chiu chow dumplings 78

    Crisp beancurd skin dumplings 87
    Deep-fried glutinous rice dumplings 72
    Eggplant with minced pork 126
    Hae mee 59
    Glass noodles with minced pork shiitake and garlic chives 50
    Nyonya pork satay 132–3
    Pearl balls 68
    Penang Nyonya braised pork 142
    Pork and Chinese cabbage dumplings 80–1
    Pork chop bun, Macanese style 129
    Potsticker dumplings 96
    Rice rolls with pork and wood-ear mushrooms 74–5
    Sichuan twice-cooked pork 153
    Slow-cooked duck with fragrant stuffing – the duck that won 1000 hearts 192–3
    Steamed mussels with XO sauce 232
    Steamed pork buns with fermented black beans and chilli 92
    Steamed pork spare-ribs 97
    stock 59
    Taiwan pepper bun 86
    Tamarind pork 158
    the gelatinised 'soup' 88
    Vietnamese stuffed squid or calamari 220
    Xiao long bao 88–9
    XO sauce 232
    see also lap cheong
potatoes
    banh cuon batter 74
    Beef cooked in sweet soy sauce 148
    Massaman curry of beef 139
    My mother's roast chicken 189
    Roast potatoes with fermented bean sauce 276
    Slow-cooked duck with cumin and black pepper 183
    Taro gnocchi two ways 278–9
potstickers *see* dumplings
prawns
    Butter prawns 225
    Cantonese fried rice 44
    Char kway teow 37
    Chicken and prawn windmill dumplings 71
    Chicken buah keluak 199
    Chinese olive fried rice 45
    Crisp beancurd skin dumplings 87
    Eggplant with minced pork 126
    Fried rice with pineapple 46
    Hae mee 59
    Har gow 84
    Laksa lemak 42
    Roti john 104
    shellfish oil 101
    Shellfish with garlic, coriander and Thai basil 210
    Spicy pomelo and prawn salad 218
    Squid-ink potstickers 90
    Steamed prawns with pickled leeks, ginger and spring onions 226
    Stir-fried prawns with duck-liver sausage 236

Stir-fried squid ink noodles with prawns, lap cheong and tomato 39
Thai green papaya salad 209
Top hats 109
Prosperity toss 41
puddings
Black rice pudding with roasted-coconut ice-cream 302
Indian rice pudding 303
Steamed seafood pudding 221

Q
quail: Vietnamese honey-roasted quail 198

R
radishes
Jewelled-rice congee with sweetcorn and whitebait fritters 49
Macanese beef 'curry' with daikon 138
Rajasthani watermelon curry 269
red curry paste 175
red rubies 288
rhubarb
Rhubarb, cardamom and rosewater sorbet, boozy watermelon and sago 300
Rhubarb crumble with rhubarb sorbet 313
rhubarb sorbet 300, 313
rice 28, 53, 55
Balinese-style roast spatchcock with glutinous rice 182
Black rice pudding with roasted-coconut ice-cream 302
Cantonese fried rice 44
Chinese olive fried rice 45
Fried rice with chicken, salted fish and bean shoots 43
Fried rice with pineapple 46
Glutinous rice with coconut custard 298
Grilled chicken with savoury coconut sauce 176–7
Indian rice pudding 303
Jewelled-rice congee with sweetcorn and whitebait fritters 49
kerabu rice salad 177
Nasi lemak 52
Pearl balls 68
Roast stuffed spatchcock with daikon 186
Rose-scented chicken biryani 54–5
Slow-cooked duck with fragrant stuffing – the duck that won 1000 hearts 192–3
Snow skin moon cake with custard filling 311
Steamed rice cake 274
Thai grilled beef salad 125
Traders' rice 53
Rice rolls with pork and wood-ear mushrooms 74–5
Roast lamb with saffron and tandoori spices 155
Roast potatoes with fermented bean sauce 276
Roast stuffed spatchcock with daikon 186
roasted-coconut ice-cream 302
Rose-scented chicken biryani 54–5

Roti canai 106–7
Roti jala 108
Roti john 104

S
sago 28
Matcha ice-cream with sago and dried persimmon 293
Rhubarb, cardamom and rosewater sorbet, boozy watermelon and sago 300
sago 293, 300
salads
Beef salad with roasted beetroot, preserved lemon and herb dressing 128
beetroot salad 128
Calamari and green mango salad 217
Edible chrysanthemum leaf and tofu salad 262
fruit salad 304
Grilled eggplant salad with chilli jam 254
kerabu rice salad 177
Spicy mung bean noodle salad 62
Spicy pomelo and prawn salad 218
spicy witlof salad 243
Thai green papaya salad 209
Thai grilled beef salad 125
Wood-ear mushrooms and shredded chicken, Nyonya style 261
salmon
Oysters with my dressing 206
Prosperity toss 41
salt, spiced 198
sambals 29
sambal belacan 261
sambal ikan bilis 52
sambol, Sri Lankan coconut 271
satay sauce, pineapple 133
satay spice paste 133
sauces 78, 147, 153, 173, 186, 194, 201, 211, 242, 273
black bean sauce 181
chilli sauce 125, 167, 174
chilli-vinegar sauce 227
coconut sauce 221
coconut sauce 297
curry sauce 77
fermented chilli 280
green herb sauce 128
nuoc cham 75, 220
pineapple satay sauce 133
Sichuan chilli sauce 252
Sichuan sauce 141
sweetcorn sauce 222
walnut pesto 264
XO sauce 232
see also sambals
scallops
Grilled scallops with sweetcorn sauce and curry leaves 222
Shellfish with garlic, coriander and Thai basil 210
Squid-ink potstickers 90
Steamed mussels with XO sauce 232
XO sauce 232

Scrambled eggs with curry leaves and green chillies 110
seitan
Seitan 272
Stir-fried seitan with mushrooms and capsicum 273
Sesame doughnut with custard and chocolate 114
shellfish oil 101
Shellfish with garlic, coriander and Thai basil 210
shrimp
chilli jam 254
Chiu chow dumplings 78
Deep-fried glutinous rice dumplings 72
Grilled eggplant salad with chilli jam 254
mushrooms and dried shrimp gnocchi 279
Slow-cooked duck with fragrant stuffing – the duck that won 1000 hearts 192–3
Spicy pomelo and prawn salad 218
Steamed mussels with XO sauce 232
Stir fried pipis with Malaysian flavours 214
Taro gnocchi two ways 278–9
Thai green papaya salad 209
Top hats 109
Watermelon with crisp fish 219
XO sauce 232
shrimp paste see belacan
Sichuan chilli sauce 252
Sichuan pepper-salt dip 190
Sichuan sauce 141
Sichuan twice-cooked pork 153
Sichuan-style dipping sauce 68
Silken tofu with roasted capsicum and fermented chilli 280
Singapore chilli crab 211
skewers, Xinjiang lamb 131
Slow-cooked duck with cumin and black pepper 183
Slow-cooked duck with fragrant stuffing – the duck that won 1000 hearts 192–3
Slow-cooked spatchcock with jicama, brussels sprouts and vadouvan 202
Snow skin moon cake with custard filling 311
Soba noodles with seafood 58
sorbet, rhubarb 300, 313
soups
Asam laksa 38
Laksa lemak 42
the gelatinised 'soup' 88
Xiao long bao 88–9
soy dipping sauce 81
soy-vinegar dipping sauce 96, 99
spice blends
curry paste 266
massaman curry paste 139
satay spice paste 133
spice mix 139
spice pastes 38, 42, 53, 54–5, 59, 142, 157, 158, 177, 182, 183, 191, 197, 199, 210, 221, 235, 239, 241, 265, 270, 284,
spiced salt 198

vadouvan 202
  see also belacan, bean pastes
spices 136–7
Spicy fried tempeh 275
Spicy mung bean noodle salad 62
Spicy pickled Chinese cabbage 281
Spicy pomelo and prawn salad 218
Spicy Sichuan mung bean noodles 252
spicy witlof salad 243
spinach
  Pandan crêpes with coconut filling 297
  Stir fried Chinese spinach or amaranth 255
  see also water spinach
spring onion oil 198
Spring onion pancakes 103
sprouts, pickled bean 145
squid: Vietnamese stuffed squid or calamari 220
squid-ink dumpling dough 90
squid-ink noodles 39
Squid-ink potstickers 90
Sri Lankan coconut custard with pear and persimmon 304
Sri Lankan spicy cashew curry 270
steamed buns 147
Steamed chicken bao 73
steamed mussels 232
Steamed mussels with XO sauce 232
Steamed pork buns with fermented black beans and chilli 92
Steamed pork spare-ribs 97
Steamed prawns with pickled leeks, ginger and spring onions 226
Steamed rice cake 274
Steamed seafood pudding 221
Stir-fried bean shoots with salted fish 260
Stir-fried chicken with cashew nuts 201
Stir-fried chicken with ginger and wood-ear mushrooms 164
Stir-fried Chinese spinach or amaranth 255
Stir-fried pipis with Malaysian flavours 214
Stir-fried lamb with spring onions and steamed buns 147
Stir-fried mixed vegetables 259
Stir-fried prawns with duck-liver sausage 236
Stir-fried seitan with mushrooms and capsicum 273
Stir-fried squid ink noodles with prawns, lap cheong and tomato 39
Stir-fried vegetarian hokkien noodles 63
stir-fries, mastering 256–7
stock 59, 162–3
  chicken stock 163
  Chinese superior stock 163
  dashi 100
  duck stock 193
  vegetable stock 163
sweet potatoes: Onde onde 308
sweetcorn sauce 222

T
Taiwan pepper bun 86
tamarind 31

Asam laksa 38
Beef salad with roasted beetroot, preserved lemon and herb dressing 128
Chicken buah keluak 199
Fish head curry 241
Massaman curry of beef 139
Nasi lemak 52
Nyonya pork satay 132–3
Penang Nyonya fish 'curry' with spicy tamarind sauce 235
pineapple satay sauce 133
sambal ikan bilis 52
Slow-cooked duck with cumin and black pepper 183
Spicy fried tempeh 275
Tamarind pork 158
Taro gnocchi two ways 278–9
tarts
  Egg tart 115
  egg tart pastry 115
  Pineapple tarts 312
tempeh 31
  Spicy fried tempeh 275
tempering ingredients 271
Teochew duck 174
Thai duck curry dumplings 77
Thai green papaya salad 209
Thai grilled beef salad 125
Thai red duck curry with lychee 175
the gelatinised 'soup' 88
tofu 31
  Edible chrysanthemum leaf and tofu salad 262
  Grilled asparagus with walnut pesto 264
  Lemongrass tofu 251
  Silken tofu with roasted capsicum and fermented chilli 280
  Soba noodles with seafood 58
  Stir-fried vegetarian hokkien noodles 63
  walnut pesto 264
  see also beancurd
tomatoes
  Beef cooked in sweet soy sauce 148
  Fish head curry 241
  Fried rice with pineapple 46
  Rose-scented chicken biryani 54–5
  Scrambled eggs with curry leaves and green chillies 110
  shellfish oil 101
  Soba noodles with seafood 58
  Sri Lankan spicy cashew curry 270
  Stir-fried squid ink noodles with prawns, lap cheong and tomato 39
  Thai green papaya salad 209
Top hats 109
Traders' rice 53
Typhoon shelter crab 237

V
vadouvan 202
Vietnamese honey-roasted quail 198
Vietnamese shaking beef 145
Vietnamese stuffed squid or calamari 220
vinegar, blanching 284

vinegar wash 173
vinegar-ginger dipping sauce 96, 99

W
walnuts
  Grilled asparagus with walnut pesto 264
  walnut pesto 264
water chestnuts 28
  Braised lamb with beancurd sticks and tangerine peel 152
  Crisp beancurd skin dumplings 87
  Har gow 84
  Pandan panna cotta with red rubies 288
  Pearl balls 68

  red rubies 288
  Rice rolls with pork and wood-ear mushrooms 74–5
  Squid-ink potstickers 90
  Steamed chicken bao 73
water dough 94
water spinach 24
  Hae mee 59
watermelon
  boozy watermelon 300
  Rajasthani watermelon curry 269
  Rhubarb, cardamom and rosewater sorbet, boozy watermelon and sago 300
  Watermelon granita with coconut jelly and berry compote 291
  Watermelon with crisp fish 219
wheat starch dough 84
whitebait fritters 49
wine marinade 173
woks 228–31, 256–7
wombok 24
  Lamb dumplings, Xi'an style 69
  Potsticker dumplings 96
  Spicy pickled Chinese cabbage 281
  Stir-fried mixed vegetables 259
Wood-ear mushrooms and shredded chicken, Nyonya style 261

X
Xiao long bao 88–9
Xinjiang lamb skewers 131
XO sauce 31, 232

Y
yeast pastry 86

Z
Zucchini dumplings 99

Published in 2024 by Murdoch Books, an imprint of Allen & Unwin

Murdoch Books Australia
Cammeraygal Country
83 Alexander Street
Crows Nest NSW 2065
Phone: +61 (0)2 8425 0100
murdochbooks.com.au
info@murdochbooks.com.au

Murdoch Books UK
Ormond House
26–27 Boswell Street
London WC1N 3JZ
Phone: +44 (0) 20 8785 5995
murdochbooks.co.uk
info@murdochbooks.co.uk

For corporate orders and custom publishing, contact our business development team at salesenquiries@murdochbooks.com.au

Publisher: Jane Willson
Editorial manager: Justin Wolfers
Design manager: Kristy Allen
Designer: George Saad
Editor: David Matthews
Photographer: Mark Roper
Stylist: Lee Blaylock
Production director: Lou Playfair

Text © Tony Tan 2024
The moral right of the author has been asserted.
Design © Murdoch Books 2024
Photography © Mark Roper 2024
Cover photography © Mark Roper 2024

Murdoch Books acknowledges the Traditional Owners of the Country on which we live and work. We pay our respects to all Aboriginal and Torres Strait Islander Elders, past and present.

All rights reserved. No part of this publication may be reproduced, stored in a retrieval system or transmitted in any form or by any means, electronic, mechanical, photocopying, recording or otherwise, without the prior written permission of the publisher.

ISBN 9 781 92261 691 3

 A catalogue record for this book is available from the National Library of Australia

A catalogue record for this book is available from the British Library

Colour reproduction by Splitting Image Colour Studio Pty Ltd, Wantirna, Victoria
Printed by 1010 Printing International Limited, China

OVEN GUIDE: You may find cooking times vary depending on the oven you are using. For fan-forced ovens, as a general rule, set the oven temperature to 20°C (35°F) lower than indicated in the recipe.

IMPORTANT: Those who might be at risk from the effects of salmonella poisoning (the elderly, pregnant women, young children and those suffering from immune deficiency diseases) should consult their doctor with any concerns about eating raw eggs. Please ensure that all seafood and beef to be eaten raw or lightly cooked are very fresh and of the highest quality.

TABLESPOON MEASURES: We have used 20 ml (4 teaspoon) tablespoon measures. If you are using a 15 ml (3 teaspoon) tablespoon add an extra teaspoon of the ingredient for each tablespoon specified.

10 9 8 7 6 5 4 3 2 1